HARDEN'S

London
Party
Guide

Where to buy Harden's guides
Harden's guides are on sale in most major bookshops
in the UK, and may be ordered from any bookshop.
In case of difficulty, call Harden's Guides on
0171-839 4763.

mail@hardens.com
We now have an e-mail address. We invite your
comments on this publication, including any
corrections or suggestions for the next edition.

© Harden's Guides, 1997

ISBN 1-873721-11-0

British Library Cataloguing-in-Publication data:
a catalogue record for this book is available from
the British Library.

Printed and bound in Finland by
Werner Söderström Osakeyhtiö

Harden's Guides
29 Villiers Street
London WC2N 6ND

CONTENTS

HOW TO USE

Price bands

The price bands indicate, in the most general terms, the overall minimum level of expenditure per head you are likely to incur in giving a party at a particular venue.

£B – *Budget:* it should be possible to organise a drinks party for about the same cost per head as an evening in a wine bar, or a party with food and drink for about the same cost as eating in a modestly priced restaurant.

£M – *Medium:* the costs of a party with wine and food will generally run at, or a little above, those of providing similar catering in a middle to high class restaurant. Drinks parties will probably cost as much per head as a meal in a modestly priced restaurant.

£E – *Expensive:* outside the budget of most private individuals and mainly, therefore, used for corporate events.

Where two levels are shown (eg £B-M), the likely range of expenditure straddles two bands.

Capacities – eg (150, 100)

The maximum normal capacity of the venue for a private function is given in bold at the beginning of each entry.

Individual room capacities are given in the smaller print. This list of rooms may not be exhaustive – details are given only for the more important or interesting rooms, or, in some cases, rooms which are representative of other similar rooms.

If a room or venue is particularly suited to a dinner-dance, three capacities are given, eg (250, 150, 100)

(standing, seated, dinner-dance)

If a room or venue is not particularly suited to a dinner-dance, two capacities are given, eg (150, 100)

(standing, seated)

The fact that no dinner-dance capacity is indicated does not necessarily mean that it is not possible to dance.

Smoking, amplified music and dancing

Permitted, unless otherwise indicated.

Restrictions on use

Any explicit restrictions upon hirers or types of function are noted. The absence of such a note does not, of course, mean that the venue may not be selective about the functions and hirers which it will accept.

Catering

Restaurants, hotels, wine bars and pubs will, of course, generally expect to provide all the food and drink for any event on their premises. For other venues, we give a guide to stipulations re catering arrangements, as follows:

"In-house catering" – you must use the resident caterer

"Xco catering" – using the specified caterer is obligatory

"List of caterers" – one of a list of approved outside caterers must be used.

"Hirer's choice of caterer" – you can, in principle, bring in the caterer of your choice, though some venues may wish to vet your proposed arrangements. Even where there is no obligation to use a particular caterer, you may find that there is a resident caterer which is able to offer keener prices than an outsider.

Finishing times

There are venues where the finishing time for functions is not at all open to negotiation, and others which are almost completely flexible. For many, the question is a grey area – you may find that there is a 'preferred' finishing time, but that, for an extra payment, a later conclusion is perfectly feasible. For venues which have a meaningful general rule about the finishing time for events, we give the time in the small print – we must, emphasise, however, that this can be no more than a broad indication. In some cases, the time given is subject to a licensing extension being obtained, but this will generally be dealt with by the venue.

Days and times available and annual closures

Except as indicated (immediately after the finishing time, where applicable), venues are generally available daily throughout the year for day and evening functions.

Telephone and (fax) numbers

All seven-digit telephone numbers are 0171- numbers – other numbers have an 0181- or STD prefix. Where appropriate, the fax number is given in brackets after the telephone number.

CHECKLIST

*This is a list for a ball –
many of the same issues
will arise for smaller
parties.*

Getting the ball rolling

Venue
Theme
Timetable for evening
Set-up schedule
Marquee
Loos
Furniture
Guest list
Invitations (and other
    information for guests)
Seating plan
Programme
Place cards
Menus
Inform police/neighbours

Food

Cooking facilities
Special food, eg cake
Snack food
Utensils
Crockery
Table linen/napkins
Catering for bands,
    performers and staff
Ashtrays

Drink

Cold storage
Glasses
Ice
Mixers and soft drinks
Fruit for cocktails, etc.
Serving trays

Decoration

Balloons, streamers
Flower, fruit or ice
    displays

Entertainments

Dance floor
Disco & DJ
Bands
Performers
Fireworks/laser
Diversions, eg casino,
    funfair attractions
Retiring room for bands
    and performers

Transport

Parking space
Signs to parking, and
    from parking to event
Cars, buses, train,
    helicopter

Staff

Security
Car parking
Reception
Cloakroom
Loos
Waiters/waitresses
Toastmaster
Seamstress
Clearing up

Cleaning up

Brushes
Water/buckets
Detergents
Cloths

Don't forget

Plan entry procedure
Insurance
Access for furniture/
    equipment
Photography
Power ("3 phase"?)

Icing on the cake

Gifts for guests
Accommodation for
    guests

INTRODUCTION

This is the second edition of our guide to venues for parties in and around the capital. Almost four years have passed since the first edition. In the light of the number of changes which are recorded in this guide, we must acknowledge that the interval has been too long.

It has been gratifying in the course of preparing this second edition to find out how many of the professionals of the party world still find the first edition a useful reference in the course of their daily work. We hope they will find this enlarged and completely revised edition of even greater assistance. We also hope that those who are organising their own special event – whatever its scale – will find the information of use.

The principal focus of this guide is on private venues – at every price level – for exclusive hire. Those who use this book primarily to find 'new' venues will find that we have increased the number of venues in the capital, and particularly in the Home Counties.

Increasing the scope of the book has been facilitated by the fact that the number of potential London venues which disdain function business from third parties continues to decline. There are now relatively few obviously suitable buildings in and around the metropolis which are – to appropriate hirers, of course – not available. In the course or our researches, we have also noted that some facilities whose availability once appeared grudging is now rather more whole-hearted.

The scope of party services available has increased, if anything, even more than the range of venues. We now list almost 100 firms in and around the capital whose main business is outside catering. And, as parties become bigger and better, professional party organisers are proliferating. A whole new trade – which barely existed 20 years ago and which was still in its infancy a decade ago – is coming into being. We now list nearly 50 firms which organise parties of all types.

We would like to thank all those who have assisted us by telling us about their facilities and their services.

In addition, we particularly thank Lady Elizabeth Anson – who could fairly lay claim to being London's original party planner – who has been kind enough to share with readers of this book 15 'Top Tips' (as we have termed them) for giving a successful event.

Richard Harden   **Peter Harden**

COSTS

Introduction

Giving a party at the venues listed in this book can cost anything between £10 and £350 a head – more if you really try. If you are organising a major party for the first time, the following guidelines on expenditure may help to set you in the right direction.

Do ensure that you keep an eye on the "big picture" – it is very important not to compare specific costs in isolation. Look at the total costs involved in plan A and compare them with the total costs involved in plan B. For example, you may find that one venue is apparently, on the basis of its hire charge, cheaper than another but that, after taking the respective catering costs into account, the true picture is entirely different.

Where choice is possible, you should, of course, always get competing estimates for each of the different items.

Catering and drink will almost inevitably consume the greater part of a party budget. The other main costs are usually venue hire and decoration. Sometimes, a marquee and/or entertainments can make up a significant part of the total cost.

Catering and drink

As a rule of thumb, expenditure on food and drink provided by an outside caterer will be roughly the same as eating in a restaurant providing comparable fare. (The difference, of course, is that generally you also have to bear the cost of the venue.) Like restaurants, caterers' charges vary widely.

The quite significant wine mark-ups and/or high corkage charges sometimes demanded can make quite a difference to total costs and you should make sure you include them in your sums.

Entertainments

Examples: a disco can cost anything from £100 to £1000, although you should be able to get something very respectable for £400 or so. A top after-dinner speaker or a well-known dance band might command £4000-£10,000, or in some cases more, for an evening's work. A 'function band' will probably charge something between £500 and £2,500.

Venue hire

The costs of hiring the venues themselves usually fall within the following ranges:

£0-£100 – most pubs and wine bars. You may have to guarantee a certain level of total 'spend'.

£100-£1,000 – most of the private venues listed in this book.

£1,000-£7,500 – grander galleries, museums, houses and livery halls, and large nightclubs.

£7,500 and up – the top 20 or so largest and most prestigious venues listed.

Hire charges can be affected by the day of the week, length of hire, purpose of hire and time of year (prices in the quiet first quarter of the year often being 'softer'). In some cases, hire charges will be greater if you do not use the services of the resident caterer. Some, but certainly not all, venues will make an allowance if you wish to use a venue to less than its full capacity. Don't be afraid to negotiate.

Decoration and theming

It is worth bearing in mind that seemingly inexpensive venues may be less of a bargain when you factor in the expenditure on decoration which will be required to make them festive. Apparently expensive venues which are decorated to a high standard can be better value than they initially appear because they require much less work and expense to get them ready for a party.

To dress a medium size ballroom, you can spend several hundred pounds on balloons and other decoration. For floral decoration on any scale it is not difficult to spend several thousand pounds – you *can* spend tens, or even hundreds of thousands of pounds, if you really want to.

The cost of fully theming a party can be very considerable, especially if a set is to be built. A more economical option is to find a venue that comes ready-themed, at least to an extent, and to build upon the base which it offers.

Marquee hire

As an example, the hire of a frame marquee large enough to hold a dinner dance for 100 people will generally cost upwards of £1,500.

TOP PARTY TIPS

Lady Elizabeth Anson of Party Planners has more than three decades' experience of organising events around the capital. Here are her 'top tips' for organising a successful event.

Drinks

Should be offered to guests when they first arrive. Do not keep people waiting in a long queue to be formally received without a drink. In hot weather ensure there is plenty of chilled mineral water and soft drinks.

Photographers and video operators

Should be inconspicuous and flexible. Do not permit them to start orchestrating an event – taking too many pictures can delay a party getting going and spoil the atmosphere. No photography should take place while guests are eating. At weddings, ensure all the people to be included in official photographs know where they should be and when, so that pictures can be taken as quickly as possible. (Avoid the best man having to search for missing guests.)

Temperature

It is very important that this is as comfortable as possible: if guests become too hot or cold they will complain and then depart early. For events in a marquee, remember that heating may be required even at the height of summer. When the temperature drops a marquee can become very cold very quickly and even with heating can take a long time to warm up.

Cocktail food

Should be bite-sized to avoid spillages and for ease of eating. For a cocktail party of two hours, allow 10 bites per head and for a longer event allow 15-20. Very pretty crudités are ideal for vegetarians, diabetics and dieters.

Equipment

Should be delivered in good time before an event to allow you to count and check it thoroughly (particularly tablecloths – these may also need ironing.) Very often hire equipment does not match up to expectation, so leave enough time to change or add incorrect or incomplete items. Equally make sure drinks are delivered in good time – increasingly couriers are unreliable.

Dance floor

Should be snug. Guests are daunted by large and empty spaces, and if overly intimidated, will not dance. In fact, a successful party should seem overcrowded at some point.

Lighting

Integral to formation of ambience.

Waiting staff

Should be efficient, responsive and well turned out.
They should be briefed on what drinks and food they are
serving and on any guests who require special attention.

PA system for speeches

May be required, however experienced the speaker. Have
a sound check – never underestimate the noise of guests
in an echoey building or on a boarded floor.

Entertainment

This should not be overly long. Even if you have put on
an expensive cabaret, which you really like, some guests
will not. If not properly arranged it can break up a party.
But it can be useful – for instance, one can move to
another area for a cabaret after the main course, and
return with the room reorganised for pudding or dancing.

Fireworks

These can be excellent and useful if professionally
organised, and can encourage guests to move out of the
marquee/dining area to enable its reorganisation.
Alternatively they make a great grand finale. Five minutes
or so are sufficient. If budget allows, it is worth investing
in electronically detonated fireworks, with music.

Invitations

Should be sent out at least two months prior to a large
event to facilitate guests making their travel plans and
arrangements. (Sometimes it is worth sending an
informal card forewarning guests, particularly those with
many commitments, of your plans and the date.) A reply
card, with a reply-by date, helps discipline guests.

Flowers

If on a limited budget, do not waste money on small
arrangements which will be lost, but have fewer, larger
displays. Generous foliage with fewer flowers keeps costs
down. Do not have flowers on pedestals which are the
same height as guests – they will be hidden by the first
arrivals – place them over doors or suspend them from
ceilings. Ensure guests can see over table arrangements.

Glasses

Take note that if guests are being served from trays they
will put a glass back on the tray and take another one –
therefore allow three or four glasses per person.

Dress

Make sure – ideally on the invitation – that guests are
aware of what they should be wearing. It wrecks an
occasion for many people if they are incorrectly attired.
Make sure you work out what you are going to wear in
good time, that your shoes are comfortable, and that
your clothes are back from the dry-cleaners.

PRIVATE VENUES

PRIVATE VENUES

Abbaye EC1   £B-M, (400,160,160)
55 Charterhouse St   253 1612   (251 5259)
These Smithfield premises, (formerly Hubble & Co, and now a
Belgian restaurant) are well suited to a big party – especially one
that's to go on till late. The cellars are particularly characterful. / 3am,
Fri & Sat 6am; Wine Bar (200,60); Basement Restaurant (200,100).

Abbey Community Centre SW1   £B, (200,150)
34 Great Smith St   222 0303   (233 3308)
No-frills Westminster hall and other rooms, with school-gym décor,
suitable for a wide range of budget events. / midnight; in-house caterers;
smoking restricted; Main Hall (200,150); Bar (100,50).

Academy of Live &
Recorded Arts SW18   £B-M, (300,250,200)
Royal Victoria Patriotic Building, Fitzhugh Grove, Trinity Rd
0181-870 6475   (0181-875 0789)
Particularly popular for weddings, this extraordinary overblown
Victorian building, in a Wandsworth park, houses a large, mirrored
rehearsal room with one of the largest sprung wooden floors in
London. It's a characterful space, and opens off the very pretty
cloister garden. / 1am; vacations and weekends; hirer's choice of caterer.

Accademia Italiana/
European Academy SW1   £M-E, (350,150,150)
8 Grosvenor Pl   235 0303   (235 0404)
The Accademia – whose prime function is to hold art and cultural
exhibitions – has moved to two converted c19 French Renaissance
town houses in Belgravia. The function rooms are on the second floor,
overlooking the gardens of Buckingham Palace. / midnight;
hirer's choice of caterer; smoking restricted.

Addington Palace, Surrey   £M-E, (500,200)
Gravel Hill, Croydon   0181-654 4404   (0181-655 2858)
This imposing listed Georgian building is set in grounds landscaped by
"Capability" Brown. The bright and airy Winter Garden is licensed to
hold 90 for weddings. It can be combined with the Great Hall and a
marquee to accommodate larger groups. / in-house caterers;
smoking restricted; Great Hall (150,150); Robing Rm (120,80); Norman Shaw
Rm (100,80); Library (50,40); Winter Garden (90,70); Music Rm (70,50);
marquee site.

Adrenaline Village SW8   £M, (2500,1700)
Chelsea Bridge   622 1188   (622 7519)
This complex at the south end of Chelsea Bridge, comprises Film
Studios and the Boogie Boat. The former is divided into the Club (with
fully fitted bar) and the Venue (which can be sub-divided into four
studios). The Boogie Boat, a converted Grimsby trawler, is licensed to
hold 200 below decks, but larger parties can be accommodated in
summer. / 2am; list of caterers; Venue (2500,1700); Club (350,300); Boogie
Boat (200,–); marquee site.

Africa Centre WC2   £B, (150,150)
38 King St   836 1973   (836 1975)
This quirky, atmospheric place, just off Covent Garden, has as its
main space a c18 galleried hall which, with a little decoration, could
be used for fairly traditional events. With catering from the on-site
restaurant (Calabash), however, it has great theme potential. / Mon-
Thu midnight, Fri-Sat 2.30am; in-house (Calabash African restaurant); Main
Hall (150,150); Rear Hall (80,80).

Ajimura WC2   £M, (–,20)
51-53 Shelton St   240 9424
Covent Garden Japanese restaurant – the oldest in the UK – which has acquired a little more character than most Nipponese establishments.

Al Basha W8   £M, (–,60)
222 Kensington High St   938 1794
Good, if pricey, food comes graciously served at this Holland Parkside Lebanese restaurant, which has a glitzy basement private room. / Private Rm (–,60).

Alexandra Palace Ice Rink N22   £M, (1200,–)
Alexandra Palace Way, Wood Gn
0181-365 2121   (0181-444 3439)
You can take over the whole Ally Pally rink by the hour. You could use it for ice go-karting (40 people per session) or a skating birthday party. (It has even hosted a wedding reception on ice.) / not Mon or Thu eve; Any Time Any Place.

Alexandra Palace & Park N22   £M, (7250,5500,5000)
Wood Gn   0181-365 2121   (0181-883 3999)
They boast that parties of between 10 and 7,250 can be catered for at this enormous Victorian hall complex. Set in 196 acres of park, it has great views over London, and parking for 2000 cars. What's impressive – apart from the sheer scale of the place, of course – is that they really do have rooms of suitable scale for almost any function. / 2am; in-house caterers; Great Hall (6500,5500,5000); West Hall (2500,2200,2000); Palm Court (1500,–); Palace Restaurant (400,250,200); Loneborough Rm (200,130,100); Palm Court 5 (100,50); Palm Court 1 (25,10); marquee site.

Alma SW18   £B, (130,60)
499 Old York Rd   0181-870 2537   (0181-874 9055)
This popular Wandsworth pub – which offers quite decent food, too – has an upstairs parlour available for dinners, drinks and "quiet discos". / midnight; not Sun; in-house caterers; Private Rm (130,60).

Amadeus Centre W9   £M, (200,160,160)
50 Shirland Rd   286 1686   (266 1225)
This converted, late Victorian Little Venice Chapel is dominated by a (non-functional) organ. It is quite a characterful space, with good natural light, and is in good order – you would, however, need a lot of decoration to make it jolly. An ideal combination is a dinner in the Upper Hall and disco below. / in-house caterers; Upper Hall (200,160); Lower Hall (100,60).

L'Amico SW1   £M, (–,14)
44 Horseferry Rd   222 4680
Regularly packed with MPs, this nice, but unremarkable basement Italian restaurant, a stone's throw from Westminster, has a couple of conspiratorial private rooms. / not Sat & Sun; Private Rm (–,14); Private Rm (–,8).

Anchor SE1   £B-M, (120,50)
34 Park St   407 1577   (407 0741)
Well-known South Bank building, four centuries old and currently in use as a pub. It is scheduled for complete refurbishment in October 1997. The Shakespeare Room has a great view and 200-year-old panelling. Mrs Thrale's Room is an intimate, characterful private bar. / 11.30pm; Garden or Adjoining Bar (80,–); Mrs Thrale's Rm (50,–); Upper Chart Rm (–,50); Lower Chart Rm (–,30); Shakespeare Rm (–,22).

PRIVATE VENUES

Annabel's W1 £E, (250,125,125)
44 Berkeley Sq 629 3558
*London's – perhaps the world's – most consistently successful
nightclub occupies a comfortable, country-houseified Mayfair
basement and makes an ideal venue for a small to medium size
party. If you're not a member, however, save yourself the cost of the
telephone call. (Capacity figures are our estimates.)* / 3am.

Antelope SW1 £B-M, (70,48)
22 Eaton Ter 730 7781
*Well-known, characterful pub – just off Eaton Square – whose
comfortable upstairs room is available for civilised stand-ups and
dinners.* / 11pm; no amplified music; no dancing; Upstairs (70,48).

Apothecaries' Hall EC4 £M-E, (200,130)
Blackfriars Ln 236 1180 (329 3177)
*With its lovely approach (through a small, cream-coloured courtyard,
off a cobbled lane), charming hall, sober Court Room and Parlour
decorated with apothecaries' jars through the centuries, this is one of
the most delightful settings in London. Most bookings tend to be
sit-downs.* / 10.30pm; not Sat eve & Sun; mid Aug-mid Sep hol; Party Ingredients;
no dancing; Hall (200,130); Court Rm (–,22); Parlour (–,22).

Apsley House W1 £E, (200,110)
Hyde Park Corner 938 8366 (938 8367)
*Home to the Dukes of Wellington past and present, 'No 1 London'
(1778, and recently completely refurbished) is arguably the grandest
place for a medium size banquet to hire in London (and available
once a month only). Parties of 80 or fewer can recreate the
Waterloo Dinner, sitting at a single table.* / companies only; eve only;
list of caterers; no dancing; no smoking or candles.

Aquarium EC1 £M, (400,–)
256-260 Old Street 251 6136 (251 5212)
*London's only nightclub with integral swimming pool and Jacuzzi
(towels provided) can be booked in its entirety in the early days of the
week. On Friday night, hire the Star Bar and your guests have access
to the (almost) all-night action in the main club.* / Mon-Wed midnight, Thu-
Fri 2am, Sat 4am; Club not Fri, Sat & Sun pm, Fri only – exclusive use of Star Bar and
access to club; in-house or hirer's choice by negotiation; Club (400,–); Café Bar (250,–).

Aquarium E1 £M, (–,150)
Ivory House, St Katharine-by-the-Tower 480 6116
*This smart, rather modernistic fish and seafood restaurant benefits
from a particularly pleasant location in the centre of the Tower
Bridge-side marina.* / Private Rm (–,100).

Archduke Wine Bar SE1 £B-M, (300,80)
153 Concert Hall Approach 928 9370 (928 0839)
*This popular South Bank wine bar/restaurant, underneath railway
arches, has two large niches available for private hire. On Sunday, the
whole place can be taken.* / midnight; Sun exclusive hire only; in-house caterers;
no dancing; Bridge Rm (60,–); Conservatory (30,–).

The Argyll Arms W1 £B, (70,40)
18 Argyll St 734 6117
*Ornately decorated Victorian pub, just by Oxford Circus, with a
largish, pleasant private room – the Palladium Bar. (It's popular for
"birthdays and leaving and divorce parties", apparently).* / 11.30pm;
Palladium Bar (70,40).

The Ark SE1 £M, (–,72)
220 Lambeth Rd   633 9701   (401 8869)
The Museum of Garden History (which no longer hosts social functions at its St Mary's Church address) has acquired a Victorian school (with a new Persian-style garden), suitable for a variety of occasions. There are three connecting halls, with parquet flooring and natural light. / midnight; list of caterers; Long Gallery (–,72); East Gallery (–,48); West Gallery (–,36); Refectory (–,26).

Armourers' & Braisers' Hall EC2 £M-E, (125,80)
81 Coleman St   606 1199   (606 7481)
On the corner with London Wall, this fine, but not overbearingly grand, livery hall (1840s) is distinctively decorated. Guests are generally received in the rich comfort of the gilt-walled Drawing Room and proceed to the armour-lined, vaulted hall, lit by the candles of the impressive c18 chandeliers. / no weddings or birthdays; 11.30pm; not Sat & Sun; list of caterers; no amplified music; no dancing; Livery Hall (125,80); Drawing Rm (125,–); Court Rm (–,20).

Arts Club W1 £M-E, (200,150,120)
40 Dover St   499 8581   (409 0913)
Popular Mayfair address, whose manageable size and layout make for conviviality, and where the mixed traditional and modern styles of the rooms produce an atmosphere of easy-going charm. A paved garden leads off the dining room. / 2am; Dining & Drawing Rms not Wed eve; 2 wks hol in Aug; list of caterers; Dining Rm (200,150,120); Bar & Conservatory (100,–); Drawing Rm (80,26).

Arts Depot NW1 £M-E, (600,150,350)
Turnhalle 62, Pancras Rd   278 0999   (278 2700)
This Victorian 'Turnhalle' – the UK's earliest surviving purpose-built gymnasium, big enough for "30 squads of ten men" – offers considerable scope for theming (with the arched roof being large enough to accommodate trapeze artists, apparently). They may apply for a wedding licence. / 1am; from 6.30pm; hirer's choice of caterer.

Ascot Racecourse, Pavilions & Queen Anne Rooms, Berks £M, (1400,1200,1000)
Ascot   01344-28231   (01344-872208)
Ascot is an all-year fixture, function-wise, offering a large range of spaces for social events (and even a new Exhibition Hall). Rather confusingly, the facilities are split between two catering companies – see also the next entry. / midnight; not race days; Letheby & Christopher; Pavilion (subdivisible) (1400,1200,1000); Buckhounds (500,300,200); King Edward VII (60,40); Crocker Bulteel (20,14).

Ascot Racecourse, Royal Enclosure, Berks £M, (500,300,250)
Ascot   01344-23668   (01344-874561)
Apart from their indoor facilities, a marquee can be organised in the middle of the racecourse. / not race days; Ring & Brymer; Paddock Suite (500,300,250); Jockey Club (200,120,100); marquee site.

Athenaeum Hotel W1 £M, (60,52,40)
116 Piccadilly   499 3464   (413 0000)
Very comfortable modern Mayfair hotel, refurbished in 1994 in fairly traditional style. Two of the function rooms (Devonshire and the Boardroom) have views of Green Park. For a small and discreet gathering, consider one of the hotel's apartments, which are located in converted Edwardian townhouses. / midnight; Westminster Suite (60,52); Devonshire Suite (50,28); Richmond Suite (20,8); Apartments (–,8).

Atlantic Bar & Grill W1   £M-E, (500,300)
20 Glasshouse St   734 4888
*This trendy and atmospheric Art Deco basement bar/restaurant, near
Piccadilly Circus, is on an enormous scale. There is a stylish private
room ('Chez Cup'), or, for a big-budget event, you could take over
the whole place. / 3am; Private Rm (80,60).*

The Avenue SW1   £M-E, (400,180)
7/9 St James's St   321 2111   (321 2500)
*The Manhattanite décor of this fashionable St James's restaurant –
which may be taken over in its entirety for suitable events – makes a
good backdrop for a stylish party. / 2am.*

Avenue House N3   £M, (–,60)
East End Rd   0181-359 2082   (0181-346 3072)
*This Victorian Finchley villa was partly rebuilt in 1989 after a major
fire. There is a variety of function rooms for 12-70 people. Some are
definitely suitable only for business meetings, but the Drawing Room
is licensed for weddings. / 11.30pm; hirer's choice of caterer; no smoking;
Drawing Rm (–,60); Salon (–,20).*

Babe Ruth's E1   £M, (–,400)
172-176 The Highway   481 8181   (481 9800)
*For an American-theme party, in particular, why not take over this
impressive, modern sports bar, on the way to the Docklands.*

Badbobs WC2   £B-M, (650,200,580)
Chandos Place   836 8000   (836 8800)
*Covent Garden bar/restaurant with two rooms for party hire – the
Library and Lilly's Bordello – whose names hint at the respective OTT
decorative styles. Or you can hire the whole place. / 12.30am; Bar -
restaurant (350,200,200); Lilly's Bordello (350,–); Library (VIP Rm) (30,–).*

BAFTA Centre W1   £M, (300,200,200)
195 Piccadilly   734 0022   (734 1009)
*While their décor is now modern, the club bars of the erstwhile
Royal Institute of Painters in Watercolours retain traces of c19
grandeur, adding to their attractiveness for receptions. This period
character is absent from the function room, which enjoys good views
of St James's churchyard. / 1am; Roux Restaurants; Function Rm (200,200);
Foyer Bar (120,–).*

Bagleys N1   £B-M, (2500,400)
Acorn Studios, Kings Cross Freight Depot, York Way
278 2777   (713 5510)
*Street-credibly located just north of King's Cross, this ex-warehouse
nightclub is ideal for a walk on the wild side that's not too far from
the centre of town. Its four entrances and range of large rooms make
it a flexible location for a variety of events – theming is advisable.
/ not Sat eve or Sun day; in-house or hirer's choice by negotiation; three studios
(each) (750,400); Bunker Bar (500,200); marquee site.*

Bakers' Hall EC3   £B-M, (150,75)
9 Harp Ln   623 2223   (621 1924)
*This livery hall is located a short step from the Tower, at the foot of
the company's own redbrick block. Decoration throughout is in
love-it-or-hate-it, modern style – the livery hall is a dark room, with
deep-blue stained glass windows, while the basement Court Room is
more conventional, with immaculate light wood panelling and
furniture. / 11pm; Aug hol; list of caterers; no dancing; Livery Hall (120,75);
Court Rm (60,22).*

Balls Brothers   **£B**
20 St James's St, SWI   321 0882   (300,94)
Hays Galleria, Tooley St, SEI   407 4301   (150,100,100)
6-8 Cheapside, EC2   248 2708   (80,–)
3/6 Budge Row, Cannon St, EC4   248 7557   (300,40)
2-3 Old Change Ct., EC4   248 8697   (150,–)
11 Blomfield St, Bell Hse Ct, EC2   588 4643   (7,12)
5/6 Carey Ln (off Gutter Ln), EC2   600 2720   (200,60)
Mark La, EC3   623 2923   (16,16)
2 St Mary-at-HI, EC3   626 0321   (250,60)
42 Threadneedle St, EC2   628 3850   (90,–)
Moor Hse, London Wall, EC2   628 3944   (250,6)
King Arms Yd, EC2   796 3049   (100,–)
at Great Eastern: Bishopsgate, EC2   626 7919   (100,–)
Gow's Restaurant: 81 Old Broad St, EC2   920 9645   (120,90)
Marine Restaurant & Bar: 52 Lime St, EC3   283 0841
*This well-known chain of wine bars makes its branches available,
given sufficient numbers, on an exclusive basis, particularly at
weekends. You can go direct to the individual wine bars, or call the
party service on 739 6466.*

Baltic Exchange EC3   **£M-E, (350,150,150)**
38 St Mary Axe   623 5501   (369 1622)
*The 'new' Baltic Exchange – in the impressive Art Deco building it has
occupied since 1995 – offers the rare opportunity to dine, or even
dance, on a real trading floor. The grand, mahogany-panelled
Boardroom may also be hired. / 10.30pm; in-house caterers; Trading
Floor (350,150,150); Dining Rm (150,95); Boardroom (–,24).*

Bank of England Club SW15   **£M, (260,220,180)**
Priory Ln   0181-876 8417   (0181-878 7007)
*Set in 42 acres of woodlands and every type of sports field, this very
well-maintained Roehampton 'country club' is tailor-made for grown-
up sports days (including go-karting and the like). The Redgates
Lodge or club restaurant are suitable for a wide variety of functions.
/ 11pm; not Sun; in-house caterers; Redgates Lodge (150,80); marquee site.*

Bank of England Museum EC2   **£M-E, (200,75)**
Bartholomew St   601 5545   (601 5808)
*Entered through the East Wall of the Bank, this museum does not
conform to any dusty stereotype and is well suited to the restrained
receptions for which it is made available. The lofty, reconstructed
Bank Stock Office is more practical than the Rotunda, but is a less
interesting space. / charities & companies only - no functions which might imply the
Bank's approval of commerical ventures; 8.30pm; from 5.30pm, not Sat & Sun;
in-house caterers; no amplified music; no dancing; no smoking.*

The Bankers Club EC2   **£M, (150,56)**
7 Lothbury   606 5883   (600 3083)
*Behind the Bank of England, what was the Overseas Bankers Club
has around 1000 members (City and overseas). If you can find a
member to host your function (or, indeed are eligible to join) the
venue is worth considering for City entertaining, a clubby dinner or
reception. / not Sat & Sun; Directors Table; Cocktail Bar (150,–); Dining Rm (–,56);
Private Dining Rms (–,30).*

Bankside Gallery SE1   **£B-M, (150,60)**
48 Hopton St   928 7521   (928 2820)
*A pleasant, red-walled gallery, this Southwark institution (home to the
Royal Watercolour Society and Royal Society of Painter-Printmakers) is
at the foot of a modern block, set back from the river. / 11pm; not Tue-Fri
& Sun before 5pm; Table Talk; no amplified music; no smoking.*

PRIVATE VENUES

Banqueting House SW1   £M-E, (500,375,375)
Whitehall   839 8918   (930 8268)
*The sole remaining fragment of the Palace of Whitehall – Inigo
Jones's stately c17 hall, with a Rubens ceiling – offers an impressive
corporate venue. The undercroft is an elegant space, available
separately. / charities & companies only; list of caterers; smoking restricted; Main
Hall (500,375); Undercroft (350,200).*

Barbarella SW6   £M, (–,–,150)
428 Fulham Rd   385 9434   (381 0895)
*Long-established Fulham dine-and-disco venue, suitable for taking
over in its entirety. / 3am; not Sun, private hire Mon-Thu only.*

Barber-Surgeons' Hall EC2   £M, (250,120)
Monkwell Sq   600 1704   (606 3857)
*This light, panelled livery hall, near the Barbican, is a '60s remodelling
in traditional style. It is available primarily for business and livery
functions. / no weddings; 10.30pm; not Sat & Sun; Aug hol; Ring & Brymer;
no amplified music; no dancing; smoking restricted.*

Barbican Art Gallery EC2   £M, (400,300)
Barbican Centre, Silk St   382 7105   (628 0364)
*This twin-level gallery is quite reasonably priced by City standards and
is a popular venue, especially in the summer. Depending on the
layout of the current exhibition, access to the external Sculpture
Court may be possible. / weekdays only, from 6pm, 7pm or 8pm (depending
on day); Searcy's; no amplified music; no smoking.*

Barbican Centre EC2   £M-E, (550,240,240)
Barbican Centre   382 7246   (382 7247)
*The huge, jungle-like Conservatory would not be out of place in Kew
Gardens and makes a dramatic setting for a grand event. It can be
used in combination with the Barbican Art Gallery (see above).
/ 12.45pm; Searcy's; Garden Rm (400,240,240); Conservatory (120,65); Conservatory
Terrace (250,150).*

El Barco Latino WC2   £B-M, (100,70)
Victoria Embankment   379 5496
*By Victoria Embankment, close to Temple tube, this permanently-
moored barge serves a mixture of Spanish and Latin American food.
It may not be ultra-tasteful, but it is geared to dancing and has an
outside deck for warm weather. / 2am; in-house caterers.*

The Barley Mow W1   £B, (100,50)
8 Dorset St   935 7318
*Weekend trade in Marylebone is sufficiently quiet that this whole pub
is available for parties on Saturday night – there is no hire charge,
you just need to guarantee between 30 and 70 people. / midnight;
Sat only.*

Basil Street Hotel SW3   £M, (300,140,120)
8 Basil St   581 3311   (581 3693)
*This well-known Knightsbridge Edwardian establishment has a
peaceful charm and lots of creaky 'country house' character. The
large Parrot Club (downstairs) can be used for dancing. / midnight; Parrot
Club eve & weekend only; Parrot Club (300,140,120); Brompton Rm (100,60); Basil
Rm (50,35); Mezzanine Rm (30,16).*

Bath – Assembly Rooms   £M-E, (400,300,230)
Bennett St, Bath   01225-477782   (01225-477743)
*If you are planning something special, Bath is very accessible by train,
and its Georgian gentility and charm are unmatched. This beautiful
complex was purpose-built for seeing, being seen and promenading –
from Ballrm (with its five chandeliers) to Octagon to Tea Rm.
The rooms are a charming place to get married.* / 11.30pm; Aug hol;
Milburns; smoking restricted; Ballroom (400,300,230); Octagon (200,–); Tea
Rm (200,200,200); Card Rm (60,50).

Bath – Pump Room   £M, (400,350,310)
Still St, Bath   01225-477782
*These elegant rooms, right in the centre of Bath, can contribute a
great sense of occasion – especially, perhaps, to a wedding. Tours of
the amazing Roman baths can be arranged.* / 2am; eve only; Milburns;
Pump Rm (250,180,170); Concert Rm (160,110,70); Smoking or Drawing Rm (–,35).

The Battersea Barge Bistro SW8   £B-M, (120,100,100)
Nine Elms Ln   498 0004
*It's not exactly easy to find – moored on the South Bank along from
New Covent Garden Market – but this restaurant in a Dutch barge
makes a cosy and atmospheric place for a party, and is very
reasonably priced.* / Upper Deck (50,–); Captain's Cabin (–,16).

Battersea Park SW8   £M, (2000,1500,1500)
Battersea Pk   924 7505   (0181-871 7533)
*By the riverside pagoda, you can have most kinds of marquee-party
(hire your own or Wandsworth Council can provide). For large
marquee events (up to 1500 people) there is the three-acre British
Genius Site. (For the park's only permanent party venue, see Victoria
Pump House.)* / 2am; hirer's choice of caterer; British Genius Site (2000,1500,1500);
Riverside Terraces (1500,500); marquee site.

Battersea Town Hall SW11   £B, (800,400,350)
Lavender Hl   738 0908   (978 5207)
*The Grand Hall – a pretty Victorian edifice, complete with organ –
lives up to its name and offers a very characterful, economical venue
for larger gatherings. Its sprung wooden floor makes it ideal for
dancing.* / midnight; hirer's choice of caterer; Grand Hall (800,400,350);
Lower Hall (200,150,110).

Beaulieu, Hants   £M-E, (2500,250,160)
John Montagu Bldg, Beaulieu   01590-612345   (01590-612624)
*The National Motor Museum, the Domus (and ruined cloisters) of
the c13 abbey, and the '70s Brabazon complex provide a wealth of
opportunity for most occasions – from wedding receptions to large
corporate gatherings. For very grand (but smaller) affairs, the use of
Palace House is also a possibility.* / Ring & Brymer; smoking restricted; National
Motor Museum (2500,–); Brabazon (300,250,160); Domus (–,140,80); marquee site.

Beckton Alpine Centre E6   £B-M, (500,150,150)
Alpine Way   511 0351   (473 0770)
*To bring an Alpine theme to a party just north of London City Airport,
consider this site, which offers a 200m piste and three nursery
slopes. For functions, you can use different facilities in various
combinations – if appropriate with the addition of a marquee.*
/ Fri & Sat 2am, Restaurant 11.20pm; in-house caterers; Function Rm (250,100);
Bar (200,–); Restaurant (–,48); marquee site.

PRIVATE VENUES

HMS Belfast SE1   £M, (350,144,96)
Hay's Galleria   403 6246   (407 0708)
This WWII destroyer, permanently moored by Tower Bridge, offers a range of possibilities for medium size events. The decks afford a central location for a summer drinks party. / 1am; Ring & Brymer; Ship Co's Dining Hall (240,144,96); Wardroom (150,50,50); Gun Rm (120,60,60); Anteroom (75,–); Admiral's Quarters (35,20); Quarter Deck (summer eve) (350,–).

Belgo Centraal WC2   £M, (–,35)
50 Earlham St   813 2233   (209 3212)
This impressive, rather space-age Covent Garden Belgian mussels and beer hall has two private rooms. / Private Rm (–,35); Private Rm (–,25).

Belvedere W8   £M, (180,150)
Holland House, Holland Pk   602 1238   (610 4382)
Beautifully situated Holland Park restaurant, ideal for a reception after a wedding at the nearby Orangery (or you can have the ceremony here, too). Various levels of the restaurant are available individually for functions, but the best floor, giving access to the Terrace, is the top one – to have this, you must hire the whole restaurant. / 3am; lower level (–,70); top level (–,60); middle level (–,20).

Bengal Clipper SE1   £M, (–,200)
Shad Thames   357 9001
This modern, airy Indian restaurant near Tower Bridge can be taken over in its entirety for functions.

Bentleys W1   £M, (–,12)
11-15 Swallow St   734 4756
This very pretty, old-established English fish restaurant (but with a contemporary menu) boasts a civilised, light, first-floor private room. / not Sun; Private Rm (–,12).

Beotys WC2   £M, (–,60)
79 St Martin's Ln   836 8768
Solid, old-fashioned, family-owned, Franco-Greek Theatreland restaurant with notably charming service. / Private Rm (–,60).

The Berkeley SW1   £M-E, (450,180,180)
Wilton Pl   235 6000   (235 4330)
The ballroom and other banqueting rooms at this modern Savoy Group hotel in Knightsbridge – some of which used to have wonderfully wacky '70s interiors – are all now decorated in rather conventionally grand/clubby/country house styles. The hotel is licensed for weddings. / Ballroom (450,180,180); Belgravia (150,54); Tattersalls (50,34); Waterloo (50,30); Billet (12,12); Knightsbridge (10,10).

The Berkshire W1   £M, (50,26)
350 Oxford St   0181-564 7464   (0181-899 3533)
The pretty, panelled top-floor Sonning Suite – suitable for dinners and smaller receptions – is the more richly furnished and better proportioned room available in this, modern wedge-shaped hotel. / 2am; Sonning Suite (50,26); Sandhurst Suite (30,20).

The Berners Hotel W1   £M-E, (250,160,120)
10 Berners St   636 1629   (580 3972)
This hotel, not far from Oxford Street, was built in 1835 and converted to its present form at the turn of the century. It's a comfortable, clubby sort of place, with a reasonable choice of medium size accommodation, and would make quite a good place to get married. / 11pm; in-house caterers; Thomas Ashton Suite (250,160,120); Fitzrovia Suite (120,80); Ashton Rm (100,80); Slater Rm (70,50).

Bill Bentley's EC2   £B, (60,40)
18 Old Broad St   588 2655   (588 0808)
City wine bar with the unusual benefit of a paved garden. The garden cannot be reserved but, if you take the basement for an evening booking, it may be used (on a non-exclusive basis) for pre-dinner drinks. / not Sat & Sun.

Bishopsgate Institute EC2   £B-M, (360,180,130)
230 Bishopsgate   247 6844   (375 1794)
Victorian institute by Liverpool Street Station, whose large main hall, with a little decoration and theming, has possibilities for big corporate parties. / companies only; midnight; hirer's choice of caterer; no smoking.

Blackheath Concert Halls SE3   £B-M, (1000,700,700)
23 Lee Rd   0181-318 9758   (0181-852 5154)
These characterful Victorian halls (claiming to be the first purpose-built concert halls in the country) are well-appointed and a local favourite for a whole range of events from wedding receptions to college balls. The Café Bar is also available for hire. / 2am; list of caterers; Great Hall (1000,700,300); Recital Rm (250,230,120); Café Bar (200,50).

Bleeding Heart EC1   £M, (60,50)
Bleeding Heart Yard, Greville St   242 8238   (831 1402)
Characterful, cramped and difficult to find cellar restaurant/wine bar, in the thin area north of Holborn. The Back Room is available daily and the whole place can be hired at weekends. / music & dancing weekends only, events must include food; 1am; bistro or restaurant weekends only; in-house caterers; Private Rm (60,40); Bistro (ground floor) (–,50).

Blenheim Palace, Oxon   £E, (750,300,300)
Woodstock   01993-811091   (01993-813527)
The home of the 11th Duke of Marlborough (and birthplace of Sir Winston Churchill) is one of the finest houses in England. A few miles north of Oxford, and set in 2,000 acres of "Capability" Brown gardens, its state rooms offer unparalleled opportunities to impress – at a price, of course. / Jan-Feb hol; list of caterers; State Rms (750,300); Orangery (200,160); marquee site.

Bloomsbury Square Training Centre WC1   £M, (80,30)
2/3 Bloomsbury Sq   212 7662   (212 7550)
The name may sound uninviting, but accountants Coopers and Lybrands' recently refurbished, listed Bloomsbury building has some surprisingly characterful accommodation, including the Ascham Room (with its six chandeliers). The Cellars Restaurant is an atmospheric place for evening functions (including discos). / 11.20pm; in-house caterers; in restaurant; smoking restricted; Ascham Rm (80,–); Cellars Restaurant (70,30).

Bluebird SW3   £M-E, (40,20)
350 King's Rd   559 1000
Conran's mega-restaurant above his new Chelsea foodie emporium is to include a private dining room, which – we are told – is "spectacular". / Private Rm (40,20).

Boisdale SW1   £M, (–,20)
15 Eccleston St   730 6922
This clubby, cosy wine bar/restaurant, near Victoria Station, has a pleasant private room, and at less busy times you can take over the whole place. Prices are quite reasonable. / Private Rm (–,20).

PRIVATE VENUES

Bombay Bicycle Club SW12   **£M, (–,70)**
95 Nightingale Ln   0181-673 6217   (0181-673 9100)
This high-quality Indian restaurant near Wandsworth Common has a ground floor private room, or, in the earlier part of the week, you can take over the whole restaurant. / Private Rm (–,22).

Bombay Brasserie SW7   **£M, (–,150)**
Courtfield Close, Glouc Rd   370 4040
London's most famous Indian restaurant is built on an imperial scale – if you guarantee 125 people, you can use the whole of the impressive conservatory. / no dancing; Conservatory (–,150).

Bonham's SW7   **£M-E, (250,200)**
Montpelier St   393 3900   (393 3905)
Knightsbridge auction rooms which are available, subject to the constraints of the current hanging, for private hire. They particularly suit early-evening receptions. / midnight; eve only; hirer's choice of caterer; no amplified music; no dancing.

Bonjour Vietnam SW6   **£B-M, (150,80)**
593-599 Fulham Rd   385 7603   (610 2433)
The basement of this brightly-coloured and wackily-furnished Fulham oriental restaurant makes a good place for a young-at-heart party. / Basement (150,80).

Borscht & Tears SW3   **£B-M, (–,70)**
46 Beauchamp Pl   589 5003
Few private rooms in restaurants have as few frills as the 'hose-down' cellar at this notoriously rowdy Polish Knightsbridge restaurant, but few places seem as tolerant of what happens in their private room. / Private Rm (–,70).

Boston Manor House, Middx   **£B-M, (60,–)**
Boston Manor Rd, Brentford   0181-992 1612
Fine Jacobean manor house in Brentford (with some Victorian interiors), used to display a local history collection. The premises were extensively refurbished in 1997, largely with a view to attracting function business – a marriage licence has been applied for. / Sun-Thu 11pm, Fri & Sat midnight; in-house or hirer's choice by negotiation; no amplified music; no dancing; no smoking; Boston Manor Suite (60,–); State Rm (60,–); marquee site.

Boudin Blanc W1   **£B-M, (–,35)**
5 Trebeck St   499 3292
Jolly, reasonably-priced Shepherd Market bistro, with an upstairs private room. / Private Rm (–,35).

Bow Film Studios E15   **£B-M, (1500,500)**
Sugar House La, Stratford
0181-522 0878/0831 872076   (0181-522 0877)
These TV film studios under the Bow Flyover offer generous capacity for themed events. As we went to press, a bar, restaurant and canteen were being built which may be available for smaller private parties from June 1997. / companies only; list of caterers; marquee site.

Bow Wine Vaults EC4   **£B-M, (140,60)**
10 Bow Church Yd   248 1121   (248 0318)
Civilised basement restaurant, just behind St Mary-le-Bow, which makes quite a congenial spot for an inexpensive City boys' get-together, not too expensively. / 11pm; Mon-Fri eve; in-house caterers; larger Section (100,60); smaller Section (40,30).

Boyd's W8
£M, (–,40)

135 Kensington Church St   727 5452   (221 0615)

If you guarantee a minimum spend, you can take over this light and airy Kensington restaurant in its entirety. High-quality modern British cooking is among the attractions.

Bramah Tea & Coffee Museum SE1
£B-M, (250,80)

4 Maguire St   378 0222   (378 0219)

The large mezzanine floor of the Butler's Wharf Clove building – home to Mr Bramah's eccentric collection of over 1000 teapots and coffee-making machines – is an interesting possibility for a reception. It would need some decoration to be festive. / 10.30pm; from 6.30pm; hirer's choice of caterer; no amplified music; no dancing; no smoking.

Brasserie du Marché aux Puces W10
£B-M, (60,30)

349 Portobello Rd   0181-968 5828   (960 8978)

The downstairs private room at this amiable North Kensington bistro makes a congenial place for an informal party. / Private Rm (60,30).

Brasserie Rocque EC2
£B-M, (300,120,90)

37 Broadgate Circle   638 7919   (628 5899)

Stylish, large, modern Brasserie which moonlights as a venue for all kinds of occasions and is particularly popular for wedding receptions – especially in summer, when it is possible to spill onto the terrace by the Broadgate Ice Rink. / 1am; Mon-Fri eve Sat & Sun all day.

Brasserie St Quentin SW3
£M, (–,20)

243 Brompton Rd   589 8005   (584 6064)

This glittering Knightsbridge brasserie – with good French atmosphere, food, and service – has a pleasant downstairs private room. / Private Rm (–,20).

Break For The Border W1
£B-M, (375,225,200)

8-9 Argyll St   734 5776   (437 5140)

Brash and brightly coloured restaurant, occupying extensive cellars, just off Oxford Street – the place has a very unusual 'feel' to it. / 11pm, Thu-Sat 3am; in-house caterers.

The Brewers Rooms W1
£M, (250,–)

42 Portman Sq   486 4831   (935 3991)

The suite of rooms at the Brewers and Licensed Retailers Association is suitable for fairly businessy drinks receptions. / midnight; not Sun; in-house caterers; smoking restricted.

Brewers' Hall EC2
£M, (200,80)

Aldermandbury Sq   606 1301   (796 3557)

The Brewers' Company is reasonably flexible about the use of its hall, whose quite simple but pleasant interconnecting rooms are available for a range of functions. / Aug hol; list of caterers; Livery Hall (200,80); Court Rm (80,30); Committee Rm (20,10).

The Brewery EC1
£M, (850,660,660)

Chiswell St   638 8811   (638 5713)

Whitbread's former City brewery is now a leading conference and function venue. The star attraction is the Porter Tun – built in the eighteenth century as a storehouse, and boasting an unobstructed floor space of 8,400 sq ft. The rooms, tend to be rather businessy in feel, though the airy Sugar Rooms are attractive enough for purely social functions. / 1am; not Sun; Porter Tun (850,660,550); King George III (700,400,300); Queen Charlotte (250,180,120); Smeaton's Vaults (250,100,100); Sugar Rms (150,100,100); The James Watt (120,66,66); City Cellars (80,45).

Brick Lane Music Hall EC2 £M, (–,250,250)
134-146 Curtain Rd   739 9996   (739 9998)
Still in Shoreditch, but no longer in Brick Lane, this Victorian theatre is installed in a former button factory. The audience remains at table, cabaret-style, for the show and dinner. You can reserve the whole place to see the current performance. / 12.30am; in-house caterers.

Brighton Royal Pavilion, Sussex £M-E, (200,90)
Brighton   01273-603005   (01273-779108)
George IV's splendid seaside palace offers the ideal setting for a Regency banquet. / companies only; 11pm; eve only; in-house caterers; no amplified music; no dancing; smoking restricted; Banqueting Rm (and Great Kitchen) (200,90); Queen Adelaide Suite (100,80); Great Kitchen (90,40).

Brinkley's SW10 £M, (–,30)
47 Hollywood Rd   351 1683   (376 5083)
The appeal of this airy, modish, modern British restaurant, off the Fulham Road, is wide-ranging. It must be the nicest restaurant in London to be notorious for stag and hen parties, the less sober of which are held in the not-unpleasant 'Brinkley bomb room'. / 1am; Private Rm (–,30).

Britannia W8 £B, (100,35)
1 Allen St   937 1864
If you have around 40 guests, you can take over the agreeable conservatory at the rear of this Kensington pub. / 11.20pm.

Britannia Intercontinental Hotel W1 £M, (120,85,85)
Grosvenor Sq   629 9400   (629 7736)
The large banqueting facilities which might be expected in a Mayfair hotel of this size are surprisingly lacking. The cosy pine bar is perhaps the best room, though the interconnecting Grosvenor rooms have the benefit of views of the square below. / Manhattan (120,85,85); Pine Bar (75,–); Grosvenor I (45,30); Grosvenor II (18,10).

British Museum WC1 £E, (1000,450)
Great Russell St   636 1555   (323 8614)
Possibly the world's greatest museum of antiquities offers some high-prestige – and suitably expensive – options for corporate entertaining. The Egyptian Sculpture Gallery is one of the most suitable for receptions, though other possibilities include the Roman Room, the Nereid Room and the Duveen (Elgin Marbles) Gallery. / midnight; eve only; list of caterers; no music; no dancing; no smoking.

Broadgate Estates EC2 £B-E, (200,–)
Broadgate Centre   505 4000   (382 9854)
Sites available for receptions at this Manhattanite city complex include the Raised Garden Terraces around the Ice Rink, the Ice Rink and – hidden away north of Liverpool Street – Exchange Square (for which the centre has a special marquee). Local wine bars and restaurants generally provide the catering (see Corney & Barrow and Brasserie Rocque). / only Fri eve, Sat eve & Sun eve; Ice Rink not Apr-Oct; hirer's choice of caterer; Ice Rink (200,–); Exchange Square Marquee (90,–).

Brocket Hall, Herts £E, (180,150,150)
Welwyn   01707-335241   (01707-375166)
Superb c18 hall and estate, suited to the grandest of gatherings. "England's finest residential venue", they claim, and with facilities including a Chippendale library and an 18-hole golf course, they may well be right. / in-house caterers; marquee site.

Brockwell Lido SE24   £B, (1000,250)
Brockwell Park, Dulwich Rd   274 3088   (924 0232)
Go retro and hold your party at this 30s-style south London site with huge, 50m pool. It's ideal for parties with an indoor and an outdoor element, and there is a 70m x 20m marquee site. / 2am; from 7pm; not Oct-Apr; in-house caterers; no amplified music; café-restaurant (260,60); Function Rm (–,250).

Brompton Oratory
St Wilfrid's Hall SW7   £B-M, (280,200)
Brompton Rd   792 1162   (229 3506)
St Wilfrid's Hall is a gracious and central Victorian setting (next to the V&A) for receptions and recitals. Facilities include a grand piano and a large billiards room. / 11pm; not Sun; list of caterers; no amplified music; no dancing; St Wilfrid's Hall (incl Billiards Rm) (140,100); St Joseph's Hall (140,100).

Brown's Hotel W1   £M, (120,70,50)
Albemarle St   493 6020   (493 9381)
Mayfair stalwart epitomising a certain creaky, pleasantly worn, traditional English style. The ethos of the hotel and lack of sound-proofing preclude anything which might be called a bash, but it's well suited to genteel entertaining. / 11.30pm; in-house caterers; no amplified music; Clarendon (120,70,50); Niagra & Roosevelt combined (100,70); Kipling (60,40); Roosevelt (60,45); Niagara (40,40); Hellenic (32,28); Lord Byron (12,12); Graham Bell (10,8).

Browns W1   £M, (280,135)
47 Maddox St   491 4565   (491 4564)
These premises just off Savile Row started life as a tailors, and the original fittings have been retained at what is now an English brasserie. The three original changing rooms have been preserved and are available for private hire, or you can take the whole place. / 1am; Rm 54 (30,20); Rm 53 (–,11); Rm 52 (–,6).

Browns WC2   £M, (120,100)
82-84 St Martin's La   497 5050   (497 5005)
This Grade II listed building in Covent Garden was a real courtroom between 1890 and 1995 – the judge's and witness boxes as well as jurors' bench are still in situ. Now it's become a branch of the Oxford/Cambridge/Brighton chain of English brasseries. / 1.30am; in-house caterers; no music; no dancing; Courtroom 1 (120,100); Courtroom 2 (80,60); Courtroom 3 (50,40).

Browns Club WC2   £B-M, (680,–)
4 Great Queen St   831 0802   (831 2228)
For a largish nightclub, the décor of this Covent Garden spot is uncharacteristically stylish. It is a popular venue for receptions. / 3am; hirer's choice of caterer, alcohol in-house; Bar & Dance Floor (300,–); VIP Rm (300,–); Small VIP Rm (100,–).

Bubb's EC1   £M, (–,10)
329 Central Markets, Farringdon Rd   236 2435
Old-fashioned Smithfield restaurant — a rambling arrangement of parlours, some of which may be used privately. The traditional cooking is heavy, quite good and pretty expensive. / Private Rm (–,10).

Burgh House NW3   £B-M, (90,50)
New End Sq   431 0144
Charmingly located Queen Anne house in Hampstead, with a very pretty ground floor music room which is especially suited to weddings and more sedate receptions. / 10.30pm; not Mon & Tue; in-house caterers; no amplified music; no dancing; no smoking.

PRIVATE VENUES

Busabong Too SW10   £M, (–,25)
1a Langton St   352 7414
Cheerfully decorated Chelsea Thai restaurant. If you supply enough people to more or less fill the mezzanine floor – where you sit bare-foot on floor cushions – you can have it to yourself.
/ Mezzanine (–,25).

The Business Design Centre N1   £M-E, (2000,2000)
52 Upper St   359 3535   (226 0590)
Modern exhibition premises in Islington sometimes used for black tie corporate events, for at least 800 people. / corporate (black tie) only; midnight; in-house caterers.

Butchers' Hall EC1   £M, (280,170,120)
87 Bartholomew Cl   600 5777   (489 8936)
This Smithfield livery hall is in a traditional but fairly modest style, but it's a flexible venue, much used for business and socially. / 1am; 2 wks hol in Aug; Chester Boyd; live band only – no discos; Great Hall (280,170); Large Court Rm & Small Court Rm (150,80); Taurus Suite (100,80); Large Court Rm (–,45); Small Court Rm (50,24).

Cabinet War Rooms SW1   £M-E, (200,50,50)
King Charles St   930 6961   (839 5897)
Churchill's fascinating subterranean bunker, off Whitehall, composed of 21 tiny rooms, and the corridors which snake between them, is best enjoyed, on an exclusive basis, in the evening. (During daytime public opening hours, function of up to 50 can be accommodated in the Annexe.) / 11.30pm; from 6.30pm; dinner hirer's choice of caterer, lunch approved list; smoking in Annexe only.

Cabot Hall E14   £M, (800,350,350)
Canary Wharf   418 2780   (512 9117)
Like the rest of Canary Wharf, this hall at the foot of the tower (overlooking Cabot Square through a lofty bay window) is huge, finished and equipped to the highest standards, and vaguely American in feel. The smaller rooms are unimposing and quite jolly. / midnight; list of caterers; Hall (800,350,350); Sebastian Rm (100,60); St Lawrence Rm (70,40); Cape Breton Rm (30,12); Nova Scotia Rm (20,10); Newfoundland Rm (–,12).

The Cadogan SW1   £M, (80,36)
75 Sloane St   235 7141   (245 0994)
Welcoming, fashionably-located, somewhat old-fashioned Knightsbridge hotel. The main dining room (for a maximum of 36 sitting) may sometimes be used for parties too large for the private room. / midnight; Langtry Dining (50,20); Langtry Sitting (30,–).

Café de Paris W1   £M-E, (750,120)
3 Coventry St   734 7700   (734 0347)
Although this '30s Society rendezvous has been relaunched as a contemporary nightclub/bar/restaurant, much of the period elegance lingers. The Fantasy Suite is a separate area with four rooms and its own bar. / 3am; not Fri & Sat; in-house caterers; Restaurant (150,120); Fantasy Suite (80,–); Oyster Bar (70,–); Red Bar (45,–).

Café du Jardin WC2   £M, (–,70)
28 Wellington St   836 8769
Culinarily speaking, this is one of the more consistent Covent Garden restaurants. The whole place was refurbished in early 1997, and its basement makes a very good place for a private party.
/ Downstairs (–,70).

Café du Marché EC1 £M, (150,60)
22 Charterhouse Sq   608 1609   (336 7055)
*Very popular French restaurant, occupying a 'designer-rustic'
warehouse conversion near Smithfield market. The atmospheric
upstairs room would suit less formal business as well as social
occasions. / midnight; not Sun.*

Café Greenwich Park SE10 £B-M, (200,–)
Greenwich Pk   0181-858 9695   (0181-935 5894)
*This park cafeteria has a wonderful location. Although its private
room is probably best suited to kids' parties, it has its own garden
which would make a good spot for an outdoors evening party/BBQ for
grown-ups. You can have the disco inside. / midnight; from 7.30pm (winter
from 3pm); hirer's choice of caterer; including Garden (200,–); Inside only (150,–);
Upstairs Rm (60,–); marquee site.*

Café L'Institute SW7 £B-M, (100,70)
17 Queensbury Pl   584 7171   (591 0467)
*Modern South Kensington premises you can hire separately from or
with the Institut Français (the building in which the café is housed).
It's quite a stylish room, with light wood fittings, and particularly
suitable for cocktail parties. / 10.30pm; in-house caterers; Cafe (–,70).*

Café Lazeez SW7 £M, (100,50)
93-95 Old Brompton Rd   581 9993
*Elegantly decorated, modern South Kensington Indian restaurant, with
an upstairs room which can be taken in its entirety.*

Café Royal W1 £M, (3000,2500,550)
68 Regent St   287 6130   (434 0718)
*Eight remarkable floors of ballrooms, banqueting chambers, bars and
restaurants, offering size, flexibility and grandeur. The first three
Victorian floors are more characterful than the 1920s extension
upward. The cellar (ideal for a wine-tasting) and Penthouse offer
interesting options at the extremes – the one dimly-lit and
atmospheric, the other with great views, if not the most stylish décor.
Three rooms are licensed for weddings. / 11.20pm; in-house caterers;
smoking restricted; 4-Empire Napoleon (1000,650,550); 6-Dubarry (600,400,300);
2-Louis (350,270,200); 6-Dauphin (250,120); 5-Marquise (200,130,100);
1-Derby & Queensbury (150,100,70); 1-Domino (120,80,60); Cellars (70,50);
8-Penthouse (40,24).*

The Caledonian Club SW1 £M-E, (200,120,120)
9 Halkin St   235 5162   (333 8737)
*Belying the myth of Scottish dourness, this welcoming Belgravia Club
lacks some of the stuffiness of its St James's cousins and is ideal for
many kinds of receptions and dinners (with reeling possible in the
Members Dining Room). The sponsorship of a member is required,
but for an event with a genuine Scottish link, it may be worth
approaching the Secretary. / 2am; members dining rm eve only; not Dec;
no discos; jacket & tie; no children under 8; Members Dining Rm (200,120,60);
Stuart (65,52); Selkirk (40,22); Oval (–,12).*

Calthorpe Arms WC1 £B, (60,36)
252 Grays Inn Rd   278 4732
*Friendly Bloomsbury pub with quite a smart, well-maintained private
room. / Private Rm (60,36).*

Canal Brasserie W10 £B-M, (200,70)
222 Kensal Rd   0181-960 2732
*Hiding in Canalot studios (on the banks of the Grand Union Canal),
this lofty, stylish space makes a nice spot for weekend parties – there
is an outside area for summer. / Mon, Tue eve – Sat & Sun all day.*

The Candid Arts Trust EC1 £B-M, (200,100)
3 Torrens St   837 4237   (278 9327)
*The banquet room at this idiosyncratic art gallery, near Angel tube, is
one of the top bargains in town for an atmospheric party on a budget
– offering flexible and reasonably priced accommodation for a whole
range of functions. A wedding licence has been applied for. / Basement –
negotiable, ground floor 1am, First Floor Gallery 11pm; hirer's choice of caterer; Ground
Floor Gallery (200,100); Basement Gallery (150,–); Banquet Rm (60,27).*

Canning House SW1 £B-M, (150,80)
2 Belgrave Sq   235 2303   (235 3587)
*The first floor rooms of the Hispanic and Luso Brazilian Council,
which overlook the square, are extremely popular for drinks parties.
They offer affordable grandeur at a very smart address, a stone's
throw from Hyde Park Corner. / 11pm; eve only, Sat & Sun all day;
hirer's choice of caterer.*

Cannizaro House SW19 £M-E, (120,100,60)
West Side, Wimbledon Common
0181-879 1464   (0181-944 6515)
*Georgian mansion hotel, prettily situated in Cannizaro Park on the
edge of Wimbledon Common, with a good range of function rooms of
various sizes. The Queen Elizabeth Room is licensed for weddings.
/ midnight; no amplified music; no dancing; Viscount Melville Suite (120,100,60); Earl Of
Mexborough (50,44); Viscount Melville (50,44); Oak Rm (35,24); Boardroom (–,10).*

La Capannina W1 £M, (–,25)
24 Romilly St   437 2473
*Untouched by modern Italian fads, this Soho trattoria survivor from a
different culinary age serves solid fare and is a cosy place for a dinner
in the private room downstairs. / not Sat L, Sun; Private Rm (–,25).*

The Capital SW3 £M-E, (35,22)
Basil St   589 5171   (225 0011)
*The private dining rooms of this chic, small hotel – right by Harrods –
are in a fairly traditional style. The cooking is consistently among the
best offered by London hotels. / Eaton (20,12); Cadogan (35,22); Sitting
Rm (–,10).*

Capital Radio Café WC2 £M, (380,250)
29-30 Leicester Sq   484 8888   (395 3595)
*Capital Radio relocated to the heart of Theatreland in early 1997
and has taken the opportunity to open a themed restaurant –
complete with loud music and multiple video screens – on the ground
floor of its new premises. The VIP Room has its own entrance. / 3am;
not Sat & Sun; VIP Lounge (60,45).*

Captain Kidd E1 £B, (150,100,50)
108 Wapping High St   480 5759   (702 0418)
*One of the most popular places for food and drink in the Docklands,
this olde worlde riverside pub has two function rooms – the second
floor Observation Deck (which has large windows overlooking the
river) and the first floor Gallows. / midnight; not Sun; in-house caterers;
Gallows (–,50); Observation Deck (60,40).*

Caravan Serai W1   £B-M, (–,18)
50 Paddington St   935 1208   (486 0255)
London's grandest (practically only) Afghani restaurant serves some unusual, enjoyable grub. The private room, like the rest of the restaurant, is decorated in a rug-filled style and makes a jolly place for a less formal occasion. / 1am.

Cardamon Café E1   £B, (80,50)
St Peter's Centre, Reardon St   702 1579   (680 9640)
Summery café in a former Wapping schoolhouse (now an arts and community centre). / 10.30pm; in-house caterers; no amplified music.

Carlyle's House SW3   £B-M, (40,–)
24 Cheyne Row   352 7087
Queen Anne Chelsea house – home of the writer and historian Thomas Carlyle for nearly half a century (and with quite a display of memorabilia on site). It is occasionally available for sedate occasions. In fine weather, you can use the Victorian walled garden. / very restricted availability; 8pm; from 6pm; not Oct-Mar; hirer's choice of caterer; no amplified music; no dancing; no smoking.

The Carnarvon Hotel W5   £M, (200,200,180)
Ealing Common   0181-992 5399   (0181-992 7082)
Modern hotel in west London whose conference facilities double up for weddings, receptions and the like. The Edward Suite features a stage. / 1am; in-house caterers; smoking restricted; Edward Suite (200,200,180); Creffield Suite (90,80,80); Gunnersbury Suite (40,32).

Carpenters' Hall EC2   £M, (350,220)
Throgmorton Av   628 0833   (638 6286)
Forming the arch over the London Wall end of Throgmorton Avenue, this Hall, in distinctive '60s style, is quite impressive. / no weddings; not Sat & Sun; Aug hol; list of caterers; no amplified music; no dancing; smoking restricted; Livery Hall (350,220); Reception Rm (230,–); Luncheon Rm (–,32).

The Catherine Wheel W8   £B, (80,25)
23 Kensington Church St   937 3259
Kensington Pub whose private bar is like an intimate drawing room. / 11.20pm; Private Rm (80,25).

Cavalry & Guards Club W1   £M, (350,130)
127 Piccadilly   499 1261   (495 5956)
This carefully maintained Edwardian club, overlooking Green Park, has a number of charming traditional rooms. For suitable functions, it may be worth trying to find a member to sponsor your event. / not Sun; in-house caterers; smoking restricted; Coffee Rm (300,130); Balaclava Rm (100,50); Peninsula Rm (180,90); Waterloo Rm (80,24); Double Bridal Rm (30,16).

The Cavendish SW1   £M, (125,80,60)
81 Jermyn St   930 2111   (839 2125)
As we go to press, expansion and refurbishment of the banqueting facilities continues at this long-established St James's hotel. All of the rooms are on the first floor, and have natural light. / Park (125,80,60); Mayfair (40,20); Duke (15,10).

Cecil Sharp House NW1   £B-M, (500,500,300)
2 Regent's Park Rd   485 2206   (284 0523)
The Primrose Hill home of the English Folk Dance and Song Society has two panelled halls, which are available for private receptions and dances, with semi-sprung floors. There is a small, attractive walled garden. / 11pm; in-house caterers; smoking restricted; Kennedy Hall (500,500,300); Trefusis Hall (140,140,100); Bar (65,–).

PRIVATE VENUES

Central Club (YWCA) WC1 £B, (350,180,150)
16-22 Great Russell St   636 7512   (636 5278)
The Queen Mary room at this Bloomsbury building (formerly the YWCA) is a large, pleasantly worn hall. Other smaller rooms are available. / 2am; in-house caterers; library – no smoking; Queen Mary Hall (350,180,150).

Champenois EC2 £M, (250,120,110)
10 Devonshire Sq   283 7888
Large, stylish basement 'business' restaurant in the impressive Cutlers' Gardens development, near Liverpool Street. / 2am.

Charcos SW3 £M, (60,35)
1 Bray Pl   584 0765
Long-established wine bar/restaurant near Sloane Square which offers competent cooking. The basement may be taken privately. / no amplified music; Downstairs (60,35).

**Chartered Institute of
Public Finance & Accountancy WC2** £M, (60,40)
3 Robert St   543 5600   (543 5700)
Though perhaps a little institutional, this Adam house offers a fine view over the Embankment from its fourth-floor committee room, which is suitable for receptions or dinners. There are lower floor rooms, which are really only suited to business entertaining. / 10pm; not Sat & Sun; Owen Bros; no amplified music; no dancing; no smoking; Committee Rm 4 (60,40); Council Chamber (60,34).

Chartered Accountants' Hall EC2 £M, (400,280,200)
Moorgate Pl   920 8100   (920 0547)
Elegant, attractive, extremely well-maintained City complex, including two interesting, traditional style rooms (Members' and Main Reception) and a tasteful modern hall. / 1am; Leith's; Great Hall (400,280,200); Main Reception Rm (120,80); Members' Rm (70,30); Small Reception Rm (30,18).

Chatham Hall SW11 £B, (70,–)
Northcote Rd   0181-871 6394
Former Battersea stables, available for children's events (around 50 youngsters) or restrained cocktail receptions. / children's parties & quieter cocktail events; 11pm; hirer's choice of caterer; no amplified music.

The Chelsea SW1 £M-E, (200,100,100)
17 Sloane St   235 4377   (235 3705)
This modern Knightsbridge hotel has unusually crisp style. Its modern banqueting rooms all open off the balcony of a small glazed atrium, giving quite an intimate effect. / 2am; Sloane Suite (200,100,100); Beauchamp Rm (60,24); Chelsea Rm (18,10).

Chelsea Football Club SW6 £B-M, (600,220,220)
Fulham Rd   915 1916   (381 4831)
No-frills, large banqueting suites. Fanatics can get married here. / not match days; London Catering Services; Executive Club Rm (400,220); Trophy Rm (120,–); Sponsors Lounge (100,60); Box (–,12).

The Chelsea Gardener SW3 £B-M, (300,100)
125 Sydney St   352 9881   (352 3301)
There are few acre-sized gardens in Chelsea. This one – the garden centre at Chelsea Gardeners' Market – is therefore very popular for summer soirées. / 10.30pm; from 6.30pm – not Sat & Sun; hirer's choice of caterer; no dancing; smoking restricted.

Chelsea Physic Garden SW3   £M, (400,80)
66 Royal Hospital Rd   352 5646   (376 3910)
*This 3 1/2 acre botanical garden, hidden away in Old Chelsea, has
been here since 1673. It makes a fascinating spot for a summer
drinks party, but not – thanks to deadly nightshade and ponds – with
kids present.* / 10.30pm; May-Sep – Mon-Wed eve, Sat all day (marquee Sat only);
list of caterers; no amplified music; no dancing; no smoking; With marquee (Sats in
Jun-Sep only) (275,–); Reception Rm (150,80); marquee site.

Chelsea Harbour Rooms SW10   £M, (400,220,200)
Chelsea Harbour   351 4433   (352 7868)
*This purpose-built suite of banqueting/conference rooms best suits
themed events.* / midnight; list of caterers; Turner & Carlyle Rms (300,220,200);
Turner Rm (200,90); Carlyle Rm (180,70,60); Reception Rm (80,–).

Chelsea Old Town Hall SW3   £B-M, (480,300,250)
King's Rd   361 2220   (938 3468)
*For a large event, this civic hall is grand, well-maintained, centrally-
located and affordable. The adjoining register office has always been
a popular wedding venue – now the Main and Small Halls of the
Town Hall itself are also available for this purpose.* / midnight;
list of caterers; Main Hall (480,300,250); Small Hall (150,100); Cadogan Suite (150,90).

The Chesterfield Hotel W1   £M, (300,190)
35 Charles St   514 5608   (491 4793)
*Clubby, comfortable hotel near Shepherd Market offering a good
range of quite characterful rooms – from a panelled library to a
conservatory. The latter is particularly suited to stand-up receptions.*
/ midnight; Charles/Queens Suites (170,110); Conservatory (70,40); Library (40,18);
Stanhope Suite (25,8).

Chez Bruce SW17   £M, (–,25)
2 Bellevue Rd   0181-672 0114
*This Wandsworth restaurant – the best in south London – has a
pleasant upstairs private room, overlooking the Common.* / Private
Rm (–,25).

Chez Gérard (Opera Terrace) WC2   £B-M, (100,50)
45 East Terrace, The Piazza   379 0666   (497 9060)
*This restaurant (now part of the Chez Gérard steak-frites chain), with
its outside terrace overlooking the Royal Opera House building-site,
offers one of the best al fresco locations in London.* / Terrace (100,50).

Chez Gerard, Dover St W1   £B-M, (50,25)
31 Dover St   499 8171
*This Mayfair establishment (part of the chain particularly reputed for
its steak/frites) has an interesting stone-walled downstairs room.
Alternatively, the mezzanine balcony can be taken privately.*
/ Private Rm (50,25); Mezzanine (–,25).

Chez Nico at Ninety
Grosvenor House Hotel W1   £E, (–,20)
90 Park Ln   409 1290   (355 4877)
*Star chef Nico Ladenis's Mayfair temple of haute cuisine has an
elegant, conventionally decorated private room.* / not Sat & Sun; Private
Rm (–,20).

PRIVATE VENUES

Chislehurst Caves, Kent   £B-M, (100,50)
Old Hill, Chislehurst   0181-467 3264
As seen in Dr Who, these ancient chalk mines comprise around 20 miles of caverns and passages. The Club Room is a cave regularly used for wedding receptions and birthday parties. The Manager – unnecessarily we would have thought – recommends people view before booking. / 11.30pm; from 6pm; in-house or hirer's choice by negotiation; no smoking.

Chiswick House W4   £E, (150,50)
Burlington La   0181-995 0508   (0181-742 3104)
Grand Palladian house (1729) with a suite of interconnecting first-floor rooms. You might dine in the octagonal Domed Saloon, with its coffered domed ceiling – other rooms feature period paintings and furniture. / midnight; summer from 6.30pm, winter from 4.30pm; hirer's choice of caterer; no amplified music; no dancing; no smoking; no red wine; First Floor (150,50); marquee site.

Christie's SW1   £M-E, (600,200)
8 King St   839 9060   (925 2751)
The grand galleries of this St James's auctioneer are, subject to other requirements, sometimes made available for functions. / Mon-Fri from 6pm, not Sat & Sun; hirer's choice of caterer; no dancing; no smoking.

Christopher's WC2   £M-E, (–,200)
18 Wellington St   240 4222   (240 3357)
This well-known, upmarket American restaurant – which occupies an impressive Victorian building in Covent Garden – is being relaunched in mid-1997. It will have variety of dining rooms, spread over three floors, any or all of which may be made available for suitable private functions.

Chuen Cheng Ku W1   £B, (–,500)
17 Wardour St   437 1398   (434 0533)
Vast (400-seater), gaudy, Chinatown restaurant set in a building some of whose rooms retain quite a degree of period grandeur. Any (for groups of 30 people and up) may be taken privately.

Church House SW1   £M, (250,200,160)
Dean's Yd   222 2348   (233 1439)
The Church of England HQ has an impressive location, overlooking the river just by Parliament, and is well-appointed, if in a rather understated way. It enjoys quite a degree of popularity for wedding receptions. / 1am; not Sun; Crown Catering; Harvey Goodwin Suite (250,200,160); Hoare Memorial Hall (250,150); Bishop Partridge Hall (180,120); Westminster (50,30); Jubilee (20,20).

Churchill W1   £M, (300,240,192)
Portman Sq   486 5800   (487 2947)
The banqueting facilities of this '70s hotel north of Oxford Street were completely refurbished in 1995. The Library (to be renovated in August 1997) and the Chartwell Suites are licensed for weddings. / 1am; Chartwell Suite (300,240,192); Chartwell I (200,144,80); Library (120,60); Blenheim (75,48); Randolph (40,30); Marlborough Suite (80,50); Spencer (40,30); marquee site.

Cibo W14   £M, (–,55)
3 Russell Gdns   371 6271
Olympia Italian restaurant with rather unusual, bright décor and good food. It can be hired in its entirety for parties, or alternatively it subdivides into areas of varying sizes and degrees of privacy.

Circa W1   £B, (300,60,60)
59 Berkeley Sq   499 7850   (499 0051)
This Mayfair basement bar moonlights as a club and makes a good place for a party, especially with dancing. It's been redecorated in soothing colours and made much plusher than before. / *3am; Upstairs not before 11pm; hirer's choice of caterer, alcohol in-house; Downstairs (165,60,60); Upstairs (130,60).*

Circus Space EC1   £M-E, (500,–)
Old St   0181-682 4900   (0181-682 0602)
This huge, high ceilinged City-fringe venue is used as a training area for circus acts. For function use, it is available through party planners PlanIt Events, who will theme it. / *12.30am; hirer's choice of caterer; marquee site.*

Cittie of Yorke WC1   £B, (300,90,90)
22 High Holborn   242 7670   (405 6371)
By the entrance to Gray's Inn, the main bar here is one of the largest and most characterful of any pub in London– with brass pipes, wooden alcoves and a high wooden ceiling. You can also hire the Cellar Bar – a long, thin, white-walled vault, or the relatively ordinary Front Bar. / *1am; in-house caterers; Main Bar (300,90,90); Cellar Bar (120,65,40); Front Bar (80,40).*

City Brasserie EC3   £M-E, (300,180)
Plantation House, Mincing Ln   220 7094
This large and stylish City basement restaurant has no private room, but for suitable events the whole place may be hired.

City Miyama EC4   £M-E, (–,10)
17 Godliman St   489 1937
For a private Japanese dinner in the City this is one of the smartest places. The cooking is predictably pricey, but of good quality. / *Private Rm (–,10).*

City of London Club EC2   £M, (500,120,96)
19 Old Broad St   588 7991   (374 2020)
Charming, early-Victorian institution (the oldest club in the City) whose first-floor smoking room is one of a number of fine period rooms for entertaining. There are also agreeable, interconnecting, modern rooms around an internal garden. / *1am; in-house caterers; Upper Smoking Rms (200,–); Garden Rm (100,50,40); Visitors Rm (50,35); Main Dining Rm (300,120,96); Bar (50,–).*

City Rhodes EC4   £M-E, (–,98)
New Street Sq   583 1313   (353 1662)
TV heart-throb Gary Rhodes now caters mainly for City businessmen at this smart, modernistic restaurant near Fleet Street. There is no totally private area, but for appropriate events it may be possible to hire the whole restaurant. / *Private Rm (–,12).*

The Clachan W1   £B, (100,50)
34 Kingly St   734 2659   (437 5751)
With its own street entrance, this Soho pub, behind Liberty, has an upstairs function room which is comfortably furnished, by pub standards, and offers a variety of real ales. / *11.20pm; not Sun; Highland Bar (100,50).*

PRIVATE VENUES

Clandon, Surrey
£M-E, (280,200,160)
West Clandon, Guildford   01483-222482
*The marbled, ground floor rooms of this c17 National Trust house
can be used for weddings, receptions and grand dinners. For dancing
or less formal functions, the restaurant in the vaults can be used, or
you can erect a marquee on the lawn.* / midnight; in-house caterers; amplified
music in restaurant only; dancing in restaurant only; no smoking; no red wine;
no photography; Restaurant (280,200,160); Marble Hall (250,180); Saloon (180,100);
marquee site.

Claridge's W1
£M-E, (800,210,192)
Brook St   629 8860   (872 8092)
*Visiting potentates often choose this elegant Mayfair hotel not only as
their home-from-home but also as the natural place to entertain local
royalty. The place is not resting on its laurels, however, and a new,
sixth-floor suite of rooms has recently been inserted. Though these
lack the elegant proportions of the earlier rooms, they benefit from
the same restrained opulence as the rest of the hotel.* / 2am;
Ballroom (400,240,192); Drawing Rm, French Salon or Mirror Rm (120,84);
Kensington (80,50); St James's (30,20); Orangery (–,14).

The Clink SE1
£B-M, (350,230,160)
1 Clink St   403 6515   (403 5813)
*A stone's throw from London Bridge, this former prison (yes, it is the
original) and erstwhile brothel is now a tourist attraction – exhibitions
follows prostitution through the ages. It now has a new entrance with
a gibbet (and body) on the way in. Take the whole place or, in the
evening, either the museum or the medieval-style Winchester Hall.*
/ 2am; prefer Castle Catering; Winchester Hall (300,180,110); Museum (100,60).

Cliveden, Berks
£E, (250,170)
Taplow   01628-668561   (01628-661837)
*The best way to enjoy the Astors' Thames-side palazzo is to take the
whole place for a house party. For more modest entertaining, the
rococo French Dining Room is reckoned to be one of England's
prettiest rooms in which to eat. You can now get married here, too.*
/ Great Hall (170,–); Terraced Dining Rm (–,110); French Dining Rm (75,54); Macmillan
Boardroom (–,20); marquee site.

Clothworkers' Hall EC3
£M-E, (350,224)
Dunster Court, Mincing Ln   623 7041   (283 1289)
*One of the grandest halls in the City – it is made available on a
limited basis, primarily for business, livery and charity functions.
Guests proceed from a contemporary and unusual hall up to the
elegant Reception Room on the first floo., Off this opens the Livery
Hall – a '50s chamber built on traditional lines.* / no weddings; 11pm;
not Fri-Sun; Aug & Sep hol; in-house caterers; no amplified music; no dancing;
smoking restricted; Livery Hall (350,224); Reception Rm (224,–).

The Coal Hole WC2
£B, (100,–)
91 Strand   836 7503
*Large, well-known West End pub, whose downstairs bar can be taken
over exclusively.* / 11pm; not Fri night & Sun.

Coates Karaoke Bar & Restaurant EC2
£B, (200,100,100)
45 London W1   256 5148   (382 9373)
*Industrial chic City wine bar with good pizzas. If you guarantee a
good turnout, you can hold a very inexpensive knees-up here.*
/ midnight; Mon-Wed eve only, Sat by negotiation.

Cobden's Club W10   £M, (350,110,90)
170-172 Kensal Rd   0181-960 4222   (0181-968 4386)
*Street-credible North Kensington hang-out, housed above a
still-functioning working men's club. The main party space is the
'retro-baroque' Grand Hall – like all the facilities, it may be available
to non-members at 'off-peak' times.* / members club; 1.30am; in-house
caterers; Grand Hall (170,100); Restaurant (100,50); Private Rm (–,16).

The Coliseum WC2   £B-M, (120,80)
St Martin's Ln   836 0111 x440   (379 4450)
*Europe's largest lyric theatre has a number of good-looking rooms
which would make pleasant places to entertain around a
performance. The panelled Dutch bar is possibly the most convivial,
and also the most suited for a stand-alone reception, but the Terrace
bar is also worth considering.* / Gardner Merchant; Terrace Bar (120,80);
Dutch Bar (100,–); Stoll Rm (20,12); Arlen Rm (12,8).

College of Arms EC4   £M, (200,–)
Queen Victoria St   236 7708   (248 6448)
*If you're looking for a fascinating venue with real history, this c17 City
college – the ultimate arbiter of all matters heraldic – is available for
book launches or for other fairly sedate events held by charities or
those with an interest in heraldry or genealogy.* / restricted availability; 9pm;
weekdays preferred, from 5pm; preferred caterer; no dancing; smoking in rooms only;
Earl Marshal's Court (60,–); Waiting Rm (60,–).

The Comedy Store SW1   £M, (400,–)
1A Oxendon St   839 6642   (839 7037)
*It may sound a slightly odd place to get married – with its dark red
and black décor and its fixed, theatre-style seating – but this comics'
venue, near Piccadilly Circus, boasts a wedding licence. In-house video
recording of the event is also available.* / Mon all day, Tue, Thu & Fri
afternoon; hirer's choice of caterer; alcohol in-house.

Commonwealth Institute W8   £M, (2000,1200,1200)
Kensington High St   603 3412   (603 9634)
*There are few sorts of corporate events for which this unusual
Holland Park building, set in three acres of gardens, is not well suited.
The Commonwealth Galleries make an impressive, multi-level setting
for large-scale entertaining. There is also a good range of smaller
accommodation which, though quite business-like, has quite a lot of
character.* / 1am; list of caterers; Commonwealth Galleries (2000,1200,1200);
Art Gallery (500,350,250); Bradley (100,60); Tweedsmuir (50,30); marquee site.

Congress Centre WC1   £B-M, (400,250,200)
23-28 Gt Russell St   580 5664   (580 8827)
*Not only champagne socialists can party at the TUC's fine '50s
memorial building. The glass-walled Marble Hall, overlooked by a
huge Epstein statue, is an elegant modern reception space, while the
Congress Hall suits dinners and dances.* / midnight; in-house caterers;
no smoking; Congress Hall (500,250,200); Marble Hall (200,–); Board Rm (–,20).

The Connaught W1   £M-E, (–,22)
Carlos Pl   499 7070   (495 3262)
*London's most discreet hotel has nothing so brash as a ballroom.
There are two sharply contrasting private dining rooms – the
extraordinarily pretty Regency Carlos Suite, including a small glazed
ante-room, and the smaller, rather sober Georgian room.*
/ Regency Carlos Suite (–,22); Georgian Rm (–,12).

PRIVATE VENUES

Conrad Hotel SW10
£M, (300,200,160)
Chelsea Harbour 823 3000 (352 8174)
This modern waterside hotel has the benefit – or disadvantage – of feeling much further from the centre of town than it actually is. There is a wide range of accommodation which, though rather corporate in feel, is carefully fitted to a high standard. / Henley Suite (300,200,160); Compass Rose or Thames (200,100,80); Henley I (150,120); Harbour (75,50); Nelson (–,12); Wellington (–,8).

The Conservatory SW11
£B-M, (100,50)
Ransome's Dock, 35-37 Parkgate 0181-874 8505 (924 2438)
Modern rooftop conservatory (heated in winter), perched on top of a riverside building by Albert Bridge (and accessed via a spiral staircase). It boasts plants, sculptures, fountains and terraces. / midnight; hirer's choice of caterer; no amplified music; no dancing.

Conway Hall WC1
£B-M, (350,160,140)
25 Red Lion Sq 242 8032
On the corner of a Bloomsbury square, the South Place Ethical Society (the UK's largest humanist group) occupies a converted music-hall. It offers characterful, if not especially smart, accommodation, suitable for a wide range of functions. / 11 pm; Oct-Apr large Hall not available Sun pm; hirer's choice of caterer; Large Hall (350,160,140); Small Hall (100,–); Club Rm (35,–).

Coopers Arms SW3
£B-M, (60,30)
87 Flood St 376 3120 (352 9187)
Much above-average Chelsea pub with a very good upstairs dining room. Two dozen people can sit around the ship's dining table in the upstairs room. / midnight; in-house caterers; no amplified music; no dancing; Private Rm (60,30).

Coopers' Hall EC2
£M, (60,30)
13 Devonshire Sq 247 9577 (377 8061)
Livery hall – Georgian in origin – used for some business functions as well as livery dinners. It is available primarily to an established circle of former users but applications from newcomers will be considered. / 10.30pm; not Sat & Sun; Aug hol; Alexander Catering Ltd; no amplified music; no dancing.

Corney & Barrow
44 Cannon St EC4 248 1700	(120,70,70)
3 Fleet Pl EC4 329 3141 (382 9373)	(100,30)
9 Cabot Sq, Canary Wharf E14 512 0397	(65,–)
1 Leadenhall Pl (Lloyd's Of London) EC3 621 9201	(150,50)
19 Broadgate Circle, B'gate EC2 628 1251 (382 9373)	(300,60)
5 Exchange Sq, Broadgate EC2 628 4367	(70,50)
16 Royal Exchange EC3 929 3131	(–,25)
2B Eastcheap EC2 929 3220	(200,80)

Well-known chain of superior City wine bars; Cannon St is best suited to discos, though their flagship is impressively situated above the Broadgate skating rink (where use of the terrace gardens is also possible, see Broadgate Estates); the Lloyd's Building wine bar (with the benefit of an outside terrace) is particularly stylish. / sometimes available Mon-Fri, also Sat & Sun.

Costa's Grill W8
£B, (–,12)
12-14 Hillgate St 229 3794
This popular Notting Hill stalwart of a restaurant offers solid Greek food at knock-down prices, and has a basic basement room for cheap and cheerful celebrations. / not Sun; Private Rm (–,12).

Cottons Atrium SE1   £M, (250,200)
London Bridge   626 3411   (623 9459)
This large, lofty riverside office-block foyer is a mite businessy, but it's a smart place with impressive views across to the City. Waterfalls and palm trees add interest. / eve only; hirer's choice of caterer.

Courtauld Gallery WC2   £E, (400,50)
Somerset House, Strand   873 2526   (873 2589)
The c18 grandeur of Somerset House is still closed to most Londoners. This is all part of the attraction of holding an evening reception or dinner at the Courtauld – enhanced, no doubt, by the presence of one of the world's greatest collections of impressionist and postimpressionist works. / 11pm; from 6.30pm – not Sat & Sun; list of caterers; no amplified music; no dancing; no smoking; Fine Rms (250,–); Great Rm (200,50).

The Courtyard, St Peter's Hall W11   £B-M, (200,80)
59a Portobello Rd   792 8227
This Victorian school building in Notting Hill, built around a small central courtyard, makes an atmospheric place for a party. The Upper Hall is a lofty room, ideal for receptions, as is the recently built Café (which opens onto the courtyard). The North Hall is reserved for kids' parties. / midnight; North Hall not Fri & Sat, Upper Hall not Thu or Sun; hirer's choice of caterer; no amplified music; Upper Hall (120,80); Café (100,50); North Hall (60,30).

Crazy Larry's SW10   £B-M, (450,–)
533 King's Rd   376 5555   (352 1659)
This rather seedy (if undoubtedly popular) Chelsea nightclub is available early in the week for exclusive hire. Theming would almost certainly be necessary. / 2.30am; Mon, Tue eve only, hirer's choice of caterer, alcohol in-house.

The Criterion W1   £M-E, (400,200)
Piccadilly Circus   925 0909
Hugely impressive, gilded and mosaicked neo-Byzantine restaurant, off Piccadilly Circus – now part of Marco Pierre White's burgeoning restaurant empire.

The Cross Keys SW3   £B-M, (–,50)
1 Lawrence St   349 9111
This very much smartened-up Chelsea pub/restaurant has an impressive new conservatory dining room at the rear. / Conservatory (–,50).

Crown & Goose NW1   £B-M, (40,20)
100 Arlington Rd   485 8008
Trendily updated Camden Town pub – complete with candelabra and fake oils – with a pleasant private room in the same vaguely arty style. The modern British pub grub is quite good too. / Private Rm (40,20).

Crown & Greyhound SE21   £B, (150,80,50)
73 Dulwich Village   0181-693 2466   (0181-693 5616)
The only pub in Dulwich Village has a second floor private room (with its own entrance) and is, of its kind, one of London's best. The restaurant is also available for hire. / midnight; no smoking area in Restaurant; Restaurant (–,42).

The Crown and Two Chairmen W1   £B, (120,40)
31 Dean St   437 8192
Well-known Soho media watering hole with characterful upstairs bar available for hire. / 11.20pm; not Sun & Sat in winter; Upstairs Bar (120,40).

PRIVATE VENUES

The Crown Tavern EC1   £B, (200,30)
43 Clerkenwell Gn   250 0757
*At weekends, this pleasant pub, peacefully situated north of
Smithfield, can be taken over in its entirety if you have sufficient
numbers. For the rest of the week there is an upstairs bar which can
be used by parties of 40 and up. / whole pub Sat, possibly Sun; Upstairs
Bar (60,30).*

Crystal Palace Park SE20   £B-E, (1000,1000,1000)
Contact Peter Kilby, Crystal Palace Park, Thicket Rd, Penge
0181-778 7148   (0181-659 8397)
*Greenfield site and open-air amphitheatre (with, from July 1997, a
permanent concert platform with stage, roof, kitchen and changing
room facilities). The concert bowl is a secure and private place for a
marquee, but local concerns about noise enforce an early cut-off
time. / 10pm; marquee site.*

Cuba Libre N1   £M, (100,60,60)
72 Upper St   354 9998
*Early on in the week, you can take over the whole of this Islington
establishment. It's a vibrant, get-up-and-dance sort of place that is
particularly suited to a buffet. / 2am.*

Cumberland Hotel W1   £M-E, (800,576,540)
Marble Arch   724 0087   (262 2248)
*The Production Box at this large hotel at the West End of Oxford
Street offers 3000 cubic metres of space, with a very high level of
technical facilities and support, so you can create a set for anything
from a fully-themed ball to a car launch. The more traditional
function rooms are surprisingly pleasant, too, especially the
ballroom-like Carlisle Suite. / 3am; Production Box (800,576,540);
Carlisle (500,400,360); Gloucester (200,100).*

Cutty Sark SE10   £M-E, (180,80)
King William Wk   0181-858 2698   (0181-858 6976)
*In its riverside Greenwich dry dock, the most famous tea clipper plays
host to many types of function. The pillars and permanent displays
reduce the space available, but in summer, access to the open top
deck offers much compensation. The Captain's Room (open for
viewing during functions) can be used for dinners only with special
permission from the trust. / from 6pm (winter 5pm); hirer's choice of caterer;
no amplified music; no dancing; no smoking, not even on outside decks; Tween
Decks (180,80); Lower Hold (180,80); Captain's Rm (–,12).*

Dan's SW3   £M, (–,30)
119 Sydney St   352 2718   (352 3265)
*Chelsea townhouse restaurant – pretty or twee, to taste – with an
attractive conservatory which is available for private hire.
/ Conservatory (–,30).*

Dartmouth House W1   £M, (240,150,150)
37 Charles St   493 3328   (495 6108)
*The imposing Georgian/Victorian Mayfair HQ of the English Speaking
Union offers some well-maintained and characterful rooms, that are
particularly suitable for weddings and other receptions. / midnight;
Crown Catering; Long Drawing Rm (120,100); Ballroom (100,80); Small Drawing
Rm (50,50).*

Davy's

Bangers: 2-12 Wilson St, EC2   377 6326 (250,200)
Bangers Too: 1 St Mary at Hl, EC3   283 4443 (75,–)
Bishop of Norwich: 91-93 Moorgate, EC2   920 0857 (200,80)
Bishops Parlour: 91-93 Moorgate, EC2   588 2581 (–,30)
Boot & Flogger: 10/20 Redcross Way, SE1   407 1184 (100,10)
Bottlescrue: 53/60 Holborn Viaduct, EC1   248 2157 (–,12)
Bung Hole: 57 High Holborn, WC1   242 4318 (250,–)
Burgundys Ben's:
102/108 Clerkenwell Rd, EC1   251 3783 (200,85)
Champagne Charlies: 17 The Arches, WC2   930 7737 (200,–)
Chiv: 90-92 Wigmore St, W1   224 0170 (250,80)
Chopper Lump: 10c Hanover St, W1   499 7569 (200,100)
City Boot: 7 Moorfields High Wk, EC2   588 4766 (200,85)
City Flogger: 120 Fenchurch St, EC3   623 3251 (250,120)
City FOB: Lower Thames St, EC3   621 0619 (150,75)
City Pipe: Foster Ln, EC1   606 2110 (200,18)
City Vaults: 2 St Martins-le-Grand, EC1   606 8721 (120,50)
Colonel Jaspers: 161 Greenwich High Rd, London, SE10
0181-853 0585   (0181-853 3331) (200,100)
Colonel Jaspers: 190/196 City Rd, EC1   608 0925 (250,120)
Cooperage: 48-50 Tooley St, SE1   403 5775 (150,60,60)
Crown Passage Vaults: 20 King St, SW1   930 6157 (250,120)
Crusting Pipe: 27 The Market, Cov Gdn, London, WC2
836 1415   (836 1415) (–,33)
Davy's of Creed Lane: 10 Creed Ln, EC4   236 5317 (200,100)
Davys at Canary Wharf: 31/35 Fishermans' Walk, Cabot Sq,
Canary Wharf, London, E14   363 6633 (–,60)
Davys of Long Lane: 15-17 Long Ln, EC1   726 8858 (100,45)
Davys Wine Vaults:
165 Greenwich High Rd, SE10
0181-858 7204   (0181-853 3331) (–,8)
Davys' at Russia Court: 1-6 Milk St, EC2   600 2165 (150,100)
Dock Blida: 50-54 Blandford St, W1   486 3590 (120,65)
Docks Bar & Diner: 66A Royal Mint St, E1
488 4144   (488 3035) (200,54)
Grapeshots: 2-3 Artillery Passage, E1   247 8215 (40,–)
Guinea Butt:
White Hart Yd, Borough High St, SE1   407 2829 (200,70)
Gyngleboy: 27 Spring St, W2   723 3351 (–,30)
Habit: 65 Crutched Friars, EC3   481 1131 (200,100)
Lees Bag: 4 Gt Portland St, W1   636 5287 (200,100)
Pulpit: 63 Worship St, EC2   377 1574 (150,100)
Shotberries: 167 Queen Victoria St, EC2   329 4759 (100,45)
Skinkers: 42 Tooley St, SE1   407 9189 (300,250,200)
Tappit-Hen:
5 William IV St, Strand, London, WC2   836 9839 (200,–)
Tapster:
3 Brewers Green, Buckingham Gt, SW1   222 0561 (150,75)
Truckles Of Pied Bull Yard:
Off Bury Pl, WC1   404 5338 (200,80)
Tumblers: 1 Kensington High St, W8   937 0393 (150,100)
Vineyard: 1 St Katharine's Way, E1   480 6680 (250,100)

It may be true that if you've seen one branch of Davy's, you've seen 'em all, but if you're looking to hire a weekend venue at reasonable cost, London's leading wine bar chain offers a wide (if City-slanted) variety of locations and capacities. For function hire, there is a central enquiry number (0181-858 6011)

PRIVATE VENUES

Deacons EC4 £B, (100,30)
1 St Brides Passage, Bridge Ln   936 2554
Hidden off Fleet Street, this is an agreeable wine bar/restaurant with large windows overlooking a small garden terrace. It's available in its entirety at weekends. / Private Rm (–,10).

Delfina Studio SE1 £M, (500,260)
50 Bermondsey St   357 9159   (357 7944)
This bright and attractive South Bank gallery makes a flexible venue for functions social and corporate. / in-house caterers; Rear Gallery (300,250); Front Gallery (200,150).

Denbies Wine Estate, Surrey £M, (250,200)
London Rd, Dorking   01306-876616   (01306-888930)
England's largest wine-producing estate is in the Mole Valley of the North Downs. The Denbies Suite is a purpose-built naturally-lit function room with an arched roof. Tastings are encouraged. / midnight; in-house caterers; no amplified music; no dancing; no smoking; Garden Atrium Conservatory (250,200); Denbies Suite (–,150).

Design Museum SE1 £M, (300,200,200)
Shad Thames   403 6933   (378 6540)
Next to Butler's Wharf, Sir Terence Conran's International-style museum has a large, white-walled foyer available for parties – for those who wish to view them, the collections above can be left open. Summer receptions can spill through the large floor-to-ceiling windows on to the riverside area, which has a magnificent view of Tower Bridge. See also Blue Print Café. / 11.20pm; from 6.30pm; list of caterers; Entrance Hall (300,–); Collection Gallery (–,200).

Detroit WC2 £B-M, (120,–)
35 Earlham St   240 2662   (240 8084)
This interestingly decorated, sci-fi cave-style bar/restaurant in Covent Garden makes an unusual setting for a drinks party. It's available in the early part of the week or (less frequently) at weekends. / midnight; no amplified music.

Dickens Inn E1 £B-M, (110,110,110)
St Katherine's Way   488 1226   (702 3610)
Prettily located, at the edge of St Katherine's Dock, this sizable inn has a large warehouse-conversion function room used for discos and, on occasions, wedding receptions. For fine days, there's also a beer garden. / midnight; Nickleby Suite (110,110,110).

The Dickens' House Museum WC1 £B-M, (50,25)
48 Doughty St   405 2127   (831 5175)
Oliver Twist's Bloomsbury birthplace is a four-floor c19 house, for the most part filled with display cabinets detailing his, and his creator's, life. Entertaining takes place in the atmospheric basement Library, whose period bookcases are filled with rare editions of Dickens's work. / 11pm; eve only, possibly all day Sun; hirer's choice of caterer; no amplified music; no dancing; smoking in gardens only.

Docklands Sailing & Watersports Centre E14 £B-M, (250,124)
235A Westferry Rd, Kingsbridge, Millwall Dock
537 2626   (537 7774)
Purpose-built Docklands premises with one large and one much smaller room on the first floor for hire. The main hall, which is very bright and has huge windows and a balcony overlooking the river, is suitable for wedding receptions. / midnight; hirer's choice of caterer, alcohol in-house; Function Rm (250,124); Teaching Rm (40,24).

The Dog & Duck W1   £B, (35,–)
18 Bateman St   437 4447
*Media-heartland pub with original tiles and mirrors, whose attractive
upstairs bar is available for exclusive hire. / 11.20pm; no amplified music;
no dancing.*

The Dog and Fox Ballroom SW19   £M, (250,150)
24 High St   0181-946 6565   (0181-946 3459)
*Wimbledon pub ballroom, decorated in Victorian style. / no 18ths;
11.20pm; not Wimbledon fortnight; Ballroom (250,150).*

Doggetts Coat & Badge SE1   £M, (200,80)
1 Blackfriars Bridge Rd   633 9081   (928 7299)
*Huge, Thames-side, modern pub complex with excellent views
(especially from the large terraces) of the City and St Paul's. It can be
taken over in its entirety at the weekends. The Terrace Bar offers a
barbecue facility. / 12.30am; only large parties Sat & Sun; Restaurant (140,80);
Boardroom/Terrace Bar (80,30).*

Dolphin Square SW1   £B-M, (240,200,125)
Dolphin Square, Chichester St   798 8783   (798 8735)
*The main interest at this huge, very '30s apartment block in Pimlico
is the unique ground floor restaurant, with its ocean liner feel and
view over the internal swimming-pool – ideal for nautical or '30s
theme balls. The low-ceilinged Chichester Suite is one of the few
central London rooms in which you can cater for your own dinner
party. / 12.30am; hirer's choice of caterer, alcohol in-house; Restaurant only and only
live music; Restaurant (240,200,125); Chichester Suite (100,55).*

Dora House SW7   £B-M, (120,70)
108 Old Brompton Rd   373 5554   (370 3721)
*The Royal Society of British Sculptors, housed in an elegant 1826
house, offers an agreeable and not too expensive South Kensington
venue. As we went to press there were plans to get a wedding
licence. / over 30s preferred; midnight; hirer's choice of caterer; no amplified music;
Studio (80,70); Salon (40,20).*

The Dorchester W1   £M-E, (1000,550,450)
53 Park Ln   495 7353   (317 6363)
*Glamorous opulence distinguishes the rooms at this Mayfair hotel –
all of the rooms have real style, from the subtly-mirrored Ballroom
down (or rather up) to the extraordinary fairy-tale setting of the
eighth floor Penthouse with terrace, fountain and spectacular view. All
the larger rooms are licensed for weddings. / 1am; in-house caterers;
Ballroom (1000,550,450); Orchid (250,160,120); the Terrace (200,100); Park
Suite (100,70,60); Holford (100,50); Pavilion (60,40); Penthouse (30,18); Library (10,–).*

La Dordogne W4   £M, (–,28)
5 Devonshire Rd   0181-747 1836
*Chiswick's number one restaurant is a cosy, very Gallic spot, with a
private room. For large parties, one of the main restaurant rooms can
be used. / only large parties Sat L & Sun L; Private Section (–,28); Private Rm (–,14).*

Downstairs At 190 SW7   £M, (100,70)
190 Queensgate   581 5666   (581 8172)
*South Kensington fish restaurant housed in an impressive basement.
The private room – sumptuous, fun and overblown – comes complete
with exotic tented ceiling – for bigger parties, the whole restaurant
can be hired. / not Sun; Private Rm (40,30).*

PRIVATE VENUES

Dr Johnsons' House EC4 £B-M, (80,–)
17 Gough Sq 353 3745
Apart from its literary associations (and associated bric-à-brac), the charm of this five-storey house, hidden away off Fleet Street, is that it is, most unusually, a plain Georgian house in central London – the décor is authentically neutral. The house is generally available only for early evening receptions, but occasionally for wedding receptions and the like. / 9pm – possibly later; from 6.30pm, Sun by arrangement; hirer's choice of caterer; no amplified music; no dancing; no smoking.

Drakes EC4 £B, (200,30)
5 Abchurch Yard, Abchurch Ln 623 2355
Prettily located subterranean City wine bar whose restaurant is available in the evenings for drinks parties or smaller dinners. It's popular for birthdays and work-related events. / 11.20pm; Mon-Fri eve; no dancing.

Drapers' Hall EC2 £M-E, (400,250)
Throgmorton Av 588 5001 (628 1988)
Behind the Bank of England, this livery hall, remodelled in Victoria's day, is one of the City's finest. It is now made generally available for functions to suitable hirers. / Aug hol; in-house caterers; no amplified music; no dancing; Livery Hall (400,250); Court Rm/Court Dining (100,60); marquee site.

Drones SW1 £M, (250,180)
1 Pont St 259 6166
This chic Mediterranean restaurant in Belgravia has a basement private room with a piano – or you can take over the whole restaurant. / Private Rm (120,40).

Duke of Albemarle W1 £B, (40,20)
6 Stafford St 493 9051 (409 0427)
Comfortable, slightly old-fashioned, room over Mayfair pub, available without charge for functions.

Duke of Clarence W11 £B, (100,50)
203 Holland Park Av 603 5431
Hospitable Notting Hill pub whose quite large rear conservatory can be used privately. / 11.20pm; Conservatory (100,50).

Duke of York's HQ SW3 £B-M, (350,300,250)
King's Rd 414 5513 (414 5560)
This fashionably located TA HQ is a stone's throw from Sloane Square. The Cadogan Hall is very popular by virtue of its size plus the affordability and flexibility it offers (although some effort on decoration is a good investment). / music ends 1am; hirer's choice of caterer; Cadogan Hall (350,300,250); London Irish Mess (220,72); Mercury House (50,20); marquee site.

Dukes Hotel SW1 £M-E, (150,60,50)
35 St James's Pl 491 4840 (493 1264)
Traditional, late-Victorian St James's hotel where, perhaps surprisingly, it's an attractive roof terrace which is the star attraction (but not for its view). Winter entertaining is in one of the three more conventional private rooms, which suit intimate dinners or perhaps a wedding. / midnight, Roof Terrace 10pm; Roof Terrace (100,–); Marlborough Suite (150,60,50); Sheridan Rm (25,12); Duke of Montrose Suite (35,18).

Dulwich College SE21 £B-M, (500,400,300)
Dulwich Common   0181-693 3737   (0181-693 6319)
*Impressively equipped Victorian school – in extensive and leafy
grounds – which offers a variety of possibilities for functions and
entertainments (especially sports-related). Moderate prices are
helped by a no-corkage policy – as long as catering is in-house.
The Old Library has a wedding licence.* / midnight; in-house caterers;
smoking restricted; Christenson Hall and Upper Dining Rms (500,400,300); Great
Hall (500,250,200); Cricket Pavilion (100,75); Lower Hall (120,–); Old Library (–,50);
marquee site.

Dulwich Picture Gallery SE21 £M-E, (300,150)
College Rd   0181-693 5254   (0181-693 0923)
*England's oldest, purpose-built picture gallery – designed by Soane
and housing works by, inter alia, Rembrandt and Canaletto – offers
an unusual, atmospheric and rather charming venue.* / midnight; Mon all
day, otherwise from 5pm; list of caterers; no dancing; no smoking; no candles;
marquee site.

Durrants Hotel W1 £B-M, (80,60)
George St   935 8131   (487 3510)
*Now one of London's few privately-owned hotels, these comfortable
and characterful Marylebone premises were built in 1790 as a row of
townhouses. There are two old-fashioned panelled, ground floor
rooms which are particularly attractive.* / midnight; Edward VII Rm (80,50);
Oak Rm (60,24); Spy Rm (80,60); Armfield Rm (25,12).

Dyers' Hall EC4 £M-E, (–,57)
10 Dowgate Hl   236 7197   (248 0774)
*Small, early Victorian hall, available to suitable hirers for luncheons
and dinners only.* / not Aug & Sep; in-house caterers; no amplified music; no dancing.

Earlsfield Library SW18 £B, (120,80)
Magdalen Rd   0181-871 6389   (0181-944 6912)
*The library has a pleasant barrel-vaulted art gallery, available for
social functions.* / 11.30pm; Sat & Sun only; hirer's choice of caterer; no smoking.

East India Club SW1 £M, (250,150)
16 St James's Sq   930 1000   (321 0217)
*This imposing St James's Club makes no efforts to market its facilities
to non-members. However, if you can find one of their number
(6,000 or so) to act as host (and be present), the rooms are convivial
places for dinners and receptions.* / in-house caterers.

Eatons EC3 £B-M, (400,160,150)
1 Minster Pavt   283 2838   (283 7275)
*Off Mincing Lane, this pleasant modern City wine bar/restaurant has
a banqueting suite which can be used for various types of function
(and for parties as small as 10). At evenings and weekends, you can
take over the whole place.* / Banqueting Suite (300,160,150).

Edwin Shirley Productions E3 £B-M, (6000,–)
Three Mills Island Studios, Three Mill La   363 0033   (363 0034)
*Ten east London studios suitable for larger parties (from 500 people)
and offering much scope for theming.* / hirer's choice of caterer; marquee site.

Electric Ballroom NW1 £B, (1100,–)
184 Camden High St   485 9006   (284 0745)
*Rather nice, old-established, Camden Town dance hall, ideal for a
large dance or major themed event.* / 2am; not Fri, Sat & Sun, Tues;
hirer's choice of caterer; alcohol in-house.

PRIVATE VENUES

Elena's L'Etoile W1   £M, (–,70)
30 Charlotte St   636 7189   (580 0109)
*This long-established, but recently revamped, Fitzrovia French
restaurant still maintains quite a lot of period charm. There is an
upstairs private room or, in the evening, you could take over the
whole place.* / Private Rm (–,24).

Embargo SW10   £B-M, (200,150)
533B Kings Rd, Chelsea   351 5038   (352 6526)
*In the early evening (till 11pm), you can hire this intimate Chelsea
nightclub for a drinks or dinner party. Such of your guests as wish to
can then stay on for the rest of the evening.* / in-house caterers.

Empress Garden W1   £M, (–,36)
15-16 Berkely St   493 1381   (491 2655)
*This expensive, rather businessy, Mayfair Chinese has three basement
private rooms.* / Private Rm 1 (–,36); Private Rm 2 (–,12); Private Rm 3 (–,10).

Engineer NW1   £B-M, (50,32)
65 Gloucester Av   722 0950   (483 0592)
*Well-known Camden Town super-pub, with ambitious grub.
The upstairs dining room is much smarter than your average boozer,
and a good venue for a less formal dinner.* / midnight; closed Sun L and Tue;
Large Rm (50,32); Mirror Rm (–,16).

English Garden SW3   £M-E, (–,50)
10 Lincoln St   584 7272   (581 2848)
*A restaurant very similar to the English House (below). We find the
décor of the upstairs private rooms preferable to that of the rather
overblown main restaurant (which may be taken in its entirety for
larger parties).* / Rm 1 (–,20); Rm 2 (–,10).

English House SW3   £M-E, (–,26)
3 Milner St   584 3002   (581 2848)
*Chelsea townhouse restaurant decorated in a lavish Laura
Ashleyesque style which is carried through to the upstairs private
rooms (of which the smaller opens onto a small outside terrace).*
/ Front Rm (–,12); Blue Rm (–,6).

Epsom Downs, Surrey   £M, (–,400,360)
Epsom Downs, Epsom   01372-726311   (01372-748253)
*Extensive views make this suite overlooking Epsom racecourse a
popular choice for wedding receptions and banqueting. Rooms are
light if rather bland.* / not race days; in-house caterers; Blue Riband Rm (–,400,360);
Derby Suite (–,230,200); Jockey Club Rm (–,180,140); Boardroom (–,90,70);
marquee site.

Equinox at the Empire WC2   £B-M, (1850,600,600)
Leicester Sq   437 1446   (287 2944)
*Recent works mean the largest dance floor in the West End
(they claim) just got bigger. This nightclub boasts all the hi-tec gizmos
you would expect and is used for a large range of day and evening
functions. The Square, effectively a mini-nightclub, is available
independently.* / weekdays during day also Sun & Mon eve; Crown Catering;
Club (1500,300); The Square (150,60,60).

L'Escargot W1   £M, (–,40)
48 Greek St   437 2679   (437 0790)
*Consistent Soho restaurant with two good quality private rooms,
of which the barrel-vaulted room with a single table is the more
distinctive.* / not Sat L & Sun; Barrel-vaulted Rm (–,40); Private Rm (–,22).

Euphorium N1 £M, (–,50)
203 Upper St   704 6909
*This strikingly designed, glazed-fronted Islington restaurant has a
private area upstairs, or you can hire the whole restaurant.
/ Private Area (–,16).*

Euten's WC2 £M, (300,110)
4-5 Neal's Yd   379 6877   (379 6877)
*Afro-Caribbean ('Black-British') restaurant – hidden away, off Covent
Garden's Neal's Yard – whose configuration (around a bar) makes it
very suitable to be taken over for a party. / 2am.*

Exxo W1 £B, (250,–)
33-34 Rathbone Pl   255 1120   (436 2686)
*This trendy basement bar, just north of Soho, offers a large venue –
with facilities for a DJ and dancing – which can be taken over in its
entirety for a large drinks or buffet party on a Saturday night. / 3am.*

La Famiglia SW10 £M, (–,40)
7 Langton St   351 0761   (351 2409)
*This ever-fashionable Chelsea Italian restaurant of long standing has a
private room downstairs. / Private Rm (–,40).*

Fan Museum SE10 £B-E, (80,35)
12 Crooms Hl   0181-305 1441   (0181-293 1889)
*Very pretty all around – both the fine collection of fans (housed in two
converted c18 Greenwich townhouses) and the mirrors-and-murals
décor of the Orangery annexe where food is served. The venue is
ideal for smaller weddings receptions but also increasingly in demand
from the corporate market. / 11pm; list of caterers; no amplified music;
no dancing; no smoking; no drinks while viewing collection; Museum (80,–);
Orangery (80,35).*

Farmers' & Fletchers' Hall EC1 £M, (220,120)
3 Cloth St   600 5777   (489 8936)
Modern livery hall, decorated in a traditional style. / 1am; Chester Boyd.

Fashion Café W1 £M-E, (800,400)
5/6 Coventry St   287 5888   (434 0635)
*Supermodel-backed, rag-trade themed restaurant, just off Leicester
Square. It will not be fully open until mid-1997, when the conversion
of the former Rialto cinema – complete with video-wall and catwalk –
will much increase capacity and provide a space ideal for lavish
parties. / midnight; Mon-Thu; Grande Salle (800,400).*

Feng Shang NW1 £M, (–,130)
Opp 15 Prince Albert Rd   485 8137   (267 2990)
*Multi-floored Chinese theme-barge – floating on Regent's Canal at the
northern tip of the Park. The style – somewhere between glamorous
and tacky – is suited to a large dinner or dinner-dance. / 1am.*

First Floor W11 £M, (100,35)
186 Portobello Rd   243 0072   (221 8387)
*This hip New York-style Notting Hill joint has a very atmospheric
private room. / Private Rm (100,35).*

Fishmongers' Hall EC4 (450,180)
London Bridge   626 3531   (929 1389)
*One of London's finest halls, included for completeness only – it is
generally unavailable to third parties, except sometimes to national
charities.*

PRIVATE VENUES

Footstool SW1   **£B-M, (250,120,90)**
St John's, Smith Sq   222 2779   (233 1618)
St John's light, flower-filled crypt is a lunch spot popular with MPs (it has a division bell) and those attending concert evenings. At other times, it's available for most types of function. / 1am.

Formula Veneta SW10   **£M, (–,40)**
14 Hollywood Rd   352 7612
Stylish, younger-scene Chelsea Italian restaurant. The private area downstairs has less charm than the main restaurant. / Private Rm (–,40).

Forte Posthouse Regent's Park W1   **£M, (500,240,200)**
Carburton St   387 6357   (388 3198)
Quietly situated, rather Continental in feel, modernish Marylebone hotel (inevitably not adjacent to the Park). The Academy – the conference and banqueting area – was refurbished in 1996. / 2am; in-house caterers; Cambridge & Oxford Suites (500,240,200); Trinity Suite (70,50); Pembroke Suite (–,12).

The Founders' Hall EC1   **£M, (125,75,50)**
1 Cloth Fair   600 5777   (489 8936)
Small, modern (1987) Smithfield hall, impressively designed. The intimate Livery Hall boasts striking contemporary décor – the Parlour is more conventional. / 1am; Aug hol; Chester Boyd; Livery Hall (125,75,50); Parlour (50,20).

Four Seasons Hotel W1   **£M-E, (750,400,325)**
Hamilton Pl   499 0888   (499 5572)
Large, '70s hotel overlooking Hyde Park. The c18-panelled Pine Room is a grand setting for smaller dinners. The larger Oak Room is also atmospheric – the Ballroom, Park and Garden Rooms are less distinctive (though the last benefits from access to a garden). Most rooms are licensed for weddings. / Ballroom (750,400,325); Garden Rm (300,100,80); Oak Rm (150,80,60); Pine Rm (60,40); Sitting and Dining Rms (35,16).

41 Queen's Gate Terrace SW7   **£M, (200,150,150)**
41 Queen's Gate Ter   581 3019   (581 3114)
Victorian hotel building in South Kensington, now converted into a series of light and pleasant spaces available for function use. / midnight, Fri & Sat 1am; hirer's choice of caterer; Pillar Suite (200,150,150); President's Club (150,–); Art Deco Rm (50,48).

Fox & Anchor EC1   **£B-M, (–,25)**
115 Charterhouse St   253 4838   (255 0696)
Famous, atmospheric Smithfield pub – the best known of those serving early breakfast with Guinness. For parties of 10-25 people you can order breakfasts, grill lunches and dinners to be taken in the agreeable upstairs parlour. / weekdays 9pm, Sat 10pm ; not Sun; Private Rm (–,25).

Foxtrot Oscar SW3   **£B-M, (–,34)**
79 Royal Hospital Rd   352 7179
This comfortably dated, Chelsea in-crowd hang-out remains popular for its relaxed atmosphere. The basement is available for hire.

Frederick's N1   **£M, (180,120,120)**
Camden Pas   359 3902   (359 5173)
Grand and spacious Islington restaurant with two private rooms – the Clarence Room is an elegant first-floor room, which is a pleasant place for a dinner or small reception (a wedding licence is being applied for). For larger events, it may be possible to use the whole restaurant. / Clarence Rm (40,26); Sussex Rm (30,18).

The Freemason's Arms WC2   £B, (100,50)
81-82 Longacre   836 3115
*Covent Garden pub with a large, pleasant upstairs bar used for much
more than typical pub functions. / 11pm; no amplified music; no dancing.*

French House W1   £M, (–,30)
49 Dean St   437 2477
*This Bohemian restaurant above a famous Soho pub offers an
intimate atmosphere in which to enjoy good modern British cooking.
The whole place is an ideal size for a birthday party or similar
celebration.*

French Institute SW7   £B-M, (80,30)
17 Queensbury Pl   838 2162   (838 2145)
*The Salon de Réception of this South Kensington centre is a quite
large, light, first-floor room that suits smartish receptions and dinners.
The café downstairs is run separately, as Café L'Institute (see also).
/ midnight; hirer's choice of caterer; no amplified music; no dancing; Salon de
Réception (80,30).*

Freud Museum NW3   £M, (120,50)
20 Maresfield Gdns   435 2002   (431 5452)
*Spacious '20s Hampstead villa in which the great man lived his last
days and where his daughter, Anna, resided until the '80s. Its
domestic ambience makes it ideal for intimate gatherings, especially
in summer when the charming, small garden can be used. / 11pm; Wed-
Sun from 5pm, Mon & Tue all day; list of caterers; no amplified music; no dancing;
no smoking; House (80,30); marquee site.*

The Fridge SW2   £B, (1100,–)
Town Hall Parade, Brixton Hl   326 5100   (274 2879)
*Large, well-known Brixton nightclub available for exclusive hire on
quieter nights – an application to increase capacity to 1600 was
being made as we went to press. The next-door basement Fridge Bar
is another possibility. / 3am; not Fri & Sat; in-house or hirer's choice by negotiation;
Fridge Bar (150,–).*

Frocks E9   £B-M, (–,30)
95 Lauriston Rd   0181-986 3161
*This intimate English restaurant near the East End's Victoria Park has
a cosy downstairs section, which would make a good place for a
birthday party. / Basement (–,30).*

Froebel Institute College SW15   £B-M, (400,140,140)
Roehampton Ln   0181-392 3305   (0181-392 3331)
*Grove House, in leafy Roehampton, is home of the Froebel Institute.
Set in 25 acres it has grounds and gardens including a large lake.
The attractive Terrace and Portrait Room are popular for wedding
receptions (and perhaps soon for weddings). / midnight; in-house caterers;
smoking restricted; Portrait Rm (160,140); Terrace (120,70).*

Front Page SW3   £B-M, (50,25)
35 Old Church St   352 2908
*Prettily located Old Chelsea pub, with a deserved reputation for food
which is pretty good by pub standards. Its panelled upstairs private
room offers a more ambitious menu than is offered below.
/ Private Rm (50,25).*

PRIVATE VENUES

Fulham House SW6   £B-M, (200,160,140)
87 Fulham High St   414 5513   (414 5560)
This listed Georgian house (with defensive cannon) houses a branch of the TA and is also a popular party venue. The main hall, a recent extension, is a flexible gym-type space with a glass-canopied ceiling. The Dining Room is formal. / 3am; hirer's choice of caterer; Main Hall (200,160,140); Dining Rm (80,52); Reception Rm (–,20).

Fulham Palace SW6   £M, (130,80,80)
Bishops Av   0181-748 3020, x4930   (381 0079)
This listed medieval palace, with courtyard, was the home of the Bishops of London until the '70s. It is prettily situated in a park, and potentially charming, but you should reckon to spend quite a lot on decoration. / midnight; hirer's choice of caterer; no smoking; Great Hall (100,80); Drawing Rm (100,80); Ante Rm (30,–); marquee site.

Fulham Road SW3   £M-E, (–,16)
257-259 Fulham Rd   351 7823
This chic modern British restaurant in Chelsea has a downstairs private room. / Private Rm (–,16).

Fulham Town Hall SW6   £B-M, (500,300,230)
Fulham Broadway   0181-576 5008   (0181-576 5459)
Fulham Town Hall has been restored to its original Edwardian splendour, and the Grand Hall with its vaulted ceiling and period chandeliers is certainly very impressive. The Concert Hall shares many of the attractions of the Great Hall, but on a smaller scale. Both halls are licensed for weddings. / 3am; hirer's choice of caterer; Grand Hall (500,300,230); Concert Hall (250,150,100).

Fung Shing WC2   £M, (–,28)
15 Lisle St   437 1539
The best reputed Cantonese restaurant in Chinatown has a first-floor private room. / Private Rm (–,28).

Gargoyle Club SW10   £B, (80,–)
363 Fulham Rd   349 0398
Underneath PizzaExpress, on the Fulham Road, this muralled basement, unusually for a nightclub, has options all week for private parties. At the weekends, you get your guests in early and – if you manage to fill the place – they don't let anyone else in. / 12.30 am; hirer's choice of caterer, alcohol in-house.

Le Gavroche W1   £M-E, (40,20)
43 Upper Brook St   408 0881   (491 4387)
London's longest-established grand restaurant has an elegant, airy, traditionally-styled private dining room, with its own small but comfortable sitting room. / not Sat & Sun; Private Rm (40,20).

Gay Hussar W1   £M, (–,24)
2 Greek St   437 0973
The atmosphere of this venerable, creaky Soho Hungarian restaurant permeates as far as the cosy private rooms above the main dining room. / not Sun; Second Floor (–,12); First Floor (–,24).

Gecko NW1   £B-M, (300,90)
7-9 Pratt St   424 0203/4   (424 0505)
Trendily minimalist oriental bar/restaurant in Camden – for a party you can take the bar or, for a large affair, the whole place. / midnight; Bar (150,–).

Geffrye Museum E2   **£M-E, (150,30)**
Kingsland Rd   739 9893   (729 5647)
*Charming former 18th century almshouses, now an interesting
museum of the history of the English domestic interior. It is made
available for functions only occasionally, usually to groups whose
interest is closely related to the subject matter of the museum.*
*/ very restricted availability; 10pm; Mon all day, Tue-Fri from 5pm; in-house caterers;
no amplified music; no dancing; no smoking; Lecture Theatre (50,30).*

George Inn SE1   **£B-M, (350,150)**
77 Borough High St   407 2056   (403 6613)
*National Trust pub, just south of London Bridge – London's only
remaining galleried coaching inn. It has three pleasant private rooms,
but the restaurant, part of which may be taken privately, is more
characterful. Best of all, however, is the Old Bar which, for 25-35
people, is available on an exclusive basis. / midnight; George (–,55);
Talbot (–,40); Lobby (–,20).*

The Gibson Hall EC2   **£M-E, (350,280,240)**
13 Bishopsgate   454 2324   (920 1522)
*NatWest has now 'gone public' about its sumptuous City hall,
dominated by crystal chandeliers. The Garden Room is plain in
comparison, but it has lots of natural light and overlooks the secluded
garden which can be used for summer receptions for up to 300. / 1am;
Aug hol; list of caterers; Hall (350,280,240); Garden Rm (240,100); marquee site.*

Gilbert's SW7   **£M, (–,30)**
2 Exhibition Rd   589 8947
*This comfortable and unpretentious restaurant, right by South
Kensington tube, offers a cosy atmosphere, good cooking and a well-
chosen and reasonably-priced wine list. It can be hired in its entirety.*

Gladwins EC3   **£M-E, (150,120)**
Minster Court, Mark Ln   444 0004
*Smart and bright, if perhaps slightly clinical, City basement
restaurant, available for exclusive hire.*

Glassblower W1   **£B, (150,56)**
42 Glasshouse St   734 8547
*This pub on the fringe of Soho has a large, relaxed upstairs lounge
bar (recently redecorated), with the odd bookshelf and lots of seating.*
/ not Fri or Sat eve.

The Glasshouse Stores W1   **£B, (200,–)**
55 Brewer St   287 5278
*Cosy wine bar beneath a Soho pub – either or both arms of its
U-configuration may be used privately. / 11.20pm; not last Fri & Sat of the
month; One side (80,–).*

Glaziers' Hall SE1   **£M, (500,280,200)**
9 Montague Cl   403 3300   (407 6036)
*A '70s renovation left these early c19 rooms feeling slightly flat,
though they are potentially very fine. The River Room's view more
than compensates, however, and the hall and other rooms offer
flexible, not-too-expensive accommodation on a good scale. / 2am;
hirer's choice of caterer; Hall (500,280,200); River Rm (200,120); Library & Court
Rm (120,100).*

PRIVATE VENUES

Gloucester Hotel SW7   £M-E, (500,310,250)
4-18 Harrington Gdns   373 6030   (373 0409)
Recently refurbished South Kensington hotel offering flexible banqueting facilities. The hotel's Millennium Conference Centre, due to open late July 1997, will increase function capacity considerably. / 2am; Cotswold & Courtfield Suites (500,310,250); Cotswold - Chalford/Dean (250,110).

The Golden Hinde SE1   £M, (120,45)
St Mary Overie Dock, Cathedral St
0541-505041   (01722-333343)
Full-scale reconstruction of Sir Francis Drake's galleon, moored between Southwark and London bridges. The rigging is floodlit at night enhancing the setting, and you can go out on deck in the summer. You can get married in the hold. / hirer's choice of caterer; smoking on deck only; marquee site.

The Golden Lion SW1   £B, (120,20)
25 King St   930 7227
This St James's pub is usually closed at weekends, but for parties of more than 80 it will open for you. Discos can be arranged in the nicer-than-usual upper room, the Theatre Bar, which is also available independently during the week for parties of 25 or more. / midnight; Mon-Fri eve only, Sat & Sun all day; in-house caterers; Theatre Bar (40,20).

Goldsmiths College SE14   £B-M, (100,250,200)
Lewisham Way   919 7132   (919 7134)
One of London's finest art schools, unglamorously located in New Cross. Its vast Great Hall has a glazed roof. The College also has three sites which can be used for marquees – at Lewisham, Blackheath and Brockley. The Orangery at the c19th Surrey House, in New Cross, has a terrace and garden and is suitable for small wedding receptions. / 2am; vacation only; in-house or hirer's choice by negotiation; smoking restricted; Great Hall (–,250,200); Orangery (100,–); marquee site.

Goldsmiths' Hall EC2   £M-E, (500,200)
Foster Ln   606 7010   (606 1511)
The epitome of majestic, classically-styled grandeur, this early c19 livery hall, a stone's throw from St Paul's, is stately rather than stiff in atmosphere. The hall is available primarily to an established circle of former users for special events, but applications from newcomers will be considered. / midnight; not Sat & Sun; list of caterers; Livery Hall (500,200); Drawing Rm & Exhbition Rm (250,–).

Gopal's of Soho W1   £B-M, (–,20)
12 Bateman St   434 1621
For a comfortable Indian meal in a central location, the private rooms of this low-key Soho restaurant are a good bet. / Private Rm (–,20).

Gordon's Wine Bar WC2   £B-M, (140,70)
47 Villiers St   01483-271676
Famously decrepit cellar wine bar. with a small terrace, near Embankment tube, whose atmospheric premises are available on an exclusive basis at the weekends. / midnight; Sat & Sun only; in-house caterers.

Goring Hotel SW1   £M, (100,50)
Beeston Pl   396 9000   (834 4393)
*Surprisingly tranquil for Victoria, this is one of the few family-owned
hotels in town. It has some pretty rooms for entertaining, including
the Garden Lounge which offers views over, if not the use of, Mr
Goring's large garden. At weekends only, wedding receptions for up to
100 can be accommodated in the Restaurant.* / Restaurant Sat & Sun only;
Archive Rm (100,50); Drawing Rm (25,12); Breakfast Rm (–,8).

Le Gothique SW18   £B-M, (400,250,200)
The Royal Victoria Patriotic Building, Fitzhugh Green, Trinity Rd
0181-870 6567   (0181-870 1645)
*The particular appeal of this French restaurant is its access to the
very pretty cloister garden of its extraordinary OTT Victorian building,
in a Wandsworth park. It may also be able to provide catering at the
adjoining Academy of Live and Recorded Arts (see also).* / 1am; with
Academy of Live & Recorded Arts (400,250,200); Patio (150,60).

The Grafton W1   £M, (400,80,70)
Tottenham Court Rd   0181-564 7464   (0181-899 3533)
*Edwardian hotel on the fringe of Bloomsbury, with a number of
smaller to medium size function rooms, decorated in traditional style.*
/ 11pm; smoking areas; Southampton Suite (200,80,70); Arlington Suite (120,60,60);
Warren (50,–,20); Duchess (30,–,20).

Granita N1   £M, (–,70)
127 Upper St   226 3222
*This well-known, minimalist, modern British restaurant in Islington can
be taken over in its entirety.*

Gray's Inn WC1   £M-E, (450,170,170)
High Holborn   405 8164   (831 8381)
*The attractively cloistered surroundings of this Inn of Court make a
good setting for social and business events. You might have dinner in
the simply decorated but attractive c17 hall and adjourn for coffee to
the Large Pension Room, before returning to the Hall for dancing.*
/ midnight; not Sun; not Jul-Sep; in-house caterers; Hall (300,170,170); Large Pension
Rm (150,40); Landing (50,–); marquee site.

Green's SW1   £M-E, (50,34)
36 Duke St   930 4566
*Club-like St James's restaurant and oyster bar offering simple English
food – as an Establishment favourite, it is priced accordingly. The
subterranean private rooms are not as characterful as the main
restaurant.* / Private Rm 1 (50,34); Private Rm 2 (–,10).

Grocers' Hall EC2   £M-E, (250,160)
Princes St   606 3113   (600 3082)
*Rebuilt in 1970, the Grocers' accommodation, by the Bank of
England, emerged relatively unscathed by the period's style-horrors.
The Piper Room, named after the designer of its striking modern wall-
hangings, may be used for a reception or dinner. The Livery Hall (with
medieval gates) is an unusual modern re-creation of traditional style.*
/ 11pm; not Sun; Aug hol; in-house caterers; negotiable; Livery Hall (250,160); Piper
Rm (150,100).

The Grosvenor SW1   £M, (150,120,120)
101 Buckingham Palace Rd   834 9494   (931 8662)
*Victoria's grand Victorian railway hotel has some very attractive,
atmospheric period rooms, including one 'find' – the imposing, very
bright Bessborough Room, a double-height treasure, complete with
minstrel's gallery.* / 1am; Gallery Rm (150,120,120); Bessborough Rm (100,70,50);
Warwick Rm (35,25); Belgrave (30,16); Wilton Rm (20,12); Hanover (12,8).

PRIVATE VENUES

The Grosvenor House Hotel W1 £M-E, (2000,1500,1500)
86-90 Park Ln   495 6363   (499 3901)
The Great Room – an enormous two-storey, unpillared space with chandeliers, originally built as an ice rink – is the largest hotel room in Europe (it is said) and hosts many major events. Its fame tends to overshadow the other facilities here, which include a pretty ballroom and 86 Park Lane – a complex of 18 dining and reception rooms all with natural light (catering for parties from six to 120) in a variety of styles, but principally clubby English. The hotel is licensed for weddings. / 2am; Great Rm (1500,1500,1500); Ballroom (800,500,500); Albemarle (150,120,80); Bourdon Suite (50,–); Spencer Rm (80,40).

Grosvenor Rooms NW2   £B-M, (700,500,450)
92 Walm Ln, Willesden   0181-451 0066   (0181-459 7676)
Unpretentious, very '70s Willesden banqueting complex where each suite has its own sprung dance floor. Large kitchens are available for use by external caterers, enabling, for example, ethnic requirements to be accommodated. The Pearl Suite (used as a nightclub Fri-Sun) is a much more informal venue suitable for a disco. / 2am; in-house caterers; Grosvenor Suite (700,500,450); Executive Suite (300,180,180); Pearl Suite (200,100,100).

Groucho Club W1   £M, (500,120)
45 Dean St   439 4685   (437 0133)
This Soho media-world club has a variety of rooms and emphasises that they are suitable for many types of function. The club can organise entertainments, discos, and so on, and makes rooms available to "members or their friends". / 1am; whole club Sat and Sun only, 1st or 2nd floors Sat eve; in-house caterers; Soho Rm (200,90); New Rm (50,35); Gennaro Rm (60,50); Bloomsbury Rm (–,20); First Floor (entire) (350,120).

Guards Museum SW1   £M, (180,80,80)
Wellington Barracks, Birdcage Wk   414 3271   (414 3411)
Below the concrete of the Guards' parade ground, these modern galleries of regimental dress, weapons and regalia make a colourful backdrop for a function. There is space for a free-standing marquee in the square, which increases capacity and permits dancing. / midnight; eve only; hirer's choice of caterer; no amplified music; no dancing; no smoking; Royal Gallery (–,80); marquee site.

Guildhall EC2   £M-E, (1500,704)
Aldermanbury   332 1118   (796 2621)
The City's imposing c14 HQ is the venue for many state and civic occasions. City (and notable London) organisations can also apply, but use of the cathedral-like Great Hall is limited to special events such as milestone anniversaries. Other rooms include the lofty, churchy Library and the Crypts which – with their painted ceilings and stained glass windows, are not at all gloomy. Dancing is allowed but discouraged by the early closing time. / 11pm; not Sun; Aug hol; list of caterers; no dancing in Great Hall; Great Hall (900,704); Old Library (600,300); West Crypt (250,180); Livery Hall (250,200).

The Guinea W1   £M, (30,20)
30 Bruton Pl   499 1210   (491 1442)
Pleasantly old-fashioned Mayfair pub which is one of the few steakhouses in London, and one of the fewer tolerable ones. For a comfortable, traditional meal it has a first-floor, panelled boardroom. / Boardroom not Sat lunch, closed Sun; Boardroom (30,20).

Gunnersbury Park W3   £B-M, (120,70)
Gunnersbury Pk   0181-862 5850   (0181-862 5847)
A huge park, just north of Kew Bridge, with three simple buildings available for wedding receptions and similar events – the Small Mansion possibly enjoys the nicest position. A wedding licence has been applied for the Terrace Room (Small Mansion) and Orangery. Restricted catering facilities and loos. / midnight; hirer's choice of caterer; Small Mansion (120,70); Orangery (120,70); Temple (100,50); marquee site.

Guy's Hospital SE1   £B-M, (180,120,80)
St Thomas's St   955 4490   (955 4181)
On the 29th Floor of London's fourth highest block, the Robens Suite is the highest venue available for hire in London. The view is, predictably, magnificent (while the walk through the building to reach the suite is, predictably, not). The earth-bound Court Room, part of a much older building, is suitable for formal dinners. / midnight; in-house caterers; Robens Suite (180,120,80); Court Rm (50,40).

Halcyon Hotel W11   £M-E, (100,60,60)
81 Holland Pk   727 7288   (229 8516)
Intimate, pretty and fashionable Holland Park villa-hotel, which offers attractive accommodation and good cooking. / 1am; Restaurant (100,60,60); Conference Rm (–,12).

The Halkin SW1   £M-E, (150,75)
5 Halkin St   333 1000   (333 1100)
Slick, minimalist Italian style distinguishes this Belgravia hotel. In "exceptional circumstances' – perhaps once or twice a year, the restaurant can be hired in its entirety. The Private Room – an extension of the restaurant – has its own entrance and much natural light. / Private Rm (40,30).

Ham House, Surrey   £M-E, (500,60)
Petersham   0181-332 6644   (0181-332 6903)
Weddings (and, very occasionally, other functions) are held in the Great Hall of this c17 National Trust house. You might use the Orangery's Tea Room for drinks, moving to the Restaurant (in the same building) for dining. The Tea Garden behind the Restaurant is available for al fresco events, and there is a marquee site overlooking the river. / 11pm; House Mon-Thu eve, Fri & Sat all day – Orangery Thu & Fri; Double Cover; no smoking in the house; no red wine, stilettoes or confetti in the house; Orangery (Restaurant) (75,60); Orangery (Tea Rm) (–,40); Great Hall (–,60); Tea Garden (–,60); marquee site.

Ham Polo Club, Surrey   £M, (200,150)
Petersham Rd, Petersham   0181-870 6202   (0181-870 0602)
London's only polo club, 10 miles from the West End, has space for a marquee of virtually any size. Or you can take over the clubhouse, with its floor-to-ceiling glass doors, which open onto a vine-clad veranda. / midnight; not Sun; in-house caterers; Club House (200,150).

Hamilton House EC4   £M, (100,50)
1 Temple Av   353 4212   (353 3325)
This bright, lofty room, nicely decorated in traditional style, has windows on three sides and an excellent view of the Inner Temple Garden. Its location in an office building and absence of cooking facilities restrict its purely function use to drinks parties,. / 11pm; not Sat & Sun; hirer's choice of caterer; no amplified music; no dancing.

PRIVATE VENUES

Hamilton Suite W1   £M, (220,140)
5a Hamilton Pl   499 6555   (499 1230)
*The subterranean setting makes this Mayfair suite of rooms –
formerly part of Les Ambassadeurs club upstairs – more suited to
evening than lunchtime functions. The vaguely exotic, lacquered red
room and relaxed Conservatory bar suit less formal functions, while
the Marble Room and wood-panelled Hamilton Room are more
sedate.* / 3am; in-house caterers; Conservatory & Red Rm (220,140);
Hamilton Rm (80,40).

Hamiltons Gallery W1   £M-E, (300,–)
13 Carlos Pl   499 9493   (629 9919)
*London's leading photographic gallery, in Mayfair, offers an
uncluttered, neutral but impressive central space for receptions.*
/ 10.30pm; not Sun; hirer's choice of caterer; no amplified music; no dancing; no smoking.

Hamleys Metropolis W1   £B-M, (250,–)
188-196 Regent St   734 3161   (494 5858)
*It's playtime for adults... The Sega Amusement centre in this world
famous toy shop offers over 100 games – anything from Virtual Cop
and Mortal Combat 3 to Air Hockey and a flight simulator.* / 11pm;
from 7pm, not Thu; not Dec; hirer's choice of caterer.

Hammersmith Palais W6   £B, (2230,650,650)
242 Shepherd's Bush Rd   0181-748 2812   (0181-748 8995)
*Well-known nightclub, just north of Hammersmith Broadway.
The areas overlooking the large dance floor may be taken privately.*
/ 3am; Wed-Sat eve restricted to Balcony, VIP Lounge or Stage Bar;
hirer's choice of caterer, alcohol in-house; Balcony Bar (400,–); VIP Bar (120,60);
Stage Bar (200,–).

Hammersmith Town Hall W6   £B-M, (1000,400,350)
King St   0181-576 5008   (0181-576 5459)
*The panelled Assembly Hall is a huge, atmospheric '30s room,
suitable for a large ball. The other rooms, including the Marble
Gallery, are also impressive. The panelled Council Chamber
(which seats 130) is licensed for weddings.* / 3am; hirer's choice of caterer;
Assembly Hall (1000,400,350); Marble Gallery (100,–); Small Hall (150,80).

Hampshire Hotel WC2   £M-E, (120,80,60)
Leicester Sq   839 9399   (976 1129)
*With its view towards Trafalgar Square, the Penthouse is the best part
of this Theatreland hotel. The basement banqueting rooms compare
well with similar hotels, but style Anglais is laid on with a trowel.*
/ Penthouse (120,80,60); Milton (20,10).

Hampton Court Palace, Surrey   £E, (400,280)
0181-781 9508   (0181-781 9669)
*Wolsey's magnificent palace, adopted by Henry VIII, is occasionally
used for major corporate and charity dinners. On a more intimate
scale, the delightful Banqueting House in the grounds is used
relatively frequently for medium size dinners.* / charities & companies only;
eve only; list of caterers; no amplified music; no dancing; no smoking; no weddings;
Great Hall (400,280); Banqueting House (80,60).

Hampton Court, Tiltyard, Surrey   £M, (300,200,160)
East Molesey   0181-943 3666   (0181-943 5457)
*A purpose-built function-room, the 'Garden Room' – adjacent to the
'20s-style tearooms and the c14 Tiltyard Tower – is the only part of
the palace within most budgets.* / 11.30pm; no amplified music.

Harrington Hall SW7   £M-E, (400,240,200)
5-25 Harrington Gdns   396 1717   (396 1719)
This modern South Kensington hotel – decorated in a smart, fairly traditional style – is well provided with panelled banqueting rooms of varying sizes. / 1am; Harrington (400,240,200); Turner & Constable (180,100,85); Reynolds & Landseer (150,110,70); Stubbs (70,45); Sutherland (50,45).

Harrods SW1   £M, (900,400)
87-135 Brompton Rd, Knightsbridge   730 1234   (225 5795)
If you are organising something for a good cause you may be able to hire the massive Georgian Restaurant for an evening event. During the day, you can hire just half the restaurant for parties of up to 250 people (Sat up to 100). / 2am; in-house caterers; smoking restricted; Georgian Restaurant (900,400).

Hartwell House, Bucks   £M-E, (100,60)
Oxford Rd, Nr Aylesbury   01296-747444   (01296-747450)
Set in 90 acres of parkland, this country house hotel (with Jacobean and Georgian façades) is located just outside Aylesbury. The Hartwell Rooms, converted from c18 coach houses, are rather anodyne. In the house itself, there are two rooms for private dining – the tented Octagon Room (with views of the gardens) and the plusher Doric Room. / midnight; in-house caterers; music in Conference Centre only; James Gibbs Rm (100,–); James Wyatt Rms (100,60); Doric Rm (–,30); Henry Keene Rm (–,12); Octagon Rm (–,18).

Hayward Gallery SE1   £E, (300,–)
Belvedere Rd   921 0725   (928 6903)
The art gallery at the South Bank centre hosts some prominent exhibitions, at which time it is booked out for evening receptions. However three two-hour slots per week are reserved for functions. Food and drink can only be consumed in the Pavilion, which has small external terraces the sides of which can be opened to provide river views in warm weather. / Mon, Thu & Fri 6.30pm-8.30pm; list of caterers; no amplified music; no dancing; no smoking; no drinking.

Hellenic Centre W1   £B-M, (350,200,200)
16-18 Paddington St   487 5060   (486 4254)
This impressive Marylebone building may not feel even vaguely Hellenic, but it does offer smart and characterful accommodation at relatively reasonable cost. / music must end by 11.30pm; in-house caterers; smoking restricted; Great Hall (350,200,200); Conference Rm (–,18).

The Hempel W2   £M-E, (600,300)
17 Craven Hill Gdns   298 9000   (402 4666)
Mega-trendy, ultra-minimalist Bayswater hotel, with a separate annexe for functions. Other options include a soundproof marquee in the garden square or a function in the modishly sepulchral I-Thai restaurant. / 3am; in-house caterers; Garden Square (400,300); Rm No 17 (200,40); Jade Rm (–,18); I-Thai Restaurant (and Shadow Bar) (–,75); marquee site.

Hendon Hall Hotel NW4   £M, (350,240,200)
Ashley La, Hendon   0181-203 3341   (0181-203 9709)
This imposing mid-c18 building was once the home of actor David Garrick. To the rear is the purpose-built Mount Charlotte Suite which is licensed for weddings. The garden has space for a marquee, and there is a terrace suitable for summer functions. / 11.45pm; Mount Charlotte Suite (350,240,200); Garrick (60,40,30); Sheridan (40,30,20); Johnson (35,30,20); marquee site.

PRIVATE VENUES

Henry J Beans SW3   £B-M, (50,–)
195 King's Rd   352 9255
Chelsea burgeria which we include solely for the rear section of its large garden, which can be used privately for summer parties.
/ no music; no dancing; Garden Section (50,–).

Herstmonceux Castle, East Sussex   £M-E, (200,200)
Hailsham   01323-834479   (01323-834499)
C15 moated castle which has in its time been a scenic ruin and a Royal Observatory. Now it is an international study centre set in 500 acres of Elizabethan gardens, farm, wood and parklands. The former chapel (the Data Room) is licensed for weddings while the Ballroom overlooks the gardens. / 11pm; in-house caterers; no smoking; Ballroom (200,200); Pub (70,–); Data Rm (–,70); marquee site.

Hever Castle, Kent   £M-E, (100,70)
nr Edenbridge   01732-861744   (01732-867860)
Rich with Tudor historical associations, this intimate moated castle, was substantially rebuilt by the Astors at the turn of the century. It now benefits from an adjacent Tudor Village which makes it especially suitable for residential events. No dancing in the castle, but facilities are available in the grounds. / 11.30pm; in-house caterers; no amplified music; no dancing; Castle Inner Hall (100,–); Tudor Suite (100,70); Great Hall (–,36).

Highclere Castle, Berks   £M-E, (200,120)
Newbury   01635-253210   (01635-255066)
Lord Carnarvon's fine high Victorian seat rather resembles the Palace of Westminster. The Saloon (richly decorated in gothic style) and the panelled Library are licensed for weddings. With 3000 acres of parkland, it's possible to find a space for a marquee of any size. / midnight; in-house caterers; no amplified music; smoking restricted; Saloon (200,–); Library (200,120); Dining Rm (–,60); marquee site.

Hillingdon Ski and Snowboard Centre, Middx   £B-M
Gatting Way, Park Rd, Uxbridge
01895-255183   (01895-255458)
If you can't afford to take your friends to the Alps, you could always take them to the Uxbridge 170m ski slope, complete with pine-clad bar restaurant. The facilities are being refurbished for the 1997/98 season – greater emphasis is to be placed on function availability. / marquee site.

Hilton on Park Lane W1   £M-E, (1250,1250,1000)
22 Park Ln   493 8000   (208 4145)
This landmark hotel has one of the capital's largest ballrooms (in a modern style) and also a full range of other accommodation for functions (especially dinner-dances). The fourth-floor Serpentine Room has one of the best views of any function room in London. / 2am; Grand Ballroom (1250,1250,1000); Grand Ballroom - Section 1 (500,380); Grand Ballroom - Section 2 (480,350); Grand Ballroom - Section 3 (250,150); Curzon Suite (300,180,130); Crystal Palace Rm (250,140,90); Serpentine Rm (30,16).

RS Hispaniola WC2   £M, (450,220)
Victoria Embankment   839 3011   (321 0547)
Moored by Hungerford Bridge for the last 30 years, this erstwhile Clyde steamer is now quite a smart place to entertain. The Top Deck has outside areas, front and rear, while the Main Deck has an external area at the side. / 1am; in-house caterers; Main Deck (300,150); Top Deck (150,80).

Hodgson's WC2   £M, (–,12)
115 Chancery Ln   242 2836
This modern British restaurant, near Fleet Street, occupies glazed-roofed premises built for a c19 book auctioneer, and benefits from a most impressive, light and airy setting. / not Sat & Sun; Private Rm (–,12).

Hogarth's House W4   £M, (40,–)
Hogarth's Lane, Great West Rd
0181-570 0622   (0181-862 7602)
Newly renovated for the tercentenary of his birth, the home of engraver and painter William Hogarth contains memorabilia of the great man's life, work and circle. There are also examples of his work – most famously, the Rake's Progress and Marriage à la Mode. There is an attractive garden. / 10.30pm; not Mon, Tue-Fri from 6pm, Sat & Sun from 7pm; Jan hol; hirer's choice of caterer; no amplified music; no dancing; no smoking; no red wine; marquee site.

Holderness House EC2   £B, (300,110,110)
51-61 Clifton St   377 9237   (414 5596)
The location of this modern TA base north of the City is hardly glamorous. However, it is an inexpensive place to hire, and with some effort spent on decoration the drill hall itself can be made into an agreeable space. / 1am; hirer's choice of caterer; Hall (300,110,110); Rifleman's Bar (50,20).

Holiday Inn – Mayair W1   £M, (90,50)
Berkeley St   493 8282   (629 2827)
As befits the area, the banqueting rooms here are fitted out with a little more class than that for which the chain is renowned. The hotel is also well-located – just off Piccadilly. / Stratton Suite (90,50); Presidential Suite (40,20); Burlington (20,10).

Holiday Inn – Nelson Dock SE16   £M, (400,300,250)
265 Rotherhithe St   231 1001   (417 7048)
On the south bank of the Thames in Rotherhithe, this modern hotel and conference centre overlooks the eponymous dock and – across the water – Canary Wharf. Part of the hotel (including the Copenhagen Room, with river terrace) occupies converted c18 warehouses. Five rooms have wedding licences. / midnight; Sweden (400,300,250); Wasa Suite (250,220,180); Denmark Suite (80,50); Rising Star (55,40); Finland I & II (35,–); Copenhagen (–,24).

Hollands W11   £B, (150,60)
6 Portland Rd   229 3130/460 3687   (0181-931 0411)
The airy conservatory at the rear of this Holland Park Thai and Filipeno restaurant and wine bar makes an ideal spot for an informal drinks party. / 2am; Conservatory (–,40); Conservatory and Balcony (–,60).

Hollington House Hotel, Berks   £M, (90,60)
Woolton Hl, Newbury   01635-255100   (01635-255075)
Edwardian country house hotel, three miles from Newbury, with gardens by Gertrude Jekyll. Weddings take place in the panelled entrance hall overlooked by a minstrels gallery. The marquee site has access to the Cedar Suite as a dance floor and bar. Hire is on an exclusive basis. / no stag nights; 1am; Cedar Suite (90,60); Oak Rm (–,26); Millard Dining Rm (–,17); marquee site.

Hollyhedge House SE3   £B-M, (250,250,250)
Blackheath   414 5513   (414 5560)
For an affordable big bash, the vast drill hall at this army centre on the edge of Blackheath is ideal. / midnight; hirer's choice of caterer; marquee site.

PRIVATE VENUES

Holy Trinity Brompton
Church Hall SW7   £B, (250,200)
Brompton Rd   581 8255
The hall at this fashionable Knightsbridge church is fairly basic.
However, it does have the benefit of large windows opening onto a
garden. Availability is very restricted. / HTB weddings, charities or parochial use
only; 10.30pm; hirer's choice of caterer; no amplified music; no dancing.

Honourable Artillery Co EC1   £B-M, (2500,1000,1000)
Armoury House, City Rd   382 1537   (628 0949)
Armoury House, the HAC's north City home, looks onto seven acres
of fields. Options include the atmospheric, if basic, Queen's Room;
the Albert Room (a large drill hall used for parties, often with a
marquee liner as decoration) and, for smarter events, the Long Room
(using the fine Court Room for pre-dinner drinks). Organisers of
mega-functions (for up to 2,500) should consider using the huge
amount of kit assembled for the annual June ball while it is still up –
a rig much cheaper than you could possibly DIY. / 11.45pm; Albert not Tue
& Wed eve; Long Rm eve only except rare whole house bookings; Graison; Court Rm —
no smoking; Marquee (2500,1000,1000); Albert Rm (500,350,300); Long
Rm (250,172); Medal Rm (60,36); Court Rm (60,–); Queen's Rm (70,50); marquee site.

Hop Cellars SE1   £B, (330,90,90)
24 Southwark St   403 6851   (403 4237)
Close to London Bridge, this large, pleasant wine bar beneath the
imposing facade of the Hop Exchange has two interconnecting
private function rooms and a restaurant and bar for hire. Parties of
100 or more can hire the facilities at weekends. / Malt Rm (150,90,70);
Porter Rm (75,50); Restaurant (–,55).

Hop Exchange SE1   £M, (350,250,220)
24 Southwark St   403 2573   (403 6848)
In the hinterland to London Bridge, this lofty, cream and green
Victorian hall – with wrought iron galleries and a modern, translucent
roof – offers a large and atmospheric venue for those prepared to
think a little about lighting and decoration. / from 7pm, Sat & Sun all day;
hirer's choice of caterer.

The Horniman at Hay's SE1   £B, (300,70)
Hay's Galleria, Tooley St   407 3611   (357 6449)
High-ceilinged Hay's Galleria riverside pub which, despite being a
recent conversion, is atmospheric and comfortable. The upstairs
Gallery, with river view, can be taken without charge for suitably sized
parties. On Saturday and Sunday evenings you can take the whole
place over if you guarantee a minimum spend. / midnight; whole pub all day
Sat & Sun night; in-house caterers; Gallery (150,60); Frederick John Horniman
Rm (80,70).

Horniman Museum and Gardens SE23   £M, (100,85)
100 London Rd   0181-699 1872, ext 138
The galleries of this intriguing, old-style museum in Forest Hill are not
available for hire, but the glass-domed conservatory is. In summer,
you can have drinks on the patio and wander around the gardens –
a nice setting for wedding receptions. / 11pm; hirer's choice of caterer;
no smoking; Conservatory (100,85).

Horwood House, Bucks
£M, (–,120)

Little Horwood, Milton Keynes
01296-722100   (01296-722300)

This manor house-style building (the oldest parts of which date from 1911) is seven miles south west of Milton Keynes. It offers 38 acres of landscaped grounds suitable for a marquee of any size. Alternatively, there is a purpose-built function suite. / in-house caterers; Restaurant (–,120); Eyre (–,70); marquee site.

Hothouse Bar & Grill E1
£M, (450,450,450)

78/80 Wapping Ln   488 4797

This attractive Docklands warehouse-conversion restaurant offers a large and characterful space for a function, especially one with a jazz band or a disco. / Lower Floor (140,70).

House of Detention EC1
£M, (120,80)

Clerkenwell Clo   253 9494   (251 1897)

For some 250 years there was a gaol on this site – Fagin was based on one of its inmates. When the rest of the prison was demolished in 1890, the basement was preserved. Private hire includes an escorted tour. Events centre on the main cell block, but guests have access to the whole place. / hirer's choice of caterer.

The House of St Barnabas-in-Soho W1
£B-M, (120,55)

1 Greek St   434 1846   (434 1746)

Imposing, listed house in a quiet(ish) corner of Soho many of whose rooms have c18 rococo plasterwork. The Soho Room has a piano and its large windows overlook the square. / midnight; list of caterers; no amplified music; smoking restricted; Council Rm (80,55); Soho Rm (80,55).

Howard Hotel WC2
£M-E, (200,70)

Temple Pl   836 3555   (379 4547)

This small, luxurious, modern hotel by the Temple offers fairly compact accommodation for functions. There are two first floor suites with river views, which are most suitable for sit-downs. The ground floor Fitzalan Suite has a view of the internal brick garden. The hotel is licensed for weddings. / no dancing; Fitzalan (200,70); Arundel Suite (150,50); Westminster (40,18); Surrey (20,12).

HQ NW1
£B, (400,120)

Camden Lock   485 6044   (267 8103)

Camden Lock music club and restaurant – an ideal spot to dance the night away, especially for a younger crowd. / 2am; Mon-Tue only; in-house caterers.

The Hudson Club SW7
£B-M, (200,50)

3 Cromwell Rd   584 7258   (0181-874 5843)

Self-avowedly a haven for grown-up (just) public schoolboys, this South Kensington nightclub has Top Floor and Middle Bars available all night on less busy days, and until 11pm on Fri or midnight on Sat. From May 1997, there will also be a restaurant. A member must sponsor any booking. / Club 3am, otherwise midnight; Top Floor (100,–); Middle Bar (100,–); Restaurant (–,50).

Hurlingham Club SW6
£M-E, (1000,650,650)

Ranelagh Gdns   731 0839   (736 7167)

Elegant Georgian Fulham 'country club' in its own extensive grounds. It is one of the prettiest places near to central London and has an impressive suite of rooms well suited to weddings, dances or summer barbecues, in all of which it does big business. Sponsorship of a member must be obtained. / 1am, Fri & Sat 2am; Searcy's; Quadrangle Suite (500,250); Palm Court Suite (200,100).

PRIVATE VENUES

Hyatt Carlton Tower SW1   £M-E, (650,320,300)
Cadogan Pl   824 7063   (823 1708)
The ballroom of this modern, but fairly traditional, Belgravia hotel was remodelled in 1996. Surprisingly, it is the hotel's only banqueting room (but see also Rib Room). It can be used for weddings.
/ Ballroom (650,320,300); Boardroom (–,–,16).

Hyde Park Hotel SW1   £M-E, (650,230,200)
66 Knightsbridge   235 2000   (235 4552)
The interior of this externally overbearing redbrick Knightsbridge edifice (now owned by Mandarin Oriental group) boasts much charming Edwardian detail, and offers one of the most impressive suites of inter-connecting entertaining rooms in London. Decorated in cream, blue and gold, they have splendid views of the park and are popular for grander weddings and receptions. / 2am;
Ballroom (400,230,200); Knightsbridge Suite (250,150); King Gustav Adolf Suite (150,70); Loggia (60,36); 19 Private Salons (–,12).

ICA SW1   £M, (300,100,100)
The Mall   930 0493   (873 0051)
Certainly an imposing venue, occupying an impressive terrace overlooking the Mall. The Nash room – a grand first-floor room, with balconies – is the high-point, or the institute's well-maintained, white-walled galleries can sometimes be made available. / 1am;
in-house caterers; Exhibition Galleries (300,–); Nash (130,100); Brandon (120,100).

Iceni W1   £B, (600,–)
11 White Horse St   495 5333   (409 2537)
With a great entrance just off Shepherd Market, this three-storey building, with two dance floors, is a budget temple to '70s kitsch. It offers an in-house theming service. / 3.30am; not Fri & Sat;
in-house caterers; Ground Floor (200,–); First Floor (200,–); Second Floor (200,–).

Ikkyu W1   £B-M, (–,12)
67 Tottenham Court Rd   636 9280
This impossible-to-locate Japanese basement, near Goodge Street tube, serves excellent quality, unusually affordable Japanese food. There is a traditional (shoes off) private tatami room. / 11pm; not Sat;
Tatami Rm (–,12).

The Imagination Gallery WC1   £M-E, (450,140,180)
South Crescent, 25 Store St   323 3300   (323 5810)
One of London's most impressive spaces. You cross a sci-fi-style, apparently fragile, metal bridge which spans the building's atrium to reach the light and airy fifth-floor gallery (which has a very good view of Bedford Square from its full-length balcony). The Atrium is also available for hire. / charities & companies only; 11pm; atrium from 6pm;
in-house caterers; no children; Atrium and Mezzanine (450,140); Gallery (250,120).

Imperial City EC3   £M, (–,12)
Cornhill   626 3437
This stylish City Chinese restaurant has an excellent location (beneath the Royal Exchange) – a side vault is available for private lunches and dinners. / not Sat & Sun; Private Vault (–,12).

Imperial College SW7   £B-M, (380,320)
Watts Way, Prince's Garden   594 9517   (594 9504)
*Imperial College has a range of facilities for social occasions.
Most imposing (but also most restrictive) is the Rector's residence at
170 Queensgate – the Council Chamber is the most used room,
but the Music Room (or Solar), with French windows to the garden,
is the most pleasant. Elsewhere, the Main Dining Hall, with its
wooden floor and function bar, is used for formal dining and dinner
dances. Patio doors lead on to Queen's Lawn, popular for garden
parties and barbecues.* / 11.20pm; Sat & Sun by rector's permission,
Mon-Fri eve only except Council Rm all day; in-house caterers; Main Dining
Hall (380,320); Council Chamber (120,60); Solar (40,–); Dining Rm (170
Queensgate (–,40); marquee site.

Imperial War Museum SE1   £M-E, (1000,400,300)
Lambeth Rd   416 5394   (416 5374)
*This historic site (it includes part of the original Bedlam hospital) is
one of the most impressive venues and comes ready-themed with
guns, planes and tanks. Various galleries can be added to the lofty
central atrium for extra reception space, while the trench and Blitz
experiences can also be open during events.* / 2am; from 6pm;
hirer's choice of caterer; smoking restricted; Exhibition Hall (800,400,300);
Festival Balconies (200,–); Boardroom 1 (75,50); Boardroom 2 (40,20); marquee site.

L'Incontro SW1   £M-E, (–,30)
87 Pimlico Rd   730 6327   (730 5062)
*Noisy, glamorous, opulent, stylish, and very expensive Italian
restaurant near Sloane Square, with a smart private basement dining
room and bar.* / 1am; Private Rm (–,30).

Inner Temple Hall EC4   £M-E, (750,250,250)
Temple   797 8181   (797 8178)
*The three rooms at this Inn of Court are interconnected – you might
have drinks in the Hall, followed by dinner in the Luncheon Room and
Parliament Chamber. A wedding licence was being applied for as we
went to press.* / 1am; eve and weekends; Aug hol; in-house caterers; Hall (400,250);
Parliament Chamber (200,80,250); Luncheon Rm (120,30); marquee site.

Innholders' Hall EC4   £M-E, (250,91)
College St   236 6703   (236 0059)
*Sombre but striking, this c17 Hall, near Cannon Street, was
substantially restored after the Blitz. It is accessed via a pretty hall
and reception room, both of recent construction.* / charities & companies
only; 11pm; not Sat & Sun; Aug hol; Alexander Catering Ltd; no amplified music;
no dancing; Hall (150,91); Court Rm (30,25).

Institute of Directors SW1   £M-E, (300,250,200)
116 Pall Mall   451 3107   (930 9060)
*The full stateliness of this large, white Nash edifice in St James's –
built as a gentlemen's club – is most apparent in the Waterloo and
Nash rooms, both of which lead off the magnificent staircase.
For business-related functions particularly, the Institute offers
affordable grandeur. Events must be sponsored by one of the
40,000+ members.* / members club; 11pm; Letheby & Christopher;
Nash (300,250,200); Burton (150,80); Waterloo (120,70);
Trafalgar II/St James (50,35); Trafalgar/Spears (40,20).

PRIVATE VENUES

Institution of Civil Engineers SW1   £M, (400,260,220)
1 Great George St   665 2323   (976 0697)
The high-ceilinged lobby, staircase, and, in particular, the huge marbled Great Hall of this impressive building, just off Parliament Square, all possess much neo-classical ('30s) grandeur. They suit a range of events, from grand dinners to wedding receptions, and the whole would make a good setting for a ball. / 2am; London Catering Services; Great Hall (400,260,220); Smeaton Rm (120,100); Brunel Rm or Council Rm (100,80).

Institution of Mechanical Engineers SW1   £M, (200,150)
1 Birdcage Wk   222 7899   (222 4557)
The common parts and entrance of this prettily located St James's institute are rather, well, institutional. However, the panelled Council room, the Hinton room (park views) and the oddly striking Marble Hall are all well suited to quite grand entertaining – the last being the best for receptions. / 10pm; London Catering Services; no amplified music; no dancing; no smoking; Marble Hall (200,150); Hinton (90,–); Council (70,45).

The Insurance Hall EC2   £M, (300,180)
20 Aldermanbury   606 3835   (726 0131)
A cosy institution, behind the Guildhall, which is flexible, by City standards. Although the hall has quite a capacity, it is much less imposing than some of its local competition – which may be no bad thing – and the feel inside is of a small Edwardian town hall. The Council Chamber (with a small museum attached) is an atmospheric corner room. / midnight; Crown Catering; smoking restricted; Great Hall (300,180); Council Chamber (100,23); Ostler Suite (150,75); Pipkin Rm (40,30); Morgan Owen Rm (20,16); President's Rm (–,8).

Inter-Continental W1   £M-E, (1400,800,700)
1 Hamilton Place, Hyde Park Corner   409 3131   (409 7460)
The banqueting facilities at this impressively-located modern hotel have been transformed in the last few years and it now offers rooms, mainly decorated in traditional style, of a size appropriate to almost any function. Most impressive, perhaps, is the seventh floor Windsor suite, with its commanding view. / 2am; Grand Ballroom (1400,800,700); Westminster (800,430,300); Piccadilly (400,210,150); Apsley (200,120); Windsor Suite I (100,60,40); Windsor Suite II (80,36,30); Hogarth (40,24,15).

The International Hotel E14   £M, (650,550,450)
163 Marsh Wall   712 0100   (712 0102)
Modern Docklands hotel – bizarrely furnished in 'traditional' style – boasting a wide range of banqueting accommodation. / 1am; in-house caterers; Grand Suite (650,550,450); Royal Lounge (250,170,120); Buckingham (100,–,80); Beaufort (40,–,20); Panorama Conference Suite (–,6).

International House E1   £B-M, (500,350,280)
St Katherine's Way   488 2400   (265 0459)
The foyer of the Centre, by the approach to Tower Bridge, has large windows giving a fine view of St Katherine's marina. / 3am; from 4pm; Quayside restaurant preferred.

International Students House W1   £B, (1000,200)
229 Portland St   631 8306   (631 8315)
Impressively-housed student hostel, geared to student and club discos (as well as conference business). The cafeteria is surprisingly stylish, with the gym-like theatre (removable seating) standing out among the other rooms. Worthy organisations may be able to organise summer parties in the Park Crescent garden. / 2am; in-house caterers; smoking restricted; Theatre (600,200); Portland Rm (250,120); Gulbenkian (150,–); Bistro (140,–).

The Irish Centre W6   £B-M, (250,80)
Black's Rd   0181-563 8232   (0181-563 8233)
*Simple Hammersmith space, with sprung dance-floor and cream
walls – a relatively inexpensive venue for a dance, dinner or wedding.*
/ 2am; not Sat, some Fris; hirer's choice of caterer; Hall (250,80).

Irish Club SW1   £M, (300,100,100)
82 Eaton Sq   235 4164   (235 4247)
*Become a member here (if you are Irish by birth, marriage or
descent) and this Eaton Square townhouse-club provides one of
London's smartest, modestly-priced addresses. A major refurbishment
was concluded in 1997.* / midnight; in-house caterers; Ballroom (150,100,100);
Ulster Rm (75,60); Leinster Rm (60,40).

Ironmongers' Hall EC2   £M, (250,168)
Shaftesbury Pl, Barbican   606 2726   (600 3519)
*Even though it is surrounded by the Barbican, from the inside this
1920s faux-medieval hall (complete with panelling, stone flags and
stained glass) manages to feel like the real thing. The Drawing Room
and Livery Hall are most impressive.* / midnight; Aug hol; list of caterers;
no dancing; Banqueting Hall (250,168); Drawing Rm (100,–); Luncheon Rm (80,50).

Ivy WC2   £M, (150,60)
1 West St   379 6077   (497 3644)
*Not only thesps are attracted to this glamorous and amazingly
popular restaurant in the heart of Theatreland.* / 2am; Private Rm (150,60).

Jason's W9   £M, (95,60)
Blomfield Rd, Little Venice   286 3428   (266 4332)
*Little Venice Mauritian fish and seafood restaurant which has the twin
advantages of much above average cooking and an unusual
canal-side location. You might go for drinks on one of the company's
two narrow boats (see Moving Venues), and then have dinner at the
restaurant.* / midnight; in-house caterers; Restaurant (60,40); Restaurant with
Terrace (–,60); marquee site.

Jazz Café NW1   £B-M, (350,100)
5 Parkway   916 6060   (916 6622)
*Stylish Camden Town venue on two floors that suits a variety of
functions. The first floor restaurant overlooks the stage, as does the
cocktail bar which is next to it but slightly partitioned and available
independently.* / Sun-Thu midnight; not Fri & Sat; in-house caterers;
Restaurant (–,80); Cocktail Bar (–,40).

Jongleurs at Camden Lock NW1   £M, (–,450,450)
Middle Yd, Camden Lock   924 3080   (924 5175)
*Comedy-cabaret theatre, in an interesting location. The party planner
owners can theme the show and/or the venue to the host's
requirements.* / 2am; Mon-Thu; in-house caterers.

Jongleurs at the Cornet SW11   £M, (–,300,300)
49 Lavender Gdns   924 3080   (924 5175)
The Battersea location of Jongleurs is a converted '20s dance hall.
/ 2am; Mon-Thu; in-house caterers.

Julie's Restaurant & Wine Bar W11   £M, (–,45)
133-137 Portland Rd   229 8331   (229 4050)
*This seductive, eclectically-decorated Holland Park labyrinth is one of
London's best known party-restaurants – though it's the atmosphere
which is the draw, not the food. The best rooms are the panelled
Banqueting Room (with its single oval table) and the Garden Room.*
/ 1am; Sat L, wb only; Gothic Rm (–,45); Garden Rm (–,32); Banqueting Rm (–,24);
Conservatory (–,17); The Tomb (wb) (–,14); The Gallery (wb) (–,10).

Kaspia W1 £M-E, (–,60)
18-18a Bruton Pl 493 2612 (408 1627)
*Discreetly but centrally located fish and caviar restaurant, just by
Bond Street, with a private room, or available in its entirety for private
hire.* / Private Rm (–,12).

Kempton Park, Middx £M, (–,–)
Sunbury-on-Thames 01372-461203
*Closed for rebuilding as we go to press, this modern racecourse
banqueting suite is due to re-open in December 1997.* / 2am;
Ring & Brymer; marquee site.

Ken Lo's Memories SW1 £M, (–,20)
67-69 Ebury St 730 7734 (730 2992)
*One of the few quality restaurants in the immediate vicinity of
Victoria, serves pricey oriental cuisine. The private room is on the
ground floor.* / midnight; not Sun; Private Rm (–,20).

The Kenilworth WC1 £M, (150,135,100)
Great Russell St 0181-564 7464 (0181-899 3533)
*The most notable function feature of this traditional-style hotel near
the British Museum is the small Louis XV suite, with stained glass
cupola.* / 11pm; smoking areas; Bloomsbury Suite (150,135,100); Louis XV (40,36).

Kensington Palace Thistle W8 £M, (200,110,140)
De Vere Gdns 937 8121 (937 2816)
*Facing Kensington Gardens, the rosily bland function rooms of this
mid-range hotel are pleasant of their type.* / Duchess (200,110,140);
Marchioness (100,90,75); Park (–,80); Countess Princess (90,40); Baroness (30,15).

Kenwood House NW3 £E, (250,80)
Hampstead Ln 973 3478
*English Heritage's policy on making this beautiful house at the top of
Hampstead Heath available for functions was under reconsideration
as we went to press.* / Orangery (–,80); marquee site.

Kenwood House, Old Kitchen NW3 £M, (100,70)
Hampstead Ln 0181-341 5384
*The only part of this delightful, grand Hampstead house currently
made available regularly is the Old Kitchen Restaurant – an airy,
attractive, stone-flagged room, often used for wedding receptions.*
/ 10.30pm; in-house caterers.

Kettners W1 £B, (100,80)
29 Romilly St 437 6437 (434 1214)
*On the grounds of its very strong atmosphere (only), this Soho
pizzeria (in a building which once housed a grand English restaurant)
may be worth considering when a central location is required at
reasonable cost.* / midnight; Oak Rm (–,80); Edward Rm (100,40); Blue Rm (–,30);
Soho Rm (–,16).

Kew (Royal Botanic) Gardens, Surrey £M-E, (300,200,200)
Kew 0181-332 5617 (0181-332 5632)
*If you want to entertain in grand style, the Temperate House is the
most suitable of the famous glasshouses – other possibilities include
use of the art gallery, or erecting a marquee. You can get married in
the Lounge of the pretty, listed Cambridge Cottage (with up to 50
people in attendance).* / 11pm; from 5.30pm weekdays, Sat from 1pm, no Sun
hire; list of caterers; no amplified music; no dancing; no smoking; Temperate
House (300,200); Gallery (entire ground floor) (150,80); Cambridge Cottage
Lounge (–,30); marquee site.

Kew Bridge Steam Museum, Middx   £M, (150,100,60)
Green Dragon Ln, Brentford   0181-568 4757   (0181-569 9978)
A dramatic setting – sometimes used for sci-fi and horror films – and much in demand for occasions ranging from wedding receptions to themed company events. / *no college events or under-30s birthdays; 1am; eve only, day sometimes; hirer's choice of caterer; Steam Hall (150,100,60).*

King's College WC2   £B-M, (450,220,160)
Strand   928 3777   (928 5777)
A very central site. The college's main hall is well maintained, quite grand and suitable for a wide range of functions. / *1am; hirer's choice of caterer; Great Hall (450,220,160); Council Rm (80,–).*

King's College School SW19   £B-M, (300,180,180)
Southside, Wimbledon Common
0181-255 5401   (0181-255 5409)
Facilities at this Wimbledon school include the panelled Great Hall, a cricket pavilion used for barbecues, the Dalziel Room (with access to a terrace and private lawn) and the Boathouse club room (overlooking the river at Putney). / *11pm, boathouse midnight; Great Hall school hols only; hirer's choice of caterer; discos only in Boathouse and Great Hall; Great Hall (300,180,180); Dalziel Rm (100,40); Boathouse (100,–).*

King's College, Hampstead NW3   £B-M, (350,150,150)
Kidderpore Av   928 3777   (928 5777)
Basic but pleasant accommodation for functions at this leafy college outpost – the rooms are available together or independently. / *midnight; hirer's choice of caterer; Bay Hall (350,150,150); Bay Lounge (100,–).*

Kingswood House SE21   £B-M, (250,160,40)
Kingswood Estate, Seeley Dr, Dulwich
0181-761 7239   (0181-766 7339)
C18 house now run by Southwark Council as a library and community centre, but retaining much of the opulence of its original decorative style, and available, inter alia, for weddings. / *midnight; hirer's choice of caterer; smoking restricted; Golden Rm, Jacobean Rm (250,160); Charles Suite (100,80,40); Hannen Rm (20,–); marquee site.*

Knebworth House, Herts   £M-E, (550,230,230)
Knebworth   01438-812661   (01438-811908)
A c15 house that has been much altered but retains features of all periods and boasts gothic turrets. It stands in 250 acres of parkland , permitting many types of activities and events. The Manor Barn is licensed for weddings. / *midnight; Apr-Sep either house or barn available after 6pm – winter both available at most times; in-house caterers; disco in barns, classical in house; dancing in barns only; smoking restricted; Manor Barn (incl Bulwer Rm) (300,230,230); Lodge Barn (250,100,100); Banqueting Hall (House) (150,60); Dining Parlour (–,30); Library (50,–); marquee site.*

The Lamb Tavern EC3   £B, (100,50)
Leadenhall Market   626 2454
One of the City's best pubs – in the centre of an atmospheric, covered market – with two bars available for private early evening hire, without charge. / *10pm; not Sat & Sun; no amplified music; no dancing; Dining Rm (100,50); the Dive (100,–).*

PRIVATE VENUES

The Landmark W1   £M-E, (500,360,310)
222 Marylebone Rd   631 8000   (631 8080)
*Impressive hotel where skilful updating of a Victorian building (once
the St Marylebone railway hotel) has provided London with some of
its grandest public rooms – the marbled Ballroom and the oak-
panelled Drawing Room are especially impressive. Sadly, despite
many enquiries, the splendid atrium cannot be used. / I am;*
in-house caterers; Ballroom (500,360,310); Empire Rm (360,160,110); Drawing
Rm (300,160,110); Champagne Rm (70,30); Boardroom (–,20); Gazebo (40,–).

The Lanesborough SW1   £M-E, (250,100,60)
Hyde Park Corner   259 5599   (259 5606)
*Neo-classical landmark, converted into a glossy hotel and furnished in
rather overblown Empire style. For functions, a variety of lofty,
medium size rooms and a prettified wine cellar are available.
Many rooms are licensed for weddings. / midnight; Belgravia (250,100,60);*
Wellington Rm (100,60); Westminster Rm (60,40); Wilkins Rm (30,15);
Wine Cellar (–,14).

Langham Hilton W1   £M, (450,300,220)
Portland Pl   636 1000   (436 7418)
*London's first purpose-built Victorian hotel has an extremely grand
Grand Ballroom, with access to the garden in fine weather. You can
marry in the Palm Court (with its fountain, fronds and pillars) or the
Ambassador Room. / I am; Ballroom (450,300,220); Palm Court (300,–);*
Portland Suite (200,100); Regent and Welbeck Rms (50,36); Cumberland Rm (15,10).

Lansdowne Club W1   £B-M, (200,120,120)
9 Fitzmaurice Pl   629 7200   (408 0246)
*This large Mayfair club has a lot of slightly worn charm and, with a
member's sponsorship, offers a very central and quite economical
venue. Highlights include the elegant ballroom and the striking Art
Deco Thirties Room. / in-house caterers; Ballroom (200,120); Thirties Rm (100,48);*
Shelburne Rm (60,24).

Larry's Wine Bar WC2   £B, (100,70,70)
Mercer St   836 0572
*Below Theatreland's Mountbatten Hotel, a pleasant and
well-proportioned brick-walled space. / 2 am.*

Lauderdale House N6   £B-M, (180,100,100)
Waterlow Park, Highgate Hl   0181-348 8716
*Pretty c16 Highgate house, overlooking the park, much used for
wedding receptions and other social events. A wedding licence has
been applied for. / I am; 3 wks hol in Jan; in-house caterers; no smoking;*
marquee site.

Launceston Place W8   £M, (–,30)
1A Launceston Pl   937 6912   (938 2412)
*One of most discreet, comfortable and English of restaurants, hidden
away in Kensington, with a comfortable private room and a larger
semi-private area. / Private Area (–,30); Private Rm (–,14).*

The Law Society WC2   £M, (280,220,150)
113 Chancery Ln   320 5901   (320 5955)
*This fine early c19 building, sensitively developed over the years and
very well maintained, has a comfortable grandeur and surprising
degrees of charm and flexibility. The Old Council Chamber stands out,
but there is a good range of rooms for most occasions. A wedding
licence is on its way as we go to press (we presume they filled the
form in correctly). / I am; Charters (Sutcliffe Group); Common Rm (280,220,150);*
Old Council Chamber (120,60); Members Dining Rm (80,50).

Lea Rowing Club E5 £B, (300,–,150)
The Boathouse, Spring Hl   0181-524 7306
*Smart, L-shaped bar overlooking the River Lea in Stamford Hill. The
massive rear gym is not a pretty space, but does substantially
increase capacity – take the bar for discos or receptions for up to
100 and the entire place for larger bashes. / 2am; Fri & Sat only;
hirer's choice of caterer, alcohol in-house; Bar (100,–).*

Leadenhall Wine Bar EC3 £B, (150,100)
27 Leadenhall Mkt   623 1818   (623 1928)
*In the evening you can hire one of the two rooms of this comfortable
City wine bar, which looks down into Leadenhall Market. / 11.20pm;
Mon-Fri eve, closed Sat/Sun; Top-floor Rm (80,60).*

Leander Club, Berks £M, (150,140,80)
Henley-on-Thames   01491-575782
*Modestly styling itself "the world's premier rowing club", this
characterful and tranquil Victorian, members' club building by the
Thames offers a reasonably-priced venue for social occasions.
/ not during Henley Royal Regatta; in-house caterers; marquee site.*

The Leathermarket SE1 £B-M, (500,65)
Weston St   357 0279   (403 3068)
*This Victorian building near London Bridge has a large courtyard
suitable for holding a barbecue or for siting a marquee. The modern,
ground floor Tannery restaurant is very light and features a sprung
pine floor. / 11.20pm; Tannery, eve only; in-house caterers; Tannery
Restaurant (150,65); Marquee (500,–); marquee site.*

Lee Valley Cycle Circuit E15 £B-M, (2000,2000,2000)
Temple Mills La, Stratford   0181-534 6085   (0181-536 0959)
*On a site of 48 acres, there is virtually unlimited capacity for a
marquee at this east London venue – we have arbitrarily suggested
figures of 2,000. / 10pm; not Oct-Mar; hirer's choice of caterer; no smoking;
marquee site.*

Lee Valley Leisure Centre N9 £B-M, (2000,–,800)
Picketts Lock La, (Meridien Way), Edmonton
0181-345 6666   (0181-884 4975)
*This flexible site is part of the Lee Valley Leisure Complex. The
modern Great Hall, with its own entrance and reception area, is
suitable for balls and wedding receptions. The Conference Room is
licensed for weddings. / no political events; 2am; hirer's choice of caterer; Great
Hall (1500,–,800); marquee site.*

Leeds Castle, Kent £M-E, (350,280,220)
Maidstone   01622-765400   (01622-735616)
*"The loveliest castle in the world", Norman in origin, provides a great
range of entertaining possibilities, both within the moated castle and
in the surrounding park. Areas for hire include a c17 tithe barn (the
Fairfax Hall) and an underground grotto at the centre of the maze.
The Terrace Room is a recent addition. / State Dining Rm - companies only; in-
house caterers; Fairfax Hall With Terrace Rm (350,280,220); Henry VIII Banqueting
Hall (250,100); State Dining Rm (150,60); Terrace Rm (100,80,60); Gate Tower (70,50);
Grotto (50,–); marquee site.*

Legends W1 £B-M, (500,100)
29 Old Burlington St   437 9933   (734 3224)
*Smart, hi-tec Mayfair nightclub (revamped in 1996), which is
frequently hired out for corporate, show biz and private parties. / 3am;
in-house caterers; Upstairs (250,100); Downstairs (200,–).*

PRIVATE VENUES

Legoland Windsor, Berks   £M-E, (2000,300)
Windsor   01753-626100   (01753-626200)
The attractions here are not all childish – they range from indoor venues, for example, the JFK Drawing Room (with a terrace overlooking the park) to the Picnic Grove (a wooded barbecue area beside the harbour). 'Stand-alone' lets are not contemplated – visitors have to spend time actually visiting the park. / 10pm; Mar-Sep, weekends in Oct; in-house caterers; no dancing; smoking restricted; Marché Restaurant (–,300); Picnic Grove (–,300); Drawing Rm (120,–).

Leighton House W14   £M-E, (150,80)
12 Holland Pk   602 3316   (371 2467)
Idiosyncratic 1870s Holland Park house – built for Frederic Lord Leighton as a showcase for Aesthetic taste – which is ideally suited to more intimate grand events. The highpoint is the Arab Hall, featuring a fountain and intricately patterned c16 and c17 tiles. / 11pm; eve only, not Sun, garden (April-Sept); Searcy's or Bovingdons; no amplified music; no dancing; smoking restricted; Studio (150,80); Arab Hall (70,–); Dining Rm (–,30).

Leith's W11   £M-E, (–,36)
92 Kensington Park Rd   229 4481   (221 1246)
This well-established Notting Hill townhouse restaurant was completely revamped in 1995. It offers good quality modern British cooking, not inexpensively. / Private Rm (–,36).

Lemonia NW1   £B-M, (–,200)
89 Regent's Park Rd   586 7454   (483 2630)
For suitable events, the whole of this popular and stylish Primrose Hill taverna can be made available. / Private Rm (–,40).

Leven is Strijd E14   £M, (50,20)
West India Quay, Hertsmere Road   987 4002   (987 4002)
This permanently moored barge in the Docklands (which has been moved somewhat from its previous mooring place) caters for dinners for 10 and more people in cosy and unusually private surroundings. / midnight.

Lexington W1   £M, (–,20)
Lexington St   434-3401   (287 2997)
Despite the rather modernistic appearance of the ground floor, the first-floor private dining room is in a charming traditional style at this modern British Soho restaurant. / Private Rm (–,20).

Limelight W1   £M, (800,200,200)
136 Shaftesbury Av   434 0572   (434 3780)
One of London's most impressive settings for a nightclub – a lofty Victorian chapel, in the heart of Theatreland. The Dome (hall) has many original fittings and lots of natural light, and is suitable for receptions and dinners – it is overlooked on three sides by the Gallery Bar. A wedding licence may be applied for. / 3am; not Wed, Fri or Sat; in-house or hirer's choice by negotiation; Gallery & Dome (450,150,150); Club VIP (Basement) (250,72,72); Study Bar (50,30); Library (50,30); Annexe (20,20).

Lincoln's Inn WC2   £M-E, (600,320,280)
Lincoln's Inn   405 1393   (831 1839)
For 'medieval' magnificence, the Great Hall (1845), set in the quiet of the Inn's gardens, is difficult to better, and the Drawing Room is perfect for a formal dinner. The real c15 Old Hall across the lawn is smaller and, in its way, more atmospheric. Summer functions on the terrace will be considered – if you are extremely grand they may let you have a party on the grass. / 11.30am; Grand Hall eve only; hirer's choice of caterer; Great Hall (600,320,280); Old Hall (250,130,90).

Lindsay House W1 £M, (–,20)
21 Romilly St   439 0450
Discreet Soho townhouse restaurant, decorated in comfortable but OTT olde worlde style, with very charming private rooms (especially the larger of the two). / no dancing; Private Rm (–,20); Private Rm (–,12).

Linford Film Studios SW8 £B-E, (1200,–)
44 Linford St   627 1133   (720 1915)
High ceilings and large capacities make this Battersea nightclub, with large stage area, a potentially impressive function venue, with considerable scope for (and need of) theming. Two of the four rooms have independent light and sound systems. A marquee could double the capacity. / 3am, Fri & Sat 6am; in-house or hirer's choice by negotiation; Studio A (main rm) (1200,–); Studio B (250,–); Back Bar (150,–); Games Rm (100,–).

The Little Ship Club EC4 £B-M, (400,100,100)
Upper Thames St   236 7729   (236 9100)
Newly redeveloped (1991), comfortable and smart riverside yacht-club whose only real disadvantage is to share its entrance with a car park (though guests may be welcomed at the river entrance). It enjoys wonderful views. / 1am; Dining & Club Rms - Mon-Fri from 6pm (summer only), all day Sat & Sun; Alexander Catering Ltd; Dining Rm (120,90); Chart Rm (–,10).

Lloyd's of London EC3 £M, (800,350,250)
1 Lime St   327 6976   (327 5014)
The large ground-floor Captain's Room of Richard Rogers' remarkable building is available at night for functions. For receptions, another possibility is the Old Library – a panelled hall from the market's old building transplanted into the frame of the new. / Captain's Rm from 5pm; in-house caterers; Captain's Rm (800,350,250); Conference Rm (100,60); Old Library (120,–).

London Aquarium SE1 £M-E, (1500,–)
County Hall, Riverside Building, Westminster Bridge Rd
967 8000   (967 8029)
London's hottest (or is it coolest?) new venue is the capital's recently-opened aquarium – one of the largest in Europe. From June 1997 up to 1,500 guests can enjoy their drinks and canapés while wandering among the examples of aquatic life. / midnight; from 8pm; list of caterers; no amplified music; no dancing; no smoking.

London Astoria WC2 £B-M, (2000,800,800)
157 Charing Cross Rd   434 9592   (437 1781)
Well-known, central rock venue, used almost exclusively for concerts, but which has potential, especially with theming, for use by large, loud parties. / usually not Fri, Sat; hirer's choice of caterer.

London Astoria 2 W1 £B, (1000,–)
165 Charing Cross Rd   434 9592   (437 1781)
Large, subterranean dive – "up for anything which is neither illegal nor destructive" – with a large dance floor, surrounded by a gallery. Smaller parties of up to 500 could take over a balcony. / in-house or hirer's choice by negotiation.

London Capital Club EC4 £M-E, (140,60)
15 Abchurch La   717 0088   (717 0099)
With the sponsorship of a member of this City club, you can use its smart, formal facilities, which include five private dining rooms. The building (1917) was formerly called the Gresham Club. / no weddings, 18ths or 21sts; midnight; Mon-Fri from 7am; in-house caterers; Boardroom (55,40); Gresham Rm (25,20); Wren Rm (10,8); Marco Polo (10,10).

PRIVATE VENUES

The London Dungeon SE1   £M-E, (400,300,150)
28 Tooley St   0181-874 4234   (0181-877 0280)
Boasting "a perfectly horrible experience", this highly successful London Bridge museum of the macabre is great fun (though the high-ceilinged vaults are at their best when full). The recently added Judgement Day boat ride and cheerily-named Jack the Ripper experience can be incorporated into an evening. / 1am; summer from 7.30pm, winter from 6.30pm; London Catering Services.

The London Hippodrome WC2   £B-M, (1650,440,440)
Leicester Sq   437 4311   (434 4225)
London's best-known central nightclub is sufficiently well maintained that it would suit any crowd. It boasts an extremely impressive light system and is technically well equipped for major corporate events, in which it does big business. From July '97 it will boast a private function room. / in-house and list; Auditorium (1600,350,350); Balcony – Restaurant (300,175,175); Private Function Rm (250,50).

London Marriott W1   £M, (900,500,500)
Grosvenor Sq   493 1232   (514 1528)
A large, surprisingly characterful, subterranean '70s ballroom – with unusual barrel-vaulted ceiling – is this Mayfair hotel's most interesting feature. / Westminster Suite (900,500,500); Hamilton Rm (65,45); John Adams Suite (40,25); Dukes Suite (30,15).

London Metropole W2   £M, (1300,840,720)
Edgware Rd   402 2400   (262 2921)
Aspects, the Rooftop Restaurant, is on the 24th floor of this Bayswater/Marylebone hotel and suitable for smaller parties and wedding receptions. It is one of the highest available for exclusive hire and benefits from the views you would expect. / 2am; Palace Suite (1300,840,720); Windsor Suite (400,240,180); Thames Suite (160,110,60); Westminster Suite (200,120,80); Park Suite (160,110); Berkshire Suite (300,210,170); Aspects (Rooftop Restaurant) (–,80); Boardroom (–,12).

London Palladium W1   £M, (300,–)
Argyll St   437 6678   (434 1217)
Atop the main staircase of this famous theatre, the large, light Cinderella bar, with its comfortably worn grandeur, attracts a fair number of daytime receptions. Stop press: a wedding licence has been granted. / until 5pm, Louis Bar eve negotiable; Gardner Merchant; Cinderella Bar (300,–).

The London Planetarium NW1   £M-E, (250,80,80)
Marylebone Rd   487 0224   (465 0884)
Surroundings are perhaps more austere than at other 'ready-themed' venues, but function packages are now on offer. / 1am; from 7pm; in-house caterers.

London Rowing Club SW15   £B, (250,100)
Embankment   0181-788 0666
The first of the line of boathouses on the Putney 'hard', 'London' is a good and economical spot for informal receptions and discos – especially in summer. / midnight; hirer's choice of caterer.

London School of Economics WC2   £B-M, (80,150)
Houghton St   955 7087   (405 1350)
The rooms listed are decorated in a rather dated style and would need flowers or other decoration. However, they offer central and reasonably priced accommodation for a dinner or drinks party. / no weddings; from 6pm (Sun only if big event); in-house caterers; no amplified music; no dancing; smoking restricted; Senior Dining Rm (–,150); Senior Common Rm (80,–).

London Scottish SW1   £B-M, (300,180,150)
95 Horseferrry Rd   414 5513   (414 5560)
*Very unusual Pimlico TA hall, reconstructed from pieces transported
from the regiment's old building. With the messes also available, it is
suitable for many different types of event.* / 1am; not Tue nor some Sat
& Sun; hirer's choice of caterer; Hall (300,180,150); Queen Elizabeth Club (80,–);
Officers' Mess (60,–).

The London Toy and Model Museum W2   £M, (150,60)
21/23 Craven Hl   706 8000   (706 1993)
*Parties – for adults as well as children – take place in the
Conservatory Café and walled garden of this Bayswater Museum.
In good weather, kids can ride on the 1920s hand-turned carousel.
A wedding licence has been applied for.* / 11.30pm; not public holidays;
in-house caterers; in Conservatory background music only, in shop disco;
smoking restricted; Conservatory (–,25); marquee site.

London Transport Conference
Facilities E14   £B-M, (100,350)
30 The South Colonnade, Canary Wharf
308 2112   (308 2041)
*You might expect these premises, in a shiny new Canary Wharf
building, to be a bit 'corporate'. They are, but the restaurant
(decorated in modern 'ocean liner' style) and the attractive atrium are
pleasant areas well endowed with natural light, and suitable for
receptions.* / midnight; eve only, wkends; in-house caterers; no smoking;
Restaurant (–,350); Atrium (100,–).

London Transport Museum WC2   £M, (400,300)
Covent Gdn   379 6344   (836 4118)
*Originally a Victorian flower market, this airy, iron and glass museum
facing Covent Garden is home to a collection of old buses, tubes,
trams and trains. It attracts a lot of (mainly corporate) function
business.* / charities & companies only; midnight; from 6.30pm; list of caterers;
smoking restricted; no spirits or fortified drinks.

London Zoo NW1   £M-E, (380,200,240)
Regent's Pk   586 3339   (722 0388)
*Few are immune to the delight of partying among the animals, so this
really is a venue for children of all ages. There are two banqueting
suites (licensed for weddings) but the real attraction is to be out
barbecuing among the tigers or drinking among the reptiles –
'animal encounters' can be arranged.* / 2am; animal houses, eve only; Leith's;
Regency Suite (380,200,240); Lion Terrace (200,–); Reptile House (200,–); Raffles Bar
and Restaurant (150,100); Tropical Bird House (100,–); Insect House (60,–);
marquee site.

The London Welsh Centre WC1   £B, (300,250,150)
157 Grays Inn Rd   837 3722   (837 3722)
*The light, gym-type hall here is largely used for rehearsals, but also
for parties. The barn-like bar upstairs is suitable for informal
get-togethers.* / midnight; not Sun; in-house caterers; dancing only in hall; Main
Hall (300,250,150); Bar (100,–).

Lord's NW8   £M, (500,350,350)
St John's Wood Rd   286 2909   (266 3170)
*The home of cricket boasts a modern, purpose-built banqueting
centre.* / 1am; not match days; Town & County.

PRIVATE VENUES

Loseley Park, Surrey   £M-E, (–,150)
Guildford   01483-304440   (01483-302036)
*Parkland-set Elizabethan house, whose timber tithe barn makes quite
an atmospheric setting for a function. As an elegant marquee site, the
park also has a lot to commend it. / midnight; not Jun-Aug, Wed-Sat; in-
house caterers; amplified music in tithe barn only; Tithe Barn (–,150); marquee site.*

Lundonia House WC1   £B, (200,80,60)
24 Old Gloucester St   242 7367   (405 1851)
*AKA the October gallery, this former C of E girls school is a good size
to be taken over in its entirety and includes a small garden. The
simple galleries have potential for numerous small to medium size
functions. Events with some kind of artistic tie-in are particularly
encouraged. / 11pm – Fri & Sat 1am; hirer's choice of caterer; smoking restricted;
Ground Floor (200,80,60); Top Floor Theatre (60,–); Club (40,10).*

Madame Tussaud's NW1   £E, (600,350,300)
Marylebone Rd   487 0224   (465 0884)
*London's most-visited, longest-running tourist attraction is also one of
the top party venues. The popularity of the Garden Party is a whisker
ahead of the more traditional Grand Hall. / 1am; from 7pm; list of caterers;
Grand Hall (600,350,300); Garden Party (250,80).*

Maison Novelli EC1   £M-E, (150,45)
29 Clerkenwell Gn   251 6606   (490 1083)
*Star chef Jean-Christophe Novelli's City-fringe French restaurant,
expanding in the course of 1997, has a large upstairs private room.
/ 1am; Top Floor (80,45); Middle Floor (60,35); Ground Floor (60,35).*

Mall Galleries SW1   £B-M, (500,250)
The Mall   930 6844   (839 7830)
*A short step from Admiralty Arch, the Main Gallery at the Federation
of British Artists offers a cavernous space for a function. The East
Gallery is smaller and more inviting. / 11pm; from 5pm;
hirer's choice of caterer; no amplified music; no dancing; Main Gallery (500,250);
East Gallery (100,75); North Gallery (80,50).*

Mao Tai SW6   £M, (–,26)
58 New King's Rd   731 2520
*Consistent Parson's Green Chinese restaurant, well-known for its good
food, efficient and friendly service and fairly high prices. The private
room is upstairs. / Private Rm (–,26).*

Marble Hill House, Surrey   £M-E, (60,–)
Richmond Rd, Twickenham   0181-892 5115   (0181-607 9976)
*Fine early c18 house, whose grounds are bordered by the Thames,
and which afford a very elegant site for a marquee. The Great Room
(based on the Cube Room at Wilton House) is decorated in white
and gilt and adorned with period paintings and furniture. / midnight; from
4.30pm winter/6.30pm summer; hirer's choice of caterer; no amplified music; no dancing;
no smoking; no red wine; the Great Rm and Tetrastyle Hall (60,–); marquee site.*

Marquis W1   £M, (75,30)
121a Mount St   499 1256   (493 4460)
*Though the main dining room has had a modernistic refit, the private
rooms of this long established restaurant retain their clubby
furnishings and atmosphere. Prices, especially by Mayfair standards,
are notably reasonable. / Downstairs Rm (75,30); Ground Floor Rm (–,24).*

Mars WC2 £B-M, (–,80)
59 Endell St 240 8077
Self-consciously quirky modern British restaurant in Covent Garden. It has no private room, but is regularly taken over on an exclusive basis. / not Mon L, Sat L & Sun.

The Mayfair Inter-Continental W1 £M-E, (400,320,260)
Stratton St 629 7777 (629 1459)
Large, quite grand '20s Mayfair hotel whose only really distinctive function room is the large rose-hued Crystal Room – named for its three huge, modern chandeliers. The hotel is licensed for weddings. / Crystal Rm (400,320,260); Danziger Suite (200,120,70); Berkeley Suite (50,36).

Mega Bowl SW2 £M, (300,–)
142 Streatham Hill 0181-678 6007 (0181-674 3463)
If a mega bowling party is your idea of a fun, this is the place. You can hire a single lane, or one, or both floors. Though there is no drinking on the 36 lanes, there are fair-sized bar areas on each floor around which to stage festivities. As an alternative you might consider the Zapp Zone – a hi-tec laser game in semi-darkness with futuristic lighting, for up to 20 people. / midnight, Fri & Sat 1am; in-house caterers; single floor (120,–).

Mercers' Hall EC2
Ironmonger Ln 726 4991 (600 1158)
What is probably the richest of the livery companies tells us its hall is never available to outsiders. We mention it only for completeness – unless you have a special 'in', you can save the cost of the call.

Merchant Centre EC4 £B-M, (500,300,250)
New Street Sq 353 6211 (353 2013)
Since a complete refurbishment in 1995 only the large Caxton Suite remains for hire at this large central venue (just off Fleet Street). The décor (now predominantly cream and blue) has been much improved. / 11.20pm; Gardner Merchant; Caxton Suite (500,300,250).

Merchant Taylors' Hall EC2 £M-E, (500,280)
30 Threadneedle St 588 7606 (528 8332)
In the heart of the City, this very grand, reconstructed (post War) medieval hall is perhaps the most imposing of the livery halls to be made available to outsiders with reasonable frequency. It comes complete with cloisters and paved garden. / 2am; not Sun; in-house caterers; Great Hall (500,280); Parlour (180,80); Cloisters (120,–); Library (40,20).

Le Mercury N1 £B, (–,50)
140 Upper St 354 4088
Atmospheric, bargain-basement Islington bistro, with a private room upstairs. / Private Rm (–,50).

Le Meridien W1 £M-E, (400,250,210)
21 Piccadilly 734 8000 (465 1631)
The elegant and understated Georgian and Adam rooms are the function accommodation highlights of this smart, central hotel, which has quite a range of facilities for business and social events (now including weddings). / Georgian (400,250,210); Edwardian (350,200,150); Adams (150,80); Regency 2 (60,40).

Mermaid Theatre EC4   £B-M, (400,150,150)
Puddle Dock, Blackfriars   236 1919   (236 1819)
The function room of this modern City-fringe theatre offer unusually good river views, especially from the second-floor Blackfriars Room. You might hold a reception in the River Room, move to dine in the Blackfriars Room, and return to the River Room for a disco. / 11.20pm; Crown Catering; Blackfriars Rm (400,150); River Rm (150,70).

Le Mesurier EC1   £M, (–,24)
113 Old St   251 8117
Small, good-quality north City restaurant, well suited to being taken over in its entirely for intimate evening or weekend functions. / not Mon-Fri L.

The Metropolitan W1   £M-E, (80,28)
Old Park La   447 1000   (447 1100)
Glamorously minimalist Mayfair hotel newcomer, which has a single, top-lit function room. / in-house caterers; Dining-Meeting Rm (80,28).

Mezzo W1   £E, (700,360,340)
100 Wardour St   314 4000   (393 0032)
The great expanses of what is claimed to be Europe's largest restaurant can be hired in its entirely for events of suitable scale. Only those with enormous budgets need apply. / Mezzonine (500,340); Mezzo (–,360,340); Pâtisserie (50,35).

Middle Temple Hall EC4   £M-E, (450,300,225)
Temple   427 4820   (427 4821)
The fine Tudor hall of this Inn of Court is an impressive, historic setting for dinners and receptions of all types. More comfortable are the Bench Apartments, available separately. The garden is a charming venue much used for summer parties. / midnight; Aug hol and legal vacations; in-house caterers; Hall (450,300,225); Parliament Chamber (100,60); Queen's Rm (75,22); Smoking Rm (95,–).

Millennium Conference Ctre SW7   £M-E, (900,420,380)
Harrington Gdns   373 6030   (373 0409)
Scheduled for completion in July 1997, this purpose-built (column-free) centre in South Kensington offers two floors of accommodation which can be configured in a number of different ways. Despite the businessy name, a wedding licence may be applied for. / 1am; in-house caterers; Lower Level (900,420,380); Ground Level (800,320,280); Rm 4 (80,30); Rm 7 (45,20).

Mimmo d'Ischia SW1   £M-E, (–,30)
61 Elizabeth St   730 5406
Sociable Belgravia Italian restaurant (completely revamped in 1996), run by the jovial Mimmo as a good but rather overpriced quasi-club. The private rooms are upstairs. / Private Rm (–,30); Private Rm (–,12).

The Ministry of Sound SE1   £B, (1200,900)
103 Gaunt St   378 6528   (403 5348)
The all-black room at this converted warehouse near Elephant and Castle that houses Europe's loudest sound system – the Box – can be hired for functions. It is usually used in conjunction with the Main Bar. For smaller events you can take one of the smaller bars. For a major extravaganza you might take over the whole club, now licensed for alcohol until 2am. / 6am; whole club not Fri, Sat; hirer's choice of caterer; The Box and Main Bar (900,300); Space Bar (VIP Rm) (300,–).

Mirabelle W1   £M-E, (200,150,100)
56 Curzon St   499 4636
Classic French Mayfair restaurant, now part of the Marco Pierre White empire. The premises are, at the time of writing, used for functions only (though the small Japanese dining rooms continue to operate normally). All details must be provisional, however, as a complete relaunch is scheduled for late-1997. / Pine Rm (–,30); Oak, Garden and Teppan-Yaki Rms (–,10).

Mitsukoshi SW1   £M-E, (–,24)
14-16 Regent St   930 0317   (839 1167)
A little bright and efficient it may appear, but by Japanese standards this smart basement (below the department store) is welcoming and stylish. There are two private rooms, one Japanese-style (tatami) and one western. / Western Rm (–,24); Tatami Rm (–,12).

Mon Plaisir WC2   £M, (–,30)
21 Monmouth St   836 7243   (379 0121)
Classic Theatreland restaurant, half a century old, with great character and good food – ideal for a not-too-expensive West End celebration. / not Sun; Private Rm (–,30).

Monkey Island Hotel, Berks   £M-E, (150,120,100)
Bray   01628-23400   (01628-784732)
Idyllic four-acre islet, accessible only by footbridge or boat. The hotel – in a building early c18 in origin – has some charming rooms and a lovely garden, making this one of the nicest places for a civil wedding. / 11.30pm; River Rm (150,120,100); Boardroom (–,16).

Monkeys SW3   £M, (–,10)
1 Cale St   352 4711
This discreetly located Chelsea Green restaurant has an attractive basement private room. It's no bargain, but food (Anglo-French), service and setting are all of high quality. / not Sun D; Private Rm (–,10).

Montana SW6   £M, (–,80)
125-129 Dawes Rd   385 9500
This stylish, much above-average Fulham restaurant – with a strong reputation for its south west USA cooking – is available for exclusive hire.

Monte's SW1   £M-E
164 Sloane St   581 1404   (245 0895)
Recently launched club, aiming to rival the likes of Annabel's. There is an ambitious first floor restaurant (consultant star-chef, Alain Ducasse), and second floor bar, but perhaps the most useful area for functions is the basement nightclub. A member must sponsor your function. / members club; 3am; not Sun; in-house caterers.

Mortons Club W1   £M, (300,100,100)
28 Berkeley Sq   499 0363   (495 3160)
Fashionable but unpretentious Mayfair townhouse club, which sometimes accommodates non-members' events. The attractive dining room overlooks the square. / 3am; restaurant eve, private rm daily; in-house caterers; Restaurant & Bar (220,100,100); Private Rm (80,32).

PRIVATE VENUES

Mosimann's Belfry SW1   £M-E, (80,115)
11b West Halkin St   235 9625   (245 6354)
*Celebrity chef Anton Mosimann's converted Belgravia chapel, now a
private dining club, has a number of private rooms decorated in the
colours of the respective corporate sponsors. Non-members may hire
the main restaurant (in its entirety) as well as the private rooms.*
/ 1am; not Sun; Dining Rm (–,115); Theo Fabergé (80,50); Wedgwood (60,30);
Veuve Clicquot (25,10); Gucci (–,14); Baulthaup (–,6).

Motcomb's SW1   £M-E, (40,30)
23 Motcomb St   235 3092   (245 6351)
*This Belgravia restaurant has its own townhouse for private dining.
There is an attractive, pine-panelled dining room especially suited to
parties of a dozen or more around a single table, and a separate
reception room.* / not Sun; no music; no dancing; McClue Suite (40,30).

Motcomb's Club SW1   £M-E, (220,140,140)
5 Halkin Arcade   235 5532   (245 6125)
*Smartly-located, comfortable nightclub, just off Belgrave Square, ideal
for taking over in its entirety. Though you can, at a cost, have it all
evening, the usual arrangement is to hire it until 11pm, at which time
the club is opened to its members.* / 3am; in-house caterers.

The Mountbatten WC2   £M, (120,80,50)
Seven Dials, 20 Monmouth St   836 4300   (240 3540)
*Off the foyer, the comfortable, elegant Broadlands Suite (limited
availability) is this Theatreland hotel's best point. See also Larry's
Wine Bar.* / Broadlands (100,60); Earl (120,80,50); Viceroy (35,18).

Moyns Park, Essex   £E, (–,80,80)
Birdbrook   01440-730073   (01440-730060)
*An Elizabethan manor house, now the home of Lord and Lady
Ivar Mountbatten, set in 250 acres of parkland (with potential for a
marquee of any size). The Great Hall is panelled and features an
ornately decorated grand piano – it would suit a range of functions,
including a small dinner dance.* / midnight; in-house caterers; no amplified music
in house; smoking restricted; Great Hall (–,80,80); Dining Rm (–,40);
Drawing Rm (–,30); marquee site.

Mr Kong WC2   £B-M, (–,40)
21 Lisle St   437 7341
*This Chinatown basement looks nothing special, but it's pleasant
enough and the good, affordable food and easy-going service make it
one of London's best places for a Chinese feast.* / Private Basement (–,40).

Mudchute Park and Farm E14   £B, (500,60)
Pier St   515 5901   (538 9530)
*Set in 32 acres of open space, this Docklands city farm has a café
seating up to 60, which is especially suitable for children's parties.
Other events may be accommodated (though alcohol may only be
served with food).* / 11pm; in-house or hirer's choice by negotiation; no smoking;
Café (40,60); marquee site.

The Mug House SE1   £B, (150,65,65)
1 Tooley St   403 8343
*Oddly situated, under the southern approach to London Bridge, a
pleasant, characterful wine bar.* / 1am; from 9am; Sat & Sun all day;
Private Rm (–,8).

Museum of London EC2   £M-E, (800,120,120)
London Wall   600 3699   (600 1058)
*This colourful museum of the capital's history is quite well suited to
function use. You might have your reception in the Lord Mayor's
Coach Gallery and a disco in the museum's reception area that
overlooks it. The large, well laid-out central garden is available in
summer. / Mon all day, Tue-Sun from 6.30pm; hirer's choice of caterer;
smoking restricted; Lord Mayor's Coach Gallery (250,120); Medieval Gallery (150,–);
Entrance Hall (120,–); Eighteenth Century Gallery (100,60).*

Museum of Mankind W1   £M-E, (200,100)
6 Burlington Gdns   323 8525   (323 8614)
*An imposing Victorian building, originally the HQ of London University,
is now the Mayfair home of the British Museum's ethnic collections.
The entrance hall is the area most suited to entertaining, but it seems
an expensive choice unless the venue is for some reason particularly
appropriate. / from 5.30pm Mon-Sat, Sun from 6.30pm; list of caterers;
no amplified music; no dancing; no smoking.*

Museum of the Moving Image SE1   £M-E, (250,70,70)
South Bank   815 1304   (815 1378)
*This South Bank museum (attached to the National Film Theatre) is
a spectacular venue for most types of party – you too can be a TV
star. You might dine in the Hollywood Studio and dance in the
adjoining TV Studio. / midnight; from 6.30pm; in-house caterers; smoking restricted;
Hollywood Studio (150,70); TV Studio (150,–).*

Music Room at Grays W1   £B-M, (350,150)
26 South Moulton La   629 7034   (493 9344)
*This unusual venue is located in a Victorian building, above a Mayfair
antiques market. The Exhibition Hall is lofty with lots of natural
daylight, and the Gallery has a grand piano. It was hoped at the time
of writing that the facilities might soon be available in the evenings.
/ 6pm; hirer's choice of caterer; no amplified music; no dancing;
Exhibition Hall (350,150); Gallery (60,50).*

National Army Museum SW3   £M, (450,90)
Royal Hospital Rd   730 0717   (823 6573)
*If you are looking for a venue with martial associations in a smart
area (next to the Royal Hospital), this rather unwelcoming building
may be worth considering. / 11pm; from 6pm; list of caterers; Art & Uniform
Galleries (450,90); Templer Galleries (100,50); Council Chamber (40,20).*

National Liberal Club SW1   £M-E, (750,260,260)
Whitehall Pl   930 9871   (839 4768)
*Especially at weekends (when access to the larger rooms is more
easily obtained) this impressive Edwardian building, just off Whitehall,
makes as interesting venue for events as disparate as a wedding or a
ball. It has the special advantage of a large outside terrace,
overlooking the river. / 2am; rms marked * avail Sat & Sun only; in-house caterers;
David Lloyd George (250,140,110); Lady Violet (70,50);
Smoking Rm * (300,–); Dining Rm * (300,124); Terrace * (250,150).*

National Portrait Gallery WC2   £E, (300,100)
2 St Martin's Pl   306 0055   (306 0058)
*Compared to many of London's major galleries, the NPG has a
relatively intimate scale that suits it well to entertaining. If you wish
to dine, the second floor Stuart galleries or, less suitably, the long, thin
first-floor Victorian galleries are available. / no wedding receptions or birthday
parties; midnight; from 6.30pm; list of caterers; no amplified music; no dancing;
no smoking.*

PRIVATE VENUES

Natural History Museum SW7   £M-E, (1200,600,500)
Cromwell Rd   938 9123   (938 9290)
*The monumental Victorian Main Hall – complete with prehistoric
monsters – particularly lends itself to dramatic, big-budget parties.
Some of the individual galleries, particularly the striking, new
Earth Galleries (with their own entrance), also offer interesting
possibilities. / I am; from 7pm (daytime functions in Spencer Rm); list of caterers; 85
dBA max; 78 dBA avg; Central Hall (1200,600,500); Earth Galleries (400,180); North
Hall (250,180,150); Spencer Gallery (–,120).*

Naval & Military Club W1   £B-M, (1200,200,200)
94 Piccadilly   499 5163   (499 2891)
*The 'In & Out' is large, rambling and faded, but its crustiness is part
of its charm and the place is not unduly imposing. Thanks to its
'secret garden' courtyard, summer receptions can be accommodated
in particularly fine style. Hurry – in August 1998, the Club is moving
to new premises. / midnight; in-house caterers; Coffee Rm (400,200,130);
Smoking Rm (300,–); Regimental Rm (100,70); Palmerston Rm or Egremont (100,50);
Courtyard (80,–); Octagon (30,15).*

Neal St WC2   £M-E, (–,20)
26 Neal St   836 8368
*Popular Covent Garden Italian, whose downstairs room maintains the
smooth styling of the main room. Prices here tend infamously
upwards. / not Sun; Private Rm (–,20).*

Neal's Lodge SW18   £M, (140,60)
On the Common, Wandsworth   622 6229   (720 8157)
*Natural light, lots of plants, and French windows opening on to a
terrace impart a countrified feeling to this former farmhouse, right on
Wandsworth Common, with the Maple Room available for dancing. / 11pm; in-house caterers;
Conservatory/Maple Rm/Bar (140,–); Conservatory (80,60); marquee site.*

New Connaught Rooms WC2   £B-M, (2600,650,560)
Gt Queen St   405 7811   (831 1851)
*One of London's oldest set of banqueting suites, two centuries old, is
now mainly used by business and the Masons – this was once an
annex of the neighbouring Temple. The Grand Hall, with three huge
chandeliers, is particularly impressive, but, with 29 rooms to choose
from, there is accommodation for most sizes of event. / in-house caterers,
but hirer's choice on Sun; Balmoral (750,650,560); Edinburgh (350,300,250);
York (210,200,150); Ulster (–,75); Durham (60,50); Penthouse (–,32).*

New World W1   £B-M, (–,200)
Gerrard Pl   734 0677
*For a big party relatively inexpensively, how about a feast for all your
friends on one of the floors of this vast Chinatown spot.*

Newham City Farm E16   £B, (50,50)
King George Ave, Custom Hse   476 1170
*The Visitors Centre of this city farm has a room particularly suited
to children's parties. The whole venue, could, however, be made
available for a suitable function. / winter 4pm, summer 5pm; from 10am;
hirer's choice of caterer; no smoking; no alcohol; Rm (50,50).*

Nôtre Dame Hall WC2   £B, (300,200,160)
6 Leicester Pl   437 5571
*Tatty but atmospheric, circular dance hall – in fact a church crypt.
Its main drawback is that its central location, just off Leicester
Square, ensures it is usually fully booked. / midnight; hirer's choice of caterer.*

Odéon SW1 £M-E, (–,20)
65 Regent St   287 1400
Modern mega-brasserie, whose first-floor private room overlooks Regent Street. / Private Rm (–,20).

Odette's NW1 £M, (–,30)
130 Regent's Park Rd   586 5486
This multi-mirrored, Primrose Hill favourite – north London's smartest restaurant – has one of the sweetest private rooms, feeling rather like eating in a nice below-stairs cupboard. The downstairs conservatory can also be hired. / not Sat L & Sun; Conservatory (–,30); Private Rm (–,9).

The Old Operating Theatre, Museum & Herb Garret SE1 £B-M, (100,–)
9a St Thomas St   955 4791   (378 8383)
Bizarre and fascinating c19 operating-theatre, up tortuous spiral stairs in the belfry of a church near London Bridge. It now houses a collection of surgical instruments and pickled internal organs – tough to beat for a drinks party with a touch of the macabre. / hirer's choice of caterer; no dancing; no smoking.

Old Refectory W8 £B-M, (250,120,80)
Campden Hl Rd   928 3777   (928 5777)
Leafily located Kensington outpost of King's College, whose attractive, barrel-roofed hall is – after a couple of years out of service – again available for weddings and parties. / midnight; in-house caterers.

Old Royal Observatory SE10 £E, (80,40)
Romney Rd   0181-858 4422   (0181-312 6632)
Survey London from this lofty, 0° vantage-point in Greenwich Park. The charming, top-floor Octagon (made available on a limited basis) is one of the few surviving Wren interiors, and its long, narrow windows have one of the best views of the metropolis. / 11pm; list of caterers; no amplified music; no dancing; no red wine.

The Old Thameside Inn SE1 £B, (150,–)
Clink St   403 4243
South Bank riverside pub, refurbished in early 1997. It has a large, stone-floored cellar bar available for private parties (and where you can also have a disco). A section of the terrace overlooking the river can be roped off for 40 or so people. / 11.20pm; Cellar Bar (150,–).

The Old Town Hall, Stratford E15 £B-M, (490,250,200)
29 The Broadway, Stratford   0181-534 7835   (0181-534 8411)
If you want old-fashioned chandeliers-and-ornate-ceilings elegance, these east London premises might suit. The Courtyard (not generally open as part of a function let) can be used for a marquee. / Mon-Fri midnight Sat 2am, Sun midnight; hirer's choice of caterer; Main Hall (490,250,200); Council Chamber (80,80,60); Conference Rm (70,–); Mayor's Parlour (20,–); marquee site.

One Whitehall Place SW1 £M-E, (400,400)
One Whitehall Pl   839 3344   (839 3366)
A sumptuous, totally refurbished Grade I listed building, now exclusively used for functions (including weddings). The balconies of the River Room and the Reading and Writing Rooms have views of Whitehall Gardens and the Thames, and there is a fine library, with minstrels' gallery. It may be possible to hire the terrace of the adjacent National Liberal Club (see also). / midnight; in-house caterers; no amplified music; Gladstone Library (400,228); Whitehall Suite (220,220); Reading and Writing Rm (250,150); Meston Suite (110,72); River Rm (100,68); Cellar (50,14); Thames Suite (80,60).

PRIVATE VENUES

L'Oranger SW1 £M-E, (–,25)
5 St James's St   839 3774
It contrives to give a traditional impression, but this St James's restaurant delivers high quality contemporary French cooking, and at prices which are very reasonable for the area. The private room is downstairs. / Private Rm (–,25).

Orangery (Holland Park) W8 £M, (150,70)
Holland Pk   602 7344   (371 2467)
This must be one of the prettiest spots in London – an enchanting c18 building, on an intimate scale and glazed on three sides. / 11.30pm; list of caterers; no amplified music; no dancing; marquee site.

Orangery (Kensington Palace) W8 £M-E, (200,100)
Kensington Palace   376 2452   (376 0198)
Beautifully situated, at the back of the Palace, this lovely, long, white-painted, Queen Anne summer house is made available ten or so times a year for prestigious celebrations. / charities & companies only; eve only; Digby Trout; no amplified music; no dancing.

Ormond's Restaurant & Club SW1 £M, (250,150)
Jermyn St   930 2842   (930 2843)
Rather louche – the management prefers the epithet "cosy" – St James's restaurant-nightclub. It is all geared up to provide fun casinos, magicians, bands and DJs, so it makes a good choice if you want an evening of dance, music and entertainments all laid on. / 3.45am; in-house caterers; Restaurant (250,150); Downstairs (120,–).

Orsino W11 £M, (–,32)
119 Portland Rd   221 3299
Chic and discreetly located Holland Park modern Italian restaurant, with a stylish private room upstairs. / Private Rm (–,32).

The Oval SE11 £M, (350,240,180)
Kennington   735 6884   (582 8151)
Large, modernish banqueting suite adjacent to the cricket ground. / Knightsbridge Catering.

Oxford & Cambridge Club SW1 £M, (120,60,60)
71 Pall Mall   930 5151   (930 9490)
Those who spent their salad days at the Varsity (or who have friends who did) should bear this St James's institution in mind. A member must be present at any function. / in-house caterers; Marlborough (120,60); Edward VII (40,20).

Painters' Hall EC4 £M, (250,180)
9 Little Trinity Ln   236 6258   (236 0500)
This hall, near Mansion House lane, is quite modest compared to some of its grand City brethren. Décor is quite spare, with the hall (re-opened in the '60s) painted in cool shades. Discos are not permitted but flexibility is otherwise the keynote. The small, yellow Painted Chamber is particularly charming. / 1am; Aug hol; Payne & Gunter; Livery Hall (250,180); Court Rm (150,60); Painted Chamber (–,14).

Palace Theatre W1 £M, (250,100)
Cambridge Circus   434 0088
Though it's mainly used privately for entertaining after shows, the beautiful Stalls Bar at this landmark on the edge of Soho can also be used for daytime receptions and lunches. / before 4.30pm & after shows; hirer's choice of caterer; no amplified music; no dancing; Stalls Bar (250,100).

Pall Mall Deposit W10   £B-M, (100,50)
124-128 Barlby Rd   0181-964 5299
*Uncluttered space in the restaurant of a North Kensington business
and media centre, located in an imposing former warehouse.*
/ Bar (–,24).

La Paquerette EC2   £B, (100,60)
Finsbury Sq   638 5134
*By the green at the centre of Finsbury Square, this small bar/café has
a garden and is available for barbecues, parties and bowling evenings.
At the weekends, you can take over the whole place.* / 1am;
in-house caterers.

Park Lane Hotel W1   £M-E, (1000,600,550)
Piccadilly   499 6321   (499 1965)
*Charming Mayfair hotel, where the star is the large Art Deco
Ballroom (refurbished in 1996), with its superb entrance. Some of the
other rooms, for example the imposing Oak Room, also offer some
unusually characterful possibilities. All the rooms are licensed for
weddings.* / 1am; in-house caterers; Ballroom (1000,600,550);
Tudor Rose Rm (200,180,150); Oak Rm (140,80,50); Garden Rm (150,120,60);
Orchard Suite (80,40); Mirror Rm (40,40); Drawing Rm (30,20).

Paulo's W6   £B-M, (–,40)
30 Greyhound Rd   385 9264
*The Torres family's home, off the Fulham Palace Road, is a
long-established, very inexpensive, Brazilian, eat-all-you-can
buffet-restaurant. Groups of 15 people may book the downstairs
room for the whole evening and it is sometimes possible to take over
the entire restaurant.* / not Sun; Downstairs Rm (–,20).

Peacock House W14   £M, (250,50)
8 Addison Rd   603 6373   (602 8652)
*Extraordinary late-Victorian Holland Park house (by the same
architect as the better-known Leighton House) with a mosaicked
entrance hall. It is popular for wedding receptions and bigger events
and has a lawn for large marquees.* / 10.30pm; eve, Sat & Sun;
hirer's choice of caterer; marquee site.

Peg's Club WC2   £M, (160,45)
17 Mercer St   240 2234
*To hire the facilities in this Covent Garden media and theatrical world
club, you'll have to know a member (or become one yourself).
You can hire the whole club on a Saturday night.* / members only;
in-house caterers; no pipes, cigars permitted; Dining Rm (–,45); Quiet Rm/Bar (75,–).

Penshurst Place, Kent   £M-E, (600,150)
Penshurst, Tonbridge   01892-870307   (01892-870866)
*The Sidney family home since 1552 and substantially still a medieval
building (set in gardens laid out in 1442). You can get married in the
Sunderland Room then go downstairs to the Baron's Hall for dinner
and dancing – you could do it the other way round, except that
dancing is not allowed in the Sunderland Room.* / midnight; list of caterers;
Baron's Hall (400,150); Sunderland Rm (150,84); Buttery (70,30); marquee site.

Pentland House SE13   £B-M, (200,200,200)
Old Rd   919 7132   (919 7134)
*The key attraction of this c17 house (one of the Goldsmiths College
lodging-houses) is a fabulous garden. The Refectory is also a
possibility, although decoration will probably be necessary.* / midnight;
hirer's choice of caterer; Marquee or Lawn (200,200); Hall (150,100); marquee site.

PRIVATE VENUES

The People's Palace SE1   £M-E, (400,240)
South Bank Centre   928 9999   (928 2355)
The enormous main dining room of the Royal Festival Hall,
overlooking the Thames, can be taken in its entirety for functions.
The general prohibition (for obvious reasons) of music during shows
precludes many uses for which the place would otherwise be suitable.
/ no music; no dancing.

Pewterers' Hall EC2   £M, (150,70)
Oat Ln   726 0470   (600 3896)
This mid-sized '60s livery hall is sometimes made available for
dinners and receptions. / no weddings; 10.30pm; no amplified music; no dancing;
Livery Rm (150,70); Court Rm (150,–).

Phene Arms SW3   £B, (80,40)
9 Phene St   352 3294   (352 7026)
Chelsea pub – known particularly for its pretty garden terrace –
which has a reasonable party room above. The heated terrace is
available for dining al fresco. / 11pm; no dancing; Upstairs Rm (80,40);
Terrace (30,16).

Phillips W1   £M-E, (500,280)
101 New Bond St   468 8382   (495 1731)
The larger galleries of this Mayfair auction house are sometimes
available for receptions and dinners. / from 5pm; hirer's choice of caterer;
no smoking; Blenheim Rm (250,160).

Photographers' Gallery WC2   £B-M, (150,80)
5 Great Newport St   831 1772   (836 9704)
The nicest parts of this modern gallery, on the fringe of Covent
Garden are rather long and thin, and the cafeteria therefore tends to
be the focus for functions. / midnight; not Tue –Sat pre 7pm; in-house or hirer's
choice by negotiation; no amplified music; no dancing; smoking restricted.

Phyllis Court, Oxon   £M-E, (600,400,300)
Marlow Rd, Henley-on-Thames
01491-574366   (01491-410725)
Picturesquely situated by Henley Bridge, this turn-of-the-century
country club (with more modern grandstand building) is a popular
choice for weddings, wedding receptions, and club or charity dinners.
/ grandstand midnight, otherwise 1 am; in-house caterers; Ballroom (600,400,300);
Grandstand (250,120,120); Thames Rm (80,60,60); marquee site.

Pimlico Wine Vaults SW1   £B, (50,38)
19-22 Upper Tachbrook St   834 7429   (828 5528)
Basement wine bar near Victoria. It's decorated in a smart, if rather
pub-like, way, and boasts a panelled private room. / Private Rm (50,38).

Pinewood Studios, Bucks   £M, (200,180,150)
Pinewood Rd, Iver   01753-656953   (01753-653616)
The country house at the centre of this famous studio complex
accommodates large parties in its Ballroom (using the adjoining
theatre for dancing). Smaller get-togethers happen in its Great Gatsby
or Green Rooms. For big gatherings – perhaps after a marriage in the
house itself – a marquee can be erected. / 1 am; in-house caterers;
Ballroom (200,180,150); Green Rm (150,80); Great Gatsby Rm (150,100);
marquee site.

Pitcher & Piano WC2   £B-E, (150,–)
40-42 King William IV St   240 6180
Lofty central branch of this chain of wine bars that is something of a mecca for young London professionals. There are two options for a private party – hire of the back raised area (with no minimum spend) or hire of the upstairs party room (which at popular times requires a large minimum spend). / 11 pm; Private Rm not available Fri & Sat; Private Rm (150,–); Platform (40,–).

Pitcher & Piano W1   £B-M, (150,25)
69-70 Dean St   434 3585   (734 6627)
Early in the week, the whole upper floor of this Soho bar can be used privately. At other times a private room is available, or, most cheaply, an area of the bar (the Cosy Area) can be roped off. / 11 pm; Upper Floor (150,–); Panelled Rm (70,25); Cosy Area (40,20).

Pitcher & Piano SW10   £B, (100,–)
214 Fulham Rd   352 9234   (352 5191)
On the divide between Chelsea and Fulham, the room over this younger-scene bar is very popular for drinks parties. / midnight.

Pizza On The Park SW1   £B-M, (–,100)
11 Knightsbridge   235 5273   (235 6853)
The subterranean room of this large, fashionably-located pizzeria – used most nights for cabaret – may be hired privately at lunchtime or on Sunday evenings. / 11.30pm; Basement (–,100).

Mandrake Club (PizzaExpress) W1   £B-M, (100,100)
18 Bruton Mews   495 1411
Located in a cute Belgravia Mews, these simple gallery-style rooms offer the opportunity for an inexpensive central function in a very good address. Although part of a branch of PizzaExpress it will, at the time of writing, let you do your own catering for a modest cover charge. / midnight; in-house or hirer's choice by negotiation.

Pizzeria Condotti W1   £B, (–,40)
4 Mill St   499 1308
This smart Mayfair spot offers possibilities for a stylish, quite inexpensive, central party in its downstairs room. / not Sun; Private Rm (–,40).

The Place Below EC2   £B-M, (–,80)
St Mary-le-Bow, Cheapside   329 0789
Parties of 20 or more can take over this high-quality City crypt vegetarian restaurant. In fine weather, by prior arrangement, you might be able to use the courtyard. / 11.30pm; in-house caterers; no smoking.

Plaisterers' Hall EC2   £M-E, (600,298)
1 London Wall   606 7908   (796 1408)
The Plaisterers' modern hall belies its relatively inconspicuous entry at the base of an office block – it is on an impressive scale and decorated in grand traditional style. Although the hall has hitherto been used mainly for City functions, a wedding licence has been applied for. / not Sun; Ring & Brymer.

Planet Hollywood W1   £M, (600,300)
13 Coventry St   287 1000   (734 0835)
The West End outpost of Tinseltown, just off Leicester Square, makes an impressive, pre-themed space for a movie-related event. / 1.30am; in-house caterers; Restaurant (600,300); VIP Suite (120,90); Screening Rm (–,75).

The Players' Theatre WC2 £B-M, (200,120)
The Arches, Villiers St, Strand   976 1307   (839 8067)
*Intimate and charming theatre (whose auditorium seats 258 people),
under the Arches at Charing Cross.* / 3am; in-house caterers;
smoking restricted; Lower Supper Rm/Bar (200,120); Mezzanine Supper Rm (100,48).

The Plough WC2 £B, (45,30)
27 Musuem St   626 7964
*Friendly, creaky, well-worn pub across from the British Museum. If you
are happy to do without a private bar, the room comes free.*
/ no amplified music; no dancing.

Poetry Society WC2 £B-M, (100,45)
22 Betterton St   240 4810   (240 4818)
*Covent Garden society whose HQ is, as one might expect, most used
for book launches and readings, but where the café is also used for
more social occasions.* / member's club; 11.30 pm; not Sun; in-house caterers;
no amplified music; Restaurant (100,50).

Poissonnerie de l'Avenue SW3 £M, (–,25)
82 Sloane Av   589 2457
*Long-established, recently revamped Chelsea fish parlour, with a
comfortable upstairs private dining room.* / not Sun; Private Rm (–,25).

Polesden Lacey, Surrey £M-E, (80,70)
Dorking   01372-458203   (01372-452023)
*National Trust property, offering a restaurant (in the former stables)
and a marquee site. The restaurant is carpeted, and has wooden
walls, high ceilings and a stone floor. It is perhaps a touch functional,
but it does have the advantage of opening onto a courtyard.* / no 18ths
or 21sts; midnight; Apr-Oct, Wed-Sun (& Bank Hols) from 6pm; in-house, but list for
marquees; smoking restricted in Rest, but not in Café; Restaurant (80,70); marquee site.

Polish Hearth Club SW7 £B-M, (200,130)
55 Exhibition Rd   589 4635   (581 7926)
*For old-fashioned charm, this South Kensington emigrés' club scores
highly. Parts have been recently refurbished but it remains a
characterful, quite grand, mid-priced venue for most kinds of event.
The Restaurant has an outside terrace, and is popular for summer
cocktails.* / 1am; Ballroom Sat & Sun only; in-house caterers; Ballroom (200,130);
Restaurant (–,120).

Polish Social & Cultural Association W6 £B, (750,200,200)
238-246 King St   0181-741 1940   (0181-746 3798)
*As with many emigrés clubs, it's the time warp atmosphere which
some may find a particular attraction of this basic '60s
Hammersmith building. On the social side, the club hosts a fair
number of wedding receptions.* / Club Disco 25 years +; 1am; Club Disco
1.30am; restaurant not Sat D & Sun L, Club Disco Fri only; in-house, but Club Disco may
be at hirer's choice; Lowiczanka Restaurant (200,150,110); Malinova Rm (200,200,200);
Ballroom (–,–,160); Club Disco (150,–).

Polygon Bar & Grill SW4 £M, (–,60)
4 The Polygon, Clapham Old Town   622 1199   (622 1166)
*This unusually stylish Clapham restaurant is available during the day
for wedding receptions and the like.*

Pomegranates SW1 £M, (–,12)
94 Grosvenor Rd   826 6560
*Pimlico basement restaurant of long standing, offering good,
old-style-eclectic cooking. Its dimly-lit, mirrored setting has a curiously
illicit atmosphere.* / not Sat L & Sun; Private Rm (–,12).

La Pomme d'Amour W11 £M, (–,35)
128 Holland Park Av   229 8532
*Prettier after the recent refurbishment, this long-established Holland
Park restaurant is a good place all round, with a very pleasant private
room.* / not Sat L & Sun; Private Rm (–,35).

Le Pont de la Tour SE1 £M-E, (–,20)
Butler's Wharf   403 8403   (403 0267)
*The private room of the leading restaurant of Conran's Tower Bridge-
side 'Gastrodrome' may lack the spectacular view of the main dining
room, but proximity to the City ensures its popularity.* / Private Rm (–,20).

Porchester Centre W2 £B-M, (630,450,450)
Queensway   792 2823   (798 3693)
*Ornate, panelled Art Deco ballroom – a gem hidden away in a
municipal-looking Bayswater building – which is not very expensive
and has lots of character. The marbled Turkish baths are occasionally
used by party givers in search of the off-beat.* / 1am; list or hirer's choice by
negotiation; Ballroom (630,450,450); Baths (200,100).

La Porte des Indes W1 £M-E, (1000,300,300)
32 Bryanston St   224 0055
*This vast Indian restaurant near Marble Arch is extremely flexible as
a function venue, and offers obvious theming potential. One or other
of the restaurant's two floors can be used to accommodate parties of
anywhere between 100 and 200, and there are some smaller private
rooms.* / 3am; Private Rm (x2) (–,12).

Portman Hotel W1 £M-E, (700,400,400)
22 Portman Sq   208 6000   (224 4928)
*The banqueting facilities of this modern hotel reflect a certain
conference-orientation (though it does have a wedding licence).
There's a good variety or rooms though, all with floor-to-ceiling
windows.* / 1am; Ballroom (700,400,400); Gloucester Suite (100,80); Berkeley
Suite (50,50); Library (30,24).

POW Bar and Restaurant SW3 £M, (60,40)
145 Dovehouse St   351 1155/7478   (351 0077)
*Mid-range Chelsea restaurant, with a light and unusually attractive
first-floor private room.*

HMS President EC4 £B-M, (350,200,160)
Victoria Embankment   583 2652   (583 2840)
*For a big, limited-budget bash, this WW1, Q-class boat, moored just
above Blackfriars Bridge, offers good value and the sense of occasion
that being afloat brings. The rooms need decoration to be festive.*
/ 2am; hirer's choice of caterer; Drill Hall (250,200,160); Gun Rm (100,50);
Wardroom (120,60); Captain's Quarters (–,40).

Quaglino's SW1 £M-E, (450,320)
16 Bury St   930 6767   (839 2866)
*What is still arguably London's most striking restaurant has a salon
privé, in slickly modernistic style. If money is no object, you can hire
the whole place.* / Private Rm (60,40).

PRIVATE VENUES

Quayside E1   £M, (250,100)
International House, St Katherine's Dock, 1 St Katherine's Way
481 0972   (488 3482)
*The view of St Katherine's dock (in summer, from the terrace) is the
special attraction of this restaurant near Tower Bridge, which is very
well geared up for weddings and for functions generally (including
having a dance floor). In conjunction with the International House
(see also), receptions for up to 400 people are possible.
/ midnight; in-house caterers;
/ Private Rm (–,50).*

The Queen Elizabeth II
Conference Centre SW1   £M-E, (600,800,600)
Broad Sanctuary, Westminster   798 4000   (798 4200)
*The appeal of this purpose-built centre by Westminster Abbey is
perhaps more obvious as a venue for conferences rather than social
events. In fact, however, the place is quite geared up for the latter,
even to the extent of having a wedding licence. / midnight; in-house caterers;
Fleming + Whittle Rms (–,800); Benjamin Britten Lounge (600,–); Pickwick
Suite (300,120); Fleming Rm (–,600,600); Caxton Lounge (–,140,200);
Guild Rm (–,50,50).*

TS Queen Mary WC2   £M, (1000,–)
Victoria Embankment   240 9404   (497 8910)
*This converted steamer moored by Waterloo Bridge is undergoing
complete refurbishment in the first half of 1997. There will be a
variety of bars (over several decks), two function rooms and a
barbecue. A disco is also being added. A wedding licence has been
obtained. / in-house caterers.*

Queen's Eyot, Berks   £M, (250,150)
Monkey Island Ln   01753-671219   (01753-671244)
*Eton College's island retreat has an impressive modern clubhouse
reached by ferry. Uses of the eyot range from corporate sports days
to wedding receptions. / midnight; in-house caterers; permanent
marquee (250,150); marquee site.*

Queen's House SE10   £E, (200,150,150)
National Maritime Museum   0181-858 4422   (0181-312 6632)
*Sandwiched picturesquely between the Royal Naval College and
Greenwich Park, a highly unusual house (by Inigo Jones et al),
comprehensively restored. The lofty, cubic Great Hall and pretty
Orangery are the areas most used, and are ideal for a wedding. / larger
functions from 6pm; list of caterers; live music only; no discos; Great Hall (150,110);
Orangery Suite (150,40); Treasury (120,–); Loggia (30,–); marquee site.*

Queens Ice Bowl W2   £B, (1000,50)
Queensway   229-0172   (229 1818)
*The action at Central London's only ice rink is no longer limited to
falling over on a slippery, cold surface. You can hire the entire
Bayswater centre and try Sega World, 10 Pin Bowling as well as
skating. For smaller groups there is a private room. / midnight; Mon-Thur
day/eve, Fri till 7pm, Sun from 7pm; Function Rm every day/eve; in-house or hirer's choice
by negotiation; smoking restricted; Sega World (500,–); Private Rm (100,50);
10 Pin Bowling (per game) (72,–).*

Quo Vadis W1   £M-E, (175,150)
26-29 Dean St   437 4809   (434 9972)
*May 1997 sees the opening of three second-floor function rooms
(all overlooking Dean Street) at this successful new Soho addition to
the Marco Pierre White restaurant empire. Precise capacities were
not available at the time of going to press. / Private Rm (175,150).*

Raffles SW3 £M-E, (150,70,70)
King's Rd 352 1091 (352 9293)
This intimate Chelsea nightclub, with separate Dining Room, is decorated in comfortable, traditional style. It is available for hire by non-members before 11pm and all day on Sunday. / *non members before 11pm & Sun only; 3am; list of caterers; Dining Rm (50,38).*

Ranger's House SE10 £M-E, (200,150)
Chesterfield Wk, Blackheath 0181-853 0035 (0181-853 0090)
On the border of Greenwich Park, overlooking Blackheath, this c18 English Heritage house has a fine Gallery Room – home to the Suffolk Paintings Collection – which is available for dinners. A marquee is erected in the summer, for which Saturday bookings are taken a year in advance. A wedding licence has been applied for. / *wedding receptions & discos in marquee only; midnight; summer from 6pm, winter from 4pm; winter closed Mon & Tue; no amplified music; no smoking; no red wine; Gallery (–,80); Marquee (200,150); marquee site.*

The RAW Club WC1 £B, (450,–)
112a Gt Russell St 637 3375 (637 3965)
Underneath the Tottenham Court Road YMCA, this high-ceilinged basement-nightclub comes heavily themed and has a large dance floor. The Gardening Room is available privately most nights. / *6am; whole club Mon-Wed only; hirer's choice of caterer, alcohol in-house; The Gardening Rm (60,–).*

Red Fort W1 £M, (–,200)
77 Dean St 437 2525
Probably the best-known Indian restaurant in the West End, this comfortable Soho spot has a basement which may be hired separately. / *Private Rm (–,200).*

Reform Club SW1 £M-E, (600,400,400)
104 Pall Mall 930 9374 (930 1857)
The beautiful, august lobby of this St James's club is an ideal centrepiece for a weekend ball. The Coffee Room and the sombre Library are also very grand and there are smaller dining rooms for as few as 14. A member must be actively involved in any function. / *1am; whole club Sat & Sun only; in-house caterers; Library (250,100); Coffee Rm (250,100); Committe Rm (–,14).*

Regency Banqueting Suite N17 £B-M, (500,300,300)
113 Bruce Gro 0181-885 2490 (0181-885 1739)
It started off as a ballroom in the mid-20s, then became a cinema, and for the last decade these Tottenham premises have been a banqueting suite. Décor is ivory, gold and white, with crystal chandeliers. / *Mon-Sat 1am, Sun 11pm; Aug hol; in-house caterers.*

Regent's College NW1 £M, (400,200,200)
Inner Circle, Regent's Pk 487 7540 (487 7657)
A great position, in the heart of the Park, makes this a very attractive venue. The rooms available are light and airy, in good decorative order, and only somewhat institutional. The Tuke Common Room has a particularly leafy prospect. / *2am; ARA; Refectory (400,200,200); Herringham Hall (200,90); Tuke Common Rm (80,–); marquee site.*

The Rembrandt Hotel SW7 £M, (200,180,180)
11 Thurloe Pl 589 8100 (225 3363)
This agreeable South Ken hotel, near the V&A, offers good, flexible banqueting accommodation, all licensed for civil weddings. / *1am; Elizabeth & Victoria (Queen Suite) (90,60); Elizabeth (60,40); Princes (20,20); Victoria (15,10).*

PRIVATE VENUES

Rib Room
Hyatt Carlton Tower Hotel SW1 £M-E, (–,16)
2 Cadogan Pl   235 1234
*This luxurious Knightsbridge roasts, grill and seafood restaurant has a
dark-panelled Boardroom for private dining.* / Boardroom (–,16).

The Ritz W1 £M-E, (90,50)
150 Piccadilly   493 8181   (493 2687)
*The Ritz's strength is in stylish small to medium size rooms – in décor,
the Marie Antoinette suite lives up to its name, and the Trafalgar
Suite is also impressive. The function rooms are licensed for weddings.*
/ no discos, live music restricted to pianos; Marie Antoinette Suite (90,50); Berkeley Suite
Reception Rm & Dining Rm (–,30); Trafalgar Suite (–,20).

Riverside Studios W6 £B-M, (1000,–)
Crisp Rd, Hammersmith
0181-741 2251   (0181-563 0336/0181 846 8083)
*TV studios and arts centre, offering flexible spaces. The studios are
without windows, but the café-bar and gallery are quite light and
bright, and the terrace has views towards Hammersmith Bridge.*
/ in-house caterers; Studio 1 (498,–); Café-Bar (200,–); Terrace/Marquee (150,–);
marquee site.

Rochesters SW1 £B, (70,–)
69 Vincent Sq   828 6611   (233 6724)
*High-ceilinged, light, street-side Pimlico wine bar, which lends itself to
casual drinks parties. Dancing can be organised.* / 3am; eve only.

Rock Circus W1 £M-E, (350,–)
London Pavilion, Piccadilly Circus   734 7203   (734 8023)
*This homage to rock stars comes complete with moving Animatronic
figures and is available for receptions for events with some musical
link. As we went to press, the possibility of applying for a wedding
licence was being considered.* / parties with a musical link preferred; 2am;
from 6.30pm; list of caterers; no smoking.

Rock Garden WC2 £B, (600,60)
6-7 The Piazza   497 3154   (379 4793)
*Though better-known for its touristy upstairs burger joint, the vaults
downstairs are among London's older rock venues. It's all very clean-
cut, and offers combinations for parties of many sizes. Bigger events
are organised in conjunction with the neighbouring nightclub, the
Gardening Club.* / Gardening Club 8pm, restaurant midnight; Rock Garden not Fri or
Sat eve; in-house caterers; Rock Garden (300,–); Upstairs Restaurant (60,–).

Rock Spiders Opera SW10 £B-M, (70,–)
138 Fulham Rd   259 2667
*Discreetly trendy Chelsea bar, which marks the start of the short strip
of the Fulham Road currently being glamourised in the press as "The
Beach". The downstairs area can be hired for parties.* / Mon-Wed
midnight, Thur-Sat 1am, Sun 11.30pm; from 4pm; in-house or hirer's choice by
negotiation; no dancing.

Rodos WC2 £B, (–,40)
59 St Giles High St   836 3177
*Stuck out on a limb, behind Centre Point, this long-established, family-
run taverna offers good grub. The atmospheric upper room is great
for those feeling hungry and boisterous.* / not Sat L & Sun; Private Rm (–,40).

Roehampton Club SW15 £M-E, (330,220,180)
Roehampton La   0181-876 2057   (0181-392 2386)
It is no longer necessary to be a member to book function rooms at this impressive club, and those attending events can have the run of the sports facilities which include an 18-hole golf course, 28 tennis and five squash courts, three croquet lawns, indoor and outdoor pools, and a gymnasium. The Roehampton and Garden Rooms benefit from huge windows overlooking the garden. / 11pm; in-house caterers; Roehampton Rm (250,160,120); Garden Rm (80,60,60); marquee site.

The Roof Gardens W8 £M-E, (420,200,180)
99 High St Kensington (entrance off Derry St)
937 7994   (938 2774)
A nightclub set in two acres of beautiful gardens would be a popular venue anywhere. Eight floors above Kensington it seems all the more remarkable, and the place is constantly in demand for events of all types. / 1am; not Thu eve or Sat eve; in-house caterers.

Rose Garden Buffet NW1 £B-M, (500,150)
Inner Circle, Regent's Pk   935 5729   (935 5894)
The Prince Regent room of this park café opens onto a large rose garden area available, for example, for barbecues. (The owners also run the tea rooms and cafés in Hyde and Greenwich Parks with space for a marquee, though the Rose Garden Restaurant is the only area suitable for formal seated occasions. The central booking contact details are those given.) / restaurant eve only; hirer's choice of caterer; Prince Regent Rm (75,50); Rose Garden Restaurant (–,150); marquee site.

Rossway Park, Herts £E, (100,40)
Berkhamsted   01442-865160   (01442-863697)
This Victorian country house retains many original architectural features, and makes an ideal venue for those looking for grandeur with a degree of intimacy. / hirer's choice of caterer; Dining Rm (–,40); marquee site.

Royal Academy of Arts W1 £E, (1000,250)
Burlington House, Piccadilly   494 5701   (287 6312)
The c17/18 private rooms of the Royal Academy are among the most charmingly impressive of any in London. It may also be possible to organise functions around gallery exhibitions (particularly the Summer Exhibition). Sit-down events are for corporate members only. / 11.30pm; from 6.30pm; list of caterers; no smoking; Summer Exhibition (1000,250); Private Rms (400,100); General Assembly Rm (–,40).

Royal Aeronautical Society W1 £M, (175,130,130)
4 Hamilton Pl   499 3515   (499 6230)
Although slightly institutional in feel, much of the original grandeur of this impressive c19 townhouse, just off Hyde Park corner, remains. A terrace opens off the Argyll room. / midnight; London Catering Services; Argyll Rm & Hawker Rm (175,130); Council Rm & Bar (100,40); Hawker Rm (25,12); Sopwith Rm (60,30).

The Royal Air Force Club W1 £M, (250,140,100)
128 Piccadilly   499 3456   (355 1516)
Functions need to be sponsored by a member but, once you're in, this club is more flexible than many others as it has a ballroom and also a bar/disco area. The Mezzanine Suite offers adaptable accommodation, and in the basement, the Running Horse (the 'Pub within the club') and Buttery are suitable for discos, dances and wedding receptions. / 12.30am; in-house caterers; disco in buttery; in the buttery; Ballroom (250,140); Presidents Rm (80,–); Drawing Rm (40,20); Mezzanine Suite (–,20); Boardroom (–,8); Running Horse/Buttery (–,–,100).

PRIVATE VENUES

Royal Air Force Museum NW9   £M-E, (1400,370,300)
Grahame Pk Way, Hendon   0181-205 2266   (0181-205 8044)
*Although other galleries are available, the Battle of Britain Hall of this
Hendon venue is the most used for functions. As well as aircraft (from
both sides), it has interesting displays on the Blitz, making it a natural
for themed events.* / from 6pm; list of caterers; no smoking; Bomber Command
Hall (700,–); Main Aircraft Hall (700,–); Battle of Britain Hall (400,370,300);
marquee site.

Royal Albert Hall SW7   £M-E, (1450,1450,1000)
Kensington Gore   589 3203   (823 7725)
*You can entertain huge numbers in great style here, although, once
more than just the arena is used it is necessary to use the stalls and
the boxes – a rather odd arrangement. Smaller events may be
arranged in private rooms – the Prince of Wales and Henry Cole are
particularly attractive.* / 3am; Letheby & Christopher; smoking restricted;
Cabaret or Ball (1450,1450,1000); Arena (750,360,350); Picture Gallery (200,140);
Victoria Rm (120,80); Henry Cole Rm (30,20).

Royal College of Art SW7   £B-M, (900,500,400)
Kensington Gore   590 4444   (590 4500)
*Large, white-walled galleries looking on to Kensington Gardens, which
offer large, open spaces for inexpensive events – from a private view
to a party – or are an ideal blank canvas on which to create more
lavish themed events. The first-floor Fellows' rooms suit smaller,
formal occasions.* / 2am; large functions in term eve & Sat & Sun only;
hirer's choice of caterer; some areas, no red wine; Henry Moore Gallery (900,500,400);
Gulbenkian Upper Gallery (350,200); Gulbenkian Lower Gallery (150,80); Senior
Common Rm and Dining Rm (–,70).

Royal College of Music SW7   £M-E, (400,250,200)
Prince Consort Rd   589 3643   (589 7740)
*The Concert Hall of this grand South Kensington institution opens
directly off the college's marbled foyer. The Council Room is suitable
for small dinners, but, of all the accommodation, the Donaldson
Room (use by permission of the Director) is the most attractive.*
/ 1.30am; out of term best; hirer's choice of caterer; no smoking; some areas, no red
wine; Concert Hall (400,250,200); Donaldson Rm (80,40); Council Rm (30,24).

The Royal College of Pathologists SW1   £M-E, (350,120)
2 Carlton House Terr   930 5863   (839 1437)
*This Nash Terrace house was elegantly refurbished in understated
modern style (maple panelling and pale grey walls) in 1993. It offers
a prestigious central venue, whose outside terrace has an exceptional
view.* / 10.30pm; London Catering Services; no music; no dancing; no smoking;
Lecture Rm (200,120); Council Rm (–,42).

The Royal College of Radiologists W1   £M-E, (–,33)
38 Portland Pl   636 4432   (323 3100)
*Adam townhouse (circa 1776), with a modernised basement but
most of the remainder of which retains its original features and is
decorated in country house-style. Only the Council Chamber is really
suitable for entertaining.* / midnight; not Sat & Sun; list of caterers; no music;
no dancing; no smoking; Council Chamber (–,33).

Royal Garden Hotel W8　　　**£M-E, (800,480,400)**
2-24 Kensington High St　361 1926　(361 1921)
*Impressive but rather soulless luxury hotel – relaunched in 1996 after
a major refurbishment – whose undoubted attraction is its sweeping
views over Kensington Gardens. It has accommodation suitable for all
but the largest functions, and is licensed for weddings.* / 1am;
in-house caterers; Palace Suite (800,450,400); Kensington Suite (150,100,70);
'The Tenth' Restaurant (–,90); Lancaster Suite (80,70,50); Bertie's Bar (–,50);
Westminster Rm (25,18); Windsor Rm (–,10).

Royal Geographical Society SW7　　**£B-M, (350,110,110)**
1 Kensington Gore　591 3090　(591 3091)
*Although it is a mite institutional, this Society, just south of Hyde Park,
is comparatively flexible about what it will entertain (and a wedding
licence has been obtained). It offers a great address with very
characterful surroundings, and at competitive rates.* / midnight; Lodge;
Main Hall (150,100); New Map Rm (150,–); Tea Rm (60,40); Council Rm (–,24);
Everest Rm (–,14); Reading Rm (–,10); marquee site.

Royal Green Jackets W1　　　**£B-M, (450,180,120)**
56 Davies St　414 5514　(414 5560)
*This Mayfair TA outpost, just off Oxford Street, offers a basic, large
gym-type hall – it's most obviously suited to a bash, though, with
decoration it might be used for wedding receptions and the like. The
two mess bars are worth considering for stag nights and so on.* / 2am;
not Wed; Richmond Sundrey; Hall (450,180,120); St George's Club (200,–);
Sergeants Mess (100,–).

Royal Institute of British Architects W1　　**£M, (70,40)**
66 Portland Pl　307 3663　(255 1541)
*The impressive central hall at this '30s institute is now a dedicated
exhibition space, so the best option for entertaining is the pleasant
but less notable south room (up an imposing staircase). Other
accommodation is rather businessy.* / no weddings; 11 pm; not Sat & Sun;
Sutcliffe; no amplified music; smoking restricted; South Rm (70,40).

Royal Institution of Great Britain W1　　**£B-M, (450,120)**
21 Albemarle St　409 2992　(629 3569)
*The Mayfair institute, where Faraday discovered electricity has some
creakily impressive accommodation. Combining the Long Library and
Ante Room allows large dinner parties to be accommodated. At the
time of going to press, a wedding licence was being applied for.*
/ 9.30pm; not Sat & Sun; Crown Catering; no amplified music; no dancing;
smoking restricted; Anteroom (150,–); Library (100,–); Council Rm (60,–).

Royal Lancaster Hotel W2　　**£M-E, (2500,2000,1300)**
Lancaster Ter　262 6737　(706 3571)
*This blot on the Hyde Park landscape has one of the largest
ballrooms and the whole building is very much nicer than the exterior
might lead one to expect. The premises are unusually thinly provided
with smaller accommodation, but the two very large rooms do
subdivide. A wedding licence had been applied for as we went to
press.* / 2am; Nine Kings Suite (1500,1500,1300); Westbourne Suite (1300,1120,600);
Gloucester Suite (200,85,70).

Royal Majestic Suite NW6　　　**£M, (–,220,200)**
196 Willesden Ln　0181-459 3276　(0181-451 0920)
Pleasant, well-maintained Kosher banqueting hall in Willesden.
/ 12.30am; not Fri, not Sat in summer; in-house caterers; Ground Floor (–,220,200);
First Floor (–,70,70).

PRIVATE VENUES

Royal Mint Sovereign Gallery SW1 £M, (50,–)
7 Grosvenor Gdns   592 8601   (592 8634)
New gallery, in a large Victorian townhouse, illustrating the 500-year history of the gold sovereign. There are two interconnecting blue, cream and gilt rooms (one of which contains the display of valuable exhibits). / charities & companies only; eve and wknd only; hirer's choice of caterer; no amplified music; no dancing; no smoking.

Royal National Theatre SE1 £M, (1200,200)
South Bank   928 2033   (620 1197)
Most entertaining here happens around shows, but at other times the theatre's spaces are available for events. Ovations restaurant and the Terrace Bar café suit functions best (being used particularly for Christmas parties), while the Olivier Stalls offer a pleasant, lofty foyer-space for a reception, with outside terrace. / 2am; only related events on performance nights; in-house caterers; smoking restricted; Olivier Stalls Foyer (500,200); Terrace Café (220,150); Ovations (180,120); Olivier Circle Foyer (50,–); Richardson Rm (25,14).

Royal Over-Seas League SW1 £B-M, (200,200,100)
Park Pl   408 0214   (499 6738)
A reasonable degree of grandeur, relatively affordably, is the attraction of this clubby establishment near the Ritz. The smaller rooms of the older buildings, overlooking Green Park, are better suited to entertaining than the larger ones in the '30s annexe. / 11pm; not Sun; in-house caterers; Hall of India & Pakistan (200,200,100); St Andrew's Hall (150,80,80); Wrench (50,32); Mountbatten Rutland (45,32); Bennet-Clark (30,16); Park (15,11).

Royal Parks Agency W2
Old Police House, Hyde Pk   298 2000
Commercial events are not generally allowed in the Royal Parks (which include Hyde, Green, St James's and Greenwich), though suitable applications from charities may be entertained.

Royal Society of Arts WC2 £M, (250,170,150)
8 John Adam St   839 5049   (321 0271)
Five converted c18 houses, just off the Strand, whose vaults offer most flexibility for functions (even if the space is rather broken up). The other accommodation comprises white-walled galleries and period rooms. A wedding licence has been obtained. / 11am; Mon-Fri; 2 wks hol in Aug; in-house caterers; smoking restricted; All Vaults (250,170,150); Benjamin Franklin Rm (150,95,60); Vault 1 (100,60); Tavern Rm (70,48); Folkestone Rm (30,20).

Royal Veterinary College NW1 £B-M, (250,130)
Royal College St   468 5000
Thirties building with a comfortable ambience, a good variety of accommodation (much of it in period style) and offering a lot of flexibility. Conveniently located and not too expensive, its institutionality is part of its charm. / hirer's choice of caterer; smoking restricted; Northumberland Rm (90,70); Clarence Rm (80,70); Connaught Rm (60,20); Cambridge Rm (50,20); College Principal's Suite (–,12).

Royal Holloway College, Surrey £B-M, (550,200,170)
Egham Hl, Egham   01784-443046   (01784-437520)
The impressive Picture Gallery of this extraordinary Victorian confection (claiming the country's top collection of art of the period) makes a great venue for a dinner. Out of term you can use the adjoining Dining Hall, which is larger and, when dressed, almost as impressive. / 1am; Dining Hall only in vacs; in-house caterers; no smoking; Founder's Dining Hall (300,200,170); Picture Gallery (250,150); marquee site.

Royal Horseguards Thistle Hotel SW1   £M, (100,100)
Whitehall Ct   839 3344   (839 3366)
*At this very centrally located hotel, the Thames Suite – with access to
a terrace overlooking the river – is notably attractive, and the
Boardroom would be appropriate for business entertaining.
Other rooms are very conference-orientated.* / *midnight; Thames (80,50);
Boardroom (–,12).*

Royal Horticultural Halls SW1   £B-M, (1800,800,650)
80 Vincent Sq   828 4125   (834 2072)
*These large, flexible halls can transcend their flower show function
(although the cost of the decoration to do so is worth bearing in
mind). The older hall, bordering the Square, is traditional in style,
with a glazed, vaulted ceiling. Over the road, the '30s hall is a glass
and concrete hangar which would not be wholly out of place in a sci-fi
'B' movie.* / *11pm; London Catering Services; New Hall (1800,800,650);
Old Hall (1000,500,400).*

RSJ SE1   £M, (–,40)
13A Coin St   928 4554   (633 0489)
*This modern British South Bank restaurant offers good value for
money (and, for wine enthusiasts, a collection of 200 wines from the
Loire). The ground floor private room benefits from natural light.*
/ *Private Rm (Basement) (–,40); Private Rm (Ground Floor) (–,22).*

The Rubens SW1   £M, (250,170,140)
Buckingham Palace Rd   834 6600   (233 6037)
*Facing the Royal Mews, this Victoria hotel has agreeable banqueting
facilities that are fairly modern in style.* / *1am; in-house caterers;
Old Masters Restaurant (200,140,140); Rembrandt Rm (80,50); Rubens (40,30).*

Ruby's W1   £B, (150,–)
49 Carnaby St   287 3957
*This basement equipped with a bar – by day it's usually a dance
studio – has wood floors and mirrors on the walls. It is not nearly as
tacky as the street outside and worth considering for a budget
daytime or Sunday bash.* / *Sun 10pm, Mon-Sat 5pm; Mon-Sat pre 6pm,
Sun all day; hirer's choice of caterer.*

Rules WC2   £M, (75,48)
35 Maiden Ln   379 0258   (497 1081)
*Claiming to be London's oldest restaurant, this ultra-traditional,
panelled English establishment in Covent Garden has very attractive
private dining rooms.* / *Greene Rm (75,48); Charles Dickens Rm (60,40);
King Edward VII Rm (40,25).*

RUSI Building SW1   £M, (150,80)
Whitehall   930 5854   (321 0943)
*The airy D-shaped Lecture Theatre at these Whitehall premises is
particularly suited to receptions and has held discos. The clubby
Library (with books, for once) is a cosy and interesting place for a
formal dinner, and the Council Room would elegantly accommodate
a small dinner party.* / *2am; hirer's choice of caterer; smoking restricted; Lecture
Theatre (150,80); Reading Rm (80,35); Library (70,40); Council Rm (20,16).*

Russell Hotel WC1   £M, (650,350,300)
Russell Sq   837 6470   (278 2124)
Splendid Victorian hotel in Bloomsbury, where most of the rooms –
many of which are marbled – retain an impressive period charm.
The adjoining Warncliffe and Woburn rooms are used for
dinner-dances. The Library is suitably clubby. / midnight; in-house caterers;
music and dancing in Warncliffe Suite only; Warncliffe Suite (650,350,300); Bedford
Suite (80,36); Ormond Suite (60,48); Library (40,50); Boardrooms 1,2,6,7 (–,12);
Boardrooms 3,4,5 (–,8).

Saatchi Gallery NW8   £M-E, (1000,300)
98a Boundary Rd   328 8299   (624 3798)
An exceptional, uncluttered white space – seeming all the more
extraordinary for opening off an ordinary St John's Wood street –
whose avant-garde display changes periodically. / companies only; 11pm;
Mustard Catering; no amplified music; no dancing; no smoking.

Saddlers' Hall EC2   £M-E, (250,139)
40 Gutter Ln   726 8661   (600 0386)
This traditional livery company hall, erected in the '50s, is now made
available to a wider range of hirers than hitherto. / list of caterers;
no amplified music; no dancing.

Saint WC2   £M, (270,100)
8 Great Newport St   240 1551
This large, groovy bar-restaurant, on the fringe of Covent Garden,
can be taken over in its entirety during the day or, in the early part of
the week, for dinner.

St Andrew Golf Club EC4   £B-M, (250,80,80)
Allhallows Ln, Upper Thames St   283 1335
In the arches of Cannon Street railway bridge – the lofty main vault
bar and mezzanine restaurant are very pleasant, ideally suited to a
party, reception or dinner. You need to be, to become or to know a
member. / members club; 1am; not Sun; in-house caterers.

St Andrew's Court House EC4   £M, (130,80)
5 St Andrew St   583 7394   (583 3488)
This 1870 courthouse (refurbished in 1996), located just off
Holborn Circus, incorporates remains of earlier buildings – the ornate
and colourful fireplace in the Court Room is Jacobean, for example.
/ midnight; list of caterers; Court Rm (130,80); Archive Rm (50,20); Panelled Rm (25,12).

St Bartholomew's Hospital EC1   £M, (240,190)
West Smithfield   601 7871   (601 7080)
Ascend the Hogarth staircase to find one of the most atmospheric
halls in London (c18), all cream, gold and dark wood – a little shabby
perhaps, but only in the nicest way. Application for a wedding licence
was under consideration as we went to press. / 11.30pm; in-house caterers;
no amplified music; no dancing; no confetti; Great Hall (240,190); Henry VIII Committee
Rm (50,12); Peggy Turner Rm (40,14); Treasurer's Rm (40,18).

St Botolph's Hall EC2   £B-M, (–,150)
Bishopsgate   588 3388
Oak-panelled Victorian church hall, next to Liverpool Street Station,
used for receptions, dinners and Christmas parties by City firms.
/ midnight; hirer's choice of caterer; Upper Hall (–,150); Lower Hall (–,45).

St Bride's Foundation Institute EC4   £B, (175,90,75)
Bride Lane, Fleet St   353 3331   (353 1547)
Bright, characterful, Victorian institution, attractively situated near the 'wedding cake' church of the same name, just off Fleet Street. / 10pm; not Sat & Sun; hirer's choice of caterer; no music; no discos; no smoking; Bridewell Hall (175,90,75); Farringdon Rm (75,40).

St Etheldreda's Crypt EC1   £B, (280,120,130)
14 Ely Pl   242 8238   (831 1402)
London's oldest Catholic Church allows wedding receptions and reasonably sedate parties in its undercroft. Arrangements and catering are via the Bleeding Heart restaurant. / no 21sts; 1am; Bleeding Heart.

Saint John EC1   £M, (200,100)
26 St John's St   251 0848   (251 4090)
This Smithfield smokehouse has been converted to a bare, bright white English restaurant (whose motto is "nose-to-tail-eating") – it makes an interesting function space. / Private Rm (–,20).

St John's Gate EC1   £M, (260,120)
St John's Ln   253 6644   (490 8835)
North of Smithfield Market, this romantic medieval gatehouse – home to the Order of St John – is a local landmark. The stately Chapter Hall is a lofty, panelled room used for dinners and receptions. The Council Chamber, actually in the gatehouse, is similar but smaller. The Garden Cloisters of the order's church can be used for summer parties. / midnight; hirer's choice of caterer; no discos; Chapter Hall (200,120); Council Chamber (–,25); Lord Prior's Dining Rm (20,14); Garden Cloisters (250,–).

St John's Hill SW11   £B-M, (250,150,150)
St John's Hl   414 5514   (414 5560)
Housed in a large red-brick Victorian building, opposite Clapham Junction, the Drill Hall of this branch of the TA is used for a variety of functions – 21sts, weddings, and so on. / 1am; hirer's choice of caterer; Drill Hall (250,150,150); Sergeant's Mess (100,45).

St Martin in the Fields WC2   £B-M, (350,150,110)
5 St Martin's Pl   839 4342   (839 5163)
This atmospheric church crypt on Trafalgar Square (a café by day) offers an interesting venue for a central party. / charities & companies preferred; 2am; from 7pm, not Sun; in-house caterers; Gallery (150,–).

St Moritz W1   £B, (120,–)
159 Wardour St   437 0525
Despite its fame as a headbangers' music venue, this Soho basement of Swiss grottoes – dance-floor, bar, and seating areas – lends itself well to parties. / 3am; not Fri-Sun; hirer's choice of caterer, alcohol in-house.

St Peter's, Vauxhall SE11   £B-M, (300,200,180)
310 Kennington Ln   820 0038
Victorian gothic church now a hip function venue. A grand, affordable central choice. / 2am; Sat & Sun midnight; hirer's choice of caterer.

St Stephen's Constitutional Club SW1   £M, (450,110,100)
34 Queen Anne's Gate   222 1382   (222 8740)
Smart, yet unimposing, businessman's club boasting a garden overlooking St James's Park. It's a nice size to be taken over in its entirety, say for a wedding reception, and imparts a sense of occasion without stuffiness. A marquee substantially increases numbers. / 3am; eve only, Sat & Sun all day; in-house caterers; Dining Rm (200,100,100); Bar (80,–); Garden Rm (60,28); marquee site.

PRIVATE VENUES

St Thomas' Hospital SE1   £M, (200,100)
2 Lambeth Palace Rd   922 8181   (261 9690)
Though situated among the rather drab buildings of this hospital, opposite Parliament, the recently renovated hall and committee room offer quite grand settings for many types of function. / midnight; hirer's choice of caterer; no amplified music; smoking restricted; Governors' Hall (200,100); Grand Committee Rm (50,18); marquee site.

Salters' Hall EC2   (200,120)
Fore St   588 5216   (638 3679)
The Salters' Company now make their hall available for hire by companies and charities. / no weddings; hirer's choice of caterer; no music; no dancing.

San Martino SW3   £M, (–,20)
103 Walton St   589 3833
Marty and his merry men provide a more than usually hospitable, old-style welcome at this relatively reasonably priced Chelsea Italian restaurant. The private room, upstairs, is white-tiled and unadorned. / Private Rm (–,20).

The Sanctuary WC2   £M-E, (250,100,100)
12 Floral St   420 5110   (497 0410)
This luxury Covent Garden health spa is among the most exotic settings central London affords. You can twist by the pool (complete with palms and tropical fish). Private parties are the only times men are allowed on the premises. / Sat, Sun, Mon, Tues eve, the rest of the week by special arrangement; hirer's choice of caterer.

Sandown Park Racecourse, Surrey £M, (3000,1200,1000)
Sandown Pk, Esher   01372-461205   (01372-465205)
Modern racecourse-side facilities available for a wide range of occasions, including weddings / Ring & Brymer; Surrey Hall (3000,1200,1000); Claremont (600,500,350); Wolsey (350,250,200); Saddle Rm (250,180,120); Cavalry Bar (150,120,70); Persimmon (90,70,40); Smaller Rms (–,20); Marquee (permanent in summer) (500,350,300); marquee site.

Les Saveurs W1   £M-E, (–,10)
37a Curzon St   491 8919
Luxurious Mayfair restaurant, the style of whose ground-floor function room is, if anything, to be preferred to that of the main restaurant. The establishment changed hands soon before we went to press, and changes may be afoot. / not Sat & Sun; Private Rm (–,10).

The Savoy WC2   £M-E, (800,500,400)
Strand   836 4343   (240 6040)
This famous riverside hotel is the default choice for grander corporate and many social events – it has a range of characterful accommodation in differing period styles, some with a river view, and most licensed for wedding ceremonies. / Lancaster Rm (800,500,400); Abraham Lincoln & Manhattan Rms (400,240,180); River Rm (350,120,120); Beaufort (120,60); Pinafore (80,40); Gondoliers (50,28); Mikado (35,18); Patience (30,24); Iolanthe (25,12); Sorcerer (18,6).

Le Scandale W1   £B, (500,–)
53-54 Berwick St   437 6830
The décor has gone from glitzy to black, but the glow lights and mirrors remain at this large nightclub, just south of Oxford Street. / 3.30am; Wed & Thu only; in-house caterers; Front or Rear Bar (200,–).

School of Pharmacy WC1   £B-M, (300,150)
29-39 Brunswick Sq   753 5813   (753 5941)
Slightly institutional by nature, but pleasant, pair of '30s halls, with large windows facing onto the square, and with potential for many kinds of function. Hire of the Refectory is free if you use the in-house catering facilities. / *midnight; Refectory Fri eve, Sat & Sun; Aug hol; in-house caterers; smoking restricted; Assembly Hall (–,150); Refectory (300,140).*

Science Museum SW7   £M-E, (1500,350,300)
Exhibition Rd   938 8190   (938 8112)
The museum offers flexible party facilities – for big receptions it is not unknown for people to take the whole place. The current Science of Sport exhibition is popular, and the Challenge of Materials (from summer 1997) seems set to be so, too. / *from 6.30pm, Director's Suite all day, list of caterers; smoking restricted; no candles; Flight Gallery (500,350,300); East Hall (600,200,200); Science of Sport (300,–); Space Gallery (200,–); Director's Suite (150,90).*

Scone E14   £M, (40,28)
Millwall Dock, Selsdon Way   515 8826   (515 8826)
Clare Hunter and David Ireland's home is an old Thames sailing barge, permanently moored just by Cross Harbour DLR station. Comfortably furnished, partially gas-lit and with the galley opening onto the dining room, it is a more than usually intimate, relaxed setting for a dinner or reception, and attracts mainly corporate business. / *midnight; in-house caterers; no music; no dancing.*

Scotts W1   £M-E, (60,100)
20 Mount St   629 5248   (499 8246)
This famous and long-established Mayfair restaurant was recently relaunched in more modern style. There are two private rooms, or you could take the Oyster Terrace, the Cocktail Bar or even the whole restaurant. / *Restaurant (–,100); Cocktail Bar (60,–); Oyster Terrace (–,40); Basement Function Rm (–,22); Ground Floor Private Rm (–,16).*

Searcy's SW1   £M-E, (250,150,150)
30 Pavilion Rd   823 9212   (823 8694)
A very well-known address which, for those without their own London townhouse, makes an excellent place in which to entertain (or, now that they have a licence, to get married). The homely yet grand accommodation is flexible and smaller parties can easily be accommodated, though hire is on an exclusive basis. There are bedrooms for those who can't drag themselves away. / *1am; Searcy's; no amplified music.*

Seashell NW1   £B, (–,70)
49-51 Lisson Gr   724 1063
If you want to feast on our national dish, the whole top floor of what is probably London's most famous chippy can be made available. / *not Sun; Upstairs Rm (–,70).*

Secret Garden SE5   £B-M, (–,50)
Franklin's Antique Mkt, 161 Camberwell Rd   703 8089
You can dine all year at this Camberwell café-in-an-antiques-market. In fine weather, however, you can escape to the leafy outdoors – if you haven't got your own green patch, and want a Bohemian venue, this might well be the place. / *in-house caterers; smoking restricted; Restaurant (–,38); Garden (–,50).*

PRIVATE VENUES

The Selfridge Hotel W1   £M, (300,300,230)
Orchard St   408 2080   (493 7590)
The Drawing Room (a large, light, traditional dining room) of this woody modern hotel behind the department store is the best function facility. The long, divisible Selfridge Suite offers flexible space. / 1am; Selfridge Suite (300,300,230); Drawing Rm (–,25); Conservatory (25,16).

Selsdon Park Hotel, Surrey   £M-E, (200,190,150)
Addington Road, Sanderstead, Sth Croydon
0181-657 8811   (0181-657 3401)
Set in 200 acres, this ivy-clad, neo-Jacobean mansion near Croydon has a number of function rooms with dance floors. / in-house caterers; Tudor Rm (200,190,150); Kent Rm (90,70); Solarium (50,20).

Serpentine Gallery W2   £M-E, (350,240,170)
Kensington Gdns   823 9727
The Gallery, with its idyllic location for a summer function, will re-open in November 1997. The details given here are provisional. / 11pm (9.30pm for receptions); from 6.30pm; list of caterers; smoking sometimes restricted; marquee site.

Shakespeare Globe Centre SE1   £M, (300,100)
New Globe Wk, Bankside (was Emerson St)   928 9444
South of the river, near Southwark Bridge, the re-created theatre has an adjoining pub, restaurant and banqueting hall. No catering within the theatre itself, but the exhibition hall could be used, after a tour. Dancing and music should be appropriate to the Elizabethan theme. / companies only; midnight; from 6pm; Theatre open in summer only; in-house caterers; smoking restricted; Restaurant (100,100); Exhibition Hall (–,60); Banqueting Rm (–,60).

Shampers W1   £B, (80,45)
4 Kingly St   437 1692   (437 1217)
You can organise private dinners and receptions in the basement brasserie of this bubbling Soho wine bar. On Sundays only, the whole place is available. / 12.30am; Wine Bar (80,45); Brasserie (60,45).

Sheekey's WC2   £M-E, (–,30)
28-32 St Martins Ct   240 2565
Old-established Theatreland fish restaurant with a traditional, clubby feel. Downstairs there is an attractive function room, while upstairs a very impressive tiled and mirrored section can be curtained off. Prices are very high, considering. / not Sat L & Sun; Private Rm (–,12); Section (–,30).

Shelleys W1   £B, (70,40)
10 Stafford St   493 0337
The un-pubby, pleasant, modernish top floor bar above this Mayfair inn is suitable for informal functions. / midnight.

Shepherd's SW1   £M, (–,30)
Marsham Court, Marsham St   834 9552
Bright, art-filled, modern and clubby, this English restaurant in Westminster has a comfortable private room. It is a shade grander than the main restaurant and there is a charge for its use. / Private Rm (–,30).

Sheraton Belgravia SW1   £M, (100,50)
20 Chesham Pl   235 6040   (201 1926)
For a mid-sized dinner or reception this discreetly located Belgravia hotel has a couple of serviceable private rooms. / no dancing; Dining Rm (100,50); Study and Library (70,22).

Sheraton Park Tower SW1 £M-E, (150,120,120)
101 Knightsbridge   235 8050   (235 8231)
*Prominent, cylindrical Knightsbridge luxury hotel with a range of
first-floor function rooms in '70s/traditional style. The Trianon Room
has the benefit of an Astroturfed terrace overlooking Lowndes Square,
which may be used for barbecues. / 1am; Trianon Rm (150,120,120);
Buckingham Rm (60,22); Explorers (50,18); Balmoral (40,40).*

Ship SW18 £B-M, (80,40)
Jews Row   0181-870 9667   (0181-874 9055)
*This very popular younger-scene Wandsworth pub erects a riverside
marquee for the summer, which provides an unusual, flexible venue
for medium size parties. / 11pm; in-house caterers; Marquee (80,40);
Private Rm (–,12); marquee site.*

Shoeless Joe's SW6 £M, (200,–)
555 King's Rd   384 2333   (610 9414)
*Fashionable Fulham sports bar, with dance floor and large video
screen, which you can take in its entirety (Mon-Wed). The Members'
Bar can be taken over on any evening. / 1am; Members Bar (60,–).*

Simpsons Tavern EC3 £B, (50,74)
Ball Court, 38 1/2 Cornhill   626 9985
*This popular Dickensian City institution offers two compact bars for
function use. The restaurant is characterful, but the boothed seating
reduces suitability for functions. / Amy's Bar or Wine Bar (50,–);
Restaurant (–,74); Grill (–,50).*

Simpsons-in-the-Strand WC2 £M, (145,450,100)
100 Strand   836 9112   (836 1381)
*Nowhere can compete with the solid Edwardian charm of this most
English of restaurants. In particular, the Smoking Room downstairs
(claiming to be the oldest bar in London) is perfect for a mid-sized
dinner. Occasionally, the whole establishment may be taken over.
/ 1am; in-house caterers; South Rm (145,160,100); Smoking Rm (100,45).*

Singapura WC2 £M, (–,80)
Thomas Neal Centre   240 1083
*Stylish modern oriental restaurant in Covent Garden, whose cosy
bricks-and-pillars setting makes it well suited to convivial function use.
/ Private Rm (–,40).*

Sir John Soane's Museum WC2 £E, (100,30)
13 Lincoln's Inn Fields   405 2107   (831 3957)
*Half a dozen times a year, one of the most remarkable houses in the
world is made available, at huge expense, for parties of between 24
and 30 people. A pre-dinner tour of Soane's Egyptian treasures and
paintings (including original Rake's Progress) can be arranged, and
dinner is served in the dark, and very antique dining room and library.
/ midnight; Mon all day, Tue-Sat from 6.30pm, not Sun; list of caterers;
no amplified music; no dancing; no smoking.*

606 Club SW10 £B-M, (150,150)
90 Lots Rd   352 5953   (349 0655)
*Cellar jazz club, intriguingly located down an anonymous staircase,
opposite a power station. For private hires there is no fee – just a
minimum catering-spend. / 1.30am; not Fri & Sat; in-house caterers.*

PRIVATE VENUES

Skinners' Hall EC4   £M-E, (300,170,170)
8 1/2 Dowgate Hl   236 5629   (236 6590)
Imposing but charming, the Skinners' Company's accommodation near Cannon Street, entered via a courtyard, offers a number of possibilities. The restored c17 Hall (with Victorian murals) is rich and red. Other rooms are grand, in a relaxed country house style, and there is a modern roof garden, with fountain, for fair-weather receptions. / not Sun; 6 wks hol around Aug; list of caterers; smoking restricted.

Slaughterhouse Gallery EC1   £M, (100,–)
63 Charterhouse St   251 5888
This Smithfield gallery offers three sizable vaults, lined with raw and discoloured bricks (and so, unless you like that sort of thing, in need of quite a lot of theming). There is also a more conventional white-walled area. Loos, which need to be hired, have to be situated outside. / companies only; hirer's choice of caterer; Gallery/vaults (100,–).

Slug & Lettuce SW1   £B, (40,25)
11 Warwick Way   834 3313
Bright, well-maintained room over a comfortable and hospitable Pimlico pub. / 11pm.

Slug & Lettuce N1   £B, (150,70)
1 Islington Gn   226 3864
Homely, warm room, with sofas, overlooking Islington Green. / 11pm.

Slug & Lettuce SW15   £B, (100,100,100)
14 Putney High St   0181-785 3081   (0181-780 2355)
The private room here is self-contained (with its own entrance, bar and loo) and has a music-and-dance licence until 2am (Mon-Thu), but, rather curiously, only until midnight on Fri & Sat.

Slug & Lettuce SW18   £B, (100,60)
21 Alma Rd   0181-874 1833
Wandsworth pub with two function rooms. Both are on the first floor and have natural light, and they are popular for discos, wedding receptions and parties. / 11pm; Rm 1 (100,60); Rm 2 (70,35).

Soho House W1   £M, (100,50)
40 Greek St   734 5188   (734 1447)
Launched a few years ago, this fashionable Soho club was – in its early days – much more open to events such as launches for non-members. Still, for functions at 'off-peak' times, it may be worth exploring availability and you could always try tracking down a member. / members club; 3am; not Sun; in-house caterers; Sitting Rm, Study & Bar (100,50); Library (–,16); Study (–,12).

Soho Soho W1   £M, (80,60)
11-13 Frith St   494 3491
This ever-buzzing bright and modern Mediterranean restaurant has an attractive 'salon privé'. / Salon Privée (80,60).

Sotheby's W1   £M-E, (400,250)
34 New Bond St   493 8080   (408 5907)
Sotheby's restricts function use of its galleries to a few occasions a year, generally by companies or charities. / midnight; not Fri, Sat & Sun – café Mon-Fri 9.30-5pm except lunchtimes; Jan hol & Aug hol; list of caterers; no amplified music; no dancing; no smoking; Main Gallery (200,250); Café (–,38).

The South Bank Centre SE1   £M-E, (500,250)
Belvedere Rd   921 0600   (928 0063)
*The unadorned Chelsfield Room (in the Royal Festival Hall) is the
centre's main function room, though during the day some of the other
spaces around the centre can be used. See also People's Palace.*
/ no weddings; National Leisure Caterers; no smoking; Queen Elizabeth Hall
Foyer (500,250); Hong Kong & Chelsfield Rm (250,150); Level 5 External
Terrace (200,–); Sunley Pavilion (40,20); marquee site.

Southwark Cathedral SE1   £B-M, (175,100)
Montague Cl   407 3708   (357 7389)
*A Victorian building behind the cathedral houses a function room,
decorated in pale grey. The space is interrupted by three large pillars.*
/ 10.30pm; not Sun; list of caterers; no amplified music; no smoking; Function
Rm (175,100).

Southwark Tavern SE1   £B, (150,–)
22 Southwark St   403 0257
*On a Saturday, you can hire the whole of this pub just south of
London Bridge. It has an atmospheric, if quite cramped, cellar bar.*
/ 1.30am; Sat only.

Spaghetti House W1   £B, (–,50)
15 Goodge St   636 6582   (436 4908)
*This three-floor Fitzrovia monument to '50s Italian restaurant-kitsch
offers two private rooms.* / no music; no dancing; Private Rms x 2 (–,50).

Spanish Club W1   £M, (180,90,50)
5 Cavendish Sq   637 9061   (436 7188)
*Overlooking the square, the pretty, quite grand first floor room of the
Spanish Chamber of Commerce is available for receptions and
dinners.* / 2am; hirer's choice of caterer but have restaurant; live music only; no dancing;
Alfonso XIII Rm (180,90,50); Presidention Rm (50,40).

Spencer House SW1   £E, (450,132,120)
27 St James's Pl   409 0526   (493 5765)
*C18 palace, bordering Green Park, restored in the mid-'80s to its
former glory (with paintings from the Royal collection and furniture on
loan from the V&A). Dancing can occasionally be arranged in a
marquee in the garden or on the terrace.* / 1am; not Sun in day; Aug & Jan
hol; in-house caterers; dancing only in marquee; smoking restricted; no stilettoes;
Great Rm (–,72); Lady Spencer's Rm (–,36); Dining Rm (–,24); Music Rm (–,24).

Spitalfields Market E1   £M-E, (3000,1000,1000)
Spitalfields   0181-682 4900   (0181-682 0602)
*All year round, this covered City space, managed by PlanIt Events, is
available for suitable semi-outdoor functions. In winter, though, you
need a marquee as protection against the cold – offering an
expensive, if central, site with a large capacity.* / 12.30am; Mon-Sat from
midday; hirer's choice of caterer; Market (summer) (3000,–); Marquee
(winter) (2000,1000,1000); marquee site.

Spring Grove House, Middx   £M, (120,80)
London Rd, Isleworth   0181-569 7173   (0181-847 2421)
*Georgian house of Sir Joseph Banks (creator of Kew Gardens),
remodelled in Victorian times, and now part of West Thames College.
It is used for social and business events – the Winter Garden Room,
licensed for weddings, features potted palms, a domed glass ceiling
and mosaic floor.* / no 21sts; 11pm; preferred in-house caterer; smoking restricted;
Winter Garden Rm (100,80); Music Rm (50,50); Export Suite (40,–); marquee site.

PRIVATE VENUES

The Square W1   £M-E, (–,18)
6-10 Bruton St   495 7100
The stylish new Mayfair home (just off Bond Street) of one of London's leading modern British restaurants has an internal private room. / Private Rm (–,18).

The Stafford SW1   £M-E, (100,42)
16 St James's Pl   493 0111   (493 7121)
Dinner in its wonderful, musty, 350-year-old wine-cellars (which are still very much in use) is this cosy St James's hotel's special attraction, though it has a good range of traditionally-furnished function rooms. A wedding licence has been applied for. / 12.30am; Panel Rm & Sutherland Rm (100,40); The Cellar (75,42); Sutherland Rm (40,24); Pink Rm & Argyll Rm (50,14); Argyll Rm (30,14); Panel Rm or Pink Rm (–,8).

Stakis St Ermins SW1   £M, (350,200,200)
Caxton St   222 7888   (222 7703)
The very characterful, old-fashioned ballroom is the most striking feature of this Victoria hotel (which is licensed for weddings). The proximity to Westminster makes its smaller rooms favourites for political entertaining. / 1am; in-house caterers; Ballroom (250,200,200); Balcony (100,100); York or Clarence (40,30); Cameo (35,20).

Staple Inn WC1   £M, (250,120)
High Holborn   242 0106   (405 2482)
Prettily situated off a cobbled courtyard, this panelled Victorian medieval-style hall (the home of the Institute of Actuaries) is lofty, plain and handsome. A wedding licence was being applied for as we went to press. / midnight; hirer's choice of caterer; no amplified music; no smoking; Hall (250,120); Council Chamber (80,40).

Star Tavern SW1   £B, (50,–)
6 Belgrave Mews West   235 3019
The private bar is available for hire, at this famous, if hidden away, public house near Belgrave Square. / 11.20pm; not Sat & Sun; no music; no dancing; Bar (50,–).

Stationers' Hall EC4   £M-E, (400,205,175)
Ave Maria Ln   248 2934   (489 1975)
One of the more accommodating of the livery halls – even dancing is permitted, if at an extra charge. The c17 hall itself is dark-panelled and bannered, and the gilded Court Room and the plainer Stock Room are also agreeable. Sadly, the courtyard is entered through the arch of a '50s block. / 1am; Aug hol; list of caterers; no smoking in Court Rm; Livery Hall (400,205,175); Court Rm (150,80); Stock Rm (80,46); Ante Rm (–,20).

Stoke Newington Town Hall N16   £B-M, (500,500,500)
Stoke Newington Church St   0181-525 3299   (0181-985 3397)
The wooden-floored Assembly Room is regularly used for wedding receptions and other fairly large-scale celebrations. Theming is advised. / midnight; hirer's choice of caterer; Assembly Rm (500,500,500).

Stone Buildings WC2   £M-E, (100,60)
10 Stone Buildings, Lincoln's Inn   414 5513   (414 5560)
Clubbily furnished Inn of Court premises, in process of being extensively refurbished as a function-venue as we go to press. / midnight; in-house caterers; no music; no dancing; Dining Rm (–,30); Reception Rm (60,–).

Strand Palace Hotel WC2 £B-M, (200,140,340)
Strand   257 9029   (257 9025)
*This banqueting facilities of this central hotel have now been
revamped in a crisp modern style which is much more suited to
business than to social events. The Art Deco ballroom is sadly no
more, though the impressive entrance remains. / 2am;
Exeter Suite (200,140,120); Essex Suite (70,56); Grenville Suite (60,48);
Drake Suite (50,48).*

Streatham Ice Arena SW16 £B-M, (2000,–)
386 Streatham High Rd   0181-769 7771   (0181-769 9979)
*For a skating party, numbers are limited to 900, but if you board over
the ice, you can accommodate 2,000. There is no permanent bar
on site. / 2am; hirer's choice of caterer; no smoking.*

Le Studio Café N1 £B-M, (350,70)
49-50 Eagle Wharf Rd   251 1155
*The attractions of this Islington Regent's Canal barge/restaurant
complex are best appreciated on a summer evening. You could use
the ground floor for dining and the upstairs for a disco, or floors can
be hired individually. / Mon-Thu 12.30am, Fri & Sat, 3.30am; in-house caterers;
Restaurant (300,70); Tea Rm (150,60); Boat (45,–).*

Subterania W10 £B, (650,–)
12 Acklam Rd   0181-961 5490   (0181-961 9238)
*Trendy Notting Hill nightclub, where, once inside, you forget that its
location is under the Westway. On the most popular club nights,
you can have a private party only until the club goes into action.
/ 2am; Sun-Thu all night, Fri & Sat 6pm-9pm; in-house caterers.*

The Sun WC2 £B-M, (80,30)
Longacre   836 4520
*Bright function room, decorated in modern style, over a Covent
Garden pub. / 11.20pm; no music; no dancing.*

Suntory SW1 £M-E, (–,12)
72 St James's St   409-0201   (499 7993)
*This St James's restaurant is the top of the range for prestige
Japanese corporate entertaining. The atmosphere is dry, the food is
good, and the prices are very high. / 11pm; not Sun; Tatami (–,12);
Teppan-Yaki (–,7).*

Le Suquet SW3 £M, (–,30)
104 Draycott Av   581 1785
*West London's most authentic French fish restaurant transports you
from Chelsea to Cannes – not least in the two upstairs private rooms.
The service is no less Gallic than the atmosphere. / Private Rm 1 (–,30);
Private Rm 2 (–,16).*

Surrey Docks Watersports Centre SE16 £B-M, (100,20)
Rope St, Off Plough Way   237 4009/5555   (252 1007)
*The light and bright first floor Quay Room and Lounge at this
Rotherhithe venue overlook the Thames. They are suitable for buffets,
birthday parties and wedding receptions. / no stag nights; midnight;
in-house caterers; smoking restricted; Quay Rm/Quay Lounge (50,20).*

PRIVATE VENUES

Sutton House E9   £M, (180,80,80)
2-4 Homerton High St   0181-986 2264   (0181-533 0556)
*The oldest house in Hackney (1535), this National Trust property has
interiors ranging from dark oak panelling to lighter Georgian
additions, and an enclosed courtyard. It offers an interesting setting
for a wedding, for example. Heating is restricted, though open fires
can be arranged in some rooms.* / 11.30pm; not Mon & Tue; closed 3 wks Dec
& Jan; in-house caterers; no amplified music; no smoking; Wenlock Barn (including Café-
Bar/Linenfold Parlour) (100,50,80); Marriage Suite (Great and Little Chambers) (–,50);
Linenfold Parlour (20,14).

SW1 Club SW1   £B, (860,–)
191 Victoria St   630 8980   (630 5068)
*Centrally located nightclub/dance hall (right by Victoria Station).
Until recently, it was very scruffy, but it has been upgraded.* / 6am;
not Fri-Sun; hirer's choice of caterer; alcohol in-house.

Sweetings EC4   £M, (120,30)
39 Queen Victoria St   248 3062
*This quirky City fish parlour is a famous lunching place. It is less
well-known that it will do private evening parties, at which optional
extras include jazz, and cod 'n' chips wrapped in the newspaper of
your choice.* / midnight; eve only, not Sat & Sun; no discos.

Syon Park (Banqueting), Middx   £B-M, (600,450,350)
Brentford   0181-568 0778   (0181-568 4308)
*Modern, purpose-built banqueting complex, benefiting from views of
the garden of Syon House. The rooms all have access to a terrace.*
/ midnight; Payne & Gunter; no fireworks; Garden Rm (300,146);
Lakeside Rm (280,120); Peacock Rm (200,140); Terrace Rm (120,80);
Conservatory Lounge (60,48); marquee site.

Syon Park (Conservatory), Middx   £M, (400,250,150)
Brentford   0181-560 0881   (0181-568 0936)
*Vast and imposing 1820s glasshouse – it is suitable for a range of
events and very popular (especially for wedding receptions).
Hire includes access to the 'Capability' Brown garden.* / midnight; Apr-Sep,
Wed-Sun, not during day - Oct-Mar not at all; hirer's choice of caterer; Great
Conservatory (400,250,150); marquee site.

Syon Park (House), Middx   £E, (300,120)
Brentford   0181-560 0881   (0181-568 0936)
*The Duke of Northumberland's London seat is a Robert Adam
palace, set in its own park. It is the only great house near the capital
still privately occupied, and can be made available for suitably lavish
entertaining.* / Apr-Sep, Wed-Sun not daytime; house, list; conservatory is on-site or
DIY; no amplified music; smoking restricted; red wine only at table, no stilettoes; Great
Hall (–,120); Long Gallery (300,–); State Dining Rm (–,95); marquee site.

Tallow Chandlers' Hall EC4   £M, (120,97)
4 Dowgate Hl   248 4726   (236 0844)
*Charming c17 livery hall, set back in its own courtyard. It's quite
grand, but has a very agreeable, relaxed atmosphere.* / no weddings;
11.15pm; not Sat & Sun; not mid-Jul to end-Aug; Payne & Gunter; no amplified music;
no dancing; Livery Hall (120,97); Parlour (60,30).

La Tante Claire SW3   £M-E, (–,48)
68-69 Royal Hospital Rd   352 6045
*London's most consistent haute cuisine hot-spot, discreetly located in
Chelsea, is available for hire on an exclusive basis. There is no
private room.*

Tate Gallery SW1 £E, (500,200)
Millbank   887 8958   (887 8007)
*If you wish to hold a function in the Tate's impressive galleries you
need to become a sponsor or corporate member – which might be
worth considering for a sufficiently grand event.* / *sponsors only;
list of caterers; no amplified music; no smoking; Pre Raphaelite and 19th Century
Gallery (500,200); Clore Gallery Foyer (200,–); Lodge (25,10).*

Tatsuso EC2 £M, (–,10)
32 Broadgate Circle   638 5863   (638 5864)
*The basement of this modern City Japanese (one of the very best in
town) is much less slick than its ground floor and has two private
rooms – one is a traditional tatami room and the other is in ordinary
western style.* / *not Sat & Sun; Private Rm (–,10).*

The Tattershall Castle SW1 £B, (200,150,100)
Victoria Embankment   839 6548   (839 1139)
*Permanently moored near Hungerford Bridge, this paddle
steamer/pub is something of a tourist paradise. Exclusive hire is
restricted to Steamers Nightclub (Tue-Thu) and the Bridge – an
interesting but thin space with excellent views. No outside decks can
be taken privately.* / *3am; in-house caterers; Steamers Discotheque (200,150,100);
Bridge (30,–).*

Temple Island, Oxon £M-E, (180,40)
c/o Henley Royal Regatta HQ   01491-572153   (01491-575509)
*A fantasy location, this restored Georgian island folly, picturesquely
sited at the start of the Henley Regatta course, can be reached only
by boat. It's difficult to beat for summer entertaining.* / *list of caterers;
Indoors (70,40); marquee site.*

Texas Embassy Cantina WC2 £B-M, (500,240)
1 Cockspur St   925 0077   (925 0444)
*The lofty premises of this centrally located Tex/Mex restaurant are
well suited to use for functions. Fully themed evenings can be
arranged.* / *Upstairs (250,120).*

Theatre Museum WC2 £M-E, (250,70)
Russell St   836 7891   (836 5148)
*Guests on their way to this converted Covent Garden flower market
can match their handprints with those of celebrities in the Wall of
Fame. For a drinks reception or dinner you might hire the deep-red
Gallery. Smaller groups might take the Foyer, and the Studio Theatre
can be used for discos.* / *midnight; Studio Theatre Mondays and eve only;
hirer's choice of caterer; no smoking; Paintings Gallery (250,70); Foyer (120,70);
Beard Rm (30,–).*

Theatre Royal WC2 £M, (300,150)
Drury Lane, Catherine St   494 5200   (434 1217)
*Crimson-and-gilt theatre, whose impressive Grand Salon is regularly
used for events during the daytime and on Sundays.* / *11am; Mon-Sat until
6pm, Sun all day if no current show; Gardner Merchant; Grand Salon (300,150);
Royal Retiring Rm (40,20); Board Rm (40,20); Prince of Wales Suite (16,–);
Duke of Bedford (–,4).*

Thomas Goode Restaurant W1 £M-E, (–,37)
19 South Audley St   409 7242   (495 0552)
*The wildly OTT restaurant of London's grandest china shop, in
Mayfair, is available for private receptions. It's best appreciated with
all the guests (max 24) sitting around a single table.* / *Elephant Rm (–,10).*

PRIVATE VENUES

Thorpe Park, Surrey   £M-E, (5000,–)
Staines Rd, Chertsey 01932-569393 x 3029 (01932-566367)
*A hundred rides await you at this adventure park, located just off the
M25. For a mega-event you could take over the whole place, or hire
one of the entertainment facilities and give your guests the run of the
place. Some attractions only function in the summer. / 11pm;
in-house caterers; marquee site.*

Throgmorton's EC2   £B-M, (400,100,100)
27 Throgmorton St 588 5165 (256 8956)
*Amazing Victorian City labyrinth of underground restaurants and
bars, behind the Bank of England. The Oak Room, in the deepest
bowels, is the most flexible room. / Short & Long Rm not Mon-Fri L, whole place
Sat only, not Sun; in-house caterers; Oak Rm (200,100,100); Short Rm (100,–);
Long Rm (80,–).*

Tinseltown EC1   £B-M, (300,200)
34-36 St John St 689 2424 (689 7860)
*24-hour subterranean restaurant near Smithfield Market popular with
clubbers and taxi drivers. If your fellow party goers aren't sufficiently
interesting to hold your attention you can play 'name that star' with
the paparazzi-style photos or watch one of the 12 screens showing
videos and cable TV.*

Tower Bridge SE1   £M-E, (250,100)
Tower Bridge 403 3761 (357 7935)
*This symbol of the capital is now available for social as well as
corporate events. You can stage your dinner or reception either on the
walkways linking the towers or in the engine room. / hirer's choice of
caterer (but they have a preferred list); Walkways (250,100); Engine Rm (150,70).*

HM Tower of London EC3   £E, (150,50)
London 488 5762 (488 5763)
*For a very grand cocktail party, suitable hirers can now have access –
at considerable expense – to one of London's most historic buildings.
Areas available include the Norman White Tower, with its display of
arms, armour and instruments of torture. / charities & companies only;
11pm; from 6pm winter, 7pm summer; list of caterers; no amplified music; no dancing;
no smoking; no stilettoes; White Tower (150,–); Medieval Palace (150,–); Royal Fusiliers
Association Rm (–,50).*

Tower Thistle E1   £M, (300,200,160)
St Katharine's Way 481 2575 (488 1667)
*Some of the views (of the Tower and Tower Bridge) from the
banqueting rooms of this monolithic '70s hotel are most impressive,
and it offers a good range of accommodation for smaller to medium-
size events (including weddings). / 1am; Tower Suite (300,200,160); Raleigh or
Spencer (80,40); Mortimer Suite (50,40); Beaufort (50,40); Lewin (10,8).*

Trafalgar Tavern SE10   £B-M, (320,250,200)
Park Row 0181-858 2437 (0181-858 2507)
*Historic Thames-side Greenwich pub, with spectacular views and
whose function rooms are very much grander than the norm, and
licensed for weddings. / 2am; Nelson Suite (320,250,200); Hawke & Howe
Bar (60,–).*

Trinity House EC3   £M, (120,120,120)
Tower Hl 480-6601 (480 7662)
*Fine, late-Georgian HQ of the UK's lighthouse authority. The Court
Room is an elegant and ornate chamber, and the view of the Tower
of London from the Library is magnificent. / 1am; Aug hol; list of caterers;
smoking restricted; Court Rm (120,60); Library (120,120); Reading Rm (–,10); Luncheon
Rm (–,20).*

Turnmills EC1 £B, (1500,150)
63b Clerkenwell Rd   250 3409   (250 1046)
This Farringdon nightclub, with 24-hour dance-licence, is self-evidently suited to a certain type of large bash. There are also smaller spaces which are suitable for less grandiose events. / Club not Fri, Sat & Sun eve –
Juno Lucina Fri, Sat & Sun eve; in-house or hirer's choice by negotiation;
Juno Lucina (300,–); Café Gaudi (–,80).

Tuttons WC2 £B-M, (75,50)
11-12 Russell St   240 3228   (379 9979)
Below this large English brasserie overlooking Covent Garden, the white-painted brick vaults are very atmospheric (even if the cooking is unlikely to excite). The restaurant has been expanded to include the Conservatory, which area is available for hire during the week. / 12.30am; conservatory, Mon-Thu; in-house caterers; Conservatory (–,40);
Larger Vault (–,35); Smaller Vault (–,20).

22 Jermyn St SW1 £M, (–,10)
22 Jermyn St   734 2353   (734 0750)
For an intimate setting for a lunch or dinner party, the traditionally decorated sitting rooms of this soothing, understated, central suite-hotel are sometimes used by non-residents. / no amplified music; no dancing.

Twickenham Banqueting Centre, Middx £M, (450,400,300)
Rugby Rd, Twickenham   0181-891 4565   (0181-744 2104)
Substantial rebuilding of the home of Rugby has expanded facilities, including those of the purpose-built banqueting suite. Hire can include tours of the grounds and visits to the Museum of Rugby. A wedding licence was being applied for as we went to press. / midnight; not match days; Payne & Gunter; Rose Rm (450,400,300); Spirit of Rugby (450,330,280);
Members Lounge (330,–).

Two Chairmen SW1 £B, (50,22)
39 Dartmouth St   222 8694
Atmospheric, clubby restaurant of a Westminster pub, available for evening hire or (for suitable size parties) at lunch. / 11.20pm; closed Sat & Sun; in-house caterers; no amplified music; no dancing.

University of London Union WC1 £B, (400,150,150)
Malet St   436 5826   (436 4604)
Completely refurbished in 1995, the main hall (now called Room 101 in homage to Orwell, who used to write in the neighbouring Senate House) is sound-proofed (how appropriate) and air-conditioned, and has a disco lighting system. The smaller wine bar is popular for receptions, discos and lunches. / 11.20pm; not Mon-Fri in term time; sometimes Aug hol; in-house caterers; Rm 101 (400,150); Palms Wine Bar (120,60);
Bar 101 (80,–).

University Women's Club W1 £M, (100,50)
2 Audley Sq   499 2268   (499 7046)
With a member's sponsorship, many kinds of events are possible at this recently refurbished Mayfair club, which is ideal for smaller wedding receptions. Attractions include a pretty garden. / midnight; in-house caterers; Library (100,50); Drawing Rm (80,50).

Upper Refectory Suite SW3 £B-M, (150,75)
King's College, Manresa Rd   928 3777   (928 5777)
If you're looking for an informal venue just off the King's Road, this suite of rooms (the Old Common Room and the Quiet Room) in a King's College '60s outpost is worth considering. / midnight; in-house or hirer's choice by negotiation; no amplified music; no dancing.

Urban Learning Foundation E14   £B-M, (80,–)
56 East India Dock Rd   987 0033   (536 0107)
Companies seeking a smaller venue in the Docklands, perhaps for a drinks reception, might use the Poplar room with its pine floors and large windows. It is particularly pleasant in summer when you can open the double doors onto the garden. / *companies only; list of caterers; no amplified music; no dancing; no smoking; Conference Rm (80,–).*

Vanderbilt Hotel SW7   £M, (125,100,100)
68-86 Cromwell Rd   589 2424   (225 2293)
The listed Vanderbilt Suite of this South Kensington hotel is decorated in extraordinary French château style. The other accommodation is all much more businessy. / *Vanderbilt (40,20).*

Vats WC1   £B, (130,75,40)
51 Lamb's Conduit St   242 8963   (831 7299)
Convivial, street-level Bloomsbury wine bar, whose back room restaurant is atmospheric, in a rather dated way. On Saturdays the whole place can be hired. / *Mon-Sat only restaurant; no beer; Restaurant (100,75,40).*

The Viceroy NW1   £M, (275,200,150)
3-5 Glentworth St   486 3515   (486 3401)
Smart, spacious Indian restaurant in Marylebone, popular as a function venue both with the subcontinental community and, increasingly, with the pop world. / *Private Rm (35,20).*

Victoria & Albert Museum SW7   £E, (700,300,250)
Cromwell Rd   938 8366   (938 8367)
Two recent re-openings – The English Silver Gallery and austere Raphael Gallery – are among the impressive rooms available for functions. The ornate Gamble Room and, in summer, the Pirelli Garden are popular for more social events, such as wedding receptions. Dancing is only possible in the Dome. / *2am; eve not Wed – by day Morris and Gamble Rms are available; list of caterers; no smoking; some areas, no red wine; Dome, Medieval Treasury (& Pirelli Garden) (700,300,250); Raphael Gallery (600,300); Gamble Rm (including Morris Rm) (400,150); Silver Gallery (300,–); Morris Rm (80,40).*

Victoria & Albert Museum Café SW7   £B-M, (300,150,120)
Exhibition Rd   581 2159
This café-with-a-museum-attached offers an atmospheric, lofty, brick-vaulted space in which many kinds of party are possible. Its private room is suitable for smaller or daytime functions. / *1am; whole place eve only; Milburns; Painted Rm (60,40).*

Victoria Pump House SW11   £B, (100,60)
Battersea Pk   350 0523   (228 9062)
Prettily located by a lake in the south east corner of Battersea Park, this square tower (converted into four levels of pleasing small art galleries) makes an attractive and rather unusual place for a cocktail party. For a sit-down, it is necessary to boost the ground floor area with a marquee, and the place makes an attractive venue for weddings, in which they do brisk business. / *2 am; hirer's choice of caterer; no smoking; marquee site.*

Village Bistro N6   £M, (–,35)
38 Highgate High St   0181-340 5165   (0181-347 5584)
This cosy Highgate cottage restaurant provides rather better English cooking than you might expect, and is ideal for smaller, more intimate lunches and dinners. / *not Sat eve; Ground Floor (–,20).*

Villandry Dining Rooms W1   £M, (–,50)
89 Marylebone High St   487 3816   (486 1370)
This annexe to a Marylebone foodie shop serves delicious, fairly simple dishes in plain, cramped but quite atmospheric surroundings. It is available for private hire at evenings and weekends. / not Sun.

Waddesdon Manor, The Dairy, Bucks   £M-E, (110,100)
Queen St, Waddesdon, Aylesbury
01296-651236   (01296-651142)
Near Aylesbury, this Rothschild Victorian fantasy-château has a fine outbuilding whose grandeur belies its modest name. Recently totally revamped, the Dairy is a suite of rooms arranged around a courtyard, some of which have views over the water gardens. It makes a very charming place to get married. / no 18ths or 21sts; in-house caterers; West Hall (110,100); Winter Gardens (80,60); marquee site.

Wag W1   £B, (600,–)
35 Wardour St   437 5534   (287 1747)
Either floor of this centrally located nightclub on the fringe of Chinatown can be hired. It's not scruffy but it does not have the rather antiseptic feel of some of the major West End discos. / 7am; hirer's choice of caterer, alcohol in-house; Bottom Floor (300,–); Top Floor (300,–).

Waldorf Hotel WC2   £M, (800,420,420)
Aldwych   240 9009   (497 0351)
For large receptions and dinner-dances, this fringe-of-Covent Garden hotel will close its Palm Court restaurant and combine it with the Adelphi Suite. For smaller functions, the Aldwych is a characterful choice. The new Edwardian-style Minstrel Suite is popular for receptions. The hotel is licensed for weddings. / 1am; in-house caterers; Adelphi Suite & Palm Court (800,420,420); Charter Suite (600,–); Charter 2 (400,280,224); Minstrel Suite (200,100,80); Somerset (60,50); Kingsway (48,20); Westminster or Waterloo or Tavistock (20,12).

Walkers of St James's SW1   £B, (150,100)
32a Duke St   930 0278
St James's cellar wine bar available in its entirety at the weekend. / 12.30am; Sat only; in-house caterers; no dancing.

Wallace Collection W1   £E, (350,150)
Hertford House, Manchester Sq   935 0687 x45   (224 2155)
The sumptuous rooms of this c18 palace – home to 6,000 works of fine and decorative art, are available for receptions and dinners. Most popular are the Long ('Laughing Cavalier') Gallery, the galleries of c18 French paintings and furniture (in which the collection excels) and the armour galleries. The courtyard is available during fine weather. / no weddings; 11.30pm; from 6.30pm; list of caterers; no amplified music; no dancing; no smoking; Long Gallery (350,150); Gallery 17 (50,24); Arms and Armour (40,–).

Wandsworth Civic Suite SW18   £B, (800,800,550)
Wandsworth High St   0181-871 6394   (0181-871 7560)
Remodelled '30s suite of rooms, comfortably decorated in municipal style, and ideal for a dinner-dance. / midnight; hirer's choice of caterer; Civic Suite (800,–); Civic Hall (475,–); Banqueting Hall (400,–); Reception Rm (30,–).

The Washington W1   £M, (550,120,100)
Curzon St   499 7000   (495 6172)
This modern Mayfair establishment is perhaps more obviously suited to corporate than social use. It may be possible to use the restaurant for a small dinner-dance. / in-house caterers; Richmond Suite (110,70,60); Richmond 1 (Winchester) (60,30); Richmond 2 (Fairfax) (40,25); Restaurant (Madisons) (–,120,100).

PRIVATE VENUES

Watermen & Lightermen's Hall EC3 £M, (110,72)
16-18 St Mary-at-Hill   283 2373   (283 0477)
An appealing mix of characterful charm, flexible attitude and a fair
degree of stateliness makes this, the only Georgian livery hall, ideal
for a wide variety of business and social events. / list of caterers;
no amplified music; no dancing; Freemen's Rm (110,72); Court Rm (70,37).

Waxy O'Connors W1 £M, (700,90)
14-16 Rupert St   287 0255   (287 3962)
Huge central bar, where the Irish theming is done surprisingly well.
For a lavish party during normal opening hours it might be persuaded
to let you take over the whole place (and for a big late night party –
say the closing-party for a show – it would be ideal).
/ in-house caterers; College Bar (150,90); Mezzanine (70,40); Restaurant (–,50).

HQS Wellington WC2 £M-E, (150,120)
Victoria Embankment, Temple Stairs   600 5777   (489 8936)
The Master Mariners' hall, a Second World War naval Sloop, boasts
a fine location (opposite the National Theatre). Its hall, in the bowels
of the ship, gives little clue that you are afloat, but the other rooms
are more nautical in flavour (with superb models of ships) and have
an airy charm. The decks make a good choice for a summer party.
/ 1am; Chester Boyd; Court Rm (150,120); Quarterdeck (100,60); Model Rm and
Library (60,25); Reception Area (50,–).

Wessex House SW11 £B, (200,150)
1A St John's Hl   622 6818   (622 6818)
Characterfully seedy dance hall at Clapham Junction. It's ideal for real
bops, and particularly popular with twentysomethings. / 3.15am;
in-house caterers.

West Wycombe Caves, Bucks £M, (250,50,50)
West Wycombe Pk   01494-524411   (01494-471617)
The caves – legacy of a c18 job-creation scheme – were the meeting
place for the Hell-Fire Club and are used for a variety of functions.
/ from 6.30pm; one caterer; no smoking; Banqueting Hall (–,50); marquee site.

West Zenders WC2 £B-M, (–,40)
4a Upper St Martin's Ln   497 0376   (437 0641)
Unusually stylish Theatreland Chinese, with a double-height glazed
frontage. The basement private room offers a comfortable,
modern setting for an oriental feast. / Private Rm (–,40).

The Westbury W1 £M, (150,100,80)
Conduit St   629 7755   (495 1163)
This smartly-located '50s hotel provides four pleasant function rooms
which possess a fair degree of charm. / 11.20pm; in-house caterers;
Mount Vernon Rm (150,100,80); Pine Rm (120,80,60); Brighton Rm (60,40);
Regency Rm (40,28).

Westminster Abbey Garden SW1 £M-E, (500,230)
Westminster Abbey   222 5152   (233 2072)
A gem of a site of just over an acre. Medicinal herbs were once grown
there – it was the property of the Infirmarer of the Abbey – and it
now contains statutes and many fine trees. You should ideally book at
least a year ahead. / 10.30pm; Jul and early Aug, Mon-Fri 6pm-10pm, plus some
daytimes; list of caterers; no amplified music; smoking restricted; Marquee (500,230);
marquee site.

Westminster Boating Base SW1   £B-M, (500,230,170)
136 Grosvenor Rd   821 7389
Located on the river by Dolphin Square, the base offers an unusually central location which can be turned to most types of function. Prices are reasonable and there are good facilities. Capacity is increased in summer by tenting over the piers while for major events marquees may be erected in the adjoining park. / 1am; hirer's choice of caterer; marquee site.

Westminster Cathedral Hall SW1   £B, (300,200)
42 Francis St   798 9064   (798 9090)
This attractive and colourful Edwardian hall behind the cathedral was refurbished in 1995. It has an arched roof, natural wood floor and period chandeliers. / charities & companies only; 11pm; daytime Tue, Wed, Thu, Sat & Sun; hirer's choice of caterer; live or background music only; no dancing.

Westminster College (Battersea) SW11   £B-M, (200,30)
Battersea Park Rd   556 8005   (556 8082)
Modern offshoot of the Victoria catering college (see next). The Great Hall makes a reasonably economical choice for a party of suitable size. / 9pm; term time only; in-house caterers; no smoking; Great Hall (200,–); Restaurant (–,30); Private Dining Rm (Rm 2) (15,–).

Westminster College (Victoria) SW1   £B, (200,130)
76 Vincent Sq   828 1222   (931 9480)
These catering college premises border a Victoria square. The function rooms (with much natural light) have recently been refurbished, but remain perhaps rather better suited to corporate than social use. / 11.30pm; not during college hrs; in-house caterers; Vincent Rm (Restaurant) (200,130); Escoffier (50,36).

Westminster Conference Centre SW1   £M, (200,100)
12 Gt George St   222 7000   (334 3871)
Just off Parliament Square, the home of the Royal Institution of Chartered Surveyors offers traditional Victorian rooms with an easy-going atmosphere. The dark-panelled Lecture Theatre is the best room and is popular for receptions. The much smaller York Room, also panelled, has marble columns and is filled with antiques. / midnight; Crown Catering; no amplified music; no dancing; smoking restricted; Lecture Hall (200,100); Members Club Rm (150,–); Cambridge (80,60); Gloucester (40,24); Kent (20,16).

Westway Studios W11   £M-E, (750,500,500)
8 Olaf St   0181-469 3744
Notting Hill film studios with large, empty spaces that are ideal for theme evenings – these are usually organised by on-site Buzz Productions (see entry in Party Planners). / hirer's choice of caterer; Studio 1 (750,500); Studio 2 (590,300); Studio 4 (300,200); Studio 3 (150,100).

Whipsnade Wild Animal Park, Beds   £M, (700,400)
Dunstable   01582-872171   (01582-872649)
The park, home to 2,500 creatures, makes an interesting location for a variety of events. Packages can include animal encounters and tours in an open top double-decker bus or on a narrow-gauge railway. The two light, bright, rather functional, modern suites each has a private lawn. / midnight; in-house caterers; Griffin Suite (–,200); Phoenix Suite (–,200); marquee site.

The White Horse SW6   £B, (100,65)
Parson's Gn   736 2115   (610 6091)
Well-known, atmospheric pub overlooking Parson's Green. It has a large upstairs private room. / 12.20am; Private Rm (100,65).

PRIVATE VENUES

White House Hotel NW1   £M, (175,120,100)
Albany Street, Regent's Pk   387 1200   (872 0112)
*Rather anonymous Marylebone hotel whose kitsch, subterranean
Albany Room has most to recommend it.* / 11am; in-house caterers;
Albany (175,120,100); Chester (50,40,40).

White Swan Water W9   £M, (40,40,40)
Blomfield Rd   266 1100   (266 1926)
*Oak and walnut panelling creates a smart yet welcoming feel in this
60-year-old barge, moored in Little Venice. It now has a wedding
licence and concentrates mainly on nuptials, but it's also equipped
for more businesslike functions.* / 10pm; in-house caterers.

White Tower W1   £M, (–,35)
1 Percy St   636 8141
*This Franco/Greek Fitzrovia restaurant is one of the few in London
which could truly be described as venerable. Its comfortably-furnished
private rooms are among the most characterful in town.* / Private Rm
1 (–,20); Private Rm 2 (–,35); Private Rms 3 ,4 ,5 (each) (–,8).

Whitechapel Art Gallery E1   £B-M, (500,60,60)
80-82 Whitechapel High St   377-5015   (377 1685)
*Agreeable, spacious Edwardian gallery on the fringes of the City,
which is particularly suitable for early evening receptions.* / eve only,
not Wed; hirer's choice of caterer; alcohol in café area only.

Whitelands College SW15   £B-M, (200,200)
West Hill   0181-392 3505   (0181-391 3531)
*Roehampton college, standing in its own grounds, with a characterful
'30s interior, and popular for wedding receptions and parties.*
/ midnight; vacations and weekends; in-house caterers; Ruskin Dining Hall (–,200);
Boardroom (100,–); marquee site.

Whitewebbs Museum of Transport, Middx   £B-M, (250,150,150)
Whitewebbs Rd, Enfield   0181-367 1898   (0181-363 1904)
*You can hold receptions – and sometimes other functions –
among the veteran vehicles on display in the former Victorian
pumping station.* / midnight; in-house or hirer's choice by negotiation;
smoking restricted; entire First Floor (250,–); Meeting Rm (–,150,150);
marquee site.

Whittington's EC4   £M, (80,40)
21 College Hill, Cannon St   248 5855
*Located in the cellars of Dick's home, this characterful, if quite
cramped, restaurant and wine bar offers some of the best
Anglo-French cooking in the City.* / 11am; eve only, not Sat & Sun;
Restaurant (–,40); Wine Bar (80,–).

Will's Art Warehouse SW6   £B-M, (350,190,140)
Unit 3, Heathmans Rd   371 8787   (371 0044)
*This Parson's Green gallery, housed in a Victorian building, actively
markets itself as the party venue to which it is well suited. There's a
mezzanine floor overlooking the gallery, suitable for a DJ or band.*
/ from 8pm; hirer's choice of caterer.

Wiltons SW1   £M-E, (–,16)
55 Jermyn St   629 9955
*Clubby, old-established, expensive St James's English restaurant, with
a ground-floor private room.* / Private Rm (–,16).

Winchester House SW15   £M, (180,180,180)
10, Lower Richmond Rd   622 6229   (720 8157)
*Three characterful rooms are available at this Queen Anne house
close to Putney Bridge. The first-floor River Room overlooking the
Thames is particularly suited to wedding receptions.* / 11pm;
AM & PM Catering; River Rm (180,110); Turner Rm (–,16); Library (40,–); River Lawn
(marquee) (–,180,180); Front Lawn (marquee) (–,130); marquee site.

Windsor Guildhall, Berks   £M-E, (120,120,120)
High St, Windsor   01628-796908   (01753-620103)
*Fine c17 building, (completed by Wren), popular for wedding
receptions and dinners. The Ascot Room features stained glass
windows, paintings and a chandelier. The imposing Guildhall retains
the aspect of a courtroom and boasts a four-century sequence of
royal portraits.* / 11pm; list of caterers; Guildhall Chamber (120,120,120);
Maidenhead Rm (100,40); Ascot Rm (30,26).

Wine Gallery SW10   £B-M, (–,40)
49 Hollywood Rd   352 7572
*This cosy, unchanging informal restaurant on the fringe of Chelsea
has nooks and crannies to accommodate smaller parties, as well as a
couple of private rooms.* / Private Rm (–,40); Private Rm (–,18).

Winston Churchill's
Britain At War Experience SE1   £M, (120,35)
64/66 Tooley St   403 3171   (403 5104)
*Life in Britain during WWII is the theme of this museum near London
Bridge. Events take place among the exhibits, which include a
re-creation of the Blitz, where sounds and smells produce a 'realistic'
atmosphere.* / 11.30pm; from 7pm; hirer's choice of caterer.

WKD NW1   £B, (300,120,60)
18 Kentish Town Rd   267 1869   (284 3660)
*What was part of the Camden Town Sainsbury's car park has been
reclaimed with a mixture of breeze blocks, corrugated metal sheeting
and halogen downlighters – the result is a surprisingly stylish venue.
You might take the mezzanine, with a view of the stage, for a private
bash.* / 2.30am; in-house caterers; Mezzanine (130,60,60).

Wódka W8   £M, (–,70)
12 St Albans Grove   937 6513   (937 8621)
*This bare but chic Polish restaurant in Kensington is a good place to
take over in its entirety. Alternatively, smaller groups can use the
downstairs private room.* / 1am; in-house caterers; no amplified music; no dancing;
Private Rm (–,30).

The Worx I N1   £B-E, (300,200,200)
16-24 Underwood St   837 2353   (833 8279)
*The Worx are photographic hire studios with three sites and a total of
16 studios around the capital, suitable (with some theming, of course)
for receptions and corporate events. At this site, just off City Road,
the spaces range from 700-2,000 sq ft. Capacities we give are
nominal.* / in-house or hirer's choice by negotiation.

The Worx II N1   £B-E, (300,200,200)
45 Balfe St   837 2353   (833 8279)
*At the King's Cross location, spaces range from 600-2,000 sq ft.
Capacities we give are nominal.* / in-house or hirer's choice by negotiation.

PRIVATE VENUES

The Worx III SW6   £B-E, (1500,–)
10 Heathmans Road, Parson's Gn   837 2353   (833 8279)
At the Parsons Green complex, facilities range from 400-25,000 sq ft, and include a soundproofed area suitable for dancing. The building is U-shaped, and capacity can be increased significantly by 'in-filling' with a marquee. / hirer's choice of caterer; entire building (1000,–); Marquee (500,–); marquee site.

Wrotham Park, Herts   £E, (150,120)
Barnet   0181-441 0755   (0181-449 9359)
Elegant, privately-owned Palladian mansion, just within the M25. It's set in 300 acres of parkland and therefore highly suitable as a marquee site or for events involving activities. / list of caterers; no smoking; no children under 16; Drawing Rm (150,120); Dining Rm (100,80); Saloon (50,40); marquee site.

Ye Olde Cheshire Cheese EC4   £B, (150,60)
145 Fleet St   353 6170   (353 0845)
Rambling, historic, atmospheric pub, many of whose nooks and crannies can be used for lunch, dinners or drinks. / 11.20pm; not Sun eve; Cellar Bar (150,60); Johnson's or Williams Rm (80,55); Johnson's Bar (70,–); Snug Bar (40,–); Director's Rm (25,10).

YHA City of London EC4   £B-M, (90,70)
36 Carter La   236 4965   (236 7681)
The particular attraction of the hostel formerly used by St Paul's Choir School is the Rooftop – the former playground for the choristers – which has good views of St Paul's, and makes a rather intriguing venue for a City event. / 11pm; in-house caterers; no amplified music; no smoking in chapel; Roof Top Marquee (90,70); Chapel (20,15); marquee site.

Zen SW3   £M, (–,20)
Chelsea Cloisters, Sloane Av   589 1781
This Chelsea Chinese restaurant is comfortably worn and produces enjoyable food. There is a ground-floor private room in a similar style to the main dining room. / Private Rm (–,20).

Zen Central W1   £M-E, (–,22)
20-22 Queen St   629 8089
Grand, minimalist Chinese restaurant, in the heart of Mayfair, offering food of high quality. Its style is perhaps more suited to corporate than social entertaining. / Private Rm (–,22).

ZeNW3 NW3   £M, (–,25)
83 Hampstead High St   794 7863
This very stylish, minimalist Hampstead Chinese restaurant has a top-floor private room. / Private Rm (–,25).

MOVING VENUES

MOVING VENUES

TRAIN

Venice-Simplon Orient Express SE1   £E, (–,200)
Sea Containers House, 20 Upper Ground
805 5100   (805 5908)
*These famous railway carriages can be chartered to take you
anywhere in the UK – popular destinations include Bath, Brighton,
Leeds Castle and York.*

BOATS

*Parties on boats have a number of attractions. The sense of occasion
which being afloat brings is one of them – the absence of licensing
restrictions on the Thames may be another.*

Admiral Enterprises SE1   £B-M, (250,200)
Unit 4a Tower Workshops, Riley Rd, London
237 3108   (01959-570538)
*Operator with access to luxury boats for private and corporate
functions, with capacity for formal dining from 20 to 200, and
receptions for up to 250. / in-house caterers.*

Bateaux London WC2   £M-E, (–,150,150)
Victoria Embankment   925 2215   (839 1034)
*Symphony is a restaurant boat (similar to a Parisian bâteau-mouche),
and perhaps rather too touristy in feel for some purposes. / in-house
caterers; Symphony (–,150,150).*

Catamaran Cruisers WC2   £B-M, (300,240,240)
Charing Cross Pier, Victoria Embankment
987 1185   (839 1034)
*In terms of number of vessels, the largest operator on the river.
The boats are popular for corporate entertaining, birthday parties
and the occasional wedding reception. (Only the flagship, Naticia, is,
in fact, a catamaran.) / hirer's choice of caterer, except Naticia;
Naticia (300,240,240); Pridla (270,108); Chevening (195,–); Abercorn (160,54);
Valulla (160,–); Viceroy (100,–).*

Chas Newens Marine Co SW15   £B-M, (12,12)
The Boathouse, The Embankment
0181-788 4587   (0181-780 2339)
*Some of the pencil-thin launches seen in pursuit of the Boat Race are
available for river trips – one has a covered section. / hirer's choice of
caterer; no high heels; Panache, Majestic or Pomery (12,12).*

Chelsea Luxury Charters SW10   £M-E
The Marina Terrace, Chelsea Harbour   351 9680   (352 4534)
*Upmarket company specialising in providing small yachts,
motor-yachts or launches for luxury trips. Silver service dinner cruises
for between two and 200 people can also be organised (as, more
esoterically, can flights in ex-military jets and helicopters).
/ in-house caterers.*

City Cruises SE16   £B-M, (250,120,90)
Cherry Gdn Pier, Cherry Gdn St   237 5134   (237 3498)
*This company has three large vessels (Mayflower Garden, Eltham,
Westminster) suitable for large floating hoedowns. The pride of the
fleet is the new Millennium of London, which may be made available
for grander functions. / in-house or hirer's choice; Mayflower Garden (250,90,90);
Millennium (200,120); Eltham (175,90,90); Westminster (100,70,70).*

Crown River Cruises EC4   £B-M, (180,100,100)
HMS President, nr Blackfriars Bridge   936 2033   (936 3383)
Family-run cruise-boat company, which now has four vessels (including the luxurious, two-deck Salient which was brought into service in 1996). / in-house or hirer's choice; Suerita (150,60,60); Spirit of London (80,36,36); Salient (180,100,100).

Floating Boater W2   £B-M, (80,50,40)
Little Venice, North Wharf Rd   724 8740   (603 4755)
For canal trips from Little Venice to Camden Town, you can choose between the Prince Regent (an Edwardian-style canal boat built in 1990, for all types of entertaining, year-round) and the 85-year-old Lapwing narrow boat (which is less weatherproofed and so best suited to summer use). / midnight; in-house caterers; Prince Regent (80,50,40); Lapwing (40,22).

Jason's Trip W9   £B-M, (60,28,24)
Blomfield Rd, Little Venice   286 3428   (266 4332)
This company operates traditional-style, brightly-painted narrow boats on Regent's Canal. The smaller Lace Plate II restaurant-boat accommodates more formal sit-down functions. / midnight; Apr-Oct; hirer's choice of caterers (Jason in-house) (36,28,24); Jason (60,–); Holland (48,–).

The Jenny Wren NW1   £B-M, (60,20)
250 Camden High St   485 6210   (485 9098)
Traditionally designed and decorated narrow boat available for plying the Regent's Canal between Camden and Little Venice. After the event, you could retire to the Waterside Restaurant (same ownership). / midnight; late Apr-early Oct; in-house caterers.

The Lady Daphne SE1   £B-M, (75,35)
St Katherine's Dock   562 9562   (628 5751)
A wooden vessel built in 1923 and still sailing. Spend a day on the Thames, perhaps boarding at Hays Galleria, and sailing under Tower Bridge (which will be raised for you on the way) en route to Greenwich or the Thames Barrier. Alternatively, hold a reception while docked. / charters Apr-Oct, static events all year; approved list of caterers or DIY; no stilettos; stationary (75,35); afloat (45,35).

Maidenhead Steam Navigation, Berks   £B-M, (140,76,76)
Taplow Boatyard, Mill La, Taplow
01628-21770   (01628-773802)
Three boats for cruising the upper reaches of the Thames (Windsor to Marlow) – the SL Belle (a century-old cruiser), the Edwardian (built in 1991, less characterful but better kitted out for entertaining), and the Georgian (a new boat geared towards presentations and corporate hospitality). / midnight; in-house caterers; Georgian (140,76,76); Edwardian (110,50,50); Belle (80,28).

Mainstream Leisure SW15   £B-M, (180,148,148)
3 The Mews, 6 Putney Common
0181-788 2669   (0181-785 3406)
This established party company owns two boats – the Elizabethan paddle-steamer (on the Thames) and the Lady Rose narrow boat based in Little Venice – and also offers packages on other vessels. / midnight on canal; Elizabethan (180,148,148); Lady Rose of Regent's (50,36,36).

MOVING VENUES

My Fair Lady NW1   £M, (80,80,80)
250 Camden High St   485 6210   (485 9098)
You can have year-round receptions or dinners on the Regent's Canal, cruising between Camden Town and Little Venice in a heated, carpeted and fully enclosed narrow boat, purpose-built as a restaurant. / midnight; in-house caterers; smoking restricted.

Seahorse, Middx   £M, (40,36)
4 Thameside Centre, Kew Bridge Rd, Brentford
0181-865 3040   (0181-569 9800)
Moored at Westminster, this 90-foot, '20s Dutch barge, fitted in red cedar and oak, can be chartered, perhaps for a cruise to Henley or for a wedding reception. / no 18ths/21sts/stag nights; January; in-house caterers; smoking restricted.

Thames Leisure EC4   £B-M, (400,250,250)
Swan Pier, Swan La   623 1805   (283 4002)
Choose a package for anything from corporate cruises to college parties. The fleet now includes the London Regalia – a large, moored vessel for which a wedding licence is being sought. / in-house caterers; Regalia (400,250,250); The Miyuki Maru (250,120,120); The Tideway (100,40,40).

Thames Luxury Cruises EC3   £B-M, (150,75,50)
Tower Pier   0181-780 1562   (0181-785 3406)
The Golden Salamander is the boat better suited to formal entertaining, while the Captain James Cook, with its open top-deck, is more for summer cruising. TLC is the sister company of Mainstream Leisure (see also). / Golden Salamander (150,50,50); Captain James Cook (75,75).

Tidal Cruises SE1   £B-M, (250,220,220)
Lambeth Pier, Albert Embankment   928 9009   (401 2894)
Four large boats suitable for parties and cruises on the Thames. / hirer's choice of caterer; Royal Princess (250,220,220); Viscountess (210,150,150); Hurlingham (180,132,132); Old London (130,106,106).

Turk Launches, Surrey   £B-M, (150,100,60)
Town End Pier, 68 High St, Kingston-upon-Thames
0181-546 2434   (0181-546 5775)
A choice of boats for trips above Richmond Lock (e.g. to Hampton Court), including the Yarmouth Belle, a c19 steamer, complete with side paddle wheels. / midnight; in-house caterers; New Southern Belle (150,100,60); MV Yarmouth Belle (150,40); Kingston Royale (90,–); Richmond Royale (60,–).

Woods River Cruises SE3   £M-E, (230,400,400)
PO Box 177, Blackheath   481 2711   (481 8300)
An operator at the luxury end of the market, whose Silver Sturgeon is the largest vessel on the capital's waterways (capacity 400). The Silver Barracuda also offers style on quite a scale. / 1am; in-house caterers; Silver Sturgeon (–,400,400); Silver Barracuda (230,168,168); Silver Dolphin (90,68,68).

PLANE

Concorde, Middx   £E, (–,100)
British Airways, Compass Centre, PO Box 10, Hounslow
0181-513 0202   (0181-513 0306)
Charter Concorde for hops around the Bay of Biscay or over the Channel, and be home in time for tea. For non-exclusive hires, BA refers enquiries to Goodwood Travel (tel 01227-763336).

ACTION VENUES

ACTION VENUES

GO-KARTING

*Pro-karting, as insiders like to call it, revolves – for amateurs
anyway – around racing single-engine karts capable of about 40mph,
often over an indoor track. A session usually lasts several hours, and
can be organised in heats or as a single endurance event. Prices for
most sessions work out around £35 per person. No driving licence
is necessary.*

Adventure Events E16
Gate 14, Gallion's Reach, Royal Albert Dock Basin
476 1234   (476 3456)
*The only outdoor kart circuit within the M25 is a 370m track in
Docklands, located east of London City Airport. The owners stress
their ability to offer numerous other activities from sailing days to
Formula One, with catering and accommodation available.*

Buckmore Park Kart Circuit, Kent
Maidstone Rd, Chatham
01634-201562   (01634-686104)
*Off Junction 3 of the M2, this 900m outdoor track is set in 250 acres
of parkland.*

Formula Fun W3
2606 Western Ave   0181-752 0554   (0181-752 0710)
*This 40,000 sq ft former Acton warehouse houses a 300m track, and
can accommodate parties of up to 80. In addition to the karts, you
can also try knee-high mini-motorbike racing.*

Playscape Pro Racing SW11
Battersea Kart Raceway, Hester Rd
801 0110   (801 0111)
*The first indoor kart-racing company has two converted bus garage
raceways, at Battersea ('Monaco') and Streatham ('Silverstone'). Use
is mainly by corporate children, but a special rate is offered for the
real thing (though they must be over eight years old).*

The Raceway N1
The Central Warehouse, N London Freight Terminal
833 1000   (833 0999)
*The largest indoor track in Europe (they say) is surprisingly
conveniently located for the West End and the City, being just north
of King's Cross.*

Team Daytona W12
54 Wood Ln   0181-749 2277   (0181-749 7831)
*There are two kart tracks in this former M&S warehouse, opposite
the BBC, together totalling 600m. Track 2 is a figure-of-eight circuit
featuring a flyover.*

PAINTBALL

*Paintball is a great stag night and corporate entertaining favourite.
Most days cost between £15 and £25 a head. The price usually
includes goggles (which must be worn at all times), a gun and lunch –
pellets are extra. Some people take this 'sport' very seriously and, if
you are a smaller group, it is worth exercising some caution as to who
you are put with. For an exclusive booking, you generally need 20 to
30 people.*

Electrowerkz Two EC1
7 Torrens St   837 6419   (278 1437)
*This 30,000 sq ft converted warehouse offers urban London paintball
– right behind Angel tube. Packages are for three hours and there's a
minimum age of 16.*

Mayhem Paintball Games, Essex
Pryors Farm, Patch Park, Ongar Rd, Abridge
01708-688517   (01708-688426)
A day's play here includes woodland and urban games.

National Paintball Games – Sidcup, Kent
Sidcup 01634-864173   (01634-864173)
*Eight playing areas, including fortified positions, towers and bunkers
in woodland areas.*

National Paintball Games – Southend, Essex
Rochford, Nr Southend
01634-864173   (01634-864173)
*Features at this site include 'the Bridge Crossing' and 'Trench System',
all set in natural woodland.*

The Paintball Company NW7
40 Barnet Way   0181-959 4440
*Just outside the M25 (near junction 22) this site boasts 11 combat
areas, with possibilities for jungle, village and bridge attacks.*

Skirmish – Lasham, Hants
Manor Farm Buildings, Lasham, Alton
01256-381628   (01256-381173)
*About an hour outside London, this woodland paintball site has an
array of old WWII bunkers, trenches, etc. Provisions are generally in
the form of a spit-roast pig.*

Skirmish – South East, Surrey
Ladycross Farm, Hollow La, Dormansland
01342-870870   (01342-870016)
*One of the first UK paintball companies, with a 17-acre site close to
junction 6 of the M25. New for 1997 is No Man's Land, with
trenches, bunkers and bridges. Kids' days are possible – minimum
age is 10.*

QUASAR

*Interest in Quasar has fallen to the extent there are very few places
left in London. Just in case you don't know how it's played – teams
are equipped with laser guns to zap opponents' electronic
chestpacks. The computer keeps score.*

Megabowl SW2
142 Streatham HI   0181-678 6007   (0181-674 3463)
Groups of 20 people can book exclusive use of the Quasar facilities.

Quasar N19
13 Junction Rd   281 5001   (281 0646)
*Opposite Archway tube station. There's also an arcade with video
games and pool tables.*

ACTION VENUES

RALLY DRIVING

Real boy- (and girl-) racers can try rally driving. Those prefering a more elevated position and slower pace could try tank driving.

A-Tracks, Bucks
Tan Fan House, Cadsden Rd, Princes Risborough
01844-274921 (01844-343861)
The aim here is to give you an objective rather just a 'driving experience'. Your five missions include operating a 6x6, high load carrier with amphibious capability, and manoeuvring a gun and powder keg against the clock. Prices include medals.

Brands Hatch, Kent
Fawkham, Longfield 01474-872331
(groups requiring hospitality) or 0990-125250 (groups not requiring hospitality) (01474-874766)
Roar and rev to your heart's content on this world-famous circuit. The choice of activities includes the Nigel Mansell and Four Wheel Drive Racing Schools, multi-activity days, skid pan racing and karting.

London Rally School, Oxon
Pool Farm, Stratton Audley, Bicester
01869-278199 (01869-278899)
Play hard and fast in the rear wheel drive MkII Ford Escort RS2000s and Toyotas. Other options include quad bikes, Honda pilot racing buggies and off-road rally karts. The minimum age is 18 and you need a driving licence. Archery and paintball are also available.

MULTI-ACTIVITY EVENTS

Character or team-building? Events in the multi-activity category include kart racing, mini hovercraft driving, 'It's a Knockout', human table football and clay pigeon shooting. A great way to discover muscles – perhaps even skills – you never knew you had.

Britannia Adventure Sports, Essex
Pesterford Bridge, Forest Hall Rd, Stansted
01279-817300 (01279-817444)
Military vehicle driving, quad biking, 'It's a Knockout', clay pigeon shooting, archery, paintball and off-road driving.

Leapfrog International, Berks
Riding Court Farm, Datchet
01753-580880 (01753-580881)
Groups of up to 50 can drive mini-hovercraft and tanks or try 'It's a Knockout', Motaball, human table football, laser clay pigeon shooting, blindfold driving...

Team Spirit Leisure
35 Elspeth Rd SW11 771 0383 (771 0384)
Participation events organiser, offering a very wide range of activities at a large number of venues.

WildTracks, Suffolk
Chippenham Rd, Kennett, Newmarket
01638-751918 (01638-552173)
Good – but definitely not clean – fun days arranged for groups of between 15 and 40 wanting to try perhaps motocross (two tracks), Chieftan tank or 4x4 wheel driving, and the like.

OUT ON THE TOWN

OUT ON THE TOWN

TOP SPOTS

American Bar at the Savoy WC2
Strand   836 4343
Still, after half a century, indubitably London's top cocktail bar and one of the best ways of easing into a night on the town. Jacket and tie are de rigueur.

Atlantic Bar & Grill W1
20 Glasshouse St   734 4888
Over-40s may not see the attraction, but fans of this famous, clubby, subterranean cocktail bar/restaurant, just by Piccadilly Circus, find an unmatchable buzz on an impressive scale. Make sure you have a booking if you want to make it past the velvet rope.

Bateaux London
Victoria Embankment   925 2215
London's answer to Paris's bâteaux mouches – a hyper-modern flat-deck cruiser, which plies the river for two-hour lunch and dinner trips. As you might suspect, prices are on the high side.

Benihana
37-43 Sackville St, W1   494 2525
77 King's Rd, SW3   376 7799
100 Avenue Rd, NW3   586 9508
Stylish modern Teppan-Yaki restaurants (each table with a knife-juggling chef) which offer a flash-but-fun night out (also popular with teenagers). Order a birthday cake and the staff will sing Happy Birthday in Japanese and take a photo of the embarrassed recipient.

Blakes SW7
33 Roland Gdns   370 6701
If you are intent on blowing as much money as possible on a single meal, this still fashionable, seductively decorated South Kensington basement restaurant has its attractions. Despite the passing of the years, it maintains its reputation as an unmatched venue for romance.

Blue Elephant SW6
4 Fulham Broadway   385 6595
London's best-known Thai restaurant – with its dramatic pond, bridge and jungle décor – offers a reliable setting for a special night out.

I-Thai W2
31-35 Craven Hill Gdns   298 9000
If you want to mingle with the international fashion and media crowd, consider the dining room of this ultra-minimalist hotel, which dominates a Bayswater garden square. The exquisitely presented East-meets-West dishes come at very high prices.

L'Incontro SW1
87 Pimlico Rd   730 6327
This glamorous, opulent and noisy Pimlico Italian restaurant has a brash, buzzy, rather '80s feel which suits a hang-the-expense night out.

Ivy WC2
1 West St   836 4751
The stars' favourite restaurant, and the top choice of regular London restaurant-goers too. If you want to mark a special event at this clubby Theatreland restaurant, book well ahead.

Maroush W2
21 Edgware Rd   723 0773
For something a little different, consider the dinner and dancing (complete with belly dancing) offered nightly at this glitzy, Lebanese restaurant – one of the best of its type. Note, however, that there is high minimum charge.

Motcomb's Club SW1
5 Halkin Arcade   235 5532
This stylish Belgravia nightclub/restaurant has the advantage that, by prior reservation, it's open to non-member diners. Given the paucity of quality dine-and-disco places, that makes it well worth knowing about. Prices are quite reasonable, considering.

Nobu W1
Metropolitan Hotel, Old Park Ln   447 4747
A spring 1997 opening whose innovative Japanese-based cuisine and celebrity following instantly made it the talk of the town. A great place for a groovily hip party – it is more informal than the not inconsiderable prices might suggest.

Le Pont de la Tour SE1
Butler's Whf   403 8403
The impressive view from this stylish Tower Bridge-side restaurant (especially from the window seats) and generally reliable Anglo-French cooking make this one of the better places for a civilised, big-budget celebration.

Quaglino's W1
16 Bury St   930 6767
Sir Terence Conran's glitzy and glamorous mega-scale St James's bar/restaurant is a favourite of many for a fun night out. For a smart joint it is unusual in serving into the early hours.

The Ritz W1
150 Piccadilly   493 8181
The magnificent Louis XVI restaurant of this St James's hotel is often touted as one of the most impressive dining rooms in London. It is – certainly for dinner, when candlelight softens the gilt (and there is the added attraction of dancing on Friday and Saturday). Be prepared, though, for cooking below the standard you might hope for.

The River Café W6
Thames Wharf, Rainville Rd   385 3344 am; 381 8824 pm
This chic Hammersmith restaurant boasts a keen celeb' following. The hidden-away location adds 'something special' to a celebration, and the modern Italian cooking is the best of its type in London.

Roof Gardens W8
99 High Street Kensington   937 7994
On Thursdays and Saturdays, with advance booking, groups of up to 25 can dine and dance at this intriguing nightclub venue – set among two acres of mature gardens, eight floors above Kensington High Street. (If you want to go just to dance you have to be a member or be accompanied by one.)

OUT ON THE TOWN

Savoy River Restaurant WC2
Strand   836 4343
The most elegant dinner-dance in town tips off Monday to Saturday at this extremely romantic dining room, where the best tables overlook the river. It's a great favourite for more mature birthday and anniversary celebrations.

Stoll-Moss Theatres VIP Service
39-45 Shaftesbury Av W1   494 5151
If you think an evening at the theatre is all about being plied with champagne and smoked salmon, this service – from the biggest group of West End theatres – is for you. You are greeted and looked after throughout, with drinks and nibbles before the show and, if desired, dinner in a private room afterwards. Ideal for smaller groups with generous budgets.

Windows on the World, Hilton Hotel W1
22 Park Ln   493 8000
For an expensive dinner-dance evening in glitzy surroundings, the Hilton's rooftop restaurant – with its magnificent view – provides a unique setting. Those unwilling to spend a fortune on a meal that is unlikely to have much culinary sparkle could just have a drink in the cocktail bar – a pleasant prelude to moving on elsewhere.

MID-PRICE PLACES

Albero & Grana SW3
89 Sloane Av   225 1048
Fashionable, stylish, buzzing Chelsea Spanish restaurant – ideal for a big dinner party (as long as you don't want to talk to each other). Tapas parties in a corner of the trendily decorated bar offer an informal, less expensive option.

Anna's Place N1
90 Mildmay Pk   249 9379
One of North London's most notable restaurants, Anna Hegarty's individualistic spot offers particularly good food of an unusual type – Scandinavian – and not too expensively. It's an airy place with a very inviting atmosphere.

Babe Ruth's E1
172-176 The Highway   481 8181
This large and striking American sports bar/theme-diner, on a busy road north of Wapping, makes a good setting for a party for kids of all ages. You can even shoot a few basketball hoops.

Beach Blanket Babylon W11
45 Ledbury Rd   229 2907
In the face of more recent competition, this lively Notting Hill bar/restaurant can still claim to have one of London's best interior designs. The Mediterranean food is certainly no great shakes, but for a fun meal you could do worse than to take over the 'gothic' section.

Belgo
Centraal: 50 Earlham St, WC2   813 2233
Noord: 72 Chalk Farm Rd, NW3   267 0718
Extraordinary décor, a large collection of Belgian Beers, waiters dressed as monks and a decent moules-based menu can make a meal at these strikingly designed Chalk Farm and Covent Garden restaurants quite an occasion.

Belvedere W8
Holland House, off Abbotsbury Rd   602 1238
*A magical setting overlooking Holland Park (which is floodlit by night),
is the great strength of this airy, stylishly decorated restaurant which
does a lot of party business. The cooking is no particular attraction.*

Blue Print Café SE1
Design Museum, Butler's Whf   378 7031
*One of London's finest views from a restaurant makes a table at Sir
Terence Conran's striking Design Museum dining room a memorable
place to toast a special event.*

Bombay Brasserie SW7
Courtfield Close, Gloucester Rd   370 4040
*The scale of its setting makes London's longest-established
subcontinental restaurant an impressive venue for a special event,
even if, on a purely culinary basis, prices are rather toppish.*

Café du Marché EC1
22 Charterhouse Sq   608 1609
*Located in a designer-rustic warehouse conversion, between Smithfield
and the Barbican, this French restaurant is often praised for its
combination of good food, buzzing atmosphere and jazz (most
nights). What more could you want for a party?*

Café Lazeez SW7
93-95 Old Brompton Rd   581 9993
*Fashionable South Kensington café/restaurant that offers unusual,
subtle dishes of Indian inspiration. Regular live music makes this a
good place for a stylish but informal party.*

Café Pacifico WC2
5 Langley St   379 7728
*This noisy Tex/Mex Covent Garden restaurant has seen many
competitors come and go – it remains a classic party destination. As
it usually takes 45 minutes to get a table (no booking after early
evening), and as there is nothing to do but drink Margueritas, many
people find themselves in the party mood long before they sit down.*

The Canteen SW10
Chelsea Harbour   351 7330
*For an evening with a sense of occasion, it's worth the hike to Chelsea
Harbour, to seek out this glamorous modern British restaurant whose
standards are consistent across the board.*

Le Caprice SW1
Arlington House, Arlington St   629 2239
*Would-be glamorous restaurants spring up daily, but this chic St
James's brasserie maintains its pre-eminent reputation. It is suited to
smaller celebrations – even for these you should book well ahead.*

Caspers W1
6 Tenterden St   493 7923
*The darling of stag and hen nights – if you fancy someone on the
next table just pick up the 'phone (every table has one) and tell them
so. It's a supremely tacky but extremely popular evening out. No
jeans.*

OUT ON THE TOWN

Chez Bruce SW17
2 Bellevue Rd   0181-672 0114
Unchallenged as south London's best restaurant, this comparatively informal Wandsworth Commonsider is an excellent all-rounder – a great venue for a small party wanting to forego the schlepp to the West End.

The Collection SW3
264 Brompton Rd   225 1212
The 'catwalk' entrance guarded by 'style police' sets the tone at this striking Brompton Cross bar/restaurant. Once your booking has been identified (or you have been deemed sufficiently beautiful to be admitted) the scene inside makes a good backdrop to a celebration.

Comedy Store W1
1 Oxendon St   01426-914433
Well-known Leicester Square dive, offering basic food and surroundings, but, on the humour side, a reliable evening. There's no booking, which is a disadvantage if you're planning a celebration.

The Criterion W1
Piccadilly Circus   925 0909
The gilded, neo-Byzantine décor of this Piccadilly Circus brasserie is possibly the most striking of any London restaurant. It makes a suitably impressive venue to enjoy culinary creations of the media's favourite chef, Marco Pierre White.

Cuba Libre N1
72 Upper St   354 9998
This lavishly decorated, swinging Islington restaurant consistently attracts a fun, lively crowd, and so is a good place for louder celebrations.

Cuba W8
11 Kensington High St   938 4137
Kensington bar/restaurant where the grub upstairs is no great shakes but the basement is open Monday to Saturday until 2am. There is mixed Latin and Caribbean live music nightly.

Dell'Ugo W1
56 Frith St   734 8300
Not a place for an intimate celebration, but the advantage of this buzzy Soho fixture is that you can have a drink in the boisterous ground floor bar before progressing to the relative tranquillity of the upper floors for dinner.

Detroit WC2
35 Earlham St   240 2662
This groovy Covent Garden spot with its sci-fi cave setting, is very unusual. If you get beyond the bar (which is really the main attraction of the place), the food in the restaurant is surprisingly good.

Dover Street Wine Bar W1
8-9 Dover St   629 9813
It's perhaps seen better days, but this atmospheric Mayfair cellar is one of so few places where you can dine-and-dance in central London that it still has a good following for a party night out. Beware the no-jeans rule.

Fakhreldine W1
85 Piccadilly   493 2424
Glitzy, rather dated, Mayfair Lebanese restaurant (notable, during the day, for its excellent view of Green Park). An attraction for late parties is that service continues until well after midnight.

La Famiglia SW3
7 Langton St   351 0761
This World's End Italian restaurant has been a favourite with the in-crowd for over two decades. It remains a consistent spot for parties of all sizes – especially if you can bag a table in the garden. The downsides are that it's pricey and also that you may not be encouraged to linger.

The Fifth Floor at Harvey Nichols SW1
Knightsbridge   235 5250
For a glam' party night out, the Fifth Floor restaurant combines buzz and chic. You can kick the evening off with a drink in the adjoining cocktail bar – an infamous pick-up joint.

First Floor W11
186 Portobello Rd   243 0072
The groovy décor is the key selling point of this hip modern British restaurant, which maintains its popularity as a celebration venue for Notting Hillbillies.

Formula Veneta SW10
14 Hollywood Rd   352 7612
This Chelsea/Fulham border Italian restaurant is a good place for a stylish, young-at-heart night out.

Frederick's N1
106 Camden Pas   359 3902
This atmospheric, mid-price Islington institution is unusually spacious for a place which serves 'real' food – indeed it can absorb several parties at once without really noticing.

Gasworks SW6
87 Waterford Rd   736 3830
Despite its calculatedly disinterested service and drab food, this antique-filled Fulham spot has quite a following on account of its extraordinary, decadent atmosphere. Not recommended for small groups – the enormous central table in the main room, for a dozen or more, is the only one to have.

Halcyon Hotel W11
129 Holland Park Av   221 5411
Film stars who "want to be alone" often seek out this discreet Holland Park hotel. Its dining room feels removed from the hustle and bustle, and has a deserved reputation as a venue for romance.

Jazz Café NW1
5 Parkway   916 6060
Styled with panache, the modern décor of this Camden Town spot could not be further from the dark and smoky cliché image of a jazz joint. There's live music nightly, often of excellent quality, and the fun continues until midnight (2am Fri & Sat). The large balcony bar/restaurant overlooks the stage and serves quite OK food.

OUT ON THE TOWN

Jongleurs
at Camden Lock: Middle Yd, NW1   924 3080
at the Cornet: 49 Lavender Gdns, SW11   924 3080
On Friday you can take in a comedy show, dine and disco all in one place at these Camden and Battersea clubs. On Saturday there are two performances (and, at Camden, there is dancing after the late show).

Julie's W11
135 Portland Rd   229 8331
The seductive ambience and friendly service at this eclectically decorated restaurant labyrinth in Holland Park make it one of London's most consistent party favourites. The attraction is not the cooking (which is ordinary and expensive).

Kensington Place W8
201-205 Kensington Church St   727 3184
This large, glass-fronted restaurant, near Notting Hill Gate, maintains its popularity as one of London's better all-round modern British dining experiences. Be prepared for a high noise level and, if you want to linger, book for later in the evening.

Langan's Brasserie W1
Stratton St   493 6437
The magical atmosphere lingers at this large and famously characterful English brasserie in Mayfair, even if the cooking has yet to regain the standards of yore.

Launceston Place W8
1A Launceston Pl   937 6912
This charmingly situated Kensington townhouse restaurant has a very comfortable but not at all stuffy atmosphere. It is one of the better choices for a jolly (if not uproarious) celebration.

Madame Jo Jos W1
8 Brewer St   734 2473
Famous drag Soho cabaret (Thu-Sat) so unthreatening you could take your grandmother. It's a giggle for office parties and the like, and the evening rounds off with a disco.

Mainstream Leisure
3 The Mews, 6 Putney Common SW15   0181-788 2669
If you are stuck for inspiration, consider this 25-year-old party-planning company, which offers a wide range of events for group evenings out. Some of them do sound a mite tacky, but a wide range of possibilities is clearly set out in the publicity material.

Mezzo W1
100 Wardour St   314 4000
Europe's largest restaurant provides a sense of scale for a celebration. It benefits from a buzzing atmosphere. In the evenings there is music (for which a charge is made). All in all, prices are on the high side.

Mezzonine W1
100 Wardour St   314 4000
Smaller parties might like to join the mêlée on the less formal, ground floor section of Mezzo (see above), in the heart of Soho. It's pricey for what it is, but there's a large and extremely popular bar where you could start off an evening, and some of the oriental dishes (served at long, refectory tables) are quite interesting.

Motcomb's SW1
26 Motcomb St   235 9170
Welcoming, picture-hung, tightly-packed Belgravia basement. The attraction is to a conservative crowd, but – for a fairly mature party – the place has a very good atmosphere.

Mr Wing SW5
242-244 Old Brompton Rd   370 4450
Still the best known 'party-Chinese' restaurant in London. It is famous for a jolly atmosphere and the décor of its delightfully tacky, rather amazing jungle-basement.

Nam Long SW5
159 Old Brompton Rd   373 1926
The favourite of a fashionable, younger crowd, this stylish, low-lit South Kensington cocktail bar and restaurant is a good place for parties of up to a dozen or so.

Nikita's SW10
65 Ifield Rd   352 6326
The alcoves of this richly decorated basement Russian restaurant on the Chelsea/Fulham border provide a perfect, very unusual, spot for a small party. The range of vodkas seems to have something to do with the attraction.

Odette's NW1
130 Regent's Park Rd   586 5486
North London's only really glamorous, quality restaurant is a romantic place decorated with a huge collection of mirrors. It makes a comfortable place for a civilised celebration.

Odin's W1
27 Devonshire St   935 7296
For maturer souls, this impressive Marylebone restaurant offers an unusually good all-round package of competent cooking, pleasant service, a high level of comfort and a relaxing atmosphere. In short, it makes an ideal setting for a (fairly sedate) celebration.

Orso WC2
27 Wellington St   240 5269
To cap a night at the theatre, this long-established Covent Garden basement Italian still has a lot to recommend it, thanks to its buzzy atmosphere late on. At other times, it is not the place it once was.

Oxo Tower SE1
Barge House St   803 3888
A stunning landmark location and a fantastic view (from its eighth-floor riverside location) make this modern British bar/brasserie/restaurant an obvious spot for a celebration. The food and service may not quite live up to the rest of the experience (so opt for the less expensive brasserie section).

Le Palais du Jardin WC2
136 Long Acre   379 5353
Value and glamour don't usually go hand in hand, which is perhaps why this large and very impressive Covent Garden brasserie doesn't have nearly the profile that its consistently good quality package deserves. One of the best all-rounders in town.

OUT ON THE TOWN

Palio W11
175 Westbourne Gro 221 6624
This lofty, modern, multi-level Notting Hill restaurant (under the same management as Soho's Dell'Ugo) offers OK food, quite a lot of style and a good atmosphere.

The Party Bus
Vigilant House, 120 Wilton Rd SW1 630 6063
Double-decker (open or closed top) bus excursions – such as the Grub and Club Tour and the World-famous Nightclub Tour – where "the party never stops". You have been warned.

The Pen SW6
51 Parson's Green Ln 371 8517
This rather unusual Parson's Green restaurant (in a converted pub) offers a good all-round package, and a stylish setting for a medium-sized party.

PJ's SW3
52 Fulham Rd 581 0025
This buzzing Chelsea bar/restaurant, popular on the Euro-circuit, is always packed, creating an atmosphere ideal for a celebration. The American food, sadly, is not quite such an attraction.

Planet Hollywood W1
13 Coventry St 287 1000
Prices give nothing away at this large Tinseltown-themed burgeria near Piccadilly Circus. Still, children of all ages may enjoy dining among the movie-memorabilia. You can book for parties of 6+ (subject to availability).

Players' Theatre WC2
14 Villiers St 839 1134
A fun and unusual night out – an authentically Victorian (in concept) music hall near Charing Cross. Before or after the show, you can dine on the premises simply but inexpensively. Thursday is big band jazz night – from 11.30pm until late.

Rebato's SW8
169 South Lambeth Rd 735 6388
This out-of-the-way Vauxhall Spanish establishment is a fun spot worth the hike. The grub is better in the tapas bar, but the restaurant (go for the paella) is lively, genuinely Hispanic in feel, and good for a relaxed celebration.

Ronnie Scotts W1
47 Frith St 439 0747
Soho's international-standard jazz venue offers an excellent place for, or indeed to complete, an evening out. Admission also includes a disco and the place goes on till 3am.

Saint WC2
8 Great Newport St 240 1551
Cool décor is the strong point of this painfully trendy bar/restaurant on the fringe of Covent Garden. Be hip, or book, to get past the velvet rope.

Sale e Pepe SW1
9-15 Pavilion Rd 235 0098
Very noisy but great fun trattoria – a Knightsbridge fixture since 1974, and ideal for an unrelaxing night out.

Sarastro WC2
126 Drury Ln   836 0101
*With its OTT theatrical baroque setting – and an extrovert owner
who styles himself as "the King" – this Covent Garden restaurant is
tailor-made for a party.*

School Dinners Restaurant W1
1 Robert Adam St   486 2724
*Would-be fantasy restaurant, where (Wed-Sat) schoolgirls in gymslips
and suspenders serve lads on a night out with spotted dick, verbal
abuse and six-of-the-best. Female guests are served by
'Chippendale' waiters.*

606 Club SW10
90 Lots Rd   352 5953
*Good jazz and an interesting location (through an anonymous hole in
a wall, opposite a power station) make for a good party venue.
The food is pricey for what it is, but non-members have to eat if they
want to drink.*

Smollensky's on the Strand WC2
105 Strand   497 2101
*Luxuriously decorated, this large American formula bar/restaurant, on
the fringe of Covent Garden, has a good atmosphere. It is open until
quite late and you can dance at the weekends.*

Sofra W1
18 Shepherd Mkt   493 3320
*Very good all round, this Turkish restaurant in Shepherd Market –
the original of what is now a chain – has bright décor, pleasant
service and good food. It suits parties of all sizes.*

Star of India SW5
154 Old Brompton Rd   373 2901
*London's most fashionable Indian restaurant has extraordinary
Roman-style décor and, as it's pretty much always full, a very reliable
atmosphere. The food can be pretty good too.*

Tiroler Hut W2
27 Westbourne Gro   727 3981
*Those with a sense of humour may enjoy yodelling the night away,
to the strains of an accordion, at this Bayswater chalet-restaurant.*

Toto's SW1
Lennox Gardens Mews   589 2062
*Though it's in the centre of fashionable London (just behind Harrods)
this lofty and atmospheric Italian restaurant does not suffer from the
'attitude' which afflicts a number of restaurants thereabouts. Prices
are hardly bargain-basement, of course, but it is a convivial place for
a medium-size gathering.*

Wimbledon Greyhound Stadium
Plough Ln   0181-946 8000
*A great venue for the armchair (well, dining chair) sportsman.
Watch the racing (Tue, Fri & Sat) while eating – you don't even need
to move to bet, as they come to you. The combination of excitement
and inaction makes this a popular spot for celebrations and
entertainment generally.*

Wódka W8
12 St Alban's Gro   937 6513
Welcoming, modish Kensington restaurant popular for smaller parties. The Polish food is surprisingly sophisticated and there is a large selection of flavoured vodkas to fuel the festivities.

CHEAP AND CHEERFUL

Andrew Edmunds W1
46 Lexington St   437 5708
For sheer charm, many Londoners would rate this intimate, candle-lit Soho townhouse restaurant as the top place in town. The modern British cooking is pretty good as well as being inexpensive, making this a top party choice – if you can get a table, that is.

Anemos W1
32 Charlotte St   636 2289
In spite of Greek fare that is not exactly special this beery place remains a favourite for stag and hen nights. Learn the song before you go: A-ne-mos, A-ne-mos, A-ne-mos – A-ne-mos, A-ne-mos, A-ne-mo-o-os.

Bar Madrid W1
4 Winsley St   436 4649
This large, swinging twentysomething scene, just off Oxford Street, is a lively place for a drink and a dance.

Ben's Thai W9
93 Warrington Cr   266 3134
For an inexpensive dinner with a sense of occasion, this Maida Vale Thai restaurant is a good deal. It occupies the atmospheric first floor of a huge Victorian pub.

Big Easy SW3
334 King's Rd   352 4071
This fun and boisterous American restaurant is ideal for the sort of celebration where the quality of the cooking is beside the point.

Capital Radio Restaurant WC2
Leicester Sq   484 8888
If you like the idea of a big theme-restaurant as a setting for your party, you could do much worse than this bright and cheerful spot in the centre of town.

Caravan Serai W1
50 Paddington St   935 1208
Carpets, carpets everywhere add to the feeling that you've gone further than Marylebone when you reach this jolly Afghani restaurant. It makes a good choice for those in search of something a little out of the ordinary.

Chuen Cheng Ku W1
17 Wardour St   437 1398
For a party night out in Chinatown at modest cost, you can do much worse than this landmark establishment.

Côte à Côte SW11
74-75 Battersea Bridge Rd   738 0198
This large bistro in Battersea may have no great culinary ambitions, but it offers a reliable atmosphere – of particular appeal to the young-at-heart – at super-budget prices.

Da Mario SW7
15 Gloucester Rd   584 9078
The reliability of the PizzaExpress chain and the attraction of a basement disco combine to make this as cheap a (reasonably pleasant) spot as you will find for a big dine and dance party.

De Cecco SW6
189 New King's Rd   736 1145
This Parson's Green Italian is well known for its buzzy atmosphere – ideal for a loud party – and its good, and not too expensive, cooking.

Down Mexico Way W1
25 Swallow St   437 9895
An extraordinary place, a stone's throw from Piccadilly Circus. Now a Mexican restaurant, in the '20s it was London's first Spanish restaurant and has an amazing tiled interior. The food can be a let-down, but the bar goes on till late. The ground floor bar is a disco (Thu-Sat). In the latter part of the week, there is also live salsa.

Efes Kebab Houses
I: 80 Great Titchfield St, W1   636 1953
II: 175-177 Great Portland St, W1   436 0600
The appeal of these Turkish Marylebone institutions is wide-ranging. Efes I is darker, quieter and more relaxing, while Efes II is the place for music and belly dancing. Either way the party feast of meze and kebabs is well prepared and good value.

Florians N8
4 Topsfield Pde   081-348 8348
Popular, informal Crouch End Italian, notable for the quality of its food and its buzzing atmosphere (especially, perhaps, in the wine bar at the front).

Garlic & Shots W1
14 Frith St   734 9505
Any sane person might avoid an establishment which insists on putting garlic in all the food (yes, including the ice cream). So it must be the party atmosphere (sustained by copious shots of vodka) which ensures the continuing success of this Soho spot.

El Gaucho SW3
Chelsea Farmers Mkt   376 8514
If you can secure an outside table (or bench), this inexpensive Chelsea Argentinian restaurant offers a very relaxing spot for an informal summer party. The fact that you BYO helps keep prices under control.

Glaisters SW10
4 Hollywood Rd   351 1011
The cooking at this Fulham/Chelsea bistro is nothing special but the place is cosy and the atmosphere jolly, and there's a large walled garden. It shouldn't break the bank either.

OUT ON THE TOWN

Hard Rock Café W1
150 Old Park Ln 629 0382
The oldies are sometimes the best. Despite all the newer competition, the original theme-restaurant still outperforms its rivals. This is a great place if you think loud rock, a burger and a few beers sound like heaven.

House on Rosslyn Hill SW3
34a Rosslyn Hl 435 8037
The characterful home-from-home of Hampstead's young crowd is well known for its bustling atmosphere.

Jim Thompson's SW6
617 King's Rd 731 0999
This oriental spot, in a lavishly converted pub, is a party restaurant par excellence. That is to say the food is not much cop, but the buzzy atmosphere ensures that groups continue to seek the place out anyway.

Joe's Brasserie SW6
130 Wandsworth Bridge Rd 731 7835
Raucous young-scene Fulham brasserie, which makes a good place for a party of the 'I can't hear myself think' variety.

Kalamaras Micro W2
66 Inverness Mews 727 5082
Slightly tatty Bayswater taverna which offers decent food and lets you BYO wine (but not beer) – ideal for a cosy, cramped feast.

Khan's W2
13-15 Westbourne Gro 727 5420
This huge, notorious Bayswater experience – a cross between an Indian railway station and McDonalds – is good for a cheap, chaotic group meal. It's not a place for a whole evening though – you aren't exactly encouraged to hang around.

Lemonia NW1
89 Regent's Park Rd 586 7454
One on its own. Good, affordable Greek food and friendly service are the hallmarks of this large and fashionable, Primrose Hill super-taverna.

Marine Ices NW3
8 Haverstock Hl 485 8898
This Camden Town Italian restaurant is usually packed with representatives of all generations. Main courses are of the pizza and pasta variety, but the real point is the ices and sorbets, which are the best in London.

Mars WC2
59 Endell St 240 8077
This funky north Covent Garden restaurant has quite good modern British food. The lively atmosphere makes it particularly suitable as a younger-scene party spot.

Naked Turtle SW14
505 Upper Richmond Rd 0181-878 1995
Somewhere in East Sheen has to be pretty good to generate a more than local name for itself. This jolly wine bar/restaurant, with live music nightly, has become widely known as one of the better known places for a fun group night out.

New World W1
1 Gerrard Pl   434 2508
*Once inside this enormous Chinatown restaurant, you could be in
Hong Kong. It's all pretty unsophisticated but the novelty and festive
atmosphere of trolleyfuls of dim-sum particularly make a lunch party
worth considering.*

Osteria Basilico W11
29 Kensington Park Rd   727 9957
*This is a trendy Notting Hill restaurant which attracts a good young
following with its fashionably rustic décor and reasonable prices.
The food is generally good too.*

Pizza on the Park SW1
11 Knightsbridge   235 5550
*By Hyde Park Corner, this high-ceilinged PizzaExpress showpiece has
an enjoyable atmosphere. It makes a natural choice for an
economical party at a smart address, and the basement is quite a
well-known jazz venue.*

Pizza Pomodoro SW3
51 Beauchamp Pl   589 1278
*This must be one of the most famous places in London to be almost
invisible. It's a seedy, cramped Knightsbridge basement, where good
pizzas and live music are served till late, and there is an almost Latin
buzz. Larger parties will probably not be able to sit together.*

Ruby in the Dust
102 Camden High St, NW1   485 2744
70 Upper St, N1   359 1710
*Young and fun bar/restaurants with a friendly atmosphere buoyed by
cocktails and beers. The menu is a hotchpotch based around
Tex/Mex and burgers.*

La Rueda
642 King's Rd, SW6   384 2684
68 Clapham High St, SW4   627 2173
*The Clapham original, is a big, boisterous tapas bar/restaurant that
makes a great choice for groups wanting to let their hair down.
The newer Fulham branch is less atmospheric, but popular.*

Texas Embassy Cantina WC2
1 Cockspur St   925 0077
*Large Tex/Mex restaurant, near Trafalgar Square, whose upstairs
room in particular suits a knees up of the office party variety.*

Wine Gallery SW10
49 Hollywood Rd   352 7572
*This cosy and unchanging Chelsea/Fulham fringe wine bar/restaurant
is particularly popular with a younger crowd. The downstairs divides
into a number of semi-private areas ideal for informal dinners.*

SERVICES

CATERERS

The choice of caterer is one of the most important decisions. As with selecting any contractor for your function, it's best to start by ringing around a few apparently suitable firms. You should soon get a 'feel' for the companies you would be happiest to work with.

Most caterers listed here hold themselves out as suitable for most types of occasion. We have therefore tried to suggest why each may be more or less suitable for your requirements for any particular event. Caterers are generally only too pleased to have the opportunity to quote – it should soon emerge, in their attitude or prices, if they are appropriate for the sort of work you are enquiring about.

The following list is necessarily selective and omits many excellent local firms who do not generally take on anything but small dinner or drinks parties. For such events, the best recommendation is to ask around. For larger events too, don't hesitate to speak to friends or others who have organised functions recently.

Caterers charge for food, wine, service and crockery hire in different ways. When comparing companies, it is essential to ensure you are comparing like with like – make sure, for example, that all estimates include VAT.

Almost all caterers offer some degree of party-planning service and can, in addition to organising the food, co-ordinate a marquee, flowers and even entertainment. If you want help with any of these, you should sound the companies out at an early stage.

Above the Salt
Unit 10, Battersea Business Centre, 10 Lavender Hl SW11
801 0694   (801 0399)
Smaller-to-medium size events are the forte of this caterer particularly known for its canapés.

The Admirable Crichton
6 Camberwell Trading Estate, Denmark Rd SE5
733 8113   (733 7289)
Acknowledged by its peers as one of the leading firms in the outside catering business – grand and extraordinary events are a forte.

Admiral & Amos
Unit 4a, Tower Workshops, Riley Rd SE1   237 3108
The event caterers at Tower Bridge (who also do much of the function catering for river boats) provide a general outside catering service.

Al Hamra
31-33 Shepherd Mkt W1   493 1954
A full Lebanese outside catering service is provided by this well-known Shepherd Market restaurant.

Albero & Grana
89 Sloane Av SW3   225 1048   (581 3259)
London's only modern Spanish restaurant provides a full outside catering service. Tapas make ideal buffet fare, or they can do paella for up to 1000.

Alexander Catering
Units 11-12, Riverside, 28 Park St SE1   357 7304   (357 6109)
Well-established, family-run Surrey and London firm (formerly known as Jean Alexander), which does a wide range of government, corporate and social business. It manages or has 'exclusives' at a number of quality venues.

All in Good Taste
433 Harrow Rd W10   0181-969 6333   (0181-969 6333)
*Canapés and buffets are the specialities of this relatively new firm,
whose stock-in-trade is catering for small to medium size, mainly
corporate events.*

AM & PM Catering
Neal's Lodge, Wandsworth Common SW18   0181-870 7484
*This well-established caterer does a variety of work. It has its own
venues in Putney and Wandsworth, and a country branch in
Hampshire.*

Arte
126 Cleveland St W1   813 1011   (813 1031)
*Mediterranean dishes are a speciality of this restaurant-based caterer
which has a following in the media world.*

Bagatelle
704-711 Tudor Estate, Abbey Rd NW10
0181-453 8000   (0181-453 8001)
*It may be more generally known for its South Kensington pâtisserie,
but this firm offers a full outside catering service which specialises in
events with a traditional Gallic twist.*

Beeton Rumford
Earl's Court Exhibition Ctr SW5   370 8164   (370 8192)
*A P&O Group company which specialises in banquets, receptions,
outdoor shows and large-scale events generally.*

Blue Ribbon Catering Services
205 Camberwell Rd SE5   703 3517   (701 5103)
*Traditional, small-scale family catering operation, that charges
reasonable prices.*

Bovingdons
16 Edgel St SW18   0181-874 8032   (0181-874 6403)
*Corporate and private catering, for medium size events, is the forte
of this firm, which aims at the middle-to-upper end of the market.*

Butlers Catering
109 Great Russell St WC1   580 3890   (436 7451)
*Celia Butler has been catering for a quarter of a century. She
does all the cooking herself, but can arrange to cater for several
hundred guests.*

By Word of Mouth
22 Glenville Mews, Kimber Rd SW18
0181-871 9566   (0181-871 3691)
*Themed events are one of the strengths of this well-established
general outside catering company.*

Canapé Direct
Unit 7, 81 Southern Rd W10
0181-964 0240   (0181-964 0240)
*Boxes of canapés and 'pains surprises' (loaves hollowed out and filled
with mini-sandwiches), delivered to your door, are the specialities of
Joel Brioche – ideal if you want to arrange your own service.*

Caprice Events
28 Litchfield St WC2   379 6077   (497 3644)
*The outside catering arm of the Caprice/Ivy restaurants group
maintains its exclusivity by catering only for dinners for 100 or more,
and buffets from twice that number. All table-waiting is carried out by
experienced restaurant staff.*

Carluccio's
28a Neal St WC2   240 1487   (497 1361)
*Mediterranean fare to take away is the speciality of the traiteur
attached to Neal Street, the fashionable Covent Garden restaurant.
Staff can be provided.*

Caroline's Kitchen
13 Cornwall Cr W11   229 4114
*Everything is catered for, but small to medium size buffets are the
speciality.*

Castle Catering Services
57-66 King James St SE1   928 3242   (821 1703)
*Large, traditional, mainly corporate caterer, tending to do larger-scale
events.*

Chelsea Catering Company
305 Fulham Rd SW10   351 0538   (376 5637)
*Chelsea delicatessen which has been providing outside catering
(with or without service) for over half a century, and which prides
itself on its reasonable prices.*

Christopher's
18 Wellington St WC2   240 4222   (240 3357)
*An All-American outside catering service is provided by this
well-known Covent Garden restaurant.*

Clare's Kitchen
41 Chalcot Rd NW1   0181-586 8433   (0181-586 3613)
*Dinner parties and cocktail parties at reasonable cost are the
attractions of this firm, whose work is roughly half social and half
corporate.*

Tessa Corr Associates
30 Beckwith Rd SE24   274 6196   (274 9514)
*Medium- to larger-scale work is the forte of this well-established
company, much of whose work comprises assignments for the arts
and professional services sectors.*

Crown Society
236 London Rd, Romford RM7
01708-744101   (01708-742480)
*Catering on a very large scale is a speciality – corporate hospitality,
banquets, balls, weddings.*

Danish Catering
25 Red Lion St WC1   430 1557   (430 1557)
*Danish Catering is probably the oldest name in Scandinavian catering.
Smorgasbord, canapés and confectionery are the specialities.*

Delectable Feasts
Unit 18 Battersea Business Centre, 103 Lavender Hl SW11
585 0512   (228 3090)
*Medium-scale assignments, often for stand-up functions, form much
of the work of this business and social caterer.*

Epicure
24 Keats Cl SW19   0181-288 8882   (0181-543 5507)
Roux-trained chef whose recently-established business is developing from its wedding-reception origins to include more corporate work, mainly sit-downs.

Euten's
4-5 Neal's Yd WC2   379 6877
Afro-Caribbean (or "Black British", as they prefer to call it) outside catering – on quite a scale, if required – can be provided by this Covent Garden restaurant.

Events à la Carte
32 St John's Av SW15   0181-780 9144   (0181-780 9145)
Themed events are the speciality of this firm, which caters mainly for the City and professional markets.

Feathers
2-5 Old Bond St W1   499 9192   (499 7517)
Major events for corporate clients – including an event-planning service – are a speciality of this well-established Liverpool-based company, which offers a national service. It even boasts a 24-hour free enquiry line (0800-262329).

Fileric
12 Queenstown Rd SW8   720 4844   (207 3176)
Although it will provide more substantial eats, this quality pâtisserie specialises in canapés – either for you to serve, or with staff provided.

Fina Estampa
150 Tooley St SE1   403 1342
Outside catering for up to 100 can be provided by London's leading Peruvian restaurant. Appropriate music can also be organised.

Food Show
22-23 Hackford Wk SW9   793 1877   (793 1878)
Medium size firm which does a number of high-profile jobs – show biz clients and art gallery receptions make up a good proportion of its work.

The French House Dining Room
49 Dean St W1   437 2477   (287 9109)
The popular Bohemian restaurant in Soho offers an outside catering service for smaller to medium size events.

Annie Fryer Catering
134 Lots Rd SW10   352 7693   (352 4890)
Many of the current 'big names' of the outside catering business served their apprenticeships at this well-established firm.

Gorgeous Gourmets
Unit D, Gresham Way SW19
0181-944 7771   (0181-946 1639)
Flexible firm, providing catering for social and corporate events of all sizes.

Hamlin's of Kensington
3 Abingdon Rd W8   376 2191   (376 2191)
Delicatessen-based firm which caters for small to medium size parties on a fully-serviced or takeaway basis.

Hunt Kendall Catering
10 Barmouth Rd, SW18   0181-870 6202   (0181-870 0602)
Recently established firm (1993) trusted by HM Government to provide Food from England at exhibitions on the continent. Closer to home, it does a full range of business and social catering.

Jackson Gilmour
5 Enterprise Cl, Croydon CR0
0181-665 1855   (0181-665 5325)
What a good idea – prices quoted by this decade-old, wide-ranging caterer include service (and, with some of their menus, wine too) – considerably reducing the pain of budgeting.

Michael Jay The Freelance Chef
13 Tottenham St W1   580 5090   (580 5090)
Mr Jay, who has been in the business for over 15 years, caters for a wide range of small to medium size business and social events.

John (Personal Services)
99d Talbot Rd W11   792 1162   (229 3506)
Catering for small to medium size social events is the speciality of this long-established (1950) firm.

K & M Caterers
110 Forest Hill Rd SE22   0181-299 1057   (0181-693 9086)
"Catering to the City" is the motto here – livery halls a speciality.

Kastoori
188 Upper Tooting Rd SW17   0181-767 7027
This exemplary South Indian vegetarian restaurant in Tooting provides a full outside catering service.

Katie Parsons
Unit 56, Warriner House, 140 Battersea Park Rd SW11
498 9953   (498 1171)
For those looking for a caterer for a smaller to medium size event, Katie offers over a decade of experience in the field.

Kesslers
The Broadwalk, Regents Pk NW1   935 5729   (935 5894)
General outside catering for small to medium size events, from a firm which has particular experience of catering in and around the parks.

LCS
Counties House, Keswick Rd SW15
0181-874 4234   (0181-877 0280)
Large, well-established firm (formerly called London Catering Services), which does some prestigious corporate events.

Leith's
86 Bondway SW8   735 6303   (735 1170)
Eminent ex-restaurateur Pru Leith has a largely honorary role in the company she established – now part of the Compass group – which specialises in catering for middle to larger size corporate events.

Letheby & Christopher
Cheney House, Oaklands Pk, Wokingham RG41
01734-773000   (01734-772111)
Known as a sporting event caterer (Ascot, for example), L&C, now part of the Compass group, generally concentrates its efforts on venues where it is the resident caterer. However, it also offers general outside catering.

The Lumsden Twins
Unit 24, Sleaford St SW8   622 0087   (498 1975)
The name can deceive – a truly family firm this may be, but it is large, mainly corporate receptions which form the mainstay of the business.

Macdonald & Ronan
Unit 53, South Bank Commercial Centre,
140 Battersea Park Rd SW11   498 0017   (498 3103)
Medium size corporate and social caterer, which takes on some prestigious assignments.

Mackintosh Catering
Unit G15, Belgravia Workshops, 157-163 Marlborough Rd N19
281 0483   (272 0343)
Government work is the bread and butter of this well-established medium size firm, which also does social and corporate business.

Mange on the Move
Unit 1, 26 Hartland Rd NW1   284 0349   (483 1542)
Mainly corporate caterer, offering menus at a wide range of prices. Arts and media work is a speciality.

Mange Tout
38 Melgund Rd N5   609 0640   (700 5113)
Audrey Knight caters for small to medium size parties, often with an ethnic/vegetarian twist.

Milburns
The New Restaurant, V&A, Cromwell Rd SW7
581 2159   (225 2357)
This mainly corporate caterer is on the list of a number of the top museums and galleries.

Mimosa
16 Half Moon Lane SE24   733 8838
Small to medium size events are the forte of this delicatessen-based caterer (whose principals used to run the Brixton restaurant, Twenty Trinity Gardens). Mediterranean/French fare, with Moroccan overtones, is the speciality.

Mise en Place
21 Battersea Rise SW11   228 4392   (924 1911)
Smaller to medium size events are the forte of this delicatessen-based caterer.

Philip Moore
Unit 1, Forest Hill Business Ctr, Clyde Vale SE23
0181-699 0255   (0181-699 0856)
Mid-range outfit, catering for a wide range of predominantly social gatherings.

Mosimann's
33 Lowndes St SW1   235 4849   (259 6863)
The smart black outside catering vans of this celebrity chef grace many topnotch events.

The Moving Venue
14 Calico House, Plantation Whf SW11   924 2444   (978 5178)
Established corporate caterer on the list of many of the top venues.

Mustard Caterers
1-3 Brixton Rd SW9   582 8511   (793 1024)
Mustard's reputation for being at the very top end of the more traditional caterers attracts a blue-chip business and social following.

New Quebec Quisine
13 New Quebec St W1   402 0476   (724 6581)
International corporate clients are attracted to this centrally located firm, which puts much emphasis on presentation.

Owen Brothers Catering
Units C3 & C4, Jaggard Way SW12
0181-675 2905   (0181-675 9175)
Flexible organisation, capable of dealing with functions large and small. Package deal buffets can be delivered to your door.

Pacifico Catering
28 Maiden Ln WC2   240 7075   (836 5088)
Mexican catering and Margueritas from the company which runs Covent Garden's Café Pacifico.

Party Ingredients
Kirtling St SW8   627 3800   (720 6249)
Lord Mayor's and state banquets (for the VE50 celebrations, for example) are among the topnotch events claimed by this firm, which is still, 20 years on, run by its founders.

Payne & Gunter
Mayfair House, Belvue Rd, Northolt UB5
0181-842 2224   (0181-845 4302)
This very large firm, now part of the Compass Group, is well-known for sporting event catering but big in banqueting too. It also takes on smaller, mainly corporate work.

The Pie Man Catering Company
23 Pensbury St SW8   627 5232   (720 0094)
With three retail outlets, as well as its central kitchens, this firm takes on everything from the provision of canapés for a small cocktail party to dinner for a couple of hundred.

Alison Price
Unit 5, The Talina Centre, Bagleys Ln SW6
371 5133   (371 5671)
Top-of-the-range general operator whose catering can come in a variety of national flavours.

RGC Events
Unit 4, The Swan Centre, Riverside Rd SW17
0181-947 1213   (0181-944 1895)
Wide-ranging corporate and social caterer, formerly known as the Richard Groves Catering Company.

Rhubarb
Unit 94, Battersea Business Centre, 103-109 Lavender Hl SW11
738 9272   (738 9971)
Young company, already making waves and establishing a fashionable business and social following.

Richmond Caterers
17 Studley Grange Rd W7   0181-567 9090   (0181-566 3698)
Wide-ranging caterer, whose work comprises livery hall banquets, corporate work and larger-scale social entertaining.

Ring & Brymer
Manor House, Manor Farm Rd, Alperton, Middx HA0
0181-566 9222 (0181-991 9636)
City livery hall banqueting specialists (who, having catered for Victoria's Coronation, can claim a fair degree of experience). Otherwise, outside catering is now restricted to sporting events, with more general enquiries being directed to sister Gardner Merchant company, Town & County.

Scott Harris
The Arch, 325 Blucher Rd SE5   701 2132   (252 6313)
"From six guests to a thousand", says the brochure of this general-purpose catering firm, established in 1988 – should cover most eventualities.

Searcy's
124 Bolingbroke Grove SW11   585 0505   (350 1748)
This long-established firm is particularly well known for having its own premises at 30 Pavilion Road SW1, but it also undertakes many outside catering assignments.

Selby's
Unit 56, Warriner House, 140 Battersea Park Rd SW11
498 7455   (498 1171)
Media-world launches make up quite a large proportion of the work here, but the firm also does a fair number of weddings and the like.

Shree Krishna
192-194 Tooting High St SW17   0181-672 4250
This Tooting south Indian restaurant, especially known for its vegetarian cooking, can provide outside catering on a large scale.

Simply Delicious
Unit 5a, 15 Micawber St N1   490 4548   (490 4547)
Upmarket outfit, catering for small to medium size events and attracting a growing proportion of corporate business.

Singapura
78-89 Leadenhall St EC3   929 0089   (621 0366)
South-east Asian outside catering, for smaller to medium size events, from this small City and West End restaurant chain.

Suze Catering
1 Glentworth St NW1   486 8216   (935 3827)
Kiwi caterer for small to medium size functions. Antipodean ingredients are used when possible, and it offers a wide selection of Oz and NZ wines.

Table Talk
Friars Court, 17 Rushworth St SE1   401 3200   (401 9500)
Though quite recently established, this broad-ranging company has already built up a fashionable business and social following.

Tastes Catering
The Foundry Annexe, 65 Glasshill St SE1
721 7267   (721 7268)
Corporate events are the mainstay of this firm, which generally caters for smaller to medium size events.

Top Nosh Cuisine
39 Childebert Road SW17   0181-673 3434   (0181-673 4363)
Corporate cocktail parties are the speciality here – for a few dozen people or for a thousand. The firm is, however, quite happy to take on other jobs.

Town & County
Manor House, Manor Farm Rd, Alperton, Middx HA0
0181-998 8880   (0181-991 9636)
Successors to J Lyons – Royal garden parties are the highest profile part of the activities of this wide-ranging outside caterer (now part of the Gardner Merchant group).

Uncommon Cooks
25 Cannon Wharf, 35 Evelyn St SE8   232 1122   (232 0606)
General middle- to upper-market caterer, most of whose work is corporate.

El Vergel
8 Lant St SE1   357 0057   (357 0056)
Aromatic and spicy South American cuisine, with a moderating Mediterranean influence, is the theme of this specialist caterer.

Veronica's
3 Hereford Rd W2   229 5079   (229 1210)
Period English cooking from different centuries is the attraction of the outside catering service provided by this Bayswater restaurant.

Villandry Dining Rooms
89 Marylebone High St W1   224 3799   (486 1370)
This Marylebone delicatessen/restaurant has a reputation for the quality of its (not inexpensive) cooking, and provides a full outside catering service.

Lorna Wing
Studio 21, The Talina Centre SW6   731 5105   (731 7957)
Top-end company with a reputation for the design of many of its creations and a particular following in the fashion and media worlds.

Wódka
12 St Alban's Gro W8   937 6513   (937 8621)
Polish fare is particularly well suited to canapés (especially if you wash it down with lots of vodka ...). This fashionable Kensington restaurant provides outside catering, generally for parties of up to 100.

CATERERS, KOSHER

Oberlander
1A Cecil Rd NW9   0181-205 5994   (0181-200 8253)

Tony Page
6 Chapmans Park, 378 High Rd NW10
0181-830 4000   (0181-830 2000)

Sharett
Unit A3, Connaught Business Centre, Hyde Estate Rd NW9
0181-200 1400   (0181-200 5055)

Carole Sobell
Unit C, 2-10 Carlisle Rd, NW9
0181-200 8111   (0181-200 3444)

Steven Wolfisz Catering
18 Trevelyan Cr, Harrow HA3   724 5897

CAKES

The following firms are specialists, some of whom can take on almost any design. Harrods and Selfridges also have speciality departments, and a number of the supermarket chains (Waitrose and Safeway, for example) have sample-books from which you can order a surprisingly wide range of special cakes.

Anne Fayrer Cakes
66 Lower Sloane St SW1   730 6277
Novelty and traditional cakes, from this well-established firm.

Jane Asher
24 Cale St SW3   584 6177   (584 6179)
All kinds of celebration cakes with a tendency to the unusual – it does a lot of corporate and logo work.

Final Touch
10 Burfoot Av SW6   371 7646   (371 7649)
Wedding cakes to traditional or modern designs, or novelty cakes of any size.

La Maison des Sorbets
10 Gateway Trading Estate, Hythe Rd NW10
0181-960 0667   (0181-960 1332)
Who says cakes have to be made of, er, cake – why not have one made of ice cream or sorbet?

Margaret's Cakes of Distinction
224 Camberwell Rd SE5   701 1940
Specialists in classic ("with a twist") and West Indian cakes, to order.

Pâtisserie Valerie
215 Brompton Rd SW3   823 9971   (589 4993)
"Continental alternatives to wedding cakes", such as tiered white chocolate cakes and profiterole mountains. There are a number of other branches in central and south west London.

Pierre Péchon
127 Queensway W2   221 7923   (221 0504)
Wedding cake specialists since 1925, it claims. There are branches of these characterful pâtisseries at 27 Kensington Church St W8 (tel 937 9574) and at 4 Chepstow Rd W2 (tel 229 5289).

CATERING EQUIPMENT

If you want to organise catering yourself, but do not have enough china, glasses or chairs, the following companies can help. Practice differs as regards charges for delivery, extra charges for returning items dirty and whether VAT is included in quoted prices. As always, ensure prices you are comparing are quoted on a similar basis.

Cross Catering Hire
12 Shrubbery Rd SW16   0181-769 2267   (0181-677 7282)
General-purpose catering hire. A price list is available on request.

DCS Fairs
105 Constantine Rd NW3   485 5313   (485 4297)
Exhibition suppliers whose services extend from props and theming to the hire of more prosaic items such as coat rails and ashtrays.

Gorgeous Gourmets
Gresham Way SW19   0181-944 7771   (0181-946 1639)
A good basic range of equipment is available for hire from this outside catering company.

Jones Catering Equipment Hire
100 Warner Rd SE5   735 5577   (737 4374)
China, cutlery, glasses, etc. A detailed price list is available.

Jongor
Unit 5, Martinbridge Trading Estate, Lincon Rd, Enfield EN1
0181-443 3333   (0181-805 8710)
Very large banqueting (and conference) hire specialists. A small brochure listing items suitable for weddings is available, which cuts down the bewildering choice.

Just Hire
Unit 5, Davenport Centre, Renwick Rd, Barking IG11
0181-595 8855   (0181-984 1363)
Full range of catering equipment – you can send for an illustrated brochure.

Mitchell Linen Hire
26A Devonshire Cr NW7   0181-346 0330   (0181-346 0546)
Specialists in tablecloths and napkins – available in a wide range of colours.

Planner Catering (Equipment Hire)
Unit 9, Barratt Industrial Park, Gillender St E3
987 2102   (538 3021)
China, cutlery, glasses, etc. A detailed price list is available.

Taylor's Hire
389 Northolt Rd, South Harrow HA2   0181-422 1627
Catering equipment and furniture hire (and sale).

STAFF

If you do not need caterers, but would like some staff to help out, the following will assist.

The Admirable Crichton
6 Camberwell Trading Estate, Denmark Rd SE5
733 8113   (733 7289)
Leading caterer which can also provide staff only.

At Your Service

21B Heathmans Rd SW6   371 0912   (731 6592)
The largest event management staffing company, which has, over only a few years, built up a strong reputation.

Cooks on the Books

Friars Court, 17 Rushworth St SE1   401 3222   (401 9500)
Recently formed agency whose cooks are assessed in the firm's own kitchens before being let loose on the public.

Elite Catering

10 Oxford Circus Av, 231 Oxford St W1
494 3402   (287 4254)
Butlers and other staff from this agency which provides directors' dining room staff.

Esprit & Decorum

1st Floor, Bright Cook House, 139 Upper Richmond Rd, SW15
0181-246 6777   (0181-246 6888)
Young waiters, waitresses and butlers for corporate and private events.

Gastronomique Cooks Agency

Friars Court, 17 Rushworth St SE1   633 9363   (401 9500)
Well established agency which prides itself on matching the right cook to the job.

Edmond James

37 Marlborough, 5 Inner Park Rd SW19
0181-789 8240   (0181-789 8240)
Over just a few years, 'Eddie Walshe' (as this ex-Conran group maître d'hôtel is professionally known) has built up a list of several hundred butlers, who can officiate at everything from cocktails to a shooting party.

Massey's Agency

Premier House, 10 Greycoat Pl SW1   799 1417   (799 1069)
Staff agency (a century and a half old) mainly involved in permanent and temporary placements, but also maintaining a register of occasional staff.

Mrs Hunt's Agency

99d Talbot Rd W11   229 3506   (229 3506)
Domestic staff agency which can provide waiters (who also wash up), butlers, chefs and general staff.

Universal Aunts

PO Box 304 SW4   738 8937
"Britain's original personal service bureau", established in 1921, offers all types of temporary help, including butlers, waitresses and washers-up.

WINE

Almost all the following offer delivery (often free of charge), glass hire and sale-or-return (check the proportion you can send back). Many also supply ice. If you are buying drink in quantity you should certainly shop around – you may find even the big chains will offer special terms for larger orders.

John Armit Wines
5 Royalty Studios, 105 Lancaster Rd W11
727 6846   (727 7133)
*Upmarket merchant which has no shop but does produce an
encyclopaedic (and beautifully produced) list.*

Berry Bros & Rudd
3 St James's St SW1   396 9666   (396 9611)
*St James's merchant with wonderfully Dickensian premises, and a
long, helpfully discursive list.*

Caves de la Madeleine
82 Wandsworth Bridge Rd SW6   736 6145   (371 8324)
*Parson's Green shop whose services include timed deliveries and, if
desired, providing bottles semi-uncorked – don't forget you may want
to return some, though.*

Corney & Barrow
12 Helmet Row EC1   251 4051   (608 1373)
*Well-known City wine merchant. Most sales are from its list, but it
has a retail shop at 194 Kensington Park Road W11 (tel 221 5122).*

Fortnum & Mason
181 Piccadilly W1   734 8040   (437 3278)
*F&M's wide-ranging wine department specialises in famous name
vineyards, the unusual, and the unashamedly expensive.*

Harrods
Knightsbridge SW1   730 1234
*Harrods offers a good, if not inexpensive, selection of champagnes,
wines and spirits and a high level of service.*

Justerini & Brooks
61 St James's St SW1   493 8721   (499 4653)
*Well-known St James's merchant. Although there is a retail shop,
most sales are from their long list.*

Lay & Wheeler
117 Gosbecks Road, Gosbecks Pk, Colchester CO2
01206-764446   (01206-560002)
*Well respected out-of-town merchant which emphasises the breadth
of its "value for money" selections.*

Lea & Sandeman
301 Fulham Rd SW10   376 4767   (351 0275)
*Wines are carefully chosen by an enthusiastic team. There are three
shops – the others are at 211 Kensington Church Street W8 (tel 221
1982) and 51 High St SW13 (tel 0181-878 8643).*

Majestic Wine Warehouses
Albion Wharf Hester Rd SW11 (and other branches)
223 2983   (223 2983)
*Majestic, which has branches throughout London, offers a full service,
including ice, glasses, sale-or-return, and delivery to your door. The
minimum order of a case (which can be mixed) is unlikely to be much
of a problem if you're giving a party.*

Oddbins
Head office 0181-944 4400   (0181-944 4411)
*London's leading off-licence chain, particularly well-known for its
seven-for-six, sometimes six-for-five champagne offers.*

Roberson
348 Kensington High St W14   371 2121   (371 4010)
High quality merchant, with a particularly wide range of stock.

Selfridges
Oxford St W1   629 1234
The well-known department store has an impressive wine selection.

Soho Wine Supply
18 Percy St W1   636 8490   (916 7857)
Old-established Soho suppliers, specialising in champagnes and whiskies.

Thresher
Regional office   01707-328244
Thresher is the UK's biggest retailer of wine – the more upmarket shops are called Wine Racks.

The Vintage House
42 Old Compton St W1   437 2592   (734 1174)
Champagnes, malt whiskies, liqueurs and claret are the specialities of this Soho shop of long standing.

Waitrose
Head Office   01344-424680   (01344-825255)
One of the best supermarket wine departments. Glass hire is among the services offered.

ICE

In case your needs are greater than your local off-licence can provide…

Ace Speedy Ice
13 Claylands Rd SW8   735 4966
The proprietor, Mr Marenghi, is a third-generation icemonger. Dry ice is also available, with notice.

PARTY PLANNERS

If you are organising a big party there is a lot to be said for bringing in the professionals. With an event of any scale, it is a full-time job to ensure everything comes together on the night – a party planner does the worrying for you, and lets you get on with enjoying yourself. In addition, assuming you choose the right planners you may get a better party for your money, with greater flair and professionalism.

The term 'party planner' covers a multitude of sins. Many companies have grown out of caterers or entertainers, and their business often emphasises their original speciality. Others are independent experts who have no formal links with any particular caterers or other suppliers and are free to help you choose the right contractors for your event.

Some planners get right down to the detail, for example ensuring invitations are correctly addressed and organising the 'placement' (table seating). Others regard their job as done if they organise a good dinner and the band plays.

Some work on commission, others will charge a fee. Consider the level of service you want. As with all aspects of planning a party, try to be clear in advance about what you are looking for and how much you are prepared to pay. Don't be afraid to ask the planner about their experience of similar events – there should be no objection if you ask to speak to previous clients.

The terminology of who does what is becoming more and more confusing. In the corporate arena, some firms have decided that 'event managers' (or sometimes 'event designers') is a more dignified term for what they do – in practice, their actual work differs little from that of some of the firms which describe themselves as 'party planners'. So far as organising a bash in London is concerned, there may, therefore, be little practical difference between going to a party planner and an event manager.

The organisation and planning of themed environments – which are now, weddings aside, de rigueur for most parties on any scale – should be within the competence of most firms.

ACE
39 Guildford Rd, Lightwater GU18
01276-452131 (01276-452150)
Larger themed parties for corporate customers are the speciality.

Countess Alexander of Tunis
59 Wandsworth Common Westside SW18
0181-874 4831 (0181-877 9487)
Lady Alexander organises top-flight events, generally for corporate clients.

Bailey Carr
13 Cinnamon Row, Plantation Whf SW11
924 6400 (924 6366)
Event designer, serving the corporate market, especially the City.

Banana Split
11 Carlisle Rd NW9   0181-200 1234   (0181-200 1121)
Professional planner which puts a lot of emphasis on its design work. Its discos are well-known and it can provide its own marquees.

William Bartholomew
18 The Talina Centre, Bagleys Ln SW6   731 8328   (384 1807)
One of the top all-round party planners – often cited by competitors as the man to beat.

Beadon Daniel Events
14 Ivory House, Plantation Whf SW11   978 7400   (978 7447)
Wide-ranging private and corporate events organiser, which places a lot of emphasis on design.

Bentley's
26a Winders Rd SW11   223 7900   (978 4062)
Well-known firm which has organised some very prestigious parties.

Business Pursuits
12 Ferrier St SW18   0181-877 3600   (0181-871 2242)
Party planning is among the services of this large, exclusively corporate events manager.

Mark Butler Associates
2 Goldhawk Mews W12   0181-743 0743   (0181-743 9743)
*"Creative event management" in the UK and France, for the
corporate market.*

Buzz Productions
Westway Studios, 8 Olaf St W11
0181-469 3744   (0181-469 3744)
*Specialist themer, whose Westway Studios base is a good site for
events, but which also does much work elsewhere.*

Chance
321 Fulham Rd SW10   376 5995   (376 3598)
*Andrew Chance is one of the biggest names in party planning,
particularly for events with a strong entertainments content.*

Nicki Colwyn Associates
29 Oakley Gdns SW3   351 2875   (376 8187)
*Lady Colwyn's independent planning company does a wide range of
corporate and private work.*

Complete Events
5 Beechmore Rd SW11   610 1770   (01635-202467)
*Party organiser specialising in large parties (private and corporate),
particularly those involving marquees.*

Stephen Congdon
52 Bermondsey St SE1   357 9159   (357 9157)
*Witty design and presentation has attracted some top corporate
names to this growing company. Catering is from its own kitchen.*

Creative Practice
35 Albemarle St W1   495 6710
*Organising functions with a cultural twist – usually for corporate
clients – is one of the services offered by this arts and museum
consultancy.*

CWA Party Planners
Charlton House, Searle Rd, Farnham GU9
01252-724888   (01252-724849)
*"No party too large or small" is the claim of this relatively recent
newcomer (1992), which has a variety of corporate and individual
clients.*

Neil Duttson Party Organising
5 Cranleigh Mews, Cabul Rd SW11   738 0300   (738 2969)
*Discos and atmospheric lighting are often a feature of the mainly
social occasions organised by this recently established party planner.*

Fait Accompli
Victoria House, 1A Gertrude St SW10   352 2777   (352 8118)
*Discreet and independent party planner which does some top social
business but which has a growing element of corporate work.*

The Finishing Touch
22 The Mall SW14   0181-878 7555   (0181-878 8444)
*Event management service, specialising in corporate functions,
conference events and teambuilding.*

The German Event Management Company
116 Finchley Ln NW4   0181-203 0626   (0181-203 8996)
*The name says it all about this specialist division of Lawson Ross
Management (see also).*

I.D.E.A.S.
Broadway Studios, 28 Tooting High St
0181-672 4465   (0181-767 3247)
General event manager with, as its full name (Inventive Delegate Event Arrangement Services) suggests, a very businessy slant.

In-Event
8 Westminster Court, Hipley St, Old Woking, Surrey GU22
01483-740736   (01483-740563)
Mainly corporate planner, which takes on a wide variety of assignments.

Inventive
121b Castelnau SW13   0181-741 9099   (0181-748 0351)
Themed event planning is among the services of this young company whose clients include a number of major advertising agencies.

Juliana's
99 Geraldine Rd SW18   937 1555   (381 3872)
One of the longest-established firms, offering a full party planning service.

Lawson Ross Management
116 Finchley Ln NW4   0181-203 0626   (0181-203 8996)
Party planners, designers and entertainment consultants, specialising in events with a national flavour – Russian, French, Scottish, etc.

Lickity Split
World's End Studios, 134 Lots Rd SW10
823 3637   (376 8700)
Designer and management of larger-scale events, often with a corporate and charitable twist.

Lillingston Associates
134 Lots Rd SW10   376 8600   (376 8700)
"The historical venue and event management company", whose speciality is functions (including weddings) at castles and country houses.

Dora Lowenstein Associates
39 Thurloe Pl SW7   823 8838   (581 2053)
A very high PR profile often distinguishes the assignments of this specialist events management and marketing consultancy.

Magnum Events
19 Churton St SW1   932 0006   (932 0676)
Specialists in discreet management of social and business functions for, among others, rock and screen stars.

The Major Event Company
40 Peterborough Rd, SW6   371 8881   (371 0800)
Event management company whose business is mainly corporate, but which also includes some private and charity work.

Mark & Bert
48B The Market Place NW11
0181-455 3741   (0181-455 2325)
Mark & Bert promote trendy nightclubs, and also make their expertise available as planners of corporate and social events.

Mask Entertainments
The Arts Depot, 26 Pancras Rd NW1   278 1001   (278 9001)
Founded in 1988, Mask is a party organising company which sells itself on its creativity. As well having as its own venue (The Arts Depot), it boasts an in-house inflatables firm (The Balloon Artist).

Merlin Design & Production
29 Oakley Gdns SW3   912 0012   (912 0013)
Specialists in design and realisation of corporate events and parties.

Moyles Masterkey
Yew Tree House, Ombersley, Worcs WR9
01905-620848   (01905-621238)
If you want to entertain in the grand manner, but lack your own manor, you might like to approach this firm. It claims, over some 20 years in business, to have built up an unparalleled degree of access to a network of stately piles not generally open to the public.

Catherine Owens
33 Brookville Rd SW6   610 1698   (381 9462)
Independent party consultant, who takes on a great variety of work.

Party Planners
56 Ladbroke Gr W11   229 9666   (727 6001)
Lady Elizabeth Anson – often claimed to be the inventor of the whole party planning concept – maintains her position as doyenne of the London party scene. She is not tied to any particular suppliers and emphasises her willingness to accommodate smaller budgets.

Party Professionals
33 Kensington Park Rd W11   221 3438   (243 2985)
Discreet, independent party planner, which emphasises its detailed approach.

Planit Events
15 Nottingham Rd SW17   0181-682 4900   (0181-682 0602)
Corporate event managers probably best known for its management of the Spitalfields venue, but who also work elsewhere. For examples of its events, web surfers can check out http://www.planit.uk.com.

Philip Pleydell-Pearce
90 Gladstone Rd SW19   0181-540 3070   (0181-540 3070)
If you're looking for very personal service in organising your event, you might like to consult Mr Pleydell-Pearce (a former Deputy Banqueting Manger at the Dorchester), who has been in business on his own account since 1994.

The Jonathan Seaward Organisation
Suite 3, Unit 24, The Coda Centre, Munster Rd SW6
386 0066   (386 1929)
Well-reputed, wide-ranging party planner which takes on a good mix of work. It is strong on the technical side, and now, of course, has its own web-site at http://www.jso.co.uk.

Theme Traders
The Stadium, Oaklands Rd NW2
0181-452 8518   (0181-450 7322)
Themed event specialists, offering a very large stock of props, backdrops and costumes, and, if required, full production facilities.

Ubique
2 Drayson Mews W8   937 6446   (938 3728)
*Corporate event manager specialising in organising hospitality in
innovative locations worldwide.*

The Ultimate Experience
205 St John's Hill SW11   738 2544   (738 2556)
*Growing corporate events manager (which also does a small amount
of work for private individuals). It has its own disco business,
Ultimate Productions.*

UpStage Theatrical Events
1 Magdalen St SE1   403 6510   (403 6511)
*Events with theatrical flair, sometimes on a grand scale, are the
speciality of this recently established partnership (1993) between a
catering professional and a thesp'.*

Urban Productions
63-65 Goldney Rd W9   286 1700   (286 1709)
*"Nothing is a problem" is one of the slogans of this funky firm
(formerly called Urban Party Culture) which has attracted some very
high profile work. Might its style be right for you? Surf over to its site
at http://www.urban-productions.co.uk to find out.*

Westway Events
28 Winchester Av NW6   0181-964 3600   (0181-964 3665)
*Design-led party planner specialising in media-related events, often
on a large scale.*

ENTERTAINMENTS

*If you have the budget, do consider whether a few hundred pounds
spent on performers, perhaps some musicians, a magician or a
caricaturist, might not help turn your party into a memorable event.*

*Music is, of course, the most common type of entertainment.
The best way of finding the right musicians for your event is to go to
an agency – it should be able to find not only a good band, but also
one which is right for the party.*

*Many of the companies below deal with entertainers of all types.
Most of the general agencies can provide a disco and many can
provide casinos and other themed events. For the most
comprehensive list of every type of entertainment, refer to the
White Book, the 'bible' of the entertainment business (in major
reference libraries).*

Acker's International Jazz Agency
53 Cambridge Mansions, Cambridge Rd SW11
978 5886   (978 5882)
*Many top names on the books, not least Mr Acker Bilk and his
Paramount Jazz Band.*

Alternative Arts
47A Brushfield St E1   375 0441   (375 0484)
*Arts organisation concentrating on new artists and new ideas. It is
worth getting in touch if you are looking for ideas or introductions to
up-and-coming performers.*

American Theme Events
62 Beechwood Rd, South Croydon CR2
0181-657 2813   (0181-651 6080)
A portable Wild West town, with appropriate entertainments.

John Austin Organisation
25 Delamere Gdns NW7   0181-959 1501   (0181-959 1501)
*John Austin's specialities are theme nights, discos, casinos and
corporate events.*

Paul Bailey Agency
22 Wolsey Rd, East Molesey, KT8
0181-941 2034   (0181-941 6304)
*Entertainments and more. Mr Bailey also offers a comprehensive
events management service, mainly to corporate clients.*

Barn Dance Agency
62 Beechwood Rd, Croydon CR2
0181-657 2813   (0181-651 6080)
*Any sort of folk music – pipers, Morris Men, Irish Ceilidh – as well as
barn dancing. Wedding bookings are popular.*

Bravingers
274-276 Queenstown Rd SW8   978 2536   (978 2541)
*Mr Morrall has been providing music for parties since 1969, and
brings a lot of experience to the job of marrying the music to the
event.*

British Speakers Bureau
BSB House, 12 Nottingham Pl W1   224 5050   (224 6060)
*Celebrity after-dinner speakers are the speciality of this agency whose
work is, of necessity, mainly corporate.*

Cahill Entertainment
1 Hadley Court, 83 Hadley Rd, New Barnet, Herts EN5
0181-449 6589   (0181-441 8783)
*Ms Cahill provides all types of entertainment, including magicians and
cabaret, and music from harpists to six-piece bands.*

Caledonian Enterprises
97 Erskine Rd, Sutton SM1   0181-644 4744   (0181-641 4135)
*All types of Scottish entertainment can be provided – pipes, drums,
dancers, and Ceilidh bands.*

Capital Productions
194A Station Rd, Edgware, Middx HA8
0181-905 4550   (0181-905 4463)
*Entertainment agency in business since 1979. Its list of suggested
bands is useful if you're lacking inspiration.*

Celestial Sounds
20 Middle Mead, Steyning, W Sussex BN44   01903-812662
*All sorts of music for functions, from jazz, soul and Ceilidh bands to
string quartets, harpists and wind ensembles.*

Crowd Pullers
158 Old Woolwich Rd SE10   0181-305 0074   (0181-858 9045)
*Street performers booking agency – clowns, jugglers, fire-eaters,
street bands, etc.*

Crown Entertainments
103 Bromley Common, Bromley BR2
0181-464 0454   (0181-290 4038)
*Entertainment agency which can provide a wide range of bands,
discos, cabaret acts, TV personalities and speakers.*

Dark Blues Management
30 Stamford Brook Rd W6   0181-743 3292   (0181-740 5520)
"The live entertainment specialists" – a quality agency with a quarter of a century's experience.

Fanfare 3000
The Folly, Pinner Hill Rd, Pinner HA5
0181-429 3000   (0181-868 6497)
Music, entertainments and other support for the party organiser.

Fox Artist Management
Concorde House, 101 Shepherd's Bush Rd W6
602 8822   (603 2352)
Radio DJs, TV presenters and personalities, also after-dinner speakers.

Grosvenor Productions
12 Sherwood St W1   734 6755   (494 0608)
Large entertainment agency, owned by the Granada Group, supplying acts, artistes and themed events.

Hazemead
3rd Floor, 18 Hanover St W1   629 4817   (629 5668)
Comedians, singers and after-dinner speakers.

The Highland Gathering
135 Colchester Rd E10   0181-556 8914
Pipers.

JLA
13 Short's Gdns WC2   240 0413   (240 0371)
Business, motivational and after-dinner speakers, comedians and cabaret artistes.

Le Cap Entertainment
25 Dighton Court, John Ruskin St SE5   0976 157806
Stage event management and organisers of smaller-scale entertainments.

London Music Agency
Wayside, Epping Gn CM16   01992-578617   (01992-578618)
Although music (including some off-beat acts) is the speciality, this agency can provide any type of entertainment.

Music Management
PO Box 1105 SW1   589 8133   (584 7944)
Well-established music consultancy, now in its second decade, and with a blue-chip client list. It provides a wide range of musicians, from classical guitar to salsa, from swing to rock and roll.

Oddballs International
31-35 Pitfield St N1   250 1333   (250 3999)
Juggling suppliers, jugglers and juggling workshops.

Opus Seven Music
32 Upper Mall W6   0181-563 7253   (0181-563 7253)
Music for all occasions – corporate events to weddings.

Party Jazz
26 Harold Rd E11   0181-539 5229   (0181-556 9545)
Small jazz agency providing bands of all sizes.

Penguins Entertainment
Jester House,143 Arthur Rd, Windsor SL4
01753-833811   (01753-833754)
Bands, entertainers and discos can be provided by this party organising company.

Peter Johnson Entertainments
Hastings Road, Hawkhurst, Kent TN18
01580-754822   (01580-754808)
Gladiators, a Wild West adventure and a Bolivian folk band are just three of the acts listed in the helpful – priced, for once – colour brochure of this large entertainment agency. It can also, of course, provide more regular requirements.

Jo Peters Management
56 Macready Hse, 75 Crawford St W1   724 6555   (724 5269)
Ms Peters concentrates on finding entertainers of all types, mainly for corporate clients. She does not represent individual performers.

Norman Phillips Agency
2 Hartopp Rd, Sutton Coldfield, W Midlands B74
0121-308 1267   (0121-308 5191)
One of the largest entertainment agencies, with over 35 years' experience. After-dinner speakers are a speciality.

Nic Picot Agency
6 Thrush Gn, Harrow HA2   0181-866 5585   (0181-868 3374)
General entertainment agency specialising in magic. A helpful, priced brochure is available.

Prelude
The Old Stables, 10 Timber Ln, Caterham, Surrey CR3
01883-344300   (01883-347712)
General agency offering a wide range of music and live entertainments and specialising in corporate work.

Prime Performers
The Studio, 5 Kidderpore Av NW3   431 0211   (431 3813)
All types of performers and corporate entertainments – "the largest consultancy in the UK", it claims.

The Puppet Centre Trust
BAC, Lavender Hill SW11   228 5335
Information and advice centre for all forms of puppetry. It provides an information pack and publishes a directory of professional puppeteers.

Mike Reed Promotions
27 Ladywood Rd, Cuxton, Rochester ME2
01634-723181   (01634-721414)
Bands, discos, comedians, stag/hen nights – Mr Reed's assignments range from pubs and clubs to corporate events.

Sardi's
6 Redbridge Ln E, Redbridge, Ilford IG4
0181-551 6720   (0181-551 1200)
Entertainment for all occasions – from children's parties, via weddings, to corporate promotions and theme nights.

Sound Advice
30 Artesian Rd W2   229 2219   (229 9870)
"For 15 years, Sound Advice has been producing great live music for private, corporate and university clients". Its performers have appeared at everything from rock festivals to society weddings.

Splitting Images Lookalike Agency
29 Mortimer Ct, Abbey Rd NW8   286 8300   (286 8300)
A famous face to grace your party.

Sproule Entertaiments
29 Craven Rd W2   706 1550   (706 1546)
Piano entertainers are a speciality, but this agency can provide any type of music.

Sternberg-Clarke
Russell House, Spencer Court, 140 Wandsworth High St SW18
0181-877 1102   (0181-874 4402)
Everything from the off-beat – didgeridoo players and Chinese acrobats, for example – to the more conventional attractions of jazz and dance bands.

TOASTMASTERS

One of the most difficult events at larger parties is marshalling the guests so that they are in the right place at the right time. A toastmaster – apart from his traditional rôle of introducing speakers and so on – can be very useful as a 'sheepdog'.

National Association of Toastmasters
The Old Coach House, Gleanings Mews, St Margarets St, Rochester ME1   01634-402684   (01634-402684)
One of the two big toastmasters' associations – it is happy to send out lists of members.

Society of London Toastmasters
148 Park Cr, Erith, Kent DA8   01322-341465   (01322-402619)
The oldest of the toastmasters' organisations.

Toastmasters
21 Northcotts, Old Hatfield AL9
01707-251719   (01707-251719)
Bernard Sullivan got his MBE for being a toastmaster. His wife organises toastmasters for all types of occasion.

MILITARY BANDS

Blues & Royals
Hyde Park Barracks SW7   414 2525   (414 2599)

Grenadier Guards
Wellington Barracks SW1   414 3267   (414 3236)

Irish Guards
Chelsea Barracks SW1   414 4519   (414 4349)

The Life Guards
Combermere Barracks, Windsor, Berks SL4
01753-755209   (01753-755281)

Welsh Guards
Chelsea Barracks SW1   414 4516   (414 4530)

ENTERTAINMENTS, MURDER

Accidental Productions (Murder by Accident)
117 Cremer Business Centre, 37 Cremer St E2
613 0822   (613 0822)
Murder evenings, game shows, pantomimes and comedy videos.

Clive Panto Productions
Waters Edge, Hurley-on-Thames, Berks SL6
01628-826999   (01628-820000)
*This firm (which incorporates Murder My Lord?) writes murder
mysteries, pantomimes, game shows and movies based on the gossip
and scandal current in any particular group (or workplace).*

Initiative Unlimited
12A Station Rd NW7   0181-959 6579   (0181-801 0659)
*Providers of challenging, participative events, such as murder
mysteries, treasure hunts and themed dinners.*

CHILDREN'S ENTERTAINMENT

*There are many entertainers who help amuse the kids at parties –
some of whom are happy to take over the whole event. Local
recommendations are probably the best way to find a clown or
puppeteer. An alternative is to approach one of the general agencies
listed under Entertainments. The following are specialists in looking
after kids.*

Childsplay Event Services
Briar House, Caldbec Hl, Battle, E Sussex TN33
01424-775450   (01424-775450)
*Anything relating to larger-scale events involving children, from
entertainments to crèches.*

Crêchendo
St Luke's Hall, Adrian Mews, Ifield Rd SW10
259 2727   (259 2700)
*"Action-packed" gym-parties for children of all ages. Themed events
(with entertainers such as face-painters) and bouncy castle hire are
also available.*

Puddleduck
10 Faulkner House, Horne Way SW15
0181-788 7240   (0181-780 5024)
*All-in themed kids' party organising service for those with a fair
budget. Visits by storybook characters can be arranged.
Miniaturised real food is a speciality.*

DISCOS

Banana Split
11 Carlisle Rd NW9   0181-200 1234   (0181-200 1121)
Discos from a well-known party planner.

William Bartholomew
18 The Talina Centre, Bagleys Ln SW6   731 8328   (384 1807)
One of the top party planners, particularly well known for its discos.

Ceroc Parties
Unit 3, Glenthorne Mews, 115a Glenthorne Rd W6
0181-846 8563   (0181-846 8571)
Teach your friends the elements of continental-style rock 'n' roll dancing. The evening starts with a beginners' class, and you then twirl the night away.

Chance
321 Fulham Rd SW10   376 5995   (376 3598)
One of the biggest names in quality discos.

Christian's
1 Lovegroves, Chineham, Basingstoke RG24
01256-470041   (01256-51369)
Rather more than a disco – performs at some top venues.

Exclusive Entertainments
PO Box 90, Egham, Surrey TW20
01784-471716   (01784-437199)
Reasonably priced discos.

Guy Stevens
2-5 Old Bond St W1   499 7318   (499 7517)
Fifteen years in the disco business – weddings are a speciality.

Jade Entertainments
13 Park Pde W3   0181-993 0993   (0181-723 7904)
Mobile discos, sound and lighting equipment for sale or hire. Also Laser karaoke systems and children's disco parties.

Joffins
Suite 3, Unit 24, The Coda Centre, Munster Rd SW6
386 0066   (386 1929)
The disco arm of the Jonathan Seaward organisation, one of the leading party planners.

Juliana's
99 Geraldine Rd SW18   937 1555   (381 3872)
One of the best-known names in top quality discos provides a worldwide service.

Mobi-Deque
3 Park Road Industrial Estate, Park Rd, Swanley, Kent BR8
01322-667775   (01322-615252)
Professional disco operator, established for over a quarter of a century, who can also provide internal lighting and PA systems. It has a shop selling disco equipment and party novelties.

Penguins Entertainment
Jester House, 143 Arthur Rd, Windsor SL4
01753-833811   (01753-833754)
Entertainment agency particularly known for its discos.

Scorpio Discotheque & Event Services
26 Princes Park Av, Hayes UB3
0181-561 5944   (0181-561 4092)
Proprietor Mike Lovelock's speciality is providing quality discos – he has been under contract to the Grosvenor House hotel, for example, for over 15 years. He also offers broader technical and event management services.

Sounds Good to Me
387 Liverpool Rd N1   700 7749   (607 2727)
A range of disco systems, with or without DJs. Also stage lighting, club effects and smoke.

Ultimate Productions
205 St John's Hl SW11   738 2544   (738 2556)
Disco and night club installations – part of The Ultimate Experience event management company.

Zinos
503A Fuham Rd SW6 1HH   385 3439   (385 5706)
Well-established disco operator, which can provide lighting (on quite a scale, if required) and marquees from its own equipment.

DISCO EQUIPMENT

Abbey Acoustics
775 Harrow Road NW10   0181-960 7212   (0181-960 4220)
Disco equipment hire.

Disco-Tech
775 Harrow Rd, College Pk NW10
0181-960 4220   (0181-968 0797)
Disco equipment hire.

PA Music
172 High Rd N2   0181-883 4350   (0181-883 5117)
Sound, lighting and special effects hire.

Young's
20 Malden Rd NW5   485 1115   (267 6769)
Wide range of disco equipment for hire.

CASINOS AND INDOOR AMUSEMENTS

Casinos are a very popular after-dinner diversion, even if, thanks to the gaming laws, you can only win confetti money.

Blue Moon Casino
6R Atlas Village, Oxgate Ln NW2
0181-200 8229   (0181-200 8229)
Mobile casinos with croupiers, for hire.

Cabaret Casino Associates
Brunswick House, Brunswick Gr, Cobham KT11
01932-867486   (01932-867487)
Casinos, race nights, Scalextric, bingo and wheel of fortune.

Carnival Creative Hospitality
Half Acre, Denham, Bucks UB9
01895-833822   (01895-833456)
Casinos and indoor 'games night' equipment – basketball machines, skittle alleys, golf-swing analysers, filmed horse racing and so on.

Casino Entertainment Services
1 Kingsbridge, 172 Lordship Rd N16
0181-809 1439   (01788-890 589)
Gaming tables with or without croupiers.

FIREWORKS

End the party with a bang! The professionals emphasise that, unless you have an enormous budget, it is much better to have a short, impressive display than a longer, less intensive one.

Dynamic Fireworks
Unit 17, Pear Tree Business Ctr, Stanway, Colchester CO3
01206-762123   (01206-762162)
Display specialists also offering quality DIY packages.

Fantastic Fireworks
Rocket Hse, Redbourn, Herts   01582-485555   (01582-485545)
A speciality of this company is large-scale productions combining fireworks with music and lasers. Packs for more modest events are also available.

The Firework Company
Gunpowder Plot, Bridge St, Uffculme, Cullompton, Devon EX15
01884-840504   (01884-841142)
Send for the helpful brochure setting out the various all-in packages which cater for most price levels. Special displays can also be provided.

Le Maitre Fireworks
312 Purley Way, Croydon CR0
0181-680 2400   (0181-646 1955)
Fireworks and effects company whose work has stretched from Rolling Stones concerts to the G7 Summit display at Buck' House.

Pains Fireworks
The Old Chalkpit, Romsey Rd, Whiteparish SP5
01794-884040   (01794-884015)
A firm responsible for some of the biggest displays (and which also provides a useful brochure describing its DIY packages). 'Dancing waters' – fountains synchronised with music – can also be orchestrated.

Shell Shock
South Manor Farm, Bramfield, Nr Halesworth IP19
01986-784469   (01986-784582)
Specialist international firework display company, providing "in- and outdoor spectaculars".

LASERS

The following are the specialists. For smaller shows, consult the disco operators.

Laser Creations International
55 Merthyr Ter SW13   0181-741 5747   (0181-748 9879)
One of the top laser companies. The Royal Tournament is one of its annual fixtures.

Laser Grafix
Unit 15, Orchard Rd, Royston SG8
01763-248846   (01763-246306)
"The creative force in lasers" – like most of the big firms, it does a lot of corporate and large-scale work

MARQUEES

The most traditional type is the canvas tent supported by poles with external guy-ropes, but on constricted London sites, a clear-span, or frame tent, which is free standing, will probably be more suitable. The structure is only the beginning and you should explore the types of linings available and the availability of furniture and, if appropriate, dance floors and heating. All but linings can, of course, be organised separately, but one-stop shopping will be much simpler.

Barkers Marquees
47 Osborne Rd, Thornton Heath CR7
0181-653 1988   (0181-653 2932)
Full range supplier, a century old, also offering event organisation and allied services.

Belle Tents
Owls Gate, Davidstow, Camelford, Cornwall PL32
01840-261556   (01840-261556)
The Savile Row of the marquee world – bespoke tents.

Black & Edgington
30 Marshgate Ln E15   0181-221 3000   (0181-534 4134)
One of the leading suppliers of marquees and other temporary structures.

Alfred Bull & Co
Woolbridge Meadows, Bypass Rd, Guildford GU1
01483-575492   (01483-573448)
Long established Surrey-based company, offering marquees, frame tents and a full range of accessories.

John M Carter
Industrial Est, Winchester Rd, Basingstoke RG22
01256-24434   (01256-816209)
Suppliers of marquees, structures and related equipment for functions of all sizes, private and corporate.

Charles Dean
29 Farrer Rd N8   700 5411   (609 5125)
Steel framed clearspan marquees.

London Garden Marquees
17 Ouseley Rd SW12   0181-672 2580
Navy blue and yellow mini marquees of a size (3m x 5m) to fit most London gardens. Space permitting, multiple marquees can be fitted together.

The London Marquee Co
5 Beechmore Rd, London SW11   610 1770   (01635-202467)
The tent arm of events manager, Complete Events.

M&B Marquees
Premier House, Tennyson Dr, Pitsea, Basildon SS13
01268-558002   (01268-552783)
National network supplier of frame marquees of all sizes, and also luxurious interiors.

Marquees over London
Unit 15, Ferrier Street Industrial Est, Old York Rd SW18
0181-875 1966   (0181-875 9008)
Frame tents, suited to London's many constrained spaces, and also to larger park areas.

Owen Brown
Station Rd, Castle Donnington DE7
01332-850000 (01332-850005)
*The UK's largest supplier of marquees and temporary structures. It
does a lot of upmarket corporate work.*

Stitches
7a Highshore Rd SE15   732 4976   (277 8271)
Traditional and frame marquees, and all related equipment.

Yeo Paull Dyas Marquees
Portswood Hse, Third Av, Millbrook, Southampton SO9
01489-571797   (01489-571798)
*One of the market leaders, offering a wide range of structures for
private and corporate functions.*

FLORISTS

*The following operators are mainly specialists, often involved in lavish
arrangements and theming. In some cases the firms are effectively
designers of whole sets in which flowers may be the leading, but not
the solo, performer – sharing the limelight with herbs, fruits, shells
and other props.*

*If you have a good local florist, it should be able to help with smaller
occasions. The venue itself and friends are other possible sources of
inspiration.*

Bill & Ben's Greenhouse
3 Baker's Row EC1   696 9988   (696 9948)
*Contract and special events florist, which includes tropical plants
amongst its range.*

Blooming Marvellous
Unit 152, Battersea Business Centre, 99-109 Lavender HI SW11
228 1203   (228 1203)
*Well-established function florist, whose particular strength is the "wild
and unusual".*

Garry Cherrill
11 Thurloe Place Mews SW7   225 3725   (225 3725)
Freelance events florist, specialising in the exotic.

Caroline Dickenson
Hyde Park Hotel, 66 Knightsbridge SW1
245 9599   (259 5014)
*Society florist who does a lot of top corporate and party planners'
work. Regular flower-arranging courses are offered.*

Susie Edwards
PO Box 7704 SW1   0860-546468   (340 0349)
*A complete floral service – mainly for smaller to medium size
assignments – from a lady with three decades' experience as a
freelance arranger (and who is the author of an encyclopaedia of
flower arranging).*

The Flower Van
81 Fulham Rd SW3   589 1852   (838 0982)
*The flower shop at the entrance to the Conran Shop also does event
floristry, sometimes on a grand scale.*

Edward Goodyear at Claridge's
45 Brook St W1   629 1508   (495 0524)
'Court florist', with four warrants to prove it.

Sophie Hanna Flowers
Arch 48, New Covent Garden Market, Nine Elms Ln SW8
720 0841   (720 1756)
Upmarket firm which also offers a discreet party planning service.

David Jones
108A Bishops Rd SW6   0181-875 9040   (0181-875 9040)
*Well-reputed florists, tending to a more traditional style. Mr Jones can
also undertake more general party design work, harmonising lighting,
flowers, table linen and so on.*

Moyses Stevens
157 Sloane St SW1   259 9303   (730 3002)
*Long-established (1876) florist happy to provide flowers in any style
but perhaps best known for a fairly traditional approach.*

Jane Packer
56 James St W1   935 2673   (486 5097)
*Over 15 years, Jane Packer has built up a firm which, apart from a
large party-related business, includes schools in London and Tokyo.
She also has a branch in St John's Wood (tel 586 2766).*

Pesh Flowers
31 Denmark Hl SE5   703 9124   (703 9275)
Busy Camberwell flower shop, which also does some event work.

Detta Phillips
2 Culford Mansions, Culford Gardens SW3
581 8985   (581 8601)
*Well-reputed function florist who does a good range of work, including
some top venues.*

Michael Pickworth
99 Notting Hill Gt W11   727 3222   (727 3222)
*Mr Pickworth has been in the business for a quarter of a century and
does party business internationally. His speciality is a "natural,
country house style".*

Pulbrook & Gould
127 Sloane St SW1   730 0030   (730 0722)
*The best of the big-name, shop-based florists – the training ground
for many of the leading names who now have their own businesses.*

Town & County Flowers
131 Wandsworth Bridge Rd SW6   736 4683   (371 9706)
*Upmarket firm whose business includes a lot of work with leading
party planners.*

Kenneth Turner
1-5 Mount St W1   355 3880   (495 1607)
*The top individual name in the business, with an international
following.*

Steven Woodhams
60 Ledbury Rd W11
0181-964 9818 (functions)   (0181-964 9848)
*Function florist (also with a shop) whose services range all the way
"from providing a table decoration to the installation of an English
country garden".*

ICE SCULPTOR

Duncan Hamilton
5 Lampton House Cl SW19   0181-944 9787   (0181-944 9787)
The UK's only full-time ice-sculptor. The clarity of Mr Hamilton's blocks of ice is such that they are also in demand on the continent.

BALLOONS

With a little imagination, balloons can make even the barest space festive at relatively modest expense. The following firms provide either a full decoration service or the ingredients for DIY decorations. See also Party Shops.

The Balloon and Kite Emporium
613 Garratt Ln SW18   0181-946 5962   (0181-944 0027)
The name says it all – balloons for all occasions, and decorating service.

Balloon Factory
53e Clifton Gdns W9   289 7455   (289 7455)
Size is no object to the Jago family balloon firm, which decorates hotels, balls and banquets, and works for some of the top party planners.

Balloon Printery
27A Buckingham Rd E15   0181-536 0686   (0181-257 8029)
Small, personalised orders – it says it will do singles, but 25 is probably a more realistic quantity.

The Balloon Works
233 Sandycombe Rd, Kew TW9
0181-948 8157   (0181-332 6077)
Everything to do with balloons, from children's parties to corporate launches. Balloon printing is also available.

Balloons Today
Unit A, 9 Park Rd, Hayes UB4
0181-573 2077   (0181-573 2077)
Balloon designers, tending to do larger, corporate business.

BOC Gases
10 Priestley Rd, The Surrey Research Pk, Guildford GU2
0800-111333   (01483-505211)
'Balloon gas' (98% helium), floating balloon packs and dry ice. Ring the head office number given for details of your nearest branch.

Busy Lizzie
49 Copenhagen St N1   833 0279   (833 0279)
Floristry and balloons (including sculptures) for a wide range of clients in Islington, the City and part of the West End.

Fiesta Advertising Balloons
Buck House, Sunnyside Rd, Chesham, Bucks HP5
01494-793904   (01494-793905)
Part of B-Loony, the UK's largest balloon printers, and capable of dealing with most requirements.

Just Balloons
127 Wilton Rd SW1   434 3039   (233 8224)
Just about anything balloon-related you could think of – from wedding decorations, through product launches to blimps.

Pop-up Balloons
52 Windsor St, Uxbridge, Middx UB8
01895-251111   (01895-253291)
*Large balloon cash and carry, which also organises basic and
advanced balloon-art courses and workshops.*

West Side Balloons
43 Ormiston Gr W12   0181-749 7931   (0181-749 7931)
Balloon sculptures. Also a small retail outlet.

FLAGS AND BUNTING

Black & Edgington
30 Marshgate Ln E15   0181-221 3000   (0181-534 4134)
*The flags of the world and red, white and blue bunting for hire or
sale.*

Turtle & Pearce
31 Tanner St SE1   407 1301   (378 0267)
Old established manufacturer of flags, banners and bunting.

EQUIPMENT

*It is relatively unlikely that you will want to deal with the following
firms! If you are having a party of sufficient scale to justify their
involvement, it is probable that you will have a professional organiser
doing it for you. However, if you have decided to do it yourself, or just
need, for example, some lighting, the following firms can help.*

Audio & Acoustics
United Hse, North Rd N7   200 2900   (700 6900)
Sound systems, lighting and staging.

The AV Company
278 Forest Rd E17   0181-520 4321   (0181-520 9484)
*Stage and interior lighting, sound systems of all sizes and video
screens.*

AVE
16 South Sea Rd, Kingston, Surrey KT1
0181-549 7521   (0181-549 6876)
Speech amplification is the speciality here.

Martin Bradley Lighting and Sound
69A Broad Ln, Hampton TW12   0181-979 0672
*PA systems and effects lighting for all requirements. Also hire of
staging and dance floors.*

Canegreen Commercial Presentations
Unit 2, 12-48 Northumberland Pk N17
0181-801 8333   (0181-801 8139)
Top-of-the-range sound systems.

Classic Lighting
9 Westglade, Farnborough GU15   01252-860330
Full range of indoor and external lighting.

Ecando Systems
Earl's Court Exhibition Centre, Warwick Rd SW5
244 6233   (370 8084)
*Servicing Earl's Court for the last century gives this company
unrivalled experience of support for mega-events.*

Fisher Lighting
Unit 1, Heliport Ind Est, Lombard Rd SW11
228 6979   (924 2328)
*One of the top firms, supplying a full range of internal and external
lighting. Also son-et-lumières.*

Gemini Productions
14 Morris Place, Finsbury Park Trading Est N4
263 6336   (263 8995)
*Set builder, especially for corporate events. It also hires
dance-floors.*

GHA Hire
97-99 Dean St W1   439 8705   (437 5880)
Audio visual equipment, including large screen TVs.

Glenby's
The Wooden Hse, Manton, Oakham LE15   0181-673 2035
The Rolls-Royces of the travelling loo world, complete with attendants.

HSS Hire Shops
Have 22 London shops – Call 0800-282828 for the nearest.
*Bouncy castles, barbecues, heaters, crockery, festoon lights, balloon
gas and more – a useful source for the more DIY sorts of parties.*

RG Jones (Morden)
Beulah Rd SW19   0181-540 9881   (0181-542 4368)
PA systems for all types of events.

Jukebox Junction
12 Toneborough Abbey Rd NW8   328 6206
Modern jukeboxes for hire.

Midnight Design
Unit 1, Chelsea Business Centre, 326 Queenstown Rd SW8
498 7272   (498 8845)
*Full range decorative lighting specialists. Although it aims mainly at
the top end of the market, it also has a service for smaller themed
parties.*

Nostalgia Amusements
22 Greenwood Cl, Thames Ditton KT7   0181-398 2141
*Automata, slot machines and juke boxes, including a fully operational
Edwardian amusement parlour are available – with suitably attired
attendants – for theme evenings.*

Rent-a-Loo
Building 5, Smallford Ln, St Albans AL4
01727-822120   (01727-822886)
Individual or multiple – chemical or plumbed in.

Spaceworks Furniture Hire
Unit 1, Quarry Rd, Godstone, Surrey RH9
01883-744557   (01883-744668)
*Wide range of indoor and outdoor furniture, with larger-scale and
corporate events the speciality. A helpful colour catalogue is available.*

Starlight
5 Gateway Trading Est, Hythe Rd NW10
0181-960 6078 (0181-960 7991)
A leader in the business of party 'stage-sets', interiors, and decorations, that does many of the largest events both nationally and on the continent. Lighting is a particular strength, and services include computer-coordinated firework displays.

Water Sculptures
St George's Studios, St George's Quay, Lancaster LA1
01524-64430 (01524-60454)
Byll Elliot has been orchestrating dancing fountains, indoor cascades and water installations of all types for more than two decades.

CARS

Eccentric, classic, impressive or merely practical …

Stephen Benson
45 Sugden Rd SW11   223 8635
Open and closed '20s and '30s saloons, tourers and limousines, and some later vehicles, all with chauffeurs.

Bond Enterprises
Gate Cottage, Campden Hill W8   229 6895
'30s American classics are the speciality.

Browns
48 Gloucester Pl W1   493 4851 (491 4981)
Chauffeur-driven Bentleys, Rolls-Royces and Mercedes, including some limousines.

Carey Camelot
11-15 Headfort Pl SW1   235 0234 (823 1278)
Top-of-the-range, chauffeur-driven car hire firm (formerly called Camelot Barthropp). All of their fleet – which includes Jaguars, Mercedes and stretch limos – is equipped with 'phones and air-conditioning.

Dennis Carter
96a Clifton Hill NW8   723 9244 (372 1855)
Stretch Jaguars, Daimlers and Mercedes, with uniformed chauffeurs.

Fleetwood Classic Limousines
106 Gifford St N1   624 0869 (609 8124)
Chauffeur-driven veteran, vintage and classic vehicles of all types from 1901 to the present.

Huxley Car Hire Co
1 Donnington Rd, Kenton HA3
0181-909 2251 (0181-907 7994)
Wide range of vehicles for hire, including a 1932 white Rolls-Royce.

London Limousine Co
Carriage Hse, 6 Burrell St SE1   928 9280 (928 6150)
Chauffeur-driven Jaguars and Mercedes.

Maxwell Car Services
138-140 Hammersmith Rd W6
0181-748 3000 (0181-748 7075)
Chauffeur-driven cars – Jaguars and Mercedes a speciality.

Star Express Limousines
The Bungalow, Silvester Rd HA0   900 9611
All makes of American limos, including Cadillac and Lincoln.

Wings of Desire
2-5 Old Bond St W1   349 8811   (349 8833)
"The world's most exclusive chauffeur-drive car service", it claims, and with a fleet specialising in Bentleys (including Azures, Brooklands and Continental Convertibles) it may well be right. More humdrum cars (Mercedes, Jaguars, stretch limos and so on) are also available, and you can have motorcycle outriders with uniforms colour-matched to the cars (honestly).

OTHER VEHICLES

If you are organising a wedding reception, a bus is the ideal way of getting everyone away from the church on time. Or if you want a day away with no concerns about drinking and driving. More exotic options are also available.

Air London
Platinum Hse, Gatwick Rd, Crawley, W Sussex RH10
01293-549555   (01293-536810)
Any type of aircraft may be procured from "the world's largest corporate air charter broker", established for some 40 years.

Business Air Centre
BAC House, 112 Clerkenwell Rd, London EC1
456 7123   (456 7130)
Can arrange for the charter of anything from a Concorde to a helicopter.

Cambridge Omnibus and Carriage Hire
28 St Audrey's Close, Histon, Cambridge CB4
01223-237395   (01223-561789)
Replica 1927 omnibus (seating 11) for hire, plus other more contemporary vehicles.

Capital Carriages
The Kensington Stables, 11 Elvaston Mews SW7
589 7390   (01322-528655)
A range of horse-drawn carriages, with liveried coachmen, from a company which traces its history back to 1809.

CB Helicopters
The Blue Hangar, Biggin Hl A'port, Biggin Hl, Kent TN16
01959-540633   (01959-571357)
The quickest way of leaving the party.

CBM Services
Marsh Ln, Tottenham N17   0181-808 6160   (0181-880 3834)
"Period and modern vehicle properties hire", including the oldest bus (1925) still in regular use.

The Classic Coach Company
Mogul House, 116 Ewell Rd, Surbiton KT6
0181-390 0888   (0181-399 4214)
Olde worlde charabancs – a stylish way of transporting groups of up to 11 people.

Greenhill
152 Windmill Ln, Southall UB2
0181-574 6915   (0181-571 5916)
"Double-decker hospitality units" – ie big red buses with a bar downstairs.

Harrods
Knightsbridge SW1   225 6567
The store which sells almost everything can also provide an elegant way of getting you to the church on time – a brougham, a landau or an omnibus, all horse-drawn, and all in the famous green livery.

London Coaches
Jews Row SW18   0181-877 1722   (0181-877 1968)
Open-topped, and other, red buses and coaches.

Virgin Airship & Balloon Co
1 Stafford Park 12, Telford, Salop TF3
01952-292945   (01952-292930)
Hot air balloons for hire.

FANCY DRESS

The shops below stock everything from jokey animal outfits to authentic (and sometimes original) period clothing.

Always ring to discuss whether the shop has roughly what you might want before making the journey – also a good precaution as they do not all keep very regular hours.

Academy Costumes
50 Rushworth St SE1   620 0771   (928 6287)
High quality 20th century originals. Also fancy dress and costumes of all periods (including the future, apparently).

Angels & Bermans
119 Shaftesbury Av WC2   836 5678   (240 9527)
"The world's largest costumier" offers, as a spokesman put it, "to fulfil any costume fantasy" from its vast range of ex-film/TV/theatre stock.

Butterfield 8
4 Ravey St EC2   739 3026   (739 3026)
Twentieth century costume, with emphasis on the '60s and '70s. A helpful leaflet is available.

The Cavern
154 Commercial St E1   247 1889
Treasure-trove of '60s and '70s clobber for hire, and also some virgin items for sale.

City Dress Arcade
437 Bethnal Green Rd E2   739 2645   (613 1917)
Fifth generation family enterprise, offering nearly a thousand costumes, relatively inexpensively – send for the unusually full brochure. Also party novelties, wigs, masks, hats and make-up.

Contemporary Wardrobe
The Horse Hospital, Colonnade WC1   713 7370   (713 7269)
Original '50s-and-later kit for hire. Visits by appointment only.

Laurence Corner
62-64 Hampstead Rd NW1   813 1010   (813 1413)
Military outfits old and new for hire. Also hats and general theatrical costumes.

The Costume Studio
Montgomery House, 161 Balls Pond Rd N1
388 4481   (837 6576)
Large range of period and theatrical costumes in good condition.

Culture Vultures
200 High Rd, East Finchley N2
0181-883 5525   (0181-883 5525)
Fancy dress and costume at reasonable prices. Murder parties, '60s and '70s parties and militaria are strong points.

Escapade
150 Camden High St NW1   485 7384   (485 0950)
Well-stocked, mid-price fancy dress hire shop.

Panto Box
26 North St SW4   627 1772   (627 1772)
Large selection of animal costumes, diamante jewellery and masks, for sale or hire. Visits are by appointment only. Make-up is available by mail order.

Royal National Theatre Costume Hire Department
Chichester Hse, 1/3 Brixton Rd SW9   587 0404   (820 9324)
Top quality (and not especially expensive) period costume.

DRESS HIRE (MEN)

Dinner jackets, white tie and tails, kilts.

Austin Reed
103-113 Regent St W1   437 2140
Austin Reed's operations are based in Regent Street, but you can be measured up in their other shops.

Lipman & Sons
22 Charing Cross Rd WC2   240 2310   (497 8733)
"Never knowingly undersold", this formal wear emporium both sells and hires. Group and student discounts.

Moss Bros
27 King St WC2   240 4567   (379 5652)
The name still practically synonymous with hire of gents' formal wear.

Young's Formal Wear
19-20 Hanover St W1   437 4422   (629 7853)
Hire chain with several London branches.

DRESS HIRE (WOMEN)

Frock Around the Clock
42 Vardens Rd SW11   924 1669
Evening wear and accessories for hire or sale.

Larger than Life
2 Mortlake Ter TW9   0181-332 7661
Formal or evening wear hire for larger sizes and mothers-to-be.

One Night Stand
44 Pimlico Rd SW1   730 8708   (730 2064)
Evening wear and accessories for hire.

20th Century Frox
614 Fulham Rd SW6   731 3242
Evening wear and jewellery for hire or sale (plus hats and shoes for sale only).

PARTY SHOPS

For one-stop shopping for smaller events, the following can be recommended as suppliers of balloons, novelties, decorations, masks, disposable plates and so on. Harrods Hospitality Shop also has a good range, including paper disposables in a big range of colours.

Barnum's
67 Hammersmith Rd W14   602 1211   (603 9945)
Very large, well-stocked general party shop, opposite Olympia.

Chequers
318-320 Portobello Rd W10   0181-969 4119   (0181-960 3315)
Well-stocked general party shop, whose stock includes many different lines of tableware, sugarcraft and balloons.

Circus Circus
176 Wandsworth Bridge Rd SW6   731 4128   (371 5949)
All round party shop. Kids' party items are a speciality, and a children's party organising service is available.

Davenports Magic Shop
7 Charing X Underground Shopping Arcade, Strand WC2
836 0408   (379 8828)
Third generation supplier of magic tricks ranging from simple to professional, and also juggling balls and long, thin sculptural balloons.

Non-stop Party Shop
214/216 Kensington High St W8   937 7200   (938 5309)
Well-stocked all-round novelty shops offering a delivery service and a balloon decoration service. Also at 694 Fulham Rd SW6 (tel 384 1491) and Chelsea Farmers' Market SW3 (tel 351 5771).

Oscar's Den
127/129 Abbey Rd NW6   328 6683   (625 4130)
Full-range "party and carnival shop", offering everything you could want for kids' parties, including hire of bouncy castles (and other equipment), balloon printing, fireworks (all year) and entertainers.

Partridge's
69 Cross St N1   226 2246
Magic, balloons, party hats and masks from this shop which is open seven days a week.

Party Superstores
268 Lavender Hl SW11   924 3210   (924 4484)
Wide-ranging party supplier, which also has a range of fancy dress for hire. It's located opposite Arding & Hobbs.

PHOTOGRAPHERS

Belgrave & Portman Press Bureau
7 West Halkin St SW1   235 3227
*Old-established wedding and social photographers, with over 100,000
weddings behind them.*

Stephen Benson
45 Sugden Rd SW11   223 8635
*Mr Benson has been specalising in wedding photography for
20 years.*

Phil Conrad
1-9 Harbour Yd, Chelsea Harbour SW10
351 1550   (351 3318)
*A commercial publicity photographer, one of whose specialities is
recording party settings.*

Joanna Plumbe
43 Muncaster Rd SW11   978 4814
*Shots of interiors in full party dress and of parties in progress are a
speciality.*

Brian Russell
72 Swanley Rd, Welling DA16   0181-301 3677
Long experienced party, event and conference photographer.

BIPP & MPA PHOTOGRAPHERS

*The following list of social photographers has been derived from
information kindly provided by the two following professional bodies:*

British Institute of Professional Photographers
Fox Talbot House, Amwell End, Ware, Herts SG12
01920-464011

Master Photographers Association
Hallmark House, 2 Beaumont St, Darlington,
Co Durham DL1   01325-356555

*Letters after names indicate Licentiates, Associates and Fellows of the
two associations.*

*To be a member of both organisations is common, and in such cases,
we have – solely on the basis that the BIPP list is more extensive than
that of the MPA – shown only the BIPP qualification.*

(E & EC POSTCODES)

Ronald Blaskett LMPA
Graeme Studios,
2a Derby Rd E18
0181-505 253

Ken Bray ABIPP
221-223 High Rd E18
0181-504 846

Sidney Chevin LBIPP
24 High Rd E18
0181-989 3801

Roger Eldridge LBIPP
Roger Eldridge Photography,
41 Treby St E3
0181-980 2740

Parmjit Kirk-Verdi LBIPP
Verdi Studios,
225-227 Green St E7
0181-472 8842

Neil Lewis LMPA
Gibsons Photography,
97 Lower Clapton Rd E5
0181-985 3808

Michael Ley LBIPP
238 Chingford Mount Rd E4
0181-524 2825

Tony Limrick LBIPP
Shelton Studios, College
Camera, 623 Forest Rd E17
0181-527 7445

Bruno Medici LBIPP
The Medici Studio,
5 Back Hill EC1   278 6722

**David Neal Soloman
LMPA**
Empire Photographics,
153 Forest Rd E17
0181-531 8967

(N & NW POSTCODES)

Adam Adamou ABIPP
87 Green Lns N13
0181-888 3275

Chaim Bacon LMPA
Chaim Bacon Photography,
113a Brent St NW4
0181-203 8453

Don Bartram LBIPP
10 Hawthorn Rd N18
0181-807 1376

Joe Bulaitis LMPA
Joe Bulaitis Photography,
124 Upper St N1   226 177

David Chesner LMPA
David Chesner Find
Photography,
230 Golders Green Rd
NW10   0181-905 5665

Stephen Christmas LBIPP
52 Berkeley Gdns N21
0181-360 9894

Chris Chrysanthou LBIPP
27 Kingwell Rd, Hadley Wd,
Barnet EN4
0181-440 7073

**Natwarlal Chudasama
LBIPP**
National Arts Studio, 57 High
Rd NW10   0181-451 5697

Mrs Lupe Cunha LBIPP
Photo Art Gallery,
19 Ashfield Parade N14
0181-882 6441

Chrissy Dobson LMPA
Ronald Chapman
Photography,
832 Green Lanes N21
0181-360 9433

Chris Eady AMPA
24B Halliford St N1
0181-769 5252

Fuat Erman ABIPP
Erman Photography,
28 Park Avenue N13
0181-882 5793

Peter Gooding LMPA
Peter Gooding Photography,
23 Almeida St N1   354 3116

Ms Nicola Hollins LBIPP
67 Redston Rd N8
0181-341 2080

Ali Ibrahim LMPA
Europa Photos,
78 Turnpike Lane N8
0181-881 3095

Savvakis Kafouris LMPA
SK Photography,
Unit 7 In Shops,
37-43 South Mall N9
0181-345 6866

Paul Kaye FBIPP
Paul Kaye Studio Ltd,
20 Park Rd NW1   723 2444

Richard Kerber LMPA
Richard Kerber Photography,
1454 High Rd N20
0181-445 4105

Brian Mackett LBIPP
James Howarth Limited,
Rossendale Works,
Chase Side N14
0181-886 0181

John O'Donnell ABIPP
51 Minchenden Crescent N14
0181-882 2064

Gerard O'Sullivan LMPA
Scan Photographic Services,
16a Caedmon Rd N7
700 1063

Brian Parry LMPA
Parliament Hill Studios,
31 Grove Terrace,
Highgate Rd NW5   267-3755

Raymond Pavett LMPA
Ray Pavett Photography,
100 Hay Lane NW9
0181-205-2055

Miss Rena Pearl ABIPP
8A The Drive NW11

John Prater LMPA
Kenneth Prater Photography,
57 Station Rd N21
0181-360 2111

Paul Wilmshurst FBIPP
Flambards Photography,
6 Chaseville Parade,
Chaseville Pk Rd N21
0181-360 7187

(SW & SE POSTCODES)

**John Stuart Absolon
LMPA**
SJ Photography,
4 Ardent Cl SE25
0181-771 5046

Fatai Alao LBIPP
71 Staplefield Close,
Claremount Estate SW2
0181-678 6001

Sophocles Alexiou LBIPP
Pictorials, 8 Grand Parade,
Upper Richmond Rd West
SW14   0181-876 1740

**Miss Cristina Bellodi
LBIPP**
109 Rodenhurst Rd SW4
0181-674 0966

Alan Brown LBIPP
Brown Photographic Services,
30 Sudbrook Rd SW12
0181-673 6070

**Mrs Tessa Codrington
LBIPP**
73 The Chase SW4
622 3895

Charles Cramp FMPA
Charles R Cramp Associates,
50 Queenswood Rd SE23
0181-291 2115

Mike Curry LBIPP
61 Valleyfield Rd SW16
0181-769 2950

Danny DaCosta LBIPP
177 Dunstans Rd SE22
0181-299 3520

Miss Zoe Dominic FBIPP
Dominic Photography,
4B Moore Park Rd SW6
381 0007

Ms Desi Fontaine AMPA
Desi Fontaine Studios,
60-62 Archway St SW13
0181-878 4348

V Grandison LMPA
VG Photographic,
285 Plumstead High St SE18
0181-855 6554

Desmond Horran ABIPP
409 Lordship Ln SE22
0181-693 6663

Ron Howard FBIPP
20 Aldbourne Rd W12
0181-743 8194

Gary Italiaander LBIPP
The Portrait Studio, Harrods,
Knightsbridge SW1X
730 1234

Julian Kaye ABIPP
Cover Shots International,
30-32 Mortimer St W1
491 4123

Simon Kaye ABIPP
Cover Shots International,
30-32 Mortimer St W1
491 4123

Miss Barbara Kleiner LBIPP
76 York Mansions,
Prince of Wales Dr SW11
720 5061

James Norcott LBIPP
James Russell Studio,
4 St Marks Pl SW19
0181-946 0439

Denis O'Mahony FMPA
O'Mahony Production
Ground Fl, 472 Kingston Rd
SW20   0181-543 8073

Alan Owens LBIPP
Alan M Owens,
15 Woodbastwick Rd SE26
0181-778 2667

David Phipps LMPA
Belgrave & Portman
Photography,
7 West Halkin St SW1
235 3227

Mrs Khalida Rahman ABIPP
34 Grand Drive SW20
0181-540 4054

Barry Shapcott LMPA
Barry Shapcott Photography,
65 Hsepton Rd SW16
0181-769 2786

Alan Shawcross ABIPP
Anthony Buckley &
Constantine Ltd,
109 Mount St W1   629 5235

Raymond Peter Simmons LMPA
26 Kingshurst Rd SE12
0181-857 0595

Robert Spells LMPA
Russells of Wimbledon,
4 St Mark's Place SW19
0181-946 0439

Grant White ABIPP
Anthony Buckley &
Constantine Ltd,
109 Mount St W1   629 5235

(W POSTCODES)

David Elkington-Cole LMPA
Studio ABS,
67A Warwick Rd W5
0181-567 3468

Clifford Harris LMPA
Cliff Harris Photography,
191 Princes Garden W3
0181-992 9165

Tateo Kamada LBIPP
Kam Cresswell Photographic
Studios,
108 Chiswick High Rd W4
0181-994 3909

Neil Maffre LMPA
Freeze Frame,
25 Ellesmere Rd, Grove Park
W4   0181-995 5130

V K Verma LMPA
Ealing Photographic Studio,
103 Midhurst Rd W13
0181-840 4443

(ESSEX)

Stephen Catherall ABIPP
SC Photographers,
Riddings House, Riddings
Lane, Harlow CM18
01279-415957

John Alexander LBIPP
John Alexander Studio,
52 Broadway, Leigh-on-Sea
SS9   01702-72771

Hugh Bourn ABIPP
The Burnham Studio,
86 Station Rd, Burnham-on-
Crouch CM0   01621-784442

Stephen Chapman LBIPP
SC Studios,
3 Salmon Parade, New St,
Chelmsford CM1
01245-355831

Elden Chase LBIPP
Chase Studios,
10 South St, Rainham RM13
01708-630166

Ms Carol Colledge ABIPP
Lyttons, Chilton Close,
Great Horkesley, Colchester
C06   01206-271357

Paul Cudmore LBIPP
18 King Coel Rd,
Lexden, Colchester C03
01206-562005

Leonard Dance FBIPP
Len Dance Photography,
117-119 Rectory Grove,
Leigh-on-Sea SS9
01702-480625

Philip Dorking LBIPP
26 Rockall, Western
Approaches, Southend-on-Sea
SS2   01702-522766

Norman Feakins LBIPP
6 York Close, Shenfield,
Brentwood CM15
01277-215246

Peter Frost ABIPP
Putmans Photographers,
The Studio, 1 Naze Park Rd,
Walton-on-the-Naze C014
01255-675692

Mike Laurence LBIPP
Gilmore LBIPP
Focal Images, Lower Barn
Craft & Culture Centre,
London Rd, Raleigh SS6
01268-784828

Vic Hainsworth ABIPP
5 Magazine Farm Way,
Lexden, Colchester C03
01206-562993

Jack Harrison LBIPP
Jack Harrison Photography,
The Studio, First Floor, 71
High St, Billericay CM12
01277-656385

Stanley Hecquer LBIPP
1 Queens Mews, Queens Rd,
Buckhurst Hill IG9
0181-505 6226

Jeffrey Hopson LBIPP
The Green, Hatfield Peverel,
Chelmsford CM3
01245-380986

David Islip LBIPP
27 Brain Rd, Witham CM8
01376-517955

John James LBIPP
Lindrum Photography,
51 Ongar Rd, Brentwood
CM15   01277-212895

Michael Kellett ABIPP
Kellett Photography,
3 Guild Way, South Woodham
Ferrers, Chelmsford CM3
01245-322041

Barry Kettle LBIPP
Browns The Photographers,
22 Goldberry Mead, South
Woodham Ferrers CM3
01245-328569

**Geoffrey Meadowcroft
LBIPP**
Centre Photography,
1&2 East Bay, Colchester C03
01206-868512

Ron Prince LBIPP
33 Market Pl, Romford RM1
01708-724561

George Shiffner ABIPP
14 Coggeshall Rd, Braintree
CM7   01376-322524

Christopher Webb LBIPP
Orchid Photographic,
The Old Forge, 53 High St,
Ingatestone CM4
01277-355366

David West ABIPP
Putmans Photographers,
The Studio, 1 Naze Park Rd,
Walton-on-the-Naze C014
01255-675692

(KENT)

**Brendan Balhetchet
LBIPP**
12 Maryland Court, Rainham
ME8   01634-360781

Basil Barnes LBIPP
85 Higham Lane, Tonbridge
TN10   01732-362311

Miss Celine Barsley ABIPP
8 Oaklands Rd, Bexleyheath
DA6   0181-301 6563

Mrs Patricia Baxter LBIPP
11 Cornwall Gardens,
Cliftonville, Margate CT9
01843-291523

Michael Bolt LBIPP
Kimberley Colour, 6 Norman
Pde DA14   0181-308 0060

Brian Brown LBIPP
12 River Meadow, River,
Dover CT17   01304-822229

John Burgess LBIPP
116 Lavender Hill, Tonbridge
TN9   01732-360363

Peter Ebdon ABIPP
257 High St, Chatham ME4
01634-405347

Henry Gee LBIPP
246 High St, Bromley BR1
0181-460 8444

Ms Erica Gray LBIPP
Martin & Gray,
10 Yew Tree House, King
Sreet, Rochester ME1
01634-409166

Mark Howells LBIPP
Level Gold Photos,
7 The Broadway Centre,
Maidstone ME16
01622-690616

John Lawrence ABIPP
14 Warwick Cl, Orpington
BR6   01689-826587

Leslie Lockwood LBIPP
4 Crayford High St, Crayford
DA1   01322-529950

David Markson LBIPP
The Studio, 10A St Johns Rd,
Tunbridge Wells TN4
01892-522134

Jonathan Marsh LBIPP
20 Beechy Lees Rd, Otford,
Sevenoaks TN14
01959-522424

Brian Martin LBIPP
Martin & Gray, 10 Yew Tree
House, King Sreet, Rochester
ME1   01634-409166

William Mutler LBIPP
Bill Mutler Studio,
Chantlers Hill, Paddock
Wood TN12   01892-836586

Oliver O'Connor LBIPP
Oliver O'Connor
Photography,
8 Victoria Park, Dover CT16
01304-207876

Brian Osborne LBIPP
Lime Tree Studios,
24A London Rd, Sevenoaks
TN13   01732-451131

Jon Rowe ABIPP
80 Woodlawn St, Whitstable
CT5   01227-264902

Paul Simpson ABIPP
Sloman & Pettitt Photography,
33 High St, Maidstone ME14
01622-753158

Bernard Snell ABIPP
Fine Art Studio,
11 Frindsbury Rd, Strood,
Rochester ME2
01634-719962

John Taylor LBIPP
25 St Lawrence Avenue,
Bidborough TN4
01892-536820

(MIDDX)

Chris Austin LMPA
59 Heathfield, North
Twickenham TW2
0181-892 7670

Kaushik (Ken) Bathia FBIPP
1B Alandale Rd, Greenford
UB6   0181-903 3294

Frederick Biggs LMPA
Cranbourne Photo Services,
43 Cranbourne Waye, Hayes
UB4   0181-573 8608

David Cox LMPA
Town Studio,
80 Lancaster Rd, Enfield EN2
0181-367 7683

Mrs Pamela Dyer ABIPP
Peter Dyer Photographs Ltd,
86 London Rd, Enfield EN2
0181-363 2456

Peter Dyer FBIPP
Peter Dyer Photographs Ltd,
86 London Rd, Enfield EN2
0181-363 2456

Charles Green FBIPP
309 Hale Ln, Station Rd,
Edgware HA8
0181-958 3183

Michael Herring LBIPP
Mike Herring Photography,
High Gables Studio,
11 Wheatsheaf Ln Staines
TW18   01784-456718

Leonard Hooper LBIPP
Gem Photographics,
26 Feltham Hill Rd, Ashford
TW15   01784-255613

Jason Joyce LBIPP
117 Park Avenue, Enfield EN1
0181-360 9382

Keith Lockyer LBIPP
9 Eslinge Rd, Enfield EN1
01992-760774

Malcolm Lunn LBIPP
62 First Av, Bush Hill Pk,
Enfield EN1   0181-363 3300

Satwant Matharoo LBIPP
11 Green Walk, Norwood
Green, Southall UB2
0181-571 3863

Mrs Eileen Michel LBIPP
31 South Parade, Mollison
Way, Edgware HA8
0181-952 4711

Ian Murray LBIPP
25 Downing Drive, Greenford
UB6   0181-575 0383

Michael O'Sullivan LBIPP
74 Hedge Hill, Enfield EN2
0181-363 8350

Suresh Oza ABJPP
58 Allandale Rd, Enfield EN3
01992-719674

Maurice Rubeck ABIPP
42 Church Rd, Stanmore HA7
0181-954 8047

Vassos Vassiliou LBIPP
Studio One Photographic,
160 Edenbridge Rd, Bush Hill
Park, Enfield EN1
0181-364 1958

Michael Woollard ABIPP
186 Field End Rd, Eastcote,
Pinner HA5   0181-866 1679

(SURREY)

Bertrand Adams LBIPP
Britannia Photographic,
12 The Broadway, Cheam
SM3   0181-643 9681

Keith Ash ABIPP
Keith Ash Artistic
Photography, Runnemede
Studio, 43 Runnemede Rd,
Egham TW20   01784-437247

Mrs Jeanie Brown LBIPP
1st Focus Photography,
Mount House, The Mount
Drive, Reigate RH2
01737-22358

Anthony Bugbird FBIPP
The Old School, Compton,
Guildford GU3
01483-860816

Anthony Cooper LBIPP
1 Sundale Av, Selsdon, South
Croydon CR2
0181-651 1636

Paul Davies LBIPP
Nocturne,
1 Lacey Av, Old Coulsdon
CR5   01737-553680

Thomas Elsdon ABIPP
75 Oaklands, South
Godstone, Surrey RH9
01342-893415

Ian Franklin LBIPP
25 Mandeville Close,
Guildford GU2   01483-36363

Roger Hills LBIPP
9 Wells Rd, Merrow,
Guildford GU4
01483-67299

Colin Kearney LBIPP
'Ferndown'
113 Barnett Wood Ln,
Ashtead KT21
01372-274933

Michael Lea ABIPP
The Old Coach House,
99 Reading Rd, Yateley GU17
01252-874261

Michael Long LBIPP
Cole Studios Rd,
115 Kingston Rd, New
Malden KT3   0181-942 1600

Pierre Marcar LBIPP
44A Bensham Gro, Thornton
Heath CR7   0181-771 1233

David Murray LBIPP
David Murray Photography,
The Gardener's Cottage,
White Ln, Guildford GU4
01483-33398

Mrs Hilary Nixon LBIPP
9 Heatherdene, West Horsley
KT24   01483-282205

Mrs Hilary Palmer LBIPP
6 Copping Cl, Croydon CR0
0181-680 1070

**Mahmad Peerbacus
ABIPP**
27 St Paul's Rd, Thornton
Heath CR7   0181-771 7088

Malcolm Roberts LBIPP
Castle Studios,
40-42 Castle St, Guildford
GU1   01483-504121

Paul Saville LBIPP
Pleasure Prints,
41 Conyers Close, Hersham,
Walton-on-Thames KT12
01932-25450

Joseph Schofield ABIPP
15 Fairfield Drive, Frimley,
Camberley GU16
01276-65779

Eric Strange FBIPP
Dawson Strange Photography
Ltd, 15 Between Streets,
Cobham KT11
01932-867161

**Ms Alison Trapmore
ABIPP**
Oatlands Studio,
7 Oatlands Dr, Weybridge
KT13   01932-227935

David Ward FBIPP
Latchets, Harpesford Avenue,
Virginia Water GU25
01344-843421

Jeffrey Wightwick LBIPP
Lillieys of Hinchley Wood,
18 Manor Road Nth, Hinchley
Wood KT10   0181-398 7362

Richard Wilkinson ABIPP
6 Glenfield Rd, Brockham,
Betchworth RH3
01737-844736

CARICATURISTS

*Photography is not the only
way of capturing people, why
not consider the services of
an on-the-spot caricaturist?
The following have a lot of
experience.*

Andrea Cunningham
19 Onslow Gdns SW7
581 3433

Stephen Garner
9 Garden Farm, West Mersea,
Essex CO5   01206-383198

SECURITY

Getting into a ball is often the least satisfactory part – even if you have a ticket. A relatively small investment in planning, and security/door personnel to carry plans into effect, can make all the difference.

Corps of Commissionaires
85 Cowcross St EC1   490 1125   (250 1287)
For more than a century, the corps has been providing smart, ex-servicemen commissionaires all of whom are security-trained.

Group 4
21 Wapping Ln E1   488 3111   (480 7689)
The country's biggest security firm can provide professional event security. The minimum hire period is 10 hours.

Stargard Security Consultants
Conisgold House, 302-304 Wellingborough Rd,
Northampton NN1   01604-34105   (01604-230822)
All sorts of security services, from VIP close-quarter protection to venue and event control.

STATIONERS

Aquila Press
Unit 13C, Sawnwood Trading Est, Woodside, Sawnwood, Epping
CM16   01992-573131   (01992-561516)
Copperplate invitations are the speciality of this firm, formerly of St James's. It does a lot of diplomatic work and has a keen eye for protocol.

Papyrus
48 Fulham Rd SW3   584 8022   (581 8908)
Printed and engraved social stationery.

Smythson
40 New Bond St W1   629 8558   (495 6111)
The grandest name in stationery. There is now a branch at 135 Sloane St SW1 (tel 730 5520).

The Wren Press
26 Chelsea Wharf, 15 Lots Rd SW10   351 5887   (352 7063)
Suppliers of all types of invitations – engraving and thermography are specialities.

INSURANCE

It's certainly worth talking to your broker, but surprisingly few people seem to be involved with event insurance. The following are among the specialists.

AON/Albert G Rubin
Pinewood Studios, Pinewood Rd, Iver, Bucks SL0
01753-658200   (01753-653152)
Specialists in theatrical/musical event insurance who also quote for general event cover.

Insurex Expo-Sure
The Pantiles House, 2 Nevill St, Tunbridge Wells TN2
01892-511500   (01892-510016)
Specialists in event insurance of all types.

Pluvius
Eagle Star Insurance Company, The Grange, Bishops Cleeve, Cheltenham GL52   01242-221311   (01242-690083)
Adverse weather conditions can lead to expenditure being wasted (for example, if access to a marquee is unexpectedly bogged down) or, for commercial ventures, loss of profit (such as when rain reduces the expected attendance at an event). Both types of risk can be insured by Pluvius, specialists in this type of risk for over half a century.

GP Turner
Suite 5.09, New Loom House, 101 Back Church Ln E1
481 9393   (481 9494)
Specialists in insurance for abandonment, postponement and cancellation of events.

Wedding Plan
Travellers' Protection Services Ltd, 82 Upper St Giles St, Norwich NR2   01603-767699   (01603-766858)
Wedding, reception and honeymoon insurance packages.

INDEXES

Halls

Central
Abbey Community
 Centre *(SW1)*
Africa Centre *(WC2)*
Banqueting House *(SW1)*
Central Club (YWCA) *(WC1)*
Conway Hall *(WC1)*
Gray's Inn *(WC1)*
King's College *(WC2)*
Lincoln's Inn *(WC2)*
London Scottish *(SW1)*
The London
 Welsh Centre *(WC1)*
Nôtre Dame Hall *(WC2)*
The Queen Elizabeth II
 Conference Centre *(SW1)*
Royal Green Jackets *(W1)*
Royal
 Horticultural Halls *(SW1)*
Staple Inn *(WC1)*
Westminster Cathedral
 Hall *(SW1)*

West
Amadeus Centre *(W9)*
Brompton Oratory – St
 Wilfrid's Hall *(SW7)*
Chelsea
 Old Town Hall *(SW3)*
The Courtyard, St Peter's
 Hall *(W11)*
Duke of York's HQ *(SW3)*
Fulham Town Hall *(SW6)*
Hammersmith Town
 Hall *(W6)*
Holy Trinity Brompton
 Church Hall *(SW7)*
Millennium Conference
 Centre *(SW7)*
Old Refectory *(W8)*
Porchester Centre *(W2)*

North
Alexandra
 Palace & Park *(N22)*
The Business Design
 Centre *(N1)*
Cecil Sharp House *(NW1)*
Stoke Newington
 Town Hall *(N16)*

South
Academy of Live &
 Recorded Arts *(SW18)*
Battersea Town Hall *(SW11)*
Blackheath
 Concert Halls *(SE3)*
Chatham Hall *(SW11)*
Hop Exchange *(SE1)*
St John's Hill *(SW11)*
St Thomas' Hospital *(SE1)*
Wandsworth
 Civic Suite *(SW18)*

East
Bishopsgate Institute *(EC2)*
Brick Lane Music Hall *(EC2)*
Cabot Hall *(E14)*
Holderness House *(EC2)*
Honourable
 Artillery Co *(EC1)*
Inner Temple Hall *(EC4)*
International House *(E1)*
Middle Temple Hall *(EC4)*
St Bartholomew's
 Hospital *(EC1)*
St Botolph's Hall *(EC2)*
St Bride's Foundation
 Institute *(EC4)*
St John's Gate *(EC1)*
Urban Learning
 Foundation *(E14)*

Outside London
Royal
 Holloway College *(Surrey)*

Banqueting halls

Central
Café Royal *(W1)*
New Connaught Rms *(WC2)*
One Whitehall Place *(SW1)*
Westminster Conference
 Centre *(SW1)*

West
Chelsea Football Club *(SW6)*
Chelsea
 Harbour Rooms *(SW10)*
Commonwealth
 Institute *(W8)*

North
Grosvenor Rooms *(NW2)*
Lord's *(NW8)*
Regency Banqueting
 Suite *(N17)*
Royal Majestic Suite *(NW6)*

South
Guy's Hospital *(SE1)*
The Oval *(SE11)*

East
The Brewery *(EC1)*
The Gibson Hall *(EC2)*
The Old Town Hall,
 Stratford *(E15)*
St Andrew's Court
 House *(EC4)*

Outside London
Addington Palace *(CR9)*
Ascot Racecourse, Pavilions
 & Queen Anne
 Rooms *(Berks)*
Ascot Racecourse, Royal
 Enclosure *(Berks)*
Bath – Assembly Rooms
Kempton Park *(Middx)*

Sandown Park
  Racecourse *(Surrey)*
Syon Park
  (Banqueting) *(Middx)*
Twickenham Banqueting
  Centre *(Middx)*
Windsor Guildhall *(Berks)*

Livery halls

South
Glaziers' Hall *(SE1)*

East
Apothecaries' Hall *(EC4)*
Armourers' & Braisers'
  Hall *(EC2)*
Bakers' Hall *(EC3)*
Barber-Surgeons' Hall *(EC2)*
Brewers' Hall *(EC2)*
Butchers' Hall *(EC1)*
Carpenters' Hall *(EC2)*
Chartered
  Accountants' Hall *(EC2)*
Clothworkers' Hall *(EC3)*
Coopers' Hall *(EC2)*
Drapers' Hall *(EC2)*
Dyers' Hall *(EC4)*
Farmers' & Fletchers'
  Hall *(EC1)*
Fishmongers' Hall *(EC4)*
The Founders' Hall *(EC1)*
Goldsmiths' Hall *(EC2)*
Grocers' Hall *(EC2)*
Guildhall *(EC2)*
Innholders' Hall *(EC4)*
The Insurance Hall *(EC2)*
Ironmongers' Hall *(EC2)*
Mercers' Hall *(EC2)*
Merchant Taylors' Hall *(EC2)*
Painters' Hall *(EC4)*
Pewterers' Hall *(EC2)*
Plaisterers' Hall *(EC2)*
Saddlers' Hall *(EC2)*
Salters' Hall *(EC2)*
Skinners' Hall *(EC4)*
Stationers' Hall *(EC4)*
Tallow Chandlers' Hall *(EC4)*
Watermen &
  Lightermen's Hall *(EC3)*

Houses

Central
Apsley House *(W1)*
Canning House *(SW1)*
Dartmouth House *(W1)*
Hamilton Suite *(W1)*
The House of
  St Barnabas-in-Soho *(W1)*
Searcy's *(SW1)*
Sir John Soane's
  Museum *(WC2)*
Spencer House *(SW1)*

West
Carlyle's House *(SW3)*
Chiswick House *(W4)*
Dora House *(SW7)*
Fulham House *(SW6)*
Fulham Palace *(SW6)*
Leighton House *(W14)*
Peacock House *(W14)*

North
Avenue House *(N3)*
Burgh House *(NW3)*
Freud Museum *(NW3)*
Kenwood House *(NW3)*
Kenwood House, Old
  Kitchen *(NW3)*
Lauderdale House *(N6)*

South
Hollyhedge House *(SE3)*
Pentland House *(SE13)*
Queen's House *(SE10)*
Ranger's House *(SE10)*

East
Dr Johnsons' House *(EC4)*
Hamilton House *(EC4)*
Sutton House *(E9)*

Outside London
Beaulieu *(Hants)*
Blenheim Palace *(Oxon)*
Boston Manor House *(Middx)*
Brighton
  Royal Pavilion *(Sussex)*
Brocket Hall *(Herts)*
Clandon *(Surrey)*
Ham House *(Surrey)*
Hampton Court
  Palace *(Surrey)*
Hartwell House *(Bucks)*
Herstmonceux Castle *(East Sussex)*
Hever Castle *(Kent)*
Highclere Castle *(Berks)*
Hollington House
  Hotel *(Berks)*
Knebworth House *(Herts)*
Leeds Castle *(Kent)*
Loseley Park *(Surrey)*
Marble Hill House *(Surrey)*
Moyns Park *(Essex)*
Penshurst Place *(Kent)*
Polesden Lacey *(Surrey)*
Rossway Park *(Herts)*
Syon Park
  (Conservatory) *(Middx)*
Syon Park (House) *(Middx)*
Waddesdon Manor, The
  Dairy *(Bucks)*
Wrotham Park *(Herts)*

Museums

Central
British Museum (WC1)
Cabinet War Rooms (SW1)
The Dickens' House
Museum (WC1)
Guards Museum (SW1)
London Transport
Museum (WC2)
Museum of Mankind (W1)
Theatre Museum (WC2)

West
Hogarth's House (W4)
The London Toy and Model
Museum (W2)
National Army
Museum (SW3)
Natural
History Museum (SW7)
Science Museum (SW7)
Victoria & Albert
Museum (SW7)

North
Royal Air
Force Museum (NW9)

South
The Ark (SE1)
Bramah Tea &
Coffee Museum (SE1)
The Clink (SE1)
Cutty Sark (SE10)
Design Museum (SE1)
Fan Museum (SE10)
Horniman Museum and
Gardens (SE23)
Imperial
War Museum (SE1)
Museum of the Moving
Image (SE1)
The Old Operating Theatre,
Museum & Herb
Garret (SE1)
Old Royal
Observatory (SE10)
Winston Churchill's Britain
At War Experience (SE1)

East
Bank of England
Museum (EC2)
Geffrye Museum (E2)
Museum of London (EC2)

Outside London
Kew Bridge Steam
Museum (Middx)
Whitewebbs Museum of
Transport (Middx)

Galleries

Central
Accademia Italiana/European
Academy (SW1)
Courtauld Gallery (WC2)
Hamiltons Gallery (W1)
ICA (SW1)
The Imagination
Gallery (WC1)
Lundonia House (WC1)
Mall Galleries (SW1)
Music Room At Grays (W1)
National Portrait
Gallery (WC2)
Photographers'
Gallery (WC2)
Royal Academy of Arts (W1)
Tate Gallery (SW1)
Wallace Collection (W1)

West
Royal College of Art (SW7)
Serpentine Gallery (W2)
Will's Art Warehouse (SW6)

North
Saatchi Gallery (NW8)

South
Bankside Gallery (SE1)
Delfina Studio (SE1)
Dulwich Picture
Gallery (SE21)
Hayward Gallery (SE1)
Victoria Pump House (SW11)

East
Barbican Art Gallery (EC2)
Slaughterhouse Gallery (EC1)
Whitechapel Art Gallery (E1)

Tourist attractions

Central
Rock Circus (W1)
Royal Mint Sovereign
Gallery (SW1)

North
The London
Planetarium (NW1)
London Zoo (NW1)
Madame Tussaud's (NW1)

South
London Aquarium (SE1)
The London Dungeon (SE1)
Shakespeare Globe
Centre (SE1)

East
House of Detention (EC1)
Mudchute Park and
Farm (E14)
HM Tower of London (EC3)

Outside London
Kew (Royal Botanic) Gardens *(Surrey)*
Legoland Windsor *(Berks)*
Thorpe Park *(Surrey)*
West Wycombe Caves *(Bucks)*
Whipsnade Wild Animal Park *(Beds)*

Colleges & Universities

Central
International Students *(W1)*
London School of Economics *(WC2)*
The Royal College of Pathologists *(SW1)*
The Royal College of Radiologists *(W1)*
University of London Union *(WC1)*
Westminster College (Victoria) *(SW1)*

West
Imperial College *(SW7)*
Royal College of Music *(SW7)*
Upper Refectory Suite *(SW3)*

North
King's College, Hampstead Site *(NW3)*
Regent's College *(NW1)*
Royal Veterinary College *(NW1)*

South
Dulwich College *(SE21)*
Froebel Institute College *(SW15)*
Goldsmiths College *(SE14)*
King's College School *(SW19)*
Westminster College (Battersea) *(SW11)*
Whitelands College *(SW15)*

Outside London
Spring Grove House *(Middx)*

Institutions

Central
BAFTA Centre *(W1)*
Bloomsbury Square Training Centre *(WC1)*
Chartered Institute of Public Finance & Accountancy *(WC2)*
Church House *(SW1)*
Institute of Directors *(SW1)*
Institution of Civil Engineers *(SW1)*
Institution of Mechanical Engineers *(SW1)*

The Law Society *(WC2)*
Royal Aeronautical Society *(W1)*
Royal Institute of British Architects *(W1)*
Royal Institution of Great Britain *(W1)*
Royal Society of Arts *(WC2)*
RUSI Building *(SW1)*
School of Pharmacy *(WC1)*

West
Café L'Institute *(SW7)*
French Institute *(SW7)*
Royal Geographical Society *(SW7)*

East
Baltic Exchange *(EC3)*
College of Arms *(EC4)*
Lloyd's of London *(EC3)*
Merchant Centre *(EC4)*
Trinity House *(EC3)*

Moored boats

Central
El Barco Latino *(WC2)*
TS Queen Mary *(WC2)*
HQS Wellington *(WC2)*

West
White Swan Water *(W9)*

South
HMS Belfast *(SE1)*
The Golden Hinde *(SE1)*

East
Leven is Strijd *(E14)*
HMS President *(EC4)*
Scone *(E14)*

Theatres

Central
The Coliseum *(WC2)*
The Comedy Store *(SW1)*
London Palladium *(W1)*
Palace Theatre *(W1)*
The Players' Theatre *(WC2)*
Theatre Royal *(WC2)*

West
Royal Albert Hall *(SW7)*

South
Royal National Theatre *(SE1)*
The South Bank Centre *(SE1)*

East
Mermaid Theatre *(EC4)*

Miscellaneous

Central
Badbobs *(WC2)*
The Brewers Rooms *(W1)*

Christie's *(SW1)*
Congress Centre *(WC1)*
Dolphin Square *(SW1)*
Hamleys Metropolis *(W1)*
Hellenic Centre *(W1)*
London Astoria *(WC2)*
Phillips *(W1)*
Ruby's *(W1)*
St Martin In The Fields *(WC2)*
The Sanctuary *(WC2)*
Sotheby's *(W1)*
Stone Buildings *(WC2)*
Westminster Abbey
  Garden *(SW1)*
Westminster Boating
  Base *(SW1)*

West
Bonham's *(SW7)*
The Chelsea Gardener *(SW3)*
Chelsea Physic Garden *(SW3)*
41 Queen's Gate
  Terrace *(SW7)*
Gunnersbury Park *(W3)*
The Irish Centre *(W6)*
Orangery (Holland
  Park) *(W8)*
Orangery
  (Kensington Palace) *(W8)*
Queens Ice Bowl *(W2)*
Riverside Studios *(W6)*
Royal Parks Agency *(W2)*
Westway Studios *(W11)*
The Worx III *(SW6)*

North
Alexandra Palace Ice
  Rink *(N22)*
Arts Depot *(NW1)*
Lee Valley Leisure
  Centre *(N9)*
The Worx I *(N1)*
The Worx II *(N1)*

South
Adrenaline Village *(SW8)*
Battersea Park *(SW8)*
Brockwell Lido *(SE24)*
The Conservatory *(SW11)*
Cottons Atrium *(SE1)*
Crystal Palace Park *(SE20)*
Earlsfield Library *(SW18)*
Kingswood House *(SE21)*
The Leathermarket *(SE1)*
Mega Bowl *(SW2)*
Neal's Lodge *(SW18)*
Southwark Cathedral *(SE1)*
Streatham Ice Arena *(SW16)*
Surrey Docks Watersports
  Centre *(SE16)*
Tower Bridge *(SE1)*

East
Barbican Centre *(EC2)*
Beckton Alpine Centre *(E6)*
Bow Film Studios *(E15)*
Broadgate Estates *(EC2)*
Cardamon Café *(E1)*
Circus Space *(EC1)*
Docklands Sailing &
  Watersports Centre *(E14)*
Edwin Shirley
  Productions *(E3)*
Lea Rowing Club *(E5)*
Lee Valley Cycle Circuit *(E15)*
London Transport
  Conference Facilities *(E14)*
Newham City Farm *(E16)*
St Etheldreda's Crypt *(EC1)*
Spitalfields Market *(E1)*
YHA City of London *(EC4)*

Outside London
Bath – Pump Room *(Avon)*
Chislehurst Caves *(Kent)*
Denbies Wine Estate *(Surrey)*
Epsom Downs *(Surrey)*
Ham Polo Club *(Surrey)*
Hillingdon Ski and
  Snowboard Centre *(Middx)*
Pinewood Studios *(Bucks)*
Queen's Eyot *(Berks)*
Temple Island *(Oxon)*

Clubs

Central
Annabel's *(W1)*
Arts Club *(W1)*
The Caledonian Club *(SW1)*
Cavalry & Guards Club *(W1)*
East India Club *(SW1)*
Groucho Club *(W1)*
Irish Club *(SW1)*
Lansdowne Club *(W1)*
Monte's *(SW1)*
Mortons Club *(W1)*
Mosimann's Belfry *(SW1)*
National Liberal Club *(SW1)*
Naval & Military Club *(W1)*
Oxford & Cambridge
  Club *(SW1)*
Peg's Club *(WC2)*
Poetry Society *(WC2)*
Reform Club *(SW1)*
The Royal Air Force
  Club *(W1)*
Royal Over-Seas
  League *(SW1)*
St Stephen'
  Constitutional Club *(SW1)*
Soho House *(W1)*
Spanish Club *(W1)*
University Women's
  Club *(W1)*

West
Cobden's Club *(W10)*
Embargo *(SW10)*
Hurlingham Club *(SW6)*

Polish Hearth Club *(SW7)*
Polish Social &
   Cultural Association *(W6)*
Raffles *(SW3)*

South
Bank of England Club *(SW15)*
London Rowing Club *(SW15)*
Roehampton Club *(SW15)*
Winchester House *(SW15)*

East
The Bankers Club *(EC2)*
City of London Club *(EC2)*
The Little Ship Club *(EC4)*
London Capital Club *(EC4)*
St Andrew Golf Club *(EC4)*

Outside London
Leander Club *(Berks)*
Phyllis Court *(Oxon)*

Nightclubs
Central
Browns Club *(WC2)*
Café de Paris *(W1)*
Equinox at
   the Empire *(WC2)*
Iceni *(W1)*
Legends *(W1)*
Limelight *(W1)*
London Astoria 2 *(W1)*
The London
   Hippodrome *(WC2)*
Motcomb's Club *(SW1)*
The RAW Club *(WC1)*
Rock Garden *(WC2)*
St Moritz *(W1)*
Le Scandale *(W1)*
SW1 Club *(SW1)*
Wag *(W1)*

West
Crazy Larry's *(SW10)*
Gargoyle Club *(SW10)*
Hammersmith Palais *(W6)*
The Hudson Club *(SW7)*
The Roof Gardens *(W8)*
606 Club *(SW10)*
Subterania *(W10)*

North
Bagleys *(N1)*
Electric Ballroom *(NW1)*
HQ *(NW1)*
Jazz Café *(NW1)*
Jongleurs at Camden
   Lock *(NW1)*
WKD *(NW1)*

South
The Fridge *(SW2)*
Jongleurs at The
   Cornet *(SW11)*
Linford Film Studios *(SW8)*
The Ministry of Sound *(SE1)*
Wessex House *(SW11)*

East
Aquarium *(EC1)*
Turnmills *(EC1)*

Wine bars

Central
Balls Brothers Wine Bars
Davy's Wine Bars
Exxo *(W1)*
Gordon's Wine Bar *(WC2)*
Larry's Wine Bar *(WC2)*
Pimlico Wine Vaults *(SW1)*
Pitcher & Piano *(W1, WC2)*
Rochesters *(SW1)*
Shampers *(W1)*
Vats *(WC1)*

West
Davy's Wine Bars
Hollands *(W11)*
Pitcher & Piano *(SW10)*
Rock Spiders Opera *(SW10)*

South
Archduke Wine Bar *(SE1)*
Balls Brothers Wine Bars
Davy's Wine Bars
Hop Cellars *(SE1)*
The Mug House *(SE1)*

East
Balls Brothers
Bill Bentley's *(EC2)*
Bleeding Heart *(EC1)*
Corney & Barrow Wine
   Bars
Davy's Wine Bars
Drakes *(EC4)*
Eatons *(EC3)*
Leadenhall Wine Bar *(EC3)*

Pubs

Central
Antelope *(SW1)*
The Argyll Arms *(W1)*
The Barley Mow *(W1)*
Calthorpe Arms *(WC1)*
Circa *(W1)*
Cittie of Yorke *(WC1)*
The Clachan *(W1)*
The Coal Hole *(WC2)*
The Crown and Two
   Chairmen *(W1)*
The Dog & Duck *(W1)*
Duke of Albemarle *(W1)*
The Freemason's Arms *(WC2)*
Glassblower *(W1)*
The Glasshouse Stores *(W1)*
The Golden Lion *(SW1)*
The Plough *(WC2)*
Shelleys *(W1)*
Slug & Lettuce *(SW1)*
Star Tavern *(SW1)*

The Sun *(WC2)*
The Tattershall Castle *(SW1)*
Two Chairmen *(SW1)*
Walkers of St James's *(SW1)*
Waxy O'Conners *(W1)*

West
Britannia *(W8)*
The Catherine Wheel *(W8)*
Coopers Arms *(SW3)*
Duke of Clarence *(W11)*
Phene Arms *(SW3)*
The White Horse *(SW6)*

North
Slug & Lettuce *(N1)*

South
Alma *(SW18)*
Anchor *(SE1)*
Crown & Greyhound *(SE21)*
The Dog and Fox
  Ballroom *(SW19)*
Doggetts Coat & Badge *(SE1)*
George Inn *(SE1)*
The Horniman at Hay's *(SE1)*
The Old Thameside Inn *(SE1)*
Ship *(SW18)*
Slug & Lettuce *(SW15, SW18)*
Southwark Tavern *(SE1)*
Trafalgar Tavern *(SE10)*

East
Captain Kidd *(E1)*
The Crown Tavern *(EC1)*
Dickens Inn *(E1)*
The Lamb Tavern *(EC3)*
Ye Olde Cheshire
  Cheese *(EC4)*

Restaurants

Central
Ajimura *(WC2)*
L'Amico *(SW1)*
Atlantic Bar & Grill *(W1)*
The Avenue *(SW1)*
Belgo Centraal *(WC2)*
Bentleys *(W1)*
Beotys *(WC2)*
Boisdale *(SW1)*
Boudin Blanc *(W1)*
Break For The Border *(W1)*
Browns *(W1)*
Browns *(WC2)*
Café du Jardin *(WC2)*
La Capannina *(W1)*
Capital Radio Café *(WC2)*
Caravan Serai *(W1)*
Chez Gérard (Opera
  Terrace) *(WC2)*
Chez Gerard, Dover St *(W1)*
Chez Nico at Ninety
  Grosvenor House
  Hotel *(W1)*

Christopher's *(WC2)*
Chuen Cheng Ku *(W1)*
The Criterion *(W1)*
Detroit *(WC2)*
Drones *(SW1)*
Elena's L'Etoile *(W1)*
Empress Garden *(W1)*
L'Escargot *(W1)*
Euten's *(WC2)*
Fashion Café *(W1)*
Footstool *(SW1)*
French House *(W1)*
Fung Shing *(WC2)*
Le Gavroche *(W1)*
Gay Hussar *(W1)*
Gopal's of Soho *(W1)*
Green's *(SW1)*
The Guinea *(W1)*
Harrods *(SW1)*
RS Hispaniola *(WC2)*
Hodgson's *(WC2)*
Ikkyu *(W1)*
L'Incontro *(SW1)*
Ivy *(WC2)*
Kaspia *(W1)*
Ken Lo's Memories *(SW1)*
Kettners *(W1)*
Lexington *(W1)*
Lindsay House *(W1)*
Marquis *(W1)*
Mars *(WC2)*
Mezzo *(W1)*
Mimmo d'Ischia *(SW1)*
Mirabelle *(W1)*
Mitsukoshi *(SW1)*
Mon Plaisir *(WC2)*
Motcomb's *(SW1)*
Mr Kong *(WC2)*
Neal St *(WC2)*
New World *(W1)*
Odéon *(SW1)*
L'Oranger *(SW1)*
Ormond's Restaurant &
  Club *(SW1)*
Pizza On The Park *(SW1)*
Mandrake Club
  (PizzaExpress) *(W1)*
Pizzeria Condotti *(W1)*
Planet Hollywood *(W1)*
Pomegranates *(SW1)*
La Porte des Indes *(W1)*
Quaglino's *(SW1)*
Quo Vadis *(W1)*
Red Fort *(W1)*
Rib Room Hyatt Carlton
  Tower Hotel *(SW1)*
Rodos *(WC2)*
Rules *(WC2)*
Saint *(W1)*
Les Saveurs *(W1)*
Scotts *(W1)*
Sheekey's *(WC2)*
Shepherd's *(SW1)*

Simpsons-
in-the-Strand *(WC2)*
Singapura *(WC2)*
Soho Soho *(W1)*
Spaghetti House *(W1)*
The Square *(W1)*
Suntory *(SW1)*
Texas Embassy Cantina *(WC2)*
Thomas Goode
Restaurant *(W1)*
Tuttons *(WC2)*
Villandry Dining Rooms *(W1)*
West Zenders *(WC2)*
White Tower *(W1)*
Wiltons *(SW1)*
Zen Central *(W1)*

West
Al Basha *(W8)*
Barbarella *(SW6)*
Belvedere *(W8)*
Bluebird *(SW3)*
Bombay Brasserie *(SW7)*
Bonjour Vietnam *(SW6)*
Borscht & Tears *(SW3)*
Boyd's *(W8)*
Brasserie du Marché aux
Puces *(W10)*
Brasserie St Quentin *(SW3)*
Brinkley's *(SW10)*
Busabong Too *(SW10)*
Café Lazeez *(SW7)*
Canal Brasserie *(W10)*
Charcos *(SW3)*
Cibo *(W14)*
Costa's Grill *(W8)*
The Cross Keys *(SW3)*
Dan's *(SW3)*
La Dordogne *(W4)*
Downstairs At 190 *(SW7)*
English Garden *(SW3)*
English House *(SW3)*
La Famiglia *(SW10)*
First Floor *(W11)*
Formula Veneta *(SW10)*
Foxtrot Oscar *(SW3)*
Front Page *(SW3)*
Fulham Road *(SW3)*
Gilbert's *(SW7)*
Henry J Beans *(SW3)*
Jason's *(W9)*
Julie's Restaurant & Wine
Bar *(W11)*
Launceston Place *(W8)*
Leith's *(W11)*
Mao Tai *(SW6)*
Monkeys *(SW3)*
Montana *(SW6)*
Orsino *(W11)*
Pall Mall Deposit *(W10)*
Paulo's *(W6)*
Poissonnerie de
l'Avenue *(SW3)*
La Pomme d'Amour *(W11)*

POW Bar And
Restaurant *(SW3)*
San Martino *(SW3)*
Shoeless Joe's *(SW6)*
Le Suquet *(SW3)*
La Tante Claire *(SW3)*
Victoria & Albert
Museum Café *(SW7)*
Wine Gallery *(SW10)*
Wódka *(W8)*
Zen *(SW3)*

North
Crown & Goose *(NW1)*
Cuba Libre *(N1)*
Engineer *(NW1)*
Euphorium *(N1)*
Feng Shang *(NW1)*
Frederick's *(N1)*
Gecko *(NW1)*
Granita *(N1)*
Lemonia *(NW1)*
Le Mercury *(N1)*
Odette's *(NW1)*
Rose Garden Buffet *(NW1)*
Seashell *(NW1)*
Le Studio Café *(N1)*
The Viceroy *(NW1)*
Village Bistro *(N6)*
ZeNW3 *(NW3)*

South
The Battersea Barge
Bistro *(SW8)*
Bengal Clipper *(SE1)*
Bombay Bicycle Club *(SW12)*
Café Greenwich Park *(SE10)*
Chez Bruce *(SW17)*
Le Gothique *(SW18)*
The People's Palace *(SE1)*
Polygon Bar & Grill *(SW4)*
Le Pont de la Tour *(SE1)*
RSJ *(SE1)*
Secret Garden *(SE5)*

East
Abbaye *(EC1)*
Aquarium *(E1)*
Babe Ruth's *(E1)*
Bow Wine Vaults *(EC4)*
Brasserie Rocque *(EC2)*
Bubb's *(EC1)*
Café du Marché *(EC1)*
The Candid Arts Trust *(EC1)*
Champenois *(EC2)*
City Brasserie *(EC3)*
City Miyama *(EC4)*
City Rhodes *(EC4)*
Coates Karaoke Bar &
Restaurant *(EC2)*
Deacons *(EC4)*
Fox & Anchor *(EC1)*
Frocks *(E9)*
Gladwins *(EC3)*
Hothouse Bar & Grill *(E1)*

Imperial City (EC3)
Maison Novelli (EC1)
Le Mesurier (EC1)
La Paquerette (EC2)
The Place Below (EC2)
Quayside (E1)
Saint John (EC1)
Simpsons Tavern (EC3)
Sweetings (EC4)
Tatsuso (EC2)
Throgmorton's (EC2)
Tinseltown (EC1)
Whittington's (EC4)

Outside London
Hampton Court,
  Tiltyard (Surrey)

Hotels

Central
Athenaeum Hotel (W1)
The Berkeley (SW1)
The Berkshire (W1)
The Berners Hotel (W1)
Britannia
  Intercontinental Hotel (W1)
Brown's Hotel (W1)
The Cadogan (SW1)
The Cavendish (SW1)
The Chelsea (SW1)
The Chesterfield Hotel (W1)
Churchill (W1)
Claridge's (W1)
The Connaught (W1)
Cumberland Hotel (W1)
The Dorchester (W1)
Dukes Hotel (SW1)
Durrants Hotel (W1)
Forte Posthouse Regent's
  Park (W1)
Four Seasons Hotel (W1)
Goring Hotel (SW1)
The Grafton (W1)
The Grosvenor (SW1)
The Grosvenor House
  Hotel (W1)
The Halkin (SW1)
Hampshire Hotel (WC2)
Hilton on
  Park Lane (W1)
Holiday Inn – Mayair (W1)
Hotel Russell (WC1)
Howard Hotel (WC2)
Hyatt Carlton Tower (SW1)
Hyde Park Hotel (SW1)
Inter-Continental (W1)
The Kenilworth (WC1)
The Landmark (W1)
The Lanesborough (SW1)
Langham Hilton (W1)
London Marriott (W1)
The Mayfair
  Inter-Continental (W1)

Le Meridien (W1)
The Metropolitan (W1)
The Mountbatten (WC2)
Park Lane Hotel (W1)
Portman Hotel (W1)
The Ritz (W1)
Royal Horseguards Thistle
  Hotel (SW1)
The Rubens (SW1)
The Savoy (WC2)
The Selfridge Hotel (W1)
Sheraton Belgravia (SW1)
Sheraton Park Tower (SW1)
The Stafford (SW1)
Stakis St Ermins (SW1)
Strand Palace Hotel (WC2)
22 Jermyn St (SW1)
Waldorf Hotel (WC2)
The Washington (W1)
The Westbury (W1)

West
Basil Street Hotel (SW3)
The Capital (SW3)
The Carnarvon Hotel (W5)
Conrad Hotel (SW10)
Gloucester Hotel (SW7)
Halcyon Hotel (W11)
Harrington Hall (SW7)
The Hempel (W2)
Kensington
  Palace Thistle (W8)
London Metropole (W2)
The Rembrandt Hotel (SW7)
Royal Garden Hotel (W8)
Royal Lancaster (W2)
Vanderbilt Hotel (SW7)

North
Hendon Hall Hotel (NW4)
White House Hotel (NW1)

South
Cannizaro House (SW19)
Holiday Inn – Nelson
  Dock (SE16)

East
The International Hotel (E14)
Tower Thistle (E1)

Outside London
Cliveden (Berks)
Horwood House (Bucks)
Monkey Island Hotel (Berks)
Selsdon Park Hotel (Surrey)

Venues with wedding licences

* *licence applied for*

Central
The Berkeley (SW1)
The Berners Hotel (W1)
Café Royal (W1)
Churchill (W1)
The Comedy Store (SW1)
The Dorchester (W1)
Dukes Hotel (SW1)
Four Seasons Hotel (W1)
Goring Hotel (SW1)
The Grosvenor House
  Hotel (W1)
Howard Hotel (WC2)
Hyatt Carlton Tower (SW1)
Hyde Park Hotel (SW1)
The Lanesborough (SW1)
Langham Hilton (W1)
The Law Society (WC2)
Limelight* (W1)
London Palladium (W1)
The Mayfair Inter-
  Continental (W1)
Le Meridien (W1)
National Liberal Club (SW1)
One Whitehall Place (SW1)
Park Lane Hotel (W1)
Portman Hotel (W1)
The Queen Elizabeth II
  Conference Centre (SW1)
TS Queen Mary (WC2)
The Ritz (W1)
Rock Circus* (W1)
Royal Institution of
  Great Britain* (W1)
Royal Society of Arts (WC2)
The Savoy (WC2)
Searcy's (SW1)
The Stafford* (SW1)
Stakis St Ermins (SW1)
Staple Inn* (WC1)
Waldorf Hotel (WC2)

West
Belvedere (W8)
The Carnarvon Hotel (W5)
Chelsea Football Club (SW6)
Chelsea
  Old Town Hall (SW3)
Dora House* (SW7)
Fulham Town Hall (SW6)
Hammersmith Town
  Hall (W6)
Hurlingham Club (SW6)
The Irish Centre (W6)
The London Toy And Model
  Museum* (W2)
Millennium Conference
  Centre* (SW7)
The Rembrandt Hotel (SW7)

Royal Garden Hotel (W8)
Royal Geographical
  Society (SW7)
Royal Lancaster* (W2)
White Swan Water (W9)

North
Arts Depot* (NW1)
Avenue House (N3)
Burgh House (NW3)
Hendon Hall Hotel (NW4)
Lauderdale House* (N6)
Lee Valley Leisure
  Centre (N9)
London Zoo (NW1)

South
Academy of Live &
  Recorded Arts (SW18)
Cannizaro House (SW19)
Dulwich College (SE21)
The Golden Hinde (SE1)
Holiday Inn – Nelson
  Dock (SE16)
Kingswood House (SE21)
Queen's House (SE10)
Ranger's House* (SE10)
Trafalgar Tavern (SE10)
Victoria Pump House (SW11)

East
The Candid Arts Trust* (EC1)
Inner Temple Hall* (EC4)
Plaisterers' Hall* (EC2)
Quayside (E1)
St Bartholomew's
  Hospital* (EC1)
Sutton House (E9)
Tower Thistle (E1)

Outside London
Addington Palace (CR9)
Bath – Assembly Rooms
Bath – Pump Room (Avon)
Clandon (Surrey)
Cliveden (Berks)
Ham House (Surrey)
Herstmonceux Castle
  (East Sussex)
Highclere Castle (Berks)
Hollington House
  Hotel (Berks)
Kew Gardens (Surrey)
Knebworth House (Herts)
Monkey Island Hotel (Berks)
Penshurst Place and
  Gardens (Kent)
Phyllis Court (Oxon)
Pinewood Studios (Bucks)
Sandown Park
  Racecourse (Surrey)
Spring Grove House (Middx)
Twickenham Banqueting
  Centre* (Middx)
Waddesdon Manor, The
  Dairy (Bucks)

Venues with hirer's choice of caterer

Central
Accademia Italiana/European Academy *(SW1)*
Browns Club *(WC2)*
Cabinet War Rooms *(SW1)*
Canning House *(SW1)*
Christie's *(SW1)*
Circa *(W1)*
The Comedy Store *(SW1)*
Conway Hall *(WC1)*
The Dickens' House Museum *(WC1)*
Dolphin Square *(SW1)*
Guards Museum *(SW1)*
Hamiltons Gallery *(W1)*
Hamleys Metropolis *(W1)*
King's College *(WC2)*
Limelight *(W1)*
Lincoln's Inn *(WC2)*
London Astoria *(WC2)*
London Astoria 2 *(W1)*
London Scottish *(SW1)*
Lundonia House *(WC1)*
Mall Galleries *(SW1)*
Music Room At Grays *(W1)*
New Connaught Rms *(WC2)*
Nôtre Dame Hall *(WC2)*
Palace Theatre *(W1)*
Phillips *(W1)*
Photographers' Gallery *(WC2)*
Mandrake Club (PizzaExpress) *(W1)*
The RAW Club *(WC1)*
Royal Mint Sovereign Gallery *(SW1)*
Ruby's *(W1)*
RUSI Building *(SW1)*
St Moritz *(W1)*
The Sanctuary *(WC2)*
Spanish Club *(W1)*
Staple Inn *(WC1)*
SW1 Club *(SW1)*
Theatre Museum *(WC2)*
Wag *(W1)*
Westminster Boating Base *(SW1)*
Westminster Cathedral Hall *(SW1)*

West
Bonham's *(SW7)*
Carlyle's House *(SW3)*
The Chelsea Gardener *(SW3)*
Chiswick House *(W4)*
The Courtyard, St Peter's Hall *(W11)*
Crazy Larry's *(SW10)*
Dora House *(SW7)*
Duke of York's HQ *(SW3)*

41 Queen's Gate Terrace *(SW7)*
French Institute *(SW7)*
Fulham House *(SW6)*
Fulham Palace *(SW6)*
Fulham Town Hall *(SW6)*
Gargoyle Club *(SW10)*
Gunnersbury Park *(W3)*
Hammersmith Palais *(W6)*
Hammersmith Town Hall *(W6)*
Hogarth's House *(W4)*
Holy Trinity Brompton Church Hall *(SW7)*
The Irish Centre *(W6)*
Peacock House *(W14)*
Polish Social & Cultural Association *(W6)*
Porchester Centre *(W2)*
Queens Ice Bowl *(W2)*
Rock Spiders Opera *(SW10)*
Royal College of Art *(SW7)*
Royal College of Music *(SW7)*
Upper Refectory Suite *(SW3)*
Westway Studios *(W11)*
Will's Art Warehouse *(SW6)*
The Worx III *(SW6)*

North
Arts Depot *(NW1)*
Avenue House *(N3)*
Bagleys *(N1)*
Electric Ballroom *(NW1)*
King's College, Hampstead Site *(NW3)*
Lee Valley Leisure Centre *(N9)*
Rose Garden Buffet *(NW1)*
Royal Veterinary College *(NW1)*
Stoke Newington Town Hall *(N16)*
The Worx I *(N1)*
The Worx II *(N1)*

South
Academy of Live & Recorded Arts *(SW18)*
Battersea Park *(SW8)*
Battersea Town Hall *(SW11)*
Bramah Tea & Coffee Museum *(SE1)*
Café Greenwich Park *(SE10)*
Chatham Hall *(SW11)*
The Conservatory *(SW11)*
Cottons Atrium *(SE1)*
Cutty Sark *(SE10)*
Earlsfield Library *(SW18)*
The Fridge *(SW2)*
Glaziers' Hall *(SE1)*
The Golden Hinde *(SE1)*
Goldsmiths College *(SE14)*
Hollyhedge House *(SE3)*
Hop Exchange *(SE1)*

Horniman Museum and
  Gardens (SE23)
Imperial
  War Museum (SE1)
King's College School (SW19)
Kingswood House (SE21)
Linford Film Studios (SW8)
London Rowing Club (SW15)
The Ministry of Sound (SE1)
The Old Operating Theatre,
  Museum & Herb
  Garret (SE1)
Pentland House (SE13)
St John's Hill (SW11)
St Thomas' Hospital (SE1)
Streatham Ice Arena (SW16)
Tower Bridge (SE1)
Victoria Pump House (SW11)
Wandsworth
  Civic Suite (SW18)
Winston Churchill's Britain
  At War Experience (SE1)

East

Aquarium (EC1)
Bishopsgate Institute (EC2)
Broadgate Estates (EC2)
The Candid Arts Trust (EC1)
Circus Space (EC1)
Docklands Sailing &
  Watersports Centre (E14)
Dr Johnsons' House (EC4)
Edwin Shirley
  Productions (E3)
Hamilton House (EC4)
Holderness House (EC2)
House of Detention (EC1)
Lea Rowing Club (E5)
Lee Valley Cycle Circuit (E15)
Mudchute Park and
  Farm (E14)
Museum of London (EC2)
Newham City Farm (E16)
The Old Town Hall,
  Stratford (E15)
HMS President (EC4)
St Botolph's Hall (EC2)
St Bride Foundation
  Institute (EC4)
St John's Gate (EC1)
Salters' Hall (EC2)
Slaughterhouse Gallery (EC1)
Spitalfields Market (E1)
Turnmills (EC1)
Whitechapel Art Gallery (E1)

Outside London

Boston Manor House (Middx)
Chislehurst Caves (Kent)
Kew Bridge Steam
  Museum (Middx)
Marble Hill House (Surrey)
Rossway Park (Herts)
Spring Grove House (Middx)

Syon Park
  (Conservatory) (Middx)
Whitewebbs Museum of
  Transport (Middx)

Venues with outside areas

Central

Accademia Italiana/European
  Academy (SW1)
Arts Club (W1)
El Barco Latino (WC2)
Chez Gérard (Opera
  Terrace) (WC2)
Dartmouth House (W1)
The Dorchester (W1)
Dukes Hotel (SW1)
Gray's Inn (WC1)
Guards Museum (SW1)
RS Hispaniola (WC2)
ICA (SW1)
Iceni (W1)
The Imagination
  Gallery (WC1)
International Students (W1)
Lansdowne Club (W1)
Lincoln's Inn (WC2)
Mosimann's Belfry (SW1)
National Liberal Club (SW1)
Naval & Military Club (W1)
TS Queen Mary (WC2)
The Ritz (W1)
Royal Aeronautical
  Society (W1)
Royal Horseguards Thistle
  Hotel (SW1)
St Stephen'
  Constitutional Club (SW1)
Sheraton Park Tower (SW1)
Spencer House (SW1)
University of
  London Union (WC1)
University Women's
  Club (W1)
HQS Wellington (WC2)
Westminster Abbey
  Garden (SW1)
Westminster Boating
  Base (SW1)

West

Belvedere (W8)
Brompton Oratory – St
  Wilfrid's Hall (SW7)
Canal Brasserie (W10)
Carlyle's House (SW3)
The Chelsea Gardener (SW3)
Chelsea Physic Garden (SW3)
Chiswick House (W4)
Commonwealth
  Institute (W8)
Dan's (SW3)
Duke of York's HQ (SW3)

Fulham Palace *(SW6)*
Gunnersbury Park *(W3)*
The Hempel *(W2)*
Henry J Beans *(SW3)*
Hogarth's House *(W4)*
Hurlingham Club *(SW6)*
Imperial College *(SW7)*
Orangery (Holland
 Park) *(W8)*
Orangery
 (Kensington Palace) *(W8)*
Paulo's *(W6)*
Peacock House *(W14)*
Polish Hearth Club *(SW7)*
The Roof Gardens *(W8)*
Royal Geographical
 Society *(SW7)*
Royal Parks Agency *(W2)*
Serpentine Gallery *(W2)*
Victoria & Albert
 Museum *(SW7)*

North

Alexandra
 Palace & Park *(N22)*
Cecil Sharp House *(NW1)*
Freud Museum *(NW3)*
Kenwood House *(NW3)*
Lauderdale House *(N6)*
London Zoo *(NW1)*
Regent's College *(NW1)*
Rose Garden Buffet *(NW1)*
Royal Air
 Force Museum *(NW9)*
Royal Veterinary
 College *(NW1)*

South

Academy of Live &
 Recorded Arts *(SW18)*
Anchor *(SE1)*
Bank of England Club *(SW15)*
Battersea Park *(SW8)*
HMS Belfast *(SE1)*
Brockwell Lido *(SE24)*
Café Greenwich Park *(SE10)*
Cannizaro House *(SW19)*
The Conservatory *(SW11)*
Crystal Palace Park *(SE20)*
Cutty Sark *(SE10)*
Design Museum *(SE1)*
Doggetts Coat & Badge *(SE1)*
Dulwich College *(SE21)*
Dulwich Picture
 Gallery *(SE21)*
Froebel Institute
 College *(SW15)*
Le Gothique *(SW18)*
Horniman Museum and
 Gardens *(SE23)*
King's College School *(SW19)*
London Rowing Club *(SW15)*
Neal's Lodge *(SW18)*
Pentland House *(SE13)*

Queen's House *(SE10)*
Roehampton Club *(SW15)*
Secret Garden *(SE5)*
Victoria Pump House *(SW11)*
Whitelands College *(SW15)*
Winchester House *(SW15)*

East

Aquarium *(E1)*
Bleeding Heart *(EC1)*
Brasserie Rocque *(EC2)*
Broadgate Estates *(EC2)*
Docklands Sailing &
 Watersports Centre *(E14)*
Honourable
 Artillery Co *(EC1)*
Inner Temple Hall *(EC4)*
Lea Rowing Club *(E5)*
Merchant Taylors' Hall *(EC2)*
Middle Temple Hall *(EC4)*
Mudchute Park and
 Farm *(E14)*
Museum of London *(EC2)*
Newham City Farm *(E16)*
La Paquerette *(EC2)*
HMS President *(EC4)*
Quayside *(E1)*
St John's Gate *(EC1)*
Skinners' Hall *(EC4)*
Spitalfields Market *(E1)*

Outside London

Addington Palace *(CR9)*
Ascot Racecourse, Pavilions
 & Queen Anne
 Rooms *(Berks)*
Ascot Racecourse, Royal
 Enclosure *(Berks)*
Beaulieu *(Hants)*
Blenheim Palace *(Oxon)*
Boston Manor House *(Middx)*
Brocket Hall *(Herts)*
Chislehurst Caves *(Kent)*
Clandon *(Surrey)*
Cliveden *(Berks)*
Denbies Wine Estate *(Surrey)*
Epsom Downs *(Surrey)*
Ham House *(Surrey)*
Ham Polo Club *(Surrey)*
Hampton Court
 Palace *(Surrey)*
Hampton Court,
 Tiltyard *(Surrey)*
Herstmonceux Castle *(East
 Sussex)*
Hever Castle *(Kent)*
Highclere Castle *(Berks)*
Hollington House
 Hotel *(Berks)*
Horwood House *(Bucks)*
Kempton Park *(Middx)*
Kew (Royal Botanic)
 Gardens *(Surrey)*
Knebworth House *(Herts)*
Leander Club *(Berks)*

Leeds Castle *(Kent)*
Legoland Windsor *(Berks)*
Loseley Park *(Surrey)*
Marble Hill House *(Surrey)*
Monkey Island Hotel *(Berks)*
Moyns Park *(Essex)*
Penshurst Place *(Kent)*
Phyllis Court *(Oxon)*
Pinewood Studios *(Bucks)*
Polesden Lacey *(Surrey)*
Queen's Eyot *(Berks)*
Rossway Park *(Herts)*
Royal Holloway
   College *(Surrey)*
Sandown Park
   Racecourse *(Surrey)*
Selsdon Park Hotel *(Surrey)*
Spring Grove House *(Middx)*
Syon Park
   (Banqueting) *(Middx)*
Syon Park
   (Conservatory) *(Middx)*
Syon Park (House) *(Middx)*
Temple Island *(Oxon)*
Thorpe Park *(Surrey)*
Waddesdon Manor,
   The Dairy *(Bucks)*
West Wycombe
   Caves *(Bucks)*
Whipsnade Wild
   Animal Park *(Beds)*
Wrotham Park *(Herts)*

Venues with marquee sites

Central
Churchill *(W1)*
Gray's Inn *(WC1)*
Guards Museum *(SW1)*
St Stephen'
   Constitutional Club *(SW1)*
Westminster Abbey
   Garden *(SW1)*
Westminster Boating
   Base *(SW1)*

West
Chelsea Physic Garden *(SW3)*
Chiswick House *(W4)*
Commonwealth
   Institute *(W8)*
Duke of York's HQ *(SW3)*
Fulham Palace *(SW6)*
Gunnersbury Park *(W3)*
The Hempel *(W2)*
Hogarth's House *(W4)*
Imperial College *(SW7)*
Jason's *(W9)*
The London Toy and
   Model Museum *(W2)*
Orangery (Holland
   Park) *(W8)*
Peacock House *(W14)*

Riverside Studios *(W6)*
Royal Geographical
   Society *(SW7)*
Serpentine Gallery *(W2)*
The Worx III *(SW6)*

North
Alexandra
   Palace & Park *(N22)*
Bagleys *(N1)*
Freud Museum *(NW3)*
Hendon Hall Hotel *(NW4)*
Kenwood House *(NW3)*
Lauderdale House *(N6)*
Lee Valley Leisure
   Centre *(N9)*
London Zoo *(NW1)*
Regent's College *(NW1)*
Rose Garden Buffet *(NW1)*
Royal Air
   Force Museum *(NW9)*

South
Adrenaline Village *(SW8)*
Bank of England Club *(SW15)*
Battersea Park *(SW8)*
Café Greenwich Park *(SE10)*
Crystal Palace Park *(SE20)*
Dulwich College *(SE21)*
Dulwich Picture
   Gallery *(SE21)*
The Golden Hinde *(SE1)*
Goldsmiths College *(SE14)*
Hollyhedge House *(SE3)*
Imperial
   War Museum *(SE1)*
Kingswood House *(SE21)*
The Leathermarket *(SE1)*
Neal's Lodge *(SW18)*
Pentland House *(SE13)*
Queen's House *(SE10)*
Ranger's House *(SE10)*
Roehampton Club *(SW15)*
St Thomas' Hospital *(SE1)*
Ship *(SW18)*
The South Bank Centre *(SE1)*
Victoria Pump House *(SW11)*
Whitelands College *(SW15)*
Winchester House *(SW15)*

East
Beckton Alpine Centre *(E6)*
Bow Film Studios *(E15)*
Circus Space *(EC1)*
Drapers' Hall *(EC2)*
Edwin Shirley
   Productions *(E3)*
The Gibson Hall *(EC2)*
Honourable
   Artillery Co *(EC1)*
Inner Temple Hall *(EC4)*
Lee Valley Cycle Circuit *(E15)*
Mudchute Park and
   Farm *(E14)*

The Old Town Hall,
 Stratford *(E15)*
Spitalfields Market *(E1)*
YHA City of London *(EC4)*

Outside London
Addington Palace *(CR9)*
Ascot Racecourse, Royal
 Enclosure *(Berks)*
Beaulieu *(Hants)*
Blenheim Palace *(Oxon)*
Boston Manor House *(Middx)*
Brocket Hall *(Herts)*
Clandon *(Surrey)*
Cliveden *(Berks)*
Epsom Downs *(Surrey)*
Ham House *(Surrey)*
Herstmonceux Castle
 (East Sussex)
Highclere Castle *(Berks)*
Hillingdon Ski and
 Snowboard Centre *(Middx)*
Hollington House
 Hotel *(Berks)*
Horwood House *(Bucks)*
Kempton Park *(Middx)*
Kew (Royal Botanic)
 Gardens *(Surrey)*
Knebworth House *(Herts)*
Leander Club *(Berks)*
Leeds Castle *(Kent)*
Loseley Park *(Surrey)*
Marble Hill House *(Surrey)*
Moyns Park *(Essex)*
Penshurst Place and
 Gardens *(Kent)*
Phyllis Court *(Oxon)*
Pinewood Studios *(Bucks)*
Polesden Lacey *(Surrey)*
Queen's Eyot *(Berks)*
Rossway Park *(Herts)*
Royal Holloway
 College *(Surrey)*
Sandown Park
 Racecourse *(Surrey)*
Spring Grove House *(Middx)*
Syon Park
 (Banqueting) *(Middx)*
Syon Park
 (Conservatory) *(Middx)*
Syon Park (House) *(Middx)*
Temple Island *(Oxon)*
Thorpe Park *(Surrey)*
Waddesdon Manor,
 The Dairy *(Bucks)*
West Wycombe
 Caves *(Bucks)*
Whipsnade Wild
 Animal Park *(Beds)*
Whitewebbs Museum
 of Transport *(Middx)*
Wrotham Park *(Herts)*

ROOM CAPACITIES

CAPACITY LISTS

Note: particularly with hotels, it may be possible to divide rooms to provide a smaller space.

Function rooms listed by standing capacity

* largest entry for venue

£E

1000	British Museum WC1 *(Max*)*
	Royal Academy of Arts W1 *(Summer Exhibition*)*
750	Blenheim Palace, Oxon *(State Rooms*)*
700	Mezzo W1 *(Max*)*
	Victoria & Albert Museum SW7 *(Dome, Medieval Treasury (& Pirelli Garden)*)*
600	Madame Tussaud's NW1 *(Grand Hall*)*
	Victoria & Albert Museum SW7 *(Raphael Gallery)*
500	Mezzo W1 *(Mezzanine)*
	Tate Gallery SW1 *(Pre Raphaelite and 19th Century Gallery*)*
450	Spencer House SW1 *(Max*)*
400	Courtauld Gallery WC2 *(Max*)*
	Hampton Court Palace, Surrey *(Great Hall*)*
	Royal Academy of Arts W1 *(Private Rms)*
	Victoria & Albert Museum SW7 *(Gamble Rm including Morris Rm))*
350	Wallace Collection W1 *(Long Gallery*)*
300	Hayward Gallery SE1 *(Max*)*
	National Portrait Gallery WC2 *(Max*)*
	Syon Park (House), Middx *(Long Gallery*)*
	Victoria & Albert Museum SW7 *(Silver Gallery)*
250	Annabel's W1 *(Max*)*
	Cliveden, Berks *(Max*)*
	Courtauld Gallery WC2 *(Fine Rooms)*
	Kenwood House NW3 *(Max*)*
	Madame Tussaud's NW1 *(Garden Party)*
200	Apsley House W1 *(Max*)*
	Blenheim Palace, Oxon *(Orangery)*
	Courtauld Gallery WC2 *(Great Room)*
	Queen's House SE10 *(Max*)*
	Tate Gallery SW1 *(Clore Gallery Foyer)*
180	Brocket Hall, Herts *(Max*)*
170	Cliveden, Berks *(Great Hall)*
150	Chiswick House W4 *(First floor*)*
	Queen's House SE10 *(Great Hall or Orangery Suite)*
	HM Tower of London EC3 *(Medieval Palace or White Tower*)*
	Wrotham Park, Herts *(Drawing Room*)*
120	Queen's House SE10 *(Treasury)*
100	Rossway Park, Herts *(Max*)*
	Sir John Soane's Museum WC2 *(Max*)*
	Wrotham Park, Herts *(Dining Room)*
80	Hampton Court Palace, Surrey *(Banqueting House)*
	Old Royal Observatory SE10 *(Max*)*
	Victoria & Albert Museum SW7 *(Morris Rm)*
75	Cliveden, Berks *(French Dining Rm)*
50	Mezzo W1 *(Pâtisserie)*
	Wallace Collection W1 *(Gallery 17)*
	Wrotham Park, Herts *(Saloon)*
40	Wallace Collection W1 *(Arms and Armour)*
30	Queen's House SE10 *(Loggia)*
25	Tate Gallery SW1 *(Lodge)*

£M-E

5000	Thorpe Park, Surrey *(Max*)*
3000	Spitalfields Market E1 *(Market (summer)*)*
2500	Beaulieu, Hants *(National Motor Museum*)*
	Royal Lancaster W2 *(Max*)*
2000	The Business Design Centre N1 *(Max*)*
	The Grosvenor House W1 *(Max*)*
	Legoland Windsor, Berks *(Max*)*
	Spitalfields Market E1 *(Marquee (winter))*
1500	The Grosvenor House W1 *(Great Rm)*
	Guildhall EC2 *(Max*)*
	London Aquarium SE1 *(Max*)*
	Royal Lancaster W2 *(Nine Kings Suite)*
	Science Museum SW7 *(Max*)*
1450	Royal Albert Hall SW7 *(Cabaret or Ball*)*
1400	Inter-Continental W1 *(Grand Ballroom*)*
	Royal Air Force Museum NW9 *(Max*)*
1300	Royal Lancaster W2 *(Westbourne Suite)*
1250	Hilton on Park Lane W1 *(Grand Ballroom)*
1200	Natural History Museum SW7 *(Central Hall*)*
1000	The Dorchester W1 *(Ballroom*)*
	Hurlingham Club SW6 *(Max*)*
	Imperial War Museum SE1 *(Max*)*
	Park Lane Hotel W1 *(Ballroom*)*
	La Porte des Indes W1 *(Max*)*
	Saatchi Gallery NW8 *(Max*)*
900	Guildhall EC2 *(Great Hall)*
	Millennium Conference Centre SW7 *(Lower Level*)*
800	Claridge's W1 *(Max*)*
	Cumberland Hotel W1 *(Production Box*)*
	Fashion Café W1 *(Grande Salle*)*
	The Grosvenor House W1 *(Ballroom)*
	Imperial War Museum SE1 *(Exhibition Hall)*
	Inter-Continental W1 *(Westminster)*
	Millennium Conference Centre SW7 *(Ground Level (open))*
	Museum of London EC2 *(Max*)*
	Royal Garden Hotel W8 *(Palace Suite*)*
	The Savoy WC2 *(Lancaster Rm*)*
750	Café de Paris W1 *(Max*)*
	Four Seasons Hotel W1 *(Ballroom*)*
	Inner Temple Hall EC4 *(Max*)*
	National Liberal Club SW1 *(Max*)*
	Royal Albert Hall SW7 *(Arena)*
	Westway Studios W11 *(Studio 1*)*
700	Portman Hotel W1 *(Ballroom*)*
	Royal Air Force Museum NW9 *(Bomber Command Hall or Main Aircraft Hall)*
650	Hyatt Carlton Tower SW1 *(Ballroom*)*
	Hyde Park Hotel SW1 *(Max*)*
600	Arts Depot NW1 *(Max*)*
	Christie's SW1 *(Max*)*
	Guildhall EC2 *(Old Library)*
	The Hempel W2 *(Max*)*
	Lincoln's Inn WC2 *(Great Hall*)*
	Penshurst Place, Kent *(Max*)*
	Phyllis Court, Oxon *(Ballroom*)*
	Plaisterers' Hall EC2 *(Max*)*
	The Queen Elizabeth II Conference Centre SW1 *(Benjamin Britten Lounge*)*
	Reform Club SW1 *(Max*)*
	Science Museum SW7 *(East Hall)*
590	Westway Studios W11 *(Studio 2)*
550	Barbican Centre EC2 *(Max*)*
	Knebworth House, Herts *(Max*)*
500	Addington Palace CR9 *(Max*)*
	Atlantic Bar & Grill W1 *(Max*)*
	Banqueting House SW1 *(Main Hall*)*
	Circus Space EC1 *(Max*)*
	Cumberland Hotel W1 *(Carlisle)*
	Gloucester Hotel SW7 *(Cotswold Suite & Courtfield Suite*)*
	Goldsmiths' Hall EC2 *(Livery Hall*)*

	Ham House, Surrey *(Max*)*
	Hilton on Park Lane W1 *(Grand Ballroom - Section 1)*
	Hurlingham Club SW6 *(Quadrangle Suite)*
	The Landmark W1 *(Ballroom*)*
	Merchant Taylors' Hall EC2 *(Great Hall*)*
	Phillips W1 *(Max*)*
	Science Museum SW7 *(Flight Gallery)*
	The South Bank Centre SE1 *(Queen Elizabeth Hall Foyer*)*
	Westminster Abbey Garden SW1 *(Marquee*)*
480	Hilton on Park Lane W1 *(Grand Ballroom - Section 2)*
450	The Berkeley W1 *(Ballroom*)*
	Gray's Inn WC1 *(Max*)*
	The Imagination Gallery WC1 *(Atrium and Mezzanine*)*
	Middle Temple Hall EC4 *(Hall*)*
	Quaglino's SW1 *(Max*)*
420	The Roof Gardens W8 *(Max*)*
400	The Avenue SW1 *(Max*)*
	Barbican Centre EC2 *(Garden Rm)*
	Bath – Assembly Rooms *(Ballroom*)*
	Claridge's W1 *(Ballroom)*
	The Criterion W1 *(Max*)*
	Drapers' Hall EC2 *(Livery Hall*)*
	Harrington Hall SW7 *(Harrington*)*
	The Hempel W2 *(Garden Square)*
	Hyde Park Hotel SW1 *(Ballroom*)*
	Inner Temple Hall EC4 *(Hall)*
	Inter-Continental W1 *(Piccadilly)*
	The London Dungeon SE1 *(Max*)*
	The Mayfair Inter-Continental W1 *(Crystal Rm*)*
	Le Meridien W1 *(Georgian*)*
	Natural History Museum SW7 *(Earth Galleries)*
	One Whitehall Place SW1 *(Gladstone Library*)*
	Penshurst Place, Kent *(Baron's Hall)*
	The People's Palace SE1 *(Max*)*
	Royal Air Force Museum NW9 *(Battle of Britain Hall)*
	Royal College of Music SW7 *(Concert Hall*)*
	The Savoy WC2 *(Abraham Lincoln & Manhattan Rms)*
	Sotheby's W1 *(Max*)*
	Stationers' Hall EC4 *(Livery Hall*)*
380	London Zoo NW1 *(Regency Suite*)*
360	The Landmark W1 *(Empire Rm)*
350	Accademia Italiana/European Academy SW1 *(Max*)*
	Baltic Exchange EC3 *(Trading Floor*)*
	Banqueting House SW1 *(Undercroft)*
	Clothworkers' Hall EC3 *(Livery Hall*)*
	The Gibson Hall EC2 *(Hall*)*
	Leeds Castle, Kent *(Fairfax Hall With Terrace Room*)*
	Le Meridien W1 *(Edwardian)*
	Rock Circus W1 *(Max*)*
	The Royal College of Pathologists SW1 *(Max*)*
	The Savoy WC2 *(River Rm)*
	Serpentine Gallery W2 *(Max*)*
330	Roehampton Club SW15 *(Max*)*
300	Beaulieu, Hants *(Brabazon)*
	City Brasserie EC3 *(Max*)*
	Dulwich Picture Gallery SE21 *(Max*)*
	Four Seasons Hotel W1 *(Garden Rm)*
	Gray's Inn WC1 *(Hall)*
	Hamiltons Gallery W1 *(Max*)*
	Hilton on Park Lane W1 *(Curzon Suite)*
	Institute of Directors SW1 *(Nash*)*
	Kew (Royal Botanic) Gardens, Surrey *(Temperate House*)*
	Knebworth House, Herts *(House or Manor Barn (incl Bulwer Room))*
	The Landmark W1 *(Drawing Rm)*
	National Liberal Club SW1 *(Dining Rm * or Smoking Rm *)*
	The Queen Elizabeth II Conference Centre SW1 *(Pickwick Suite)*
	Science Museum SW7 *(Science of Sport)*
	Skinners' Hall EC4 *(Max*)*
	Westway Studios W11 *(Studio 4)*
280	Clandon, Surrey *(Restaurant*)*
250	Barbican Centre EC2 *(Conservatory Terrace)*
	The Berners Hotel W1 *(Thomas Ashton Suite*)*
	Bonham's SW7 *(Max*)*
	Clandon, Surrey *(Marble Hall)*
	The Dorchester W1 *(Orchid)*
	Gloucester Hotel SW7 *(Cotswold - Chalford/Dean)*
	Goldsmiths' Hall EC2 *(Drawing Rm & Exhbition Rm)*
	Grocers' Hall EC2 *(Livery Hall*)*
	Guildhall EC2 *(Livery Hall or West Crypt)*
	Hilton on Park Lane W1 *(Crystal Palace Rm or Grand Ballroom - Section 3)*
	Hyde Park Hotel SW1 *(Knightsbridge Suite)*
	The Imagination Gallery WC1 *(Gallery)*
	Innholders' Hall EC4 *(Max*)*
	Knebworth House, Herts *(Lodge Barn)*
	The Lanesborough SW1 *(Belgravia*)*
	Leeds Castle, Kent *(Henry VIII Banqueting Hall)*
	Lincoln's Inn WC2 *(Old Hall)*
	The London Planetarium NW1 *(Max*)*
	Museum of London EC2 *(Lord Mayor's Coach Gallery)*
	Museum of the Moving Image SE1 *(Max*)*
	National Liberal Club SW1 *(David Lloyd George or Terrace*)*
	Natural History Museum SW7 *(North Hall)*
	One Whitehall Place SW1 *(Reading And Writing Room)*
	Phillips W1 *(Blenheim Room)*
	Phyllis Court, Oxon *(Grandstand)*
	Reform Club SW1 *(Coffee Rm or Library)*
	Roehampton Club SW15 *(Roehampton Room)*
	Saddlers' Hall EC2 *(Max*)*
	The Sanctuary WC2 *(Max*)*
	Searcy's SW1 *(Max*)*
	The South Bank Centre SE1 *(Hong Kong & Chelsfield Rm)*
	Theatre Museum WC2 *(Paintings Gallery*)*
	Tower Bridge SE1 *(Walkways*)*
240	The Gibson Hall EC2 *(Garden Room)*
230	Woods River Cruises SE3 *(Silver Barracuda*)*
224	Clothworkers' Hall EC3 *(Reception Room)*
220	Motcomb's Club SW1 *(Max*)*
	One Whitehall Place SW1 *(Whitehall Suite)*
200	Apothecaries' Hall EC4 *(Hall*)*
	Arts Club W1 *(Dining Rm*)*
	Bank of England Museum EC2 *(Max*)*
	Bath – Assembly Rooms *(Octagon or Tea Room)*
	Brighton Royal Pavilion, Sussex *(Banqueting Rm (and Great Kitchen)*)*
	Cabinet War Rooms SW1 *(Max*)*
	The Caledonian Club SW1 *(Members Dining Rm*)*
	The Chelsea SW1 *(Sloane Suite*)*
	Cumberland Hotel W1 *(Gloucester)*
	The Dorchester W1 *(The Terrace)*
	The Hempel W2 *(Room No 17)*
	Herstmonceux Castle, East Sussex *(Ballroom*)*
	Highclere Castle, Berks *(Library or Saloon*)*
	Howard Hotel WC2 *(Fitzalan*)*
	Hurlingham Club SW6 *(Palm Court Suite)*
	Imperial War Museum SE1 *(Festival Balconies)*
	Inner Temple Hall EC4 *(Parliament Chamber)*
	Inter-Continental W1 *(Apsley)*
	London Zoo NW1 *(Lion Terrace or Reptile House)*
	The Mayfair Inter-Continental W1 *(Danziger Suite)*

Mirabelle W1 (Max*)
Museum of Mankind W1 (Max*)
Orangery (Kensington Palace) W8 (Max*)
Park Lane Hotel W1 (Tudor Rose Rm)
Ranger's House SE10 (Marquee*)
Royal Albert Hall SW7 (Picture Gallery)
The Royal College of Pathologists SW1 (Lecture Room)
Royal Lancaster W2 (Gloucester Suite)
Science Museum SW7 (Space Gallery)
Selsdon Park Hotel, Surrey (Tudor Room*)
Sotheby's W1 (Main Gallery)
The South Bank Centre SE1 (Level 5 External Terrace)

180 Clandon, Surrey (Saloon)
Cutty Sark SE10 (Lower Hold or Tween Decks*)
Harrington Hall SW7 (Turner & Constable)
Merchant Taylors' Hall EC2 (Parlour)
Temple Island, Oxon (Max*)

175 Quo Vadis W1 (Private Rm*)

150 Addington Palace CR9 (Great Hall)
Baltic Exchange EC3 (Dining Room)
The Berkeley SW1 (Belgravia)
Café de Paris W1 (Restaurant)
Dukes Hotel SW1 (Marlborough Suite*)
Four Seasons Hotel W1 (Oak Rm)
Geffrye Museum E2 (Max*)
Gladwins EC3 (Max*)
Gray's Inn WC1 (Large Pension Rm)
Grocers' Hall EC2 (Piper Rm)
The Grosvenor House W1 (Albemarle)
The Halkin SW1 (Max*)
Harrington Hall SW7 (Reynolds & Landseer)
Howard Hotel WC2 (Arundel Suite)
Hyde Park Hotel SW1 (King Gustav Adolf Suite)
Innholders' Hall EC4 (Hall)
Institute of Directors SW1 (Burton)
Kew (Royal Botanic) Gardens, Surrey (Gallery (entire ground floor))
Knebworth House, Herts (Banqueting Hall (House))
Leeds Castle, Kent (State Dining Rm)
Leighton House W14 (Studio*)
London Zoo NW1 (Raffles Bar and Restaurant)
Maison Novelli EC1 (Max*)
Le Meridien W1 (Adams)
Monkey Island Hotel, Berks (River Rm*)
Museum of London EC2 (Medieval Gallery)
Museum of the Moving Image SE1 (Hollywood Studio or TV Studio)
Park Lane Hotel W1 (Garden Rm)
Penshurst Place, Kent (Sunderland Room)
Raffles SW3 (Max*)
Royal Garden Hotel W8 (Kensington Suite)
Science Museum SW7 (Director's Suite)
Sheraton Park Tower SW1 (Trianon Rm*)
Stationers' Hall EC4 (Court Rm)
Tower Bridge SE1 (Engine Rm)
HQS Wellington WC2 (Court Rm*)
Westway Studios W11 (Studio 3)

140 London Capital Club EC4 (Max*)
Park Lane Hotel W1 (Oak Rm)

125 Armourers' & Braisers' Hall EC2 (Drawing Rm or Livery Hall*)

120 Addington Palace CR9 (Robing Room)
Barbican Centre EC2 (Conservatory)
The Berners Hotel W1 (Fitzrovia Suite)
Cannizaro House SW19 (Viscount Melville Suite*)
Claridge's W1 (Drawing Room, French Salon or Mirror Room)
Hampshire Hotel WC2 (Penthouse*)
Inner Temple Hall EC4 (Luncheon Rm)
Institute of Directors SW1 (Waterloo)

Legoland Windsor, Berks (Drawing Room)
Merchant Taylors' Hall EC2 (Cloisters)
Museum of London EC2 (Entrance Hall)
Royal Albert Hall SW7 (Victoria Rm)
The Savoy WC2 (Beaufort)
Theatre Museum WC2 (Foyer)
Windsor Guildhall, Berks (Guildhall Chamber*)

110 One Whitehall Place SW1 (Meston Suite)
Waddesdon Manor, The Dairy, Bucks (West Hall*)

100 Addington Palace CR9 (Norman Shaw Room)
Arts Club W1 (Bar & Conservatory)
The Berners Hotel W1 (Ashton Room)
Brighton Royal Pavilion, Sussex (Queen Adelaide Suite)
The Dorchester W1 (Holford or Park Suite)
Drapers' Hall EC2 (Court Rm/Court Dining)
Dukes Hotel SW1 (Roof Terrace)
Halcyon Hotel W11 (Restaurant*)
Hartwell House, Bucks (James Gibbs Room* or James Wyatt Rooms)
Hever Castle, Kent (Castle Inner Hall* or Tudor Suite)
Inter-Continental W1 (Windsor Suite I)
The Lanesborough SW1 (Wellington Rm)
Leeds Castle, Kent (Terrace Room)
London Zoo NW1 (Tropical Bird House)
Middle Temple Hall EC4 (Parliament Chamber)
Museum of London EC2 (Eighteenth Century Gallery)
One Whitehall Place SW1 (River Room)
Portman Hotel W1 (Gloucester Suite)
The Stafford SW1 (Panel Rm & Sutherland Rm*)
Stone Buildings WC2 (Max*)
HQS Wellington WC2 (Quarterdeck)
Windsor Guildhall, Berks (Maidenhead Room)

95 Middle Temple Hall EC4 (Smoking Room)

90 Addington Palace CR9 (Winter Garden)
Brighton Royal Pavilion, Sussex (Great Kitchen)
The Ritz W1 (Marie Antoinette Suite*)
Selsdon Park Hotel, Surrey (Kent Room)
Woods River Cruises SE3 (Silver Dolphin)

80 Arts Club W1 (Drawing Rm)
Atlantic Bar & Grill W1 (Private Room)
Café de Paris W1 (Fantasy Suite)
Claridge's W1 (Kensington)
The Grosvenor House W1 (Spencer Room)
Inter-Continental W1 (Windsor Suite II)
Maison Novelli EC1 (Top Floor)
The Metropolitan W1 (Dining-Meeting Room*)
Millennium Conference Centre SW7 (Room 4)
Mosimann's Belfry SW1 (Theo Fabergé*)
One Whitehall Place SW1 (Thames Suite)
Park Lane Hotel W1 (Orchard Suite)
Phyllis Court, Oxon (Thames Room)
Polesden Lacey, Surrey (Restaurant*)
Roehampton Club SW15 (Garden Room)
Royal College of Music SW7 (Donaldson Rm)
Royal Garden Hotel W8 (Lancaster Suite)
The Savoy WC2 (Pinafore)
Stationers' Hall EC4 (Stock Rm)
Waddesdon Manor, The Dairy, Bucks (Winter Gardens)

75 Ham House, Surrey (Orangery)
Imperial War Museum SE1 (Boardroom 1)
Middle Temple Hall EC4 (Queen's Rm)
The Stafford SW1 (The Cellar)

70 Addington Palace CR9 (Music Room)

The Berners Hotel W1 (Slater Room)
Café de Paris W1 (Oyster Bar)
Harrington Hall SW7 (Stubbs)
Herstmonceux Castle, East Sussex (Pub)
The Landmark W1 (Champagne Rm)
Leeds Castle, Kent (Gate Tower)
Leighton House W14 (Arab Hall)
National Liberal Club SW1 (Lady Violet)
Penshurst Place , Kent (Buttery)
Temple Island, Oxon (Indoors)

65 The Caledonian Club SW1 (Stuart)
60 Bath – Assembly Rooms (Card Room)
The Chelsea SW1 (Beauchamp Rm)
The Dorchester SW1 (Pavilion)
Four Seasons Hotel W1 (Pine Rm)
Hyde Park Hotel SW1 (Loggia)
The Lanesborough SW1 (Westminster Rm)
London Zoo NW1 (Insect House)
Maison Novelli EC1 (Ground Floor or Middle Floor)
Marble Hill House, Surrey (The Great Room and Tetrastyle Hall*)
Le Meridien W1 (Regency 2)
Mosimann's Belfry SW1 (Wedgwood)
Quaglino's SW1 (Private Rm)
Scotts W1 (Cocktail Bar*)
Sheraton Park Tower SW1 (Buckingham Rm)
Stone Buildings WC2 (Reception Room)
HQS Wellington WC2 (Model Rm and Library)

55 London Capital Club EC4 (Boardroom)
50 Addington Palace CR9 (Library)
The Berkeley SW1 (Tattersalls or Waterloo)
Cannizaro House SW19 (Earl Of Mexborough or Viscount Melville)
Geffrye Museum E2 (Lecture Theatre)
Gray's Inn WC1 (Landing)
Green's SW1 (Private Rm 1*)
The Grosvenor House W1 (Bourdon Suite)
Harrington Hall SW7 (Sutherland)
Institute of Directors SW1 (Trafalgar II/St James)
Knebworth House, Herts (Library)
Leeds Castle, Kent (Grotta)
The Mayfair Inter-Continental W1 (Berkeley Suite)
One Whitehall Place SW1 (Cellar)
Portman Hotel W1 (Berkeley Suite)
Raffles SW3 (Dining Rm)
The Savoy WC2 (Gondoliers)
Selsdon Park Hotel, Surrey (Solarium)
Sheraton Park Tower SW1 (Explorers)
The Stafford SW1 (Pink Rm & Argyll Rm)
HQS Wellington WC2 (Reception Area)

45 Café de Paris W1 (Red Bar)
Millennium Conference Centre SW7 (Room 7)
40 Bluebird SW3 (Private Room*)
The Caledonian Club SW1 (Selkirk)
Le Gavroche W1 (Private Rm*)
The Halkin SW1 (Private Rm)
Howard Hotel WC2 (Westminster)
Imperial War Museum SE1 (Boardroom 2)
Institute of Directors SW1 (Trafalgar/Spears)
Inter-Continental W1 (Hogarth)
The Landmark W1 (Gazebo)
Merchant Taylors' Hall EC2 (Library)
Motcomb's SW1 (McClue Suite*)
Park Lane Hotel W1 (Mirror Rm)
Sheraton Park Tower SW1 (Balmoral)
The South Bank Centre SE1 (Sunley Pavilion)
The Stafford SW1 (Sutherland Rm)

35 Cannizaro House SW19 (Oak Room)
The Capital SW3 (Cadogan*)
Dukes Hotel SW1 (Duke Of Montrose Suite)
Four Seasons Hotel W1 (Sitting and Dining Rms)

The Savoy WC2 (Mikado)
30 Claridge's W1 (St James's)
The Dorchester W1 (Penthouse)
Hilton on Park Lane W1 (Serpentine Rm)
Innholders' Hall EC4 (Court Rm)
The Lanesborough SW1 (Wilkins Rm)
Park Lane Hotel W1 (Drawing Rm)
Portman Hotel W1 (Library)
Royal Albert Hall SW7 (Henry Cole Rm)
Royal College of Music SW7 (Council Rm)
The Savoy WC2 (Patience)
The Stafford SW1 (Argyll Rm)
Theatre Museum WC2 (Beard Room)
Windsor Guildhall, Berks (Ascot Room)

25 Dukes Hotel SW1 (Sheridan Room)
London Capital Club EC4 (Gresham Room)
Mosimann's Belfry SW1 (Veuve Clicquot)
Royal Garden Hotel W8 (Westminster Room)
The Savoy WC2 (Iolanthe)

20 The Capital SW3 (Eaton)
Hampshire Hotel WC2 (Milton)
Howard Hotel WC2 (Surrey)
18 The Chelsea SW1 (Chelsea Rm)
The Savoy WC2 (Sorcerer)
12 The Berkeley SW1 (Billet)
10 The Berkeley SW1 (Knightsbridge)
The Dorchester W1 (Library)
London Capital Club EC4 (Marco Polo or Wren Room)

£M

7250 Alexandra Palace & Park N22 (Max*)
6500 Alexandra Palace & Park N22 (Great Hall)
3000 Café Royal W1 (Max*)
Sandown Park Racecourse, Surrey (Surrey Hall*)
2500 Adrenaline Village SW8 (Venue*)
Alexandra Palace & Park N22 (West Hall)
2000 Battersea Park SW8 (British Genius Site*)
Commonwealth Institute W8 (Comm Galleries*)
1500 Alexandra Palace & Park N22 (Palm Court)
Battersea Park SW8 (Riverside Terraces)
1400 Ascot Racecourse, Pavilions & Queen Anne Rooms, Berks (Pavilion (subdivisible)*)
1300 London Metropole W2 (Palace Suite*)
1200 Alexandra Palace Ice Rink N22 (Max*)
Royal National Theatre SE1 (Max*)
1000 Café Royal W1 (4-Empire Napoleon)
TS Queen Mary WC2 (Max*)
900 Harrods SW1 (Georgian Restaurant*)
London Marriott W1 (Westminster Suite*)
850 The Brewery EC1 (Porter Tun*)
800 Cabot Hall E14 (Hall*)
Limelight W1 (Max*)
Lloyd's of London EC3 (Captains' Rm*)
Waldorf Hotel WC2 (Adelphi Suite & Palm Court*)
700 The Brewery EC1 (King George III)
Waxy O'Conners W1 (Max*)
Whipsnade Wild Animal Park, Beds (Max*)
650 Hotel Russell WC1 (Warncliffe Suite*)
The International Hotel E14 (Grand Suite*)
600 Café Royal W1 (6-Dubarry)
Planet Hollywood W1 (Restaurant*)
Sandown Park Racecourse, Surrey (Claremont)
Waldorf Hotel WC2 (Charter Suite)
550 The Washington W1 (Max*)

PRIVATE VENUES | STANDING CAPACITY

500 Ascot Racecourse, Pavilions & Queen Anne Rooms, Berks *(Buckhounds)*
Ascot Racecourse, Royal Enclosure, Berks *(Paddock Suite*)*
City of London Club EC2 *(Max*)*
Commonwealth Institute W8 *(Art Gallery)*
Delfina Studio SE1 *(Max*)*
Forte Posthouse Regent's Park W1 *(Cambride & Oxford Suites*)*
Glaziers' Hall SE1 *(Hall*)*
Groucho Club W1 *(Max*)*
Lord's NW8 *(Max*)*
Royal National Theatre SE1 *(Olivier Stalls Foyer)*
Sandown Park Racecourse, Surrey *(Marquee (permanent in summer))*

450 RS Hispaniola WC2 *(Max*)*
Hothouse Bar & Grill E1 *(Max*)*
Langham Hilton W1 *(Ballroom*)*
Limelight W1 *(Gallery & Dome)*
National Army Museum SW3 *(Art & Uniform Galleries*)*
St Stephen' Constitutional Club SW1 *(Max*)*
Twickenham Banqueting Centre, • *(Rose Rm* or Spirit of Rugby)*

400 Alexandra Palace & Park N22 *(Palace Restaurant)*
Aquarium EC1 *(Club*)*
Barbican Art Gallery EC2 *(Max*)*
Bath – Pump Room *(Max*)*
Chartered Accountants' Hall EC2 *(Great Hall*)*
Chelsea Physic Garden SW3 *(Max*)*
Chelsea Harbour Rooms SW10 *(Max*)*
The Comedy Store SW1 *(Max*)*
The Grafton W1 *(Max*)*
Holiday Inn – Nelson Dock SE16 *(Sweden*)*
Institution of Civil Engineers SW1 *(Great Hall*)*
London Metropole W2 *(Windsor Suite)*
London Transport Museum WC2 *(Max*)*
Regent's College NW1 *(Refectory*)*
Syon Park (Conservatory), Middx *(Great Conservatory*)*
Waldorf Hotel WC2 *(Charter 2)*

380 Capital Radio Café WC2 *(Max*)*
350 Adrenaline Village SW8 *(Club)*
HMS Belfast SE1 *(Quarter Deck (Summer Evenings)*)*
Café Royal W1 *(2-Louis)*
Carpenters' Hall EC2 *(Livery Hall*)*
Cavalry & Guards Club W1 *(Max*)*
Cobden's Club W10 *(Max*)*
Groucho Club W1 *(First Floor (entire))*
Hendon Hall Hotel NW4 *(Mount Charlotte Suite*)*
Hop Exchange SE1 *(Max*)*
The Oval SE11 *(Max*)*
Sandown Park Racecourse, Surrey *(Wolsey)*
Stakis St Ermins SW1 *(Max*)*

330 Twickenham Banqueting Centre, *(Members Lounge)*
300 BAFTA Centre W1 *(Max*)*
Basil Street Hotel SW3 *(Parrot Club*)*
Cavalry & Guards Club W1 *(Coffee Rm)*
Chelsea Harbour Rooms SW10 *(Turner & Carlyle Rms)*
The Chesterfield Hotel W1 *(Max*)*
Churchill W1 *(Chartwell Suite*)*
City of London Club EC2 *(Main Dining Rm)*
Conrad Hotel SW10 *(Henley Suite*)*
Delfina Studio SE1 *(Rear Gallery)*
Design Museum SE1 *(Entrance Hall*)*
Euten's WC2 *(Max*)*
Hampton Court, Tiltyard, Surrey *(Max*)*
RS Hispaniola WC2 *(Main Deck)*
ICA SW1 *(Exhibition Galleries*)*
The Insurance Hall EC2 *(Great Hall*)*

Irish Club SW1 *(Max*)*
Langham Hilton W1 *(Palm Court)*
London Metropole W2 *(Berkshire Suite)*
London Palladium W1 *(Cinderella Bar*)*
Mega Bowl SW2 *(Max*)*
Mortons Club W1 *(Max*)*
The Selfridge Hotel W1 *(Selfridge Suite*)*
Shakespeare Globe Centre SE1 *(Max*)*
Theatre Royal WC2 *(Grand Salon*)*
Tower Thistle E1 *(Tower Suite*)*

280 Browns W1 *(Max*)*
Butchers' Hall EC1 *(Great Hall*)*
The Law Society WC2 *(Common Rm*)*
275 Chelsea Physic Garden SW3 *(With Marquee (Sats in Jun-Sep only))*
The Viceroy NW1 *(Max*)*
270 Saint WC2 *(Max*)*
260 Bank of England Club SW15 *(Max*)*
St John's Gate EC1 *(Max*)*
250 Aquarium EC1 *(Café Bar)*
Barber-Surgeons' Hall EC2 *(Max*)*
Bath – Pump Room *(Pump Rm)*
The Brewers Rooms W1 *(Max*)*
The Brewery EC1 *(Queen Charlotte or Smeaton's Vaults)*
Café Royal W1 *(6-Dauphin)*
Champenois EC2 *(Max*)*
Church House SW1 *(Harvey Goodwin Suite* or Hoare Memorial Hall)*
Cottons Atrium SE1 *(Max*)*
Denbies Wine Estate, Surrey *(Garden Atrium Conservatory*)*
The Dog and Fox Ballroom SW19 *(Ballroom*)*
Drones SW1 *(Max*)*
East India Club SW1 *(Max*)*
Holiday Inn – Nelson Dock SE16 *(Wasa Suite)*
The International Hotel E14 *(Royal Lounge)*
Ironmongers' Hall EC2 *(Banqueting Hall*)*
Limelight W1 *(Club VIP (Basement))*
Ormond's Restaurant & Club SW1 *(Restaurant*)*
Painters' Hall EC4 *(Livery Hall*)*
Palace Theatre W1 *(Stalls Bar*)*
Peacock House W14 *(Max*)*
Quayside E1 *(Max*)*
Queen's Eyot, Berks *(Permanent Marquee*)*
The Royal Air Force Club W1 *(Ballroom*)*
Royal Society of Arts WC2 *(All Vaults*)*
The Rubens SW1 *(Max*)*
Sandown Park Racecourse, Surrey *(Saddle Rm)*
St John's Gate EC1 *(Garden Cloisters)*
Stakis St Ermins SW1 *(Ballroom)*
Staple Inn WC1 *(Hall*)*
West Wycombe Caves, Bucks *(Max*)*

240 HMS Belfast SE1 *(Ship Co's Dining Hall)*
Dartmouth House W1 *(Max*)*
St Bartholomew's Hospital EC1 *(Great Hall*)*
230 Carpenters' Hall EC2 *(Reception Rm)*
220 Farmers' & Fletchers' Hall EC1 *(Max*)*
Hamilton Suite W1 *(Conservatory & Red Room*)*
Mortons Club W1 *(Restaurant & Bar)*
Royal National Theatre SE1 *(Terrace Café)*
200 41 Queen's Gate Terrace SW7 *(Pillar Dining*)*
Adrenaline Village SW8 *(Boogie Boat)*
Alexandra Palace & Park N22 *(Loneborough Rm)*
Amadeus Centre W9 *(Upper Hall*)*
Ascot Racecourse, Royal Enclosure, Berks *(Jockey Club)*
BAFTA Centre W1 *(Function Rm)*
Brewers' Hall EC2 *(Livery Hall*)*
Café Royal W1 *(S-Marquise)*

214

The Carnarvon Hotel W5 *(Edward Suite*)*
Chelsea Harbour Rooms SW10 *(Turner Rm)*
Churchill W1 *(Chartwell I)*
City of London Club EC2 *(Upper Smoking Rms)*
College of Arms EC4 *(Max*)*
Conrad Hotel SW10 *(Compass Rose or Thames)*
Delfina Studio SE1 *(Front Gallery)*
Doggetts Coat & Badge SE1 *(Max*)*
Glaziers' Hall SE1 *(River Rm)*
The Grafton W1 *(Southampton Suite)*
Groucho Club W1 *(Soho Room)*
Ham Polo Club, Surrey *(Club House*)*
Institution of Mechanical Engineers SW1 *(Marble Hall*)*
Kensington Palace Thistle W8 *(Duchess*)*
Langham Hilton W1 *(Portland Suite)*
London Metropole W2 *(Westminster Suite)*
Pinewood Studios, Bucks *(Ballroom*)*
Regent's College NW1 *(Herringham Hall)*
The Rembrandt Hotel SW7 *(Max*)*
The Rubens SW1 *(Old Masters Restaurant)*
Saint John EC1 *(Max*)*
Shoeless Joe's SW6 *(Max*)*
St John's Gate EC1 *(Chapter Hall)*
St Stephen' Constitutional Club SW1 *(Dining Rm)*
St Thomas' Hospital SE1 *(Governors' Hall*)*
Waldorf Hotel WC2 *(Minstrel Gallery)*
Westminster Conference Centre SW1 *(Lecture Hall*)*

180
Belvedere W8 *(Max*)*
Cavalry & Guards Club W1 *(Peninsula Rm)*
Chelsea Harbour Rooms SW10 *(Carlyle Rm)*
Church House SW1 *(Bishop Partridge Hall)*
Frederick's N1 *(Max*)*
Guards Museum SW1 *(Max*)*
Royal National Theatre SE1 *(Ovations)*
Spanish Club W1 *(Alfonso XIII Rm*)*
Sutton House E9 *(Max*)*
Winchester House SW15 *(River Rm*)*

175
Royal Aeronautical Society W1 *(Argyll Rm & Hawker Rm*)*
White House Hotel NW1 *(Albany*)*

170
The Chesterfield Hotel W1 *(Charles/Queens Suites)*
Cobden's Club W10 *(The Grand Hall)*

160
Bath – Pump Room, Berks *(Concert Rm)*
London Metropole W2 *(Park Suite or Thames Suite)*
Peg's Club WC2 *(Max*)*

150
41 Queen's Gate Terrace SW7 *(President's Club)*
Bank of England Club SW15 *(Redgates Lodge)*
The Bankers Club EC2 *(Cocktail Bar*)*
HMS Belfast SE1 *(Wardroom)*
The Brewery EC1 *(Sugar Rms)*
Butchers' Hall EC1 *(Large Court Rm & Small Court Rm)*
Café du Marché EC1 *(Max*)*
Café Royal W1 *(1-Derby & Queensbury)*
Chelsea Physic Garden SW3 *(Reception Room)*
Conrad Hotel SW10 *(Henley I)*
The Grosvenor SW1 *(Gallery Rm*)*
RS Hispaniola WC2 *(Top Deck)*
The Insurance Hall EC2 *(Ostler Suite)*
Irish Club SW1 *(Ball Room)*
Ivy WC2 *(Private Rm*)*
The Kenilworth WC1 *(Bloomsbury Suite*)*
Kew Bridge Steam Museum, Middx *(Steam Hall*)*
Leander Club, Berks *(Max*)*
The London Toy And Model Museum W2 *(Max*)*

Orangery (Holland Park) W8 *(Max*)*
Painters' Hall EC4 *(Court Rm)*
Pewterers' Hall EC2 *(Court Rm or Livery Rm*)*
Pinewood Studios, Bucks *(Great Gatsby Rm or Green Rm)*
Royal Society of Arts WC2 *(Benjamin Franklin Rm)*
RUSI Building SW1 *(Lecture Theatre*)*
Sandown Park Racecourse, Surrey *(Cavalry Bar)*
Waxy O'Conners W1 *(College Bar)*
The Westbury W1 *(Mount Vernon Rm*)*
Westminster Conference Centre SW1 *(Members Club Rm)*

145 Simpsons- in-the-Strand WC2 *(South Rm*)*

140
Doggetts Coat & Badge SE1 *(Restaurant)*
Hothouse Bar & Grill E1 *(Lower Floor)*
Neal's Lodge SW18 *(Conservatory/Maple Room/Bar*)*

130
Fulham Palace SW6 *(Max*)*
ICA SW1 *(Nash)*
St Andrew's Court House EC4 *(Court Room*)*

125
The Cavendish SW1 *(Park*)*
The Founders' Hall EC1 *(Livery Hall*)*
Vanderbilt Hotel SW7 *(Max*)*

120
BAFTA Centre W1 *(Foyer Bar)*
HMS Belfast SE1 *(Gun Rm)*
The Brewery EC1 *(The James Watt)*
Britannia Intercontinental Hotel W1 *(Manhattan*)*
Brown's Hotel W1 *(Clarendon*)*
Browns WC2 *(Courtroom 1*)*
Café Royal W1 *(1-Domino)*
Chartered Accountants' Hall EC2 *(Main Reception Rm)*
Churchill W1 *(Library)*
Dartmouth House W1 *(Long Drawing Rm)*
Drones SW1 *(Private Rm)*
Freud Museum NW3 *(Max*)*
Glaziers' Hall SE1 *(Library & Court Rm)*
The Golden Hinde SE1 *(Max*)*
The Grafton W1 *(Arlington Suite)*
House of Detention EC1 *(Max*)*
ICA SW1 *(Brandon)*
Institution of Civil Engineers SW1 *(Smeaton Rm)*
The Law Society WC2 *(Old Council Chamber)*
Lloyd's of London EC3 *(Old Library)*
Mega Bowl SW2 *(Single floor)*
The Mountbatten WC2 *(Earl*)*
Ormond's Restaurant & Club SW1 *(Downstairs)*
Oxford & Cambridge Club SW1 *(Marlborough*)*
Planet Hollywood W1 *(VIP Suite)*
Spring Grove House, Middx *(Max*)*
Sweetings EC4 *(Max*)*
Tallow Chandlers' Hall EC4 *(Livery Hall*)*
Trinity House EC3 *(Court Rm* or Library)*
The Westbury W1 *(Pine Rm)*
Winston Churchill's Britain At War Experience SE1 *(Max*)*

110
The Washington W1 *(Richmond Suite)*
Watermen & Lightermen's Hall EC3 *(Freemen's Rm*)*

100
Alexandra Palace & Park N22 *(Palm Court 5)*
Amadeus Centre W9 *(Lower Hall)*
Basil Street Hotel SW3 *(Brompton Rm)*
Brown's Hotel W1 *(Niagra & Roosevelt combined)*
Butchers' Hall EC1 *(Taurus Suite)*
Cabot Hall E14 *(Sebastian Rm)*
Café Lazeez SW7 *(Max*)*
Cavalry & Guards Club W1 *(Balaclava Rm)*
City of London Club EC2 *(Garden Rm)*
Cobden's Club W10 *(Restaurant)*
Commonwealth Institute W8 *(Bradley)*

Cuba Libre N1 *(Max*)*
Dartmouth House W1 *(Ballroom)*
Downstairs At 190 SW7 *(Max*)*
First Floor W11 *(Private Rm*)*
Fulham Palace SW6 *(Drawing Rm or Great Hall)*
Goring Hotel SW1 *(Archive Room*)*
The Grosvenor SW1 *(Bessborough Rm)*
Hamilton House EC4 *(Max*)*
Horniman Museum and Gardens SE23 *(Conservatory*)*
Institution of Civil Engineers SW1 *(Brunel Rm or Council Rm)*
The Insurance Hall EC2 *(Council Chamber)*
The International Hotel E14 *(Buckingham)*
Ironmongers' Hall EC2 *(Drawing Rm)*
Kensington Palace Thistle W8 *(Marchioness)*
Kenwood House, Old Kitchen NW3 *(Max*)*
Lloyd's of London EC3 *(Conference Rm)*
The Mountbatten WC2 *(Broadlands)*
National Army Museum SW3 *(Templer Galleries)*
Royal Aeronautical Society W1 *(Council Rm & Bar)*
Royal Society of Arts WC2 *(Vault 1)*
Royal Horseguards Thistle Hotel SW1 *(Max*)*
Shakespeare Globe Centre SE1 *(Restaurant)*
Sheraton Belgravia SW1 *(Dining Rm*)*
Simpsons- in-the-Strand WC2 *(Smoking Rm)*
Slaughterhouse Gallery EC1 *(Gallery/vaults*)*
Soho House W1 *(Sitting Room, Study & Bar*)*
Spring Grove House, Middx *(Winter Garden Room)*
Stakis St Ermins SW1 *(Balcony)*
Sutton House E9 *(Wenlock Barn (including Café-Bar/Linenfold Parlour)*)*
University Women's Club W1 *(Library*)*

95 Jason's W9 *(Max*)*
90 The Carnarvon Hotel W5 *(Creffield Suite)*
Holiday Inn – Mayair W1 *(Stratton Suite*)*
Hollington House Hotel, Berks *(Cedar Suite*)*
Institution of Mechanical Engineers SW1 *(Hinton)*
Kensington Palace Thistle W8 *(Countess Princess)*
The Rembrandt Hotel SW7 *(Elizabeth & Victoria (Queen Suite))*
Sandown Park Racecourse, Surrey *(Persimmon)*
80 Bloomsbury Square Training Centre WC1 *(Ascham Room*)*
Brewers' Hall EC2 *(Court Rm)*
The Brewery EC1 *(City Cellars)*
Browns WC2 *(Courtroom 2)*
The Cadogan SW1 *(Max*)*
Cavalry & Guards Club W1 *(Waterloo Rm)*
Chelsea Harbour Rooms SW10 *(Reception Rm)*
Churchill W1 *(Marlborough Suite)*
Doggetts Coat & Badge SE1 *(Boardroom/Terrace Bar)*
Freud Museum NW3 *(House)*
Hamilton Suite W1 *(Hamilton Rm)*
Holiday Inn – Nelson Dock SE16 *(Denmark Suite)*
Hotel Russell WC1 *(Bedford Suite)*
Ironmongers' Hall EC2 *(Luncheon Rm)*
The Law Society WC2 *(Members Dining Rm)*
Mortons Club W1 *(Private Rm)*
My Fair Lady NW1 *(Max*)*
Neal's Lodge SW18 *(Conservatory)*
Regent's College NW1 *(Tuke Common Rm)*

The Royal Air Force Club W1 *(Presidents Room)*
Royal Horseguards Thistle Hotel SW1 *(Thames)*
The Rubens SW1 *(Rembrandt Rm)*
RUSI Building SW1 *(Reading Rm)*
Soho Soho W1 *(Salon Privée*)*
St Stephen' Constitutional Club SW1 *(Bar)*
Staple Inn WC1 *(Council Chamber)*
Tower Thistle E1 *(Raleigh or Spencer)*
University Women's Club W1 *(Drawing Rm)*
Westminster Conference Centre SW1 *(Cambridge Rm)*
Whittington's EC4 *(Wine Bar*)*
75 HMS Belfast SE1 *(Anteroom)*
Britannia Intercontinental Hotel W1 *(Pine Bar)*
Churchill W1 *(Blenheim)*
Conrad Hotel SW10 *(Harbour)*
Irish Club SW1 *(Ulster Rm)*
Marquis W1 *(Downstairs Room*)*
Peg's Club WC2 *(Quiet Rm/Bar)*
Rules WC2 *(Greene Rm*)*
70 Bloomsbury Square Training Centre WC1 *(Cellars Restaurant)*
Cabot Hall E14 *(St Lawrence Rm)*
Café Royal W1 *(Cellars)*
Chartered Accountants' Hall EC2 *(Members' Rm)*
The Chesterfield Hotel W1 *(Conservatory)*
Forte Posthouse Regent's Park W1 *(Trinity Suite)*
Institution of Mechanical Engineers SW1 *(Council)*
Royal Institute of British Architects W1 *(South Rm*)*
Royal Society of Arts WC2 *(Tavern Rm)*
RUSI Building SW1 *(Library)*
Sheraton Belgravia SW1 *(Study and Library)*
Watermen & Lightermen's Hall EC3 *(Court Rm)*
Waxy O'Conners W1 *(Mezzanine)*
65 London Marriott W1 *(Hamilton Rm)*
60 Ascot Racecourse, Pavilions & Queen Anne Rooms, Berks *(King Edward VII)*
Athenaeum Hotel W1 *(Westminster Suite*)*
Bleeding Heart EC1 *(Private Room*)*
Brown's Hotel W1 *(Kipling or Roosevelt)*
Capital Radio Café WC2 *(VIP Lounge)*
Charcos SW3 *(Downstairs*)*
Chartered Institute of Public Finance & Accountancy WC2 *(Committee Rm 4* or Council Chamber)*
College of Arms EC4 *(Earl Marshal's Court or Waiting Room)*
Coopers' Hall EC2 *(Max*)*
Groucho Club W1 *(Gennaro Room)*
Hendon Hall Hotel NW4 *(Garrick)*
Hotel Russell WC1 *(Ormond Suite)*
Irish Club SW1 *(Leinster Room)*
Jason's W9 *(Restaurant)*
The Rembrandt Hotel SW7 *(Elizabeth)*
Royal Aeronautical Society W1 *(Sopwith Rm)*
Rules WC2 *(Charles Dickens Rm)*
Shoeless Joe's SW6 *(Members Bar)*
St Stephen' Constitutional Club SW1 *(Garden Rm)*
Tallow Chandlers' Hall EC4 *(Parlour)*
Waldorf Hotel WC2 *(Somerset)*
The Washington W1 *(Richmond I (Winchester))*
The Westbury W1 *(Brighton Rm)*
55 Holiday Inn – Nelson Dock SE16 *(Rising Star)*
50 41 Queen's Gate Terrace SW7 *(Art Deco Room)*
Athenaeum Hotel W1 *(Devonshire Suite)*
Basil Street Hotel SW3 *(Basil Rm)*

The Berkshire W1 (Sonning Suite*)
Browns WC2 (Courtroom 3)
Butchers' Hall EC1 (Small Court Rm)
The Cadogan SW1 (Langtry Dining)
Church House SW1 (Westminster)
City of London Club EC2 (Bar or Visitors Rm)
Commonwealth Institute W8 (Tweedsmuir)
Dartmouth House W1 (Small Drawing Rm)
The Founders' Hall EC1 (Parlour)
The Grafton W1 (Warren)
Groucho Club W1 (New Room)
Langham Hilton W1 (Regent/ Welbeck Rooms)
Leven is Strijd E14 (Max*)
Limelight W1 (Library or Study Bar)
Royal Mint Sovereign Gallery SW1 (Max*)
Royal National Theatre SE1 (Olivier Circle Foyer)
Spanish Club W1 (Presidentian Rm)
Spring Grove House, Middx (Music Room)
St Andrew's Court House EC4 (Archive Room)
St Bartholomew's Hospital EC1 (Henry VIII Committee Rm)
St Thomas' Hospital SE1 (Grand Committee Rm)
Tower Thistle E1 (Beaufort or Mortimer Suite)
White House Hotel NW1 (Chester)
48 Waldorf Hotel WC2 (Kingsway)
45 Britannia Intercontinental Hotel W1 (Grosvenor I)
44 POW Bar And Restaurant SW3 (Max*)
40 Brown's Hotel W1 (Niagara)
Café Royal W1 (B-Penthouse)
The Carnarvon Hotel W5 (Gunnersbury Suite)
The Cavendish SW1 (Mayfair)
The Chesterfield Hotel W1 (Library)
Churchill W1 (Randolph or Spencer)
Downstairs At 190 SW7 (Private Rm)
Frederick's N1 (Clarence Room)
Hendon Hall Hotel NW4 (Sheridan)
Hogarth's House W4 (Max*)
Holiday Inn – Mayair W1 (Presidential Suite)
Hotel Russell WC1 (Library)
The Insurance Hall EC2 (Pipkin Rm)
The International Hotel E14 (Beaufort)
The Kenilworth WC1 (Louis XV)
London Marriott W1 (John Adams Suite)
National Army Museum SW3 (Council Chamber)
Oxford & Cambridge Club SW1 (Edward VII)
The Royal Air Force Club W1 (Drawing Room)
The Rubens SW1 (Rubens)
Rules WC2 (King Edward VII Rm)
Scone E14 (Max*)
Seahorse, Middx (Max*)
Spring Grove House, Middx (Export Suite)
St Bartholomew's Hospital EC1 (Peggy Turner Rm or Treasurer's Rm)
Stakis St Ermins SW1 (York or Clarence)
Theatre Royal WC2 (Board Rm or Royal Retiring Rm)
Vanderbilt Hotel SW7 (Vanderbilt)
The Washington W1 (Richmond 2 (Fairfax))
The Westbury W1 (Regency Rm)
Westminster Conference Centre SW1 (Gloucester)
Winchester House SW15 (Library)
35 HMS Belfast SE1 (Admiral's Quarters)
The Grosvenor SW1 (Wilton Rm)
Hendon Hall Hotel NW4 (Johnson)
Holiday Inn – Nelson Dock SE16 (Finland I & II)
The Mountbatten WC2 (Viceroy)
Stakis St Ermins SW1 (Cameo)

The Viceroy NW1 (Private Rm)
32 Brown's Hotel W1 (Hellenic)
30 Basil Street Hotel SW3 (Mezzanine Rm)
The Berkshire W1 (Sandhurst Suite)
Browns W1 (Room 54)
Cabot Hall E14 (Cape Breton Rm)
The Cadogan SW1 (Langtry Sitting)
Cavalry & Guards Club W1 (Double Bridal Rm)
Chartered Accountants' Hall EC2 (Small Reception Rm)
Frederick's N1 (Sussex Rm)
Fulham Palace SW6 (Ante Rm)
The Grafton W1 (Duchess)
The Grosvenor SW1 (Belgrave)
The Guinea W1 (Boardroom*)
Kensington Palace Thistle W8 (Baroness)
London Marriott W1 (Dukes Suite)
Royal Society of Arts WC2 (Folkestone Rm)
25 Alexandra Palace & Park N22 (Palm Court 1)
The Chesterfield Hotel W1 (Stanhope Suite)
Goring Hotel SW1 (Drawing Rm)
Royal Aeronautical Society W1 (Hawker Rm)
Royal National Theatre SE1 (Richardson Rm)
The Selfridge Hotel W1 (Conservatory)
St Andrew's Court House EC4 (Panelled Room)
20 Ascot Racecourse, Pavilions & Queen Anne Rooms, Berks (Crocker Bulteel)
Athenaeum Hotel W1 (Richmond Suite)
Brewers' Hall EC2 (Committee Rm)
Cabot Hall E14 (Nova Scotia Rm)
Church House SW1 (Jubilee)
The Grosvenor SW1 (Wilton Rm)
Holiday Inn – Mayair W1 (Burlington)
The Insurance Hall EC2 (Morgan Owen Rm)
Limelight W1 (Annexe)
The Rembrandt Hotel SW7 (Princes)
RUSI Building SW1 (Council Room)
St John's Gate EC1 (Lord Prior's Dining Room)
Sutton House E9 (Linenfold Parlour)
Waldorf Hotel WC2 (Westminster or Waterloo or Tavistock)
Westminster Conference Centre SW1 (Kent)
18 Britannia Intercontinental Hotel W1 (Grosvenor II)
16 Theatre Royal WC2 (Prince Of Wales Suite)
15 The Cavendish SW1 (Duke)
Langham Hilton W1 (Cumberland Rm)
The Rembrandt Hotel SW7 (Victoria)
12 Brown's Hotel W1 (Lord Byron)
The Grosvenor SW1 (Hanover)
10 Brown's Hotel W1 (Graham Bell)
Tower Thistle E1 (Lewin)

£B-E

1500 The Worx III SW6 (Max*)
1200 Linford Film Studios SW8 (Studio A (main room)*)
1000 Crystal Palace Park SE20 (Max*)
The Worx III SW6 (Entire Building)
500 The Worx III SW6 (Marquee)
300 The Worx I N1 (Max*)
The Worx II N1 (Max*)
250 Linford Film Studios SW8 (Studio B)
150 Linford Film Studios SW8 (Back Bar)
Pitcher & Piano WC2 (Private Room*)
100 Linford Film Studios SW8 (Games Room)
40 Pitcher & Piano WC2 (Platform)

£B-M

6000	Edwin Shirley Productions E3 *(Max*)*
2600	New Connaught Rms WC2 *(Max*)*
2500	Bagleys N1 *(Max*)*
	Honourable Artillery Co EC1 *(Marquee*)*
2000	Lee Valley Cycle Circuit E15 *(Max*)*
	Lee Valley Leisure Centre N9 *(Max*)*
	London Astoria WC2 *(Max*)*
	Streatham Ice Arena SW16 *(Max*)*
1850	Equinox at the Empire WC2 *(Max*)*
1800	Royal Horticultural Halls SW1 *(New Hall*)*
1650	The London Hippodrome WC2 *(Max*)*
1600	The London Hippodrome WC2 *(Auditorium)*
1500	Bow Film Studios E15 *(Max*)*
	Equinox at the Empire WC2 *(Club)*
	Lee Valley Leisure Centre N9 *(Great Hall)*
1200	Naval & Military Club W1 *(Max*)*
1000	Blackheath Concert Halls SE3 *(Great Hall*)*
	Hammersmith Town Hall W6 *(Assembly Hall*)*
	Riverside Studios W6 *(Max*)*
	Royal Horticultural Halls SW1 *(Old Hall)*
900	Royal College of Art SW7 *(Henry Moore Gallery*)*
750	Bagleys N1 *(3 Studios (each))*
	New Connaught Rms WC2 *(Balmoral)*
700	Grosvenor Rooms NW2 *(Grosvenor Suite*)*
680	Browns Club WC2 *(Max*)*
650	Badbobs WC2 *(Max*)*
630	Porchester Centre W2 *(Ballroom*)*
600	Chelsea Football Club SW6 *(Max*)*
	Syon Park (Banqueting), Middx *(Max*)*
550	Royal Holloway College, Surrey *(Max*)*
500	Bagleys N1 *(Bunker Bar)*
	Beckton Alpine Centre E6 *(Max*)*
	Cecil Sharp House NW1 *(Kennedy Hall*)*
	Congress Centre WC1 *(Congress Hall*)*
	Dulwich College SE21 *(Christenson Hall and Upper Dining Rms* or Great Hall)*
	Fulham Town Hall SW6 *(Grand Hall*)*
	Honourable Artillery Co EC1 *(Albert Rm)*
	International House E1 *(Max*)*
	The Leathermarket SE1 *(Marquee*)*
	Legends W1 *(Max*)*
	Mall Galleries SW1 *(Main Gallery*)*
	Merchant Centre EC4 *(Caxton Suite*)*
	Regency Banqueting Suite N17 *(Max*)*
	Rose Garden Buffet NW1 *(Max*)*
	Stoke Newington Town Hall N16 *(Assembly Room*)*
	Texas Embassy Cantina WC2 *(Max*)*
	Westminster Boating Base SW1 *(Max*)*
	Whitechapel Art Gallery E1 *(Max*)*
498	Riverside Studios W6 *(Studio 1)*
490	The Old Town Hall, Stratford E15 *(Main Hall*)*
480	Chelsea Old Town Hall SW3 *(Main Hall*)*
450	Crazy Larry's SW10 *(Max*)*
	King's College WC2 *(Great Hall*)*
	Royal Green Jackets W1 *(Hall*)*
	Royal Institution of Great Britain W1 *(Max*)*
400	Abbaye EC1 *(Max*)*
	Chelsea Football Club SW6 *(Executive Club Rm)*
	Congress Centre WC1 *(Max)*
	Eatons EC3 *(Max*)*
	Froebel Institute College SW15 *(Max*)*

	Le Gothique SW18 *(with Academy of Live & Recorded Arts*)*
	The Little Ship Club EC4 *(Max*)*
	Mermaid Theatre EC4 *(Blackfriars Room*)*
	Naval & Military Club W1 *(Coffee Rm)*
	Thames Leisure EC4 *(Regalia*)*
	Throgmorton's EC2 *(Max*)*
380	Imperial College SW7 *(Main Dining Hall*)*
375	Break For The Border W1 *(Max*)*
360	Bishopsgate Institute EC2 *(Max*)*
350	Badbobs WC2 *(Bar/restaurant or Lilly's Bordello)*
	The Clink SE1 *(Max*)*
	Conway Hall WC1 *(Large Hall*)*
	Duke of York's HQ SW3 *(Cadogan Hall*)*
	George Inn SE1 *(Max*)*
	Hellenic Centre W1 *(Great Hall*)*
	Jazz Café NW1 *(Max*)*
	King's College, Hampstead Site NW3 *(Bay Hall*)*
	Music Room At Grays W1 *(Exhibition Hall*)*
	New Connaught Rms WC2 *(Edinburgh)*
	HMS President EC4 *(Max*)*
	Royal College of Art SW7 *(Gulbenkian Upper Gallery)*
	Royal Geographical Society SW7 *(Max*)*
	St Martin In The Fields WC2 *(Max*)*
	Le Studio Café N1 *(Max*)*
	Will's Art Warehouse SW6 *(Max*)*
320	Trafalgar Tavern SE10 *(Nelson Suite*)*
300	Academy of Live & Recorded Arts SW18 *(Max*)*
	Archduke Wine Bar SE1 *(Max*)*
	Brasserie Rocque EC2 *(Max*)*
	Browns Club WC2 *(Bar & Dance Floor or VIP Rm)*
	Catamaran Cruisers WC2 *(Naticia*)*
	The Chelsea Gardener SW3 *(Max*)*
	The Clink SE1 *(Winchester Hall)*
	Eatons EC3 *(Banqueting Suite)*
	Gecko NW1 *(Max*)*
	Grosvenor Rooms NW2 *(Executive Suite)*
	King's College School SW19 *(Great Hall*)*
	The London Hippodrome WC2 *(Balcony – Restaurant)*
	London Scottish SW1 *(Hall*)*
	Naval & Military Club W1 *(Smoking Rm)*
	Royal Holloway College, Surrey *(Founder's Dining Hall)*
	School of Pharmacy WC1 *(Refectory*)*
	Le Studio Café N1 *(Restaurant)*
	Syon Park (Banqueting), Middx *(Garden Rm)*
	Tinseltown EC1 *(Max*)*
	Victoria & Albert Museum Café SW7 *(Max*)*
280	Brompton Oratory – St Wilfrid's Hall SW7 *(Max*)*
	Syon Park (Banqueting), Middx *(Lakeside Rm)*
270	Catamaran Cruisers WC2 *(Pridla)*
250	Admiral Enterprises SE1 *(Max*)*
	Beckton Alpine Centre E6 *(Function Room)*
	Blackheath Concert Halls SE3 *(Recital Rm)*
	Bramah Tea & Coffee Museum SE1 *(Max*)*
	City Cruises SE16 *(Mayflower Garden*)*
	Docklands Sailing & Watersports Centre E14 *(Function Room*)*
	Footstool SW1 *(Max*)*
	Fulham Town Hall SW6 *(Concert Hall)*
	Hamleys Metropolis W1 *(Max*)*
	Hollyhedge House SE3 *(Max*)*
	Honourable Artillery Co EC1 *(Long Rm)*
	The Irish Centre W6 *(Hall*)*

	Kingswood House SE21 (Golden Room, Jacobean Room*)
	Legends W1 (Upstairs)
	The London Hippodrome WC2 (Private Function Rm)
	Old Refectory W8 (Max*)
	HMS President EC4 (Drill Hall)
	Royal Veterinary College NW1 (Max*)
	Royal Holloway College, Surrey (Picture Gallery)
	St Andrew Golf Club EC4 (Max*)
	St John's Hill SW11 (Drill Hall*)
	Texas Embassy Cantina WC2 (Upstairs)
	Thames Leisure EC4 (The Myuki Maru)
	Tidal Cruises SE1 (Royal Princess*)
	Whitewebbs Museum of Transport, Middx (Entire First Floor*)
240	Dolphin Square SW1 (Restaurant*)
220	Duke of York's HQ SW3 (London Irish Mess)
210	New Connaught Rms WC2 (York)
	Tidal Cruises SE1 (Viscountess)
200	Abbaye EC1 (Basement Restaurant or Wine Bar)
	Beckton Alpine Centre E6 (Bar)
	Blackheath Concert Halls SE3 (Café Bar)
	Café Greenwich Park SE10 (including Garden)
	Canal Brasserie W10 (Max*)
	The Candid Arts Trust EC1 (Ground Floor Gallery*)
	City Cruises SE16 (Millennium)
	Congress Centre WC1 (Marble Hall)
	The Courtyard, St Peter's Hall W11 (Max*)
	Embargo SW10 (Max*)
	Fulham House SW6 (Main Hall*)
	Grosvenor Rooms NW2 (Pearl Suite)
	The Hudson Club SW7 (Max*)
	Lansdowne Club W1 (Ballroom*)
	Legends W1 (Downstairs)
	Pentland House SE13 (Marquee / Lawn*)
	The Players' Theatre WC2 (Lower Supper Room/Bar*)
	Polish Hearth Club SW7 (Ballroom*)
	Porchester Centre W2 (Baths)
	Riverside Studios W6 (Café-Bar)
	Royal Green Jackets W1 (St George's Club)
	Royal Over-Seas League SW1 (Hall of India & Pakistan*)
	Strand Palace Hotel WC2 (Exeter Suite*)
	Syon Park (Banqueting), Middx (Peacock Room)
	Throgmorton's EC2 (Oak Rm)
	Westminster College (Battersea) SW11 (Great Hall*)
	Whitelands College SW15 (Max*)
195	Catamaran Cruisers WC2 (Chevening)
180	Crown River Cruises EC4 (Salient*)
	Guy's Hospital SE1 (Robens Suite*)
	Lauderdale House N6 (Max*)
	Mainstream Leisure SW15 (Elizabethan*)
	Tidal Cruises SE1 (Hurlingham)
175	City Cruises SE16 (Eltham)
	Southwark Cathedral SE1 (Function Room*)
160	Catamaran Cruisers WC2 (Abercorn or Valulla)
	Froebel Institute College SW15 (Portrait Room)
150	606 Club SW10 (Max*)
	Bakers' Hall EC3 (Max*)
	Bankside Gallery SE1 (Max*)
	Bonjour Vietnam SW6 (Basement*)
	Café Greenwich Park SE10 (Inside only)
	The Candid Arts Trust EC1 (Basement Gallery)
	Canning House SW1 (Max*)
	Chelsea Old Town Hall SW3 (Cadogan Suite or Small Hall)
	Crown River Cruises EC4 (Suerita)
	Equinox at the Empire WC2 (The Square)
	Gecko NW1 (Bar)
	Le Gothique SW18 (Patio)
	Hammersmith Town Hall W6 (Small Hall)
	The Leathermarket SE1 (Tannery Restaurant)
	Mermaid Theatre EC4 (River Rm)
	Pentland House SE13 (Hall)
	Photographers' Gallery WC2 (Max*)
	Pitcher & Piano W1 (Upper Floor*)
	Riverside Studios W6 (Terrace/Marquee)
	Royal College of Art SW7 (Gulbenkian Lower Gallery)
	Royal Geographical Society SW7 (Main Hall or New Map Rm)
	Royal Institution of Great Britain W1 (Anteroom)
	Royal Over-Seas League SW1 (St Andrew's Hall)
	St Martin In The Fields WC2 (Gallery)
	Le Studio Café N1 (Tea Room)
	Thames Luxury Cruises EC3 (Golden Salamander*)
	Turk Launches, Surrey (MV Yarmouth Belle or New Southern Belle*)
	Upper Refectory Suite SW3 (Max*)
140	Bow Wine Vaults EC4 (Max*)
	Brompton Oratory – St Wilfrid's Hall SW7 (St Joseph's Hall or St Wilfrid's Hall incl Billiards Room)
	Cecil Sharp House NW1 (Trefusis Hall)
	Gordon's Wine Bar WC2 (Max*)
	Maidenhead Steam Navigation, Berks (Georgian*)
130	Tidal Cruises SE1 (Old London)
120	Anchor SE1 (Max*)
	Bakers' Hall EC3 (Livery Hall)
	The Battersea Barge Bistro SW8 (Max*)
	Chelsea Football Club SW6 (Trophy Rm)
	The Coliseum WC2 (Terrace Bar*)
	The Courtyard, St Peter's Hall W11 (Upper Hall)
	Detroit WC2 (Max*)
	Dora House SW7 (Max*)
	Dulwich College SE21 (Lower Hall)
	Froebel Institute College SW15 (Terrace Rm)
	Gunnersbury Park W3 (Orangery or Small Mansion*)
	The House of St Barnabas-in-Soho W1 (Max*)
	Imperial College SW7 (Council Chamber)
	The Little Ship Club EC4 (Dining Rm)
	HMS President EC4 (Wardroom)
	Syon Park (Banqueting), Middx (Terrace Rm)
110	Dickens Inn E1 (Nickleby Suite*)
	Maidenhead Steam Navigation, Berks (Edwardian)
100	El Barco Latino WC2 (Max*)
	Bow Wine Vaults EC4 (Larger Section)
	Browns Club WC2 (Small VIP Rm)
	Café L'Institute SW7 (Max*)
	Catamaran Cruisers WC2 (Viceroy)
	Chelsea Football Club SW6 (Sponsors Lounge)
	Chez Gérard (Opera Terrace) WC2 (Terrace*)
	Chislehurst Caves, Kent (Max*)
	City Cruises SE16 (Westminster)
	The Clink SE1 (Museum)
	The Coliseum WC2 (Dutch Bar)
	The Conservatory SW11 (Max*)
	Conway Hall WC1 (Small Hall)
	The Courtyard, St Peter's Hall W11 (Café)
	Dolphin Square SW1 (Chichester Suite)
	Dulwich College SE21 (Cricket Pavilion)
	Goldsmiths College SE14 (Orangery*)
	Gunnersbury Park W3 (Temple)
	Hammersmith Town Hall W6 (Marble Gallery)

The Hudson Club SW7 (Middle Bar or Top Floor)
King's College School SW19 (Boathouse or Dalziel Room)
King's College, Hampstead Site NW3 (Bay Lounge)
Kingswood House SE21 (Charles Suite)
Lansdowne Club W1 (Thirties Rm)
London Transport Conference Facilities E14 (Atrium*)
Mall Galleries SW1 (East Gallery)
Mandrake Club (PizzaExpress) W1 (Max*)
Naval & Military Club W1 (Palmerston Rm or Egremont or Regimental Rm)
The Old Operating Theatre, Museum & Herb Garret SE1 (Max*)
Pall Mall Deposit W10 (Max*)
The Players' Theatre WC2 (Mezzanine Supper Room)
Poetry Society WC2 (Restaurant*)
HMS President EC4 (Gun Rm)
Royal Green Jackets W1 (Sergeants Mess)
Royal Institution of Great Britain W1 (Library)
St John's Hill SW11 (Sergeant's Mess)
Surrey Docks Watersports Centre SE16 (Max*)
Thames Leisure EC4 (The Tideway)
Throgmorton's EC2 (Short Rm)
Whitelands College SW15 (Boardroom)

90 Burgh House NW3 (Max*)
Royal Veterinary College NW1 (Northumberland Rm)
Turk Launches, Surrey (Kingston Royale)
YHA City of London EC4 (Roof Top Marquee*)

80 Anchor SE1 (Garden or Adjoining Bar)
Crown River Cruises EC4 (Spirit of London)
Dora House SW7 (The Studio)
Dr Johnsons' House EC4 (Max*)
Durrants Hotel W1 (Edward VII Rm* or Spy Room)
Floating Boater W2 (Prince Regent*)
French Institute SW7 (Salon de Réception*)
Fulham House SW6 (Dining Room)
The House of St Barnabas-in-Soho W1 (Council Room or Soho Room)
King's College WC2 (Council Rm)
London School of Economics WC2 (Senior Common Rm*)
London Scottish SW1 (Queen Elizabeth Club)
Maidenhead Steam Navigation, Berks (Belle)
Mall Galleries SW1 (North Gallery)
Naval & Military Club W1 (Courtyard)
The Old Town Hall, Stratford E15 (Council Chamber)
Royal Veterinary College NW1 (Clarence Rm)
Ship SW18 (Marquee*)
The Sun WC2 (Max*)
Throgmorton's EC2 (Long Rm)
Urban Learning Foundation E14 (Conference Room*)

75 The Lady Daphne SE1 (stationary*)
Rose Garden Buffet NW1 (Prince Regent Rm)
Thames Luxury Cruises EC3 (Captain James Cook)
Tuttons WC2 (Max*)

70 Antelope SW1 (Upstairs*)
Honourable Artillery Co EC1 (Queen's Rm)
The Old Town Hall, Stratford E15 (Conference Room)
Pitcher & Piano W1 (Panelled Room)
Rock Spiders Opera SW10 (Max*)
Strand Palace Hotel WC2 (Essex Suite)

65 Cecil Sharp House NW1 (Bar)

60 Archduke Wine Bar SE1 (Bridge Room)
Bakers' Hall EC3 (Court Rm)

Boston Manor House, Middx (Boston Manor Suite* or State Room)
Brasserie du Marché aux Puces W10 (Private Rm*)
Café Greenwich Park SE10 (Upstairs Rm)
The Candid Arts Trust EC1 (Banquet Room)
Coopers Arms SW3 (Private Rm*)
The Courtyard, St Peter's Hall W11 (North Hall)
Durrants Hotel W1 (Oak Rm)
Honourable Artillery Co EC1 (Court Rm or Medal Rm)
Jason's Trip W9 (Jason*)
The Jenny Wren NW1 (Max*)
Lansdowne Club W1 (Shelburne Rm)
London Scottish SW1 (Officers' Mess)
Music Room At Grays W1 (Gallery)
New Connaught Rms WC2 (Durham)
Royal Geographical Society SW7 (Tea Rm)
Royal Institution of Great Britain W1 (Council Rm)
Royal Veterinary College NW1 (Connaught Rm)
Strand Palace Hotel WC2 (Grenville Suite)
Syon Park (Banqueting), Middx (Conservatory Lounge)
Trafalgar Tavern SE10 (Hawke & Howe Bar)
Turk Launches, Surrey (Richmond Royale)
Victoria & Albert Museum Café SW7 (Painted Rm)

50 Anchor SE1 (Mrs Thrales Room)
The Battersea Barge Bistro SW8 (Upper Deck)
Chez Gerard, Dover St W1 (Private Rm*)
The Dickens' House Museum WC1 (Max*)
Duke of York's HQ SW3 (Mercury House)
Engineer NW1 (Large Room*)
Front Page SW3 (Private Rm*)
Guy's Hospital SE1 (Court Room)
Henry J Beans SW3 (Garden Section*)
Mainstream Leisure SW15 (Lady House of Regent's)
Royal Over-Seas League SW1 (Wrench)
Royal Veterinary College NW1 (Cambridge Rm)
Strand Palace Hotel WC2 (Drake Suite)
Surrey Docks Watersports Centre SE16 (Quay Room/Quay Lounge)

48 Jason's Trip W9 (Holland)

45 The Lady Daphne SE1 (afloat)
Royal Over-Seas League SW1 (Mountbatten Rutland)
Le Studio Café N1 (Boat)

40 Bow Wine Vaults EC4 (Smaller Section)
Carlyle's House SW3 (Max*)
Crown & Goose NW1 (Private Rm*)
Docklands Sailing & Watersports Centre E14 (Teaching Room)
Dora House SW7 (Salon)
Floating Boater W2 (Lapwing)
Imperial College SW7 (Solar)
Pitcher & Piano W1 (Cosy Area)

36 Jason's Trip W9 (Lace Plate II)

35 Conway Hall WC1 (Club Room)

30 Archduke Wine Bar SE1 (Conservatory)
Badbobs WC2 (Library (VIP Room))
Naval & Military Club W1 (Octagon)
Royal Over-Seas League SW1 (Bennet-Clark)

25 Durrants Hotel W1 (Armfield Rm)

20 The Coliseum WC2 (Stoll Rm)
Kingswood House SE21 (Hannen Room)
The Old Town Hall, Stratford E15 (Mayors Parlour)
YHA City of London EC4 (Chapel)

15 Royal Over-Seas League SW1 *(Park)*
Westminster College
(Battersea) SW11
(Private Dining Room (Room 2))
12 Chas Newens Marine Co SW15
(Panache, Majestic or Pomery")
The Coliseum WC2 *(Arlen Rm)*

£B-E

200 Broadgate Estates EC2 *(Ice Rink")*
90 Broadgate Estates EC2
(Exchange Square Marquee)
80 Fan Museum SE10 *(Museum" or Orangery)*

£B

2230 Hammersmith Palais W6 *(Max")*
1500 Turnmills EC1 *(Max")*
1200 The Ministry of Sound SE1 *(Max")*
1100 Electric Ballroom NW1 *(Max")*
The Fridge SW2 *(Max")*
1000 Brockwell Lido SE24 *(Max")*
International Students W1 *(Max")*
London Astoria 2 W1 *(Max")*
Queens Ice Bowl W2 *(Max")*
900 The Ministry of Sound SE1
(The Box and Main Bar)
860 SW1 Club SW1 *(Max")*
800 Battersea Town Hall SW11
(Grand Hall")
Wandsworth Civic Suite SW18
(Civic Suite")
750 Polish Social & Cultural
Association W6 *(Max")*
650 Subterania W10 *(Max")*
600 Iceni W1 *(Max")*
International Students W1 *(Theatre)*
Rock Garden WC2 *(Max")*
Wag W1 *(Max")*
500 Mudchute Park and Farm E14 *(Max")*
Queens Ice Bowl W2 *(Sega World)*
Le Scandale W1 *(Max")*
475 Wandsworth Civic Suite SW18
(Civic Hall)
450 The RAW Club WC1 *(Max")*
400 Hammersmith Palais W6 *(Balcony Bar)*
HQ NW1 *(Max")*
University of London Union WC1
(Room 101")
Wandsworth Civic Suite SW18
(Banqueting Hall)
350 Central Club (YWCA) WC1
(Queen Mary Hall")
330 Hop Cellars SE1 *(Max")*
300 Balls Brothers SW1 *(Max")*
Circa W1 *(Max")*
Cittie of Yorke WC1 *(Main Bar)*
Corney & Barrow EC2 *(Max")*
Holderness House EC2 *(Hall")*
The Horniman at Hay's SE1 *(Max")*
Lea Rowing Club E5 *(Max")*
The London Welsh Centre WC1
(Main Hall")
The Ministry of Sound SE1
(Space Bar (VIP Room))
Nôtre Dame Hall WC2 *(Max")*
Rock Garden WC2 *(Rock Garden)*
Davy's – Skinkers SE1 *(Max")*
Turnmills EC1 *(Juno Lucina)*
Wag W1 *(Bottom Floor or Top Floor)*
Westminster Cathedral Hall SW1
(Max")
WKD NW1 *(Max")*
280 St Etheldreda's Crypt EC1 *(Max")*
260 Brockwell Lido SE24 *(Café-restaurant)*
250 Balls Brothers EC2 *(Max")*
Balls Brothers EC3 *(Max")*
Davy's – Bangers EC2 *(Max")*
Davy's – Bung Hole WC1 *(Max")*

Davy's – The Chiv W1 *(Max")*
Davy's – City Flogger EC3 *(Max")*
Davy's – Colonel Jaspers EC1 *(Max")*
Davy's – Crown Passage
Vaults SW1 *(Max")*
Exxo W1 *(Max")*
Holy Trinity Brompton Church
Hall SW7 *(Max")*
International Students W1
(Portland Rm)
London Rowing Club SW15 *(Max")*
Davy's – The Vineyard E1 *(Max")*
200 Abbey Community Centre SW1
(Main Hall")
Balls Brothers EC2 *(Max)*
Battersea Town Hall SW11
(Lower Hall)
Davy's – Bishop of Norwich EC2
(Max")
Davy's – Burgundys Ben's EC1
(Max")
Davy's – Champagne
Charlies WC2 *(Max")*
Davy's – Chopper Lump W1 *(Max")*
Davy's – City Boot EC2 *(Max")*
Davy's – City Pipe EC1 *(Max")*
Coates Karaoke Bar &
Restaurant EC2 *(Max")*
Davy's – Colonel Jaspers SE10
(Max")
The Crown Tavern EC1 *(Max")*
Davy's – Davy's of Creed
Lane EC4 *(Max")*
Davy's – Docks Bar & Diner E1
(Max")
Drakes EC4 *(Max")*
The Glasshouse Stores W1 *(Max")*
Davy's – Guinea Butt SE1 *(Max")*
Davy's – The Habit EC3 *(Max")*
Hammersmith Palais W6 *(Stage Bar)*
Iceni W1 *(First Floor, Ground Floor or
Second Floor)*
Davy's – Lees Bag W1 *(Max")*
Lundonia House WC1 *(Ground Floor")*
Polish Social & Cultural
Association W6 *(Lowiczanka Restaurant
or Malinova Rm)*
Le Scandale W1 *(Front or Rear Bar)*
Davy's – Tappit-Hen WC2 *(Max")*
The Tattershall Castle SW1
(Steamers Discotheque")
Davy's – Truckles Of Pied Bull
Yard WC1 *(Max")*
Wessex House SW11 *(Max")*
Westminster College
(Victoria) SW1
(Vincent Room (Restaurant)")
175 St Bride Foundation Institute EC4
(Bridewell Hall")
165 Circa W1 *(Downstairs)*
150 Africa Centre WC2 *(Main Hall")*
Balls Brothers EC4 *(Max)*
Balls Brothers SE1 *(Max")*
Balls Brothers EC2 *(Weekday function)*
Captain Kidd E1 *(Max")*
Davy's – City FOB EC3 *(Max")*
Davy's – The Cooperage SE1 *(Max")*
Corney & Barrow EC3 *(Max")*
Crown & Greyhound SE21 *(Max")*
Davy's – Davys' at Russia
Court EC2 *(Max")*
The Fridge SW2 *(Fridge Bar)*
Glassblower W1 *(Max")*
Hollands W11 *(Max")*
Hop Cellars SE1 *(Malt Rm)*
The Horniman at Hay's SE1 *(Gallery)*
International Students W1 *(Gulbenkian)*
Leadenhall Wine Bar EC3 *(Max")*
Davy's – The Mug House SE1 *(Max")*
The Old Thameside Inn SE1
(Cellar Bar")
Polish Social & Cultural
Association W6 *(Club Disco)*
Davy's – The Pulpit EC2 *(Max")*
Ruby's W1 *(Max")*

Slug & Lettuce N1 *(Max")*
Southwark Tavern SE1 *(Max")*
Davy's – Tapster SW1 *(Max")*
Davy's – Tumblers W8 *(Max")*
Walkers of St James's SW1 *(Max")*
Ye Olde Cheshire Cheese EC4
(Cellar Bar")

140 Balls Brothers SW1 *(Weekday function)*
International Students W1 *(Bistro)*
130 Alma SW18 *(Private Rm")*
Balls Brothers EC2 *(Weekday function)*
Balls Brothers EC4 *(Weekday function)*
Circa W1 *(Upstairs)*
Vats WC1 *(Max")*
WKD NW1 *(Mezzanine)*
120 Cittie of Yorke WC1 *(Cellar Bar)*
Davy's – City Vaults EC1 *(Max")*
Corney & Barrow EC4 *(Max")*
The Crown and Two
    Chairmen W1 *(Upstairs Bar")*
Davy's – Dock Blida W1 *(Max")*
Earlsfield Library SW18 *(Max")*
The Golden Lion SW1 *(Max")*
Hammersmith Palais W6 *(VIP Bar)*
St Moritz W1 *(Max")*
Davy's – Tappit-Hen WC2
(Wine Rooms)
University of London Union WC1
(Palms Wine Bar)
100 Abbey Community Centre SW1
(Bar)
Balls Brothers EC2 *(Max)*
Balls Brothers EC3 *(Weekday function)*
Balls Brothers at Great Eastern
    Hotel EC2 *(Max")*
The Barley Mow W1 *(Max")*
Davy's – Boot & Flogger SE1 *(Max")*
Britannia W8 *(Max")*
The Clachan W1 *(Highland Bar")*
The Coal Hole WC2 *(Max")*
Corney & Barrow EC4 *(Max)*
Davy's – The Davys of
    Long Lane EC1 *(Max")*
Deacons EC4 *(Max")*
Duke of Clarence W11 *(Conservatory")*
The Freemason's Arms WC2 *(Max")*
Kettners W1 *(Edward Room")*
The Lamb Tavern EC3
(Dining Rm" or The Dive)
Larry's Wine Bar WC2 *(Max")*
Lea Rowing Club E5 *(Bar)*
The London Welsh Centre WC1
(Bar)
La Paquerette EC2 *(Max")*
Pitcher & Piano SW10 *(Max")*
Queens Ice Bowl W2 *(Private Room)*
Davy's – Shotberries EC2 *(Max")*
Slug & Lettuce SW15 *(Max")*
Slug & Lettuce SW18 *(Room 1")*
Vats WC1 *(Restaurant)*
Victoria Pump House SW11 *(Max")*
The White Horse SW6 *(Private Rm")*
90 Balls Brothers EC2 *(Max)*
80 Africa Centre WC2 *(Rear Hall)*
Balls Brothers EC2 *(Weekday function)*
The Catherine Wheel W8
(Private Rm")
Davy's – The Chiv W1 *(Dining Rm)*
Cittie of Yorke WC1 *(Front Bar)*
Gargoyle Club SW10 *(Max")*
The Glasshouse Stores W1 *(One side)*
The Horniman at Hay's SE1
(Frederick John Horniman Rm)
Leadenhall Wine Bar EC3
(Top-floor Room)
Phene Arms SW3 *(Upstairs Rm")*
Shampers W1 *(Wine Bar")*
University of London Union WC1
(Bar 101)
Ye Olde Cheshire Cheese E4
(Johnson's or Williams Rm)
75 Davy's – Bangers Too EC3 *(Max")*
Hop Cellars SE1 *(Porter Rm)*
St Bride Foundation Institute EC4
(Farringdon Rm)

72 Queens Ice Bowl W2
(10 Pin Bowling (per Game))
70 The Argyll Arms W1 *(Palladium Bar")*
Davy's – Bung Hole WC1
(Private Room)
Chatham Hall SW11 *(Max")*
Rochesters SW1 *(Max")*
Shelleys W1 *(Max")*
Slug & Lettuce SW18 *(Room 2)*
Ye Olde Cheshire Cheese EC4
(Johnson's Bar)
65 Corney & Barrow E14 *(Max")*
60 Balls Brothers EC2 *(Weekday function)*
Bill Bentley's EC2 *(Max")*
Calthorpe Arms WC1 *(Private Rm")*
Captain Kidd E1 *(The Observation Deck)*
The Crown Tavern EC1 *(Upstairs Bar)*
Lundonia House WC1
(Top Floor Theatre)
The RAW Club WC1
(The Gardening Rm)
Rock Garden WC2 *(Upstairs Restaurant)*
Shampers W1 *(Brasserie)*
50 Balls Brothers EC4 *(Weekday function)*
Corney & Barrow EC2 *(Max")*
Holderness House EC2 *(Rifleman's Bar)*
Newham City Farm E16 *(Room")*
Pimlico Wine Vaults EC1 *(Private Rm")*
Simpsons Tavern EC3
(Amy's Bar or Wine Bar")
Star Tavern SW1 *(Bar")*
Two Chairmen SW1 *(Max")*
Westminster College
    (Victoria) SW1 *(Escoffier)*
45 The Plough WC2 *(Max")*
40 Balls Brothers EC2 *(Weekday function)*
Balls Brothers at Great Eastern
    Hotel EC2 *(Weekday function)*
Duke of Albemarle W1 *(Max")*
The Golden Lion SW1 *(Theatre Bar)*
Davy's – Grapeshots E1 *(Max")*
Lundonia House WC1 *(Club)*
Mudchute Park and Farm E14 *(Café)*
Slug & Lettuce SW1 *(Max")*
Ye Olde Cheshire Cheese EC4
(Snug Bar)
35 The Dog & Duck W1 *(Max")*
Davy's – Skinkers SE1 *(Boardroom)*
30 Phene Arms SW3 *(Terrace)*
The Tattershall Castle SW1 *(Bridge)*
Wandsworth Civic Suite SW18
(Reception Rm)
25 Ye Olde Cheshire Cheese EC4
(Director's Rm)
20 Davy's – Skinkers SE1
(Second private room)

Function rooms listed
by seated capacity

* largest entry for venue

£E

450	British Museum WC1 (Max*)
360	Mezzo W1 (Mezzo*)
350	Madame Tussaud's NW1 (Grand Hall*)
340	Mezzo W1 (Mezzanine)
300	Blenheim Palace, Oxon (State Rooms*)
	Victoria & Albert Museum SW7 (Dome, Medieval Treasury & Pirelli Garden)* or Raphael Gallery)
280	Hampton Court Palace, Surrey (Great Hall*)
250	Royal Academy of Arts W1 (Summer Exhibition*)
200	Tate Gallery SW1 (Pre Raphaelite and 19th Century Gallery*)
170	Cliveden, Berks (Max*)
160	Blenheim Palace, Oxon (Orangery)
150	Brocket Hall, Herts (Max*)
	Queen's House SE10 (Max*)
	Victoria & Albert Museum SW7 (Gamble Rm including Morris Rm)
	Wallace Collection W1 (Long Gallery*)
132	Spencer House SW1 (Max*)
125	Annabel's W1 (Max*)
120	Syon Park (House), Middx (Great Hall*)
	Wrotham Park, Herts (Drawing Room*)
110	Apsley House W1 (Max*)
	Cliveden, Berks (Terraced Dining Room)
	Queen's House SE10 (Great Hall)
100	National Portrait Gallery WC2 (Max*)
	Royal Academy of Arts W1 (Private Rms)
95	Syon Park (House), Middx (State Dining Room)
80	Kenwood House NW3 (Orangery*)
	Madame Tussaud's NW1 (Garden Party)
	Moyns Park, Essex (Great Hall*)
	Wrotham Park, Herts (Dining Room)
72	Spencer House SW1 (Great Room)
60	Hampton Court Palace, Surrey (Banqueting House)
54	Cliveden, Berks (French Dining Rm)
50	Chiswick House W4 (First floor*)
	Courtauld Gallery WC2 (Great Room*)
	HM Tower of London EC3 (Royal Fusiliers Association Room*)
40	Moyns Park, Essex (Dining Room)
	Old Royal Observatory SE10 (Max*)
	Queen's House SE10 (Orangery Suite)
	Rossway Park, Herts (Dining Room*)
	Royal Academy of Arts W1 (General Assembly Rm)
	Victoria & Albert Museum SW7 (Morris Rm)
	Wrotham Park, Herts (Saloon)
36	Spencer House SW1 (Lady Spencer's Room)
35	Mezzo W1 (Pâtisserie)
30	Moyns Park, Essex (Drawing Room)
	Sir John Soane's Museum WC2 (Max*)
24	Spencer House SW1 (Dining Room or Music Room)
	Wallace Collection W1 (Gallery 17)
20	Chez Nico at Ninety Grosvenor House Hotel W1 (Private Rm*)
	Cliveden, Berks (Macmillan Boardroom)
10	Tate Gallery SW1 (Lodge)

£M-E

2000	Business Design Centre N1 (Max*)
	Royal Lancaster W2 (Max*)
1500	The Grosvenor House Hotel W1 (Great Rm*)

	Royal Lancaster W2 (Nine Kings Suite)
1450	Royal Albert Hall SW7 (Cabaret or Ball*)
1250	Hilton on Park Lane W1 (Grand Ballroom*)
1120	Royal Lancaster W2 (Westbourne Suite)
1000	Spitalfields Market E1 (Marquee (winter)*)
800	Inter-Continental W1 (Grand Ballroom*)
	The Queen Elizabeth II Conference Centre SW1 (Fleming + Whittle Rooms*)
704	Guildhall EC2 (Great Hall*)
650	Hurlingham Club SW6 (Max*)
600	Natural History Museum SW7 (Central Hall*)
	Park Lane Hotel W1 (Ballroom*)
	The Queen Elizabeth II Conference Centre SW1 (Fleming Room)
576	Cumberland Hotel W1 (Production Box*)
550	The Dorchester W1 (Ballroom*)
500	The Grosvenor House Hotel W1 (Ballroom)
	The Savoy WC2 (Lancaster Rm*)
	Westway Studios W11 (Studio 1*)
480	Royal Garden Hotel W8 (Max*)
450	Royal Garden Hotel W8 (Palace Suite)
430	Inter-Continental W1 (Westminster)
420	Millennium Conference Centre SW7 (Lower Level*)
400	Cumberland Hotel W1 (Carlisle)
	Fashion Café W1 (Grande Salle*)
	Four Seasons Hotel W1 (Ballroom*)
	Imperial War Museum SE1 (Exhibition Hall*)
	One Whitehall Place SW1 (Max*)
	Phyllis Court, Oxon (Ballroom*)
	Portman Hotel W1 (Ballroom*)
	Reform Club SW1 (Max*)
	Woods River Cruises SE3 (Silver Sturgeon*)
380	Hilton on Park Lane W1 (Grand Ballroom - Section 1)
375	Banqueting House SW1 (Main Hall*)
370	Royal Air Force Museum NW9 (Battle of Britain Hall*)
360	The Landmark W1 (Ballroom*)
	Royal Albert Hall SW7 (Arena)
350	Hilton on Park Lane W1 (Grand Ballroom - Section 2)
	Science Museum SW7 (Flight Gallery*)
320	Hyatt Carlton Tower SW1 (Ballroom*)
	Lincoln's Inn WC2 (Great Hall*)
	The Mayfair Inter-Continental W1 (Crystal Rm*)
	Millennium Conference Centre SW7 (Ground Level (open))
	Quaglino's SW1 (Max*)
310	Gloucester Hotel SW7 (Cotswold Suite & Courtfield Suite*)
300	Atlantic Bar & Grill W1 (Max*)
	Bath – Assembly Rooms, (Ballroom*)
	Guildhall EC2 (Old Library)
	The Hempel W2 (Garden Square*)
	Legoland Windsor, Berks (Marché Restaurant* or Picnic Grove)
	The London Dungeon SE1 (Max*)
	Middle Temple Hall EC4 (Hall*)
	La Porte des Indes W1 (Max*)
	Saatchi Gallery NW8 (Max*)
	Westway Studios W11 (Studio 2)
298	Plaisterers' Hall EC2 (Max*)
280	The Gibson Hall EC2 (Hall*)
	Leeds Castle, Kent (Fairfax Hall With Terrace Room*)
	Merchant Taylors' Hall EC2 (Great Hall*)
	Phillips W1 (Max*)
260	National Liberal Club SW1 (Max*)
250	Beaulieu, Hants (Brabazon*)
	Drapers' Hall EC2 (Livery Hall*)
	Hurlingham Club SW6 (Quadrangle Suite)
	Inner Temple Hall EC4 (Hall*)
	Institute of Directors SW1 (Nash*)
	Le Meridien W1 (Georgian*)
	Royal College of Music SW7 (Concert Hall*)
	Sotheby's W1 (Main Gallery*)

The South Bank Centre SE1 *(Queen Elizabeth Hall Foyer*)*
240 Barbican Centre EC2 *(Garden Rm*)*
Claridge's W1 *(Ballroom*)*
Harrington Hall SW7 *(Harrington*)*
The People's Palace SE1 *(Max*)*
The Savoy WC2 *(Abraham Lincoln & Manhattan Rms)*
Serpentine Gallery W2 *(Max*)*
230 Hyde Park Hotel SW1 *(Ballroom*)*
Knebworth House, Herts *(Manor Barn (incl Bulwer Room*))*
Westminster Abbey Garden SW1 *(Marquee*)*
228 One Whitehall Place SW1 *(Gladstone Library)*
224 Clothworkers' Hall EC3 *(Livery Hall*)*
220 One Whitehall Place SW1 *(Whitehall Suite)*
Roehampton Club SW15 *(Max*)*
210 Claridge's W1 *(Max)*
Inter-Continental W1 *(Piccadilly)*
205 Stationers' Hall EC4 *(Livery Hall*)*
200 Addington Palace CR9 *(Max*)*
Banqueting House SW1 *(Undercroft)*
Bath – Assembly Rooms, *(Tea Room)*
Bonham's SW7 *(Max*)*
Christie's SW1 *(Max*)*
Christopher's WC2 *(Max*)*
Clandon, Surrey *(Restaurant*)*
The Criterion W1 *(Max*)*
Goldsmiths' Hall EC2 *(Livery Hall*)*
Guildhall EC2 *(Livery Hall)*
Herstmonceux Castle, East Sussex *(Ballroom*)*
Kew (Royal Botanic) Gardens, Surrey *(Temperate House*)*
London Zoo NW1 *(Regency Suite*)*
Le Meridien W1 *(Edwardian)*
The Roof Gardens W8 *(Max*)*
Science Museum SW7 *(East Hall)*
Westway Studios W11 *(Studio 4)*
190 Selsdon Park Hotel, Surrey *(Tudor Room*)*
180 The Avenue SW1 *(Max*)*
The Berkeley SW1 *(Ballroom*)*
City Brasserie EC3 *(Max*)*
Clandon, Surrey *(Marble Hall)*
Guildhall EC2 *(West Crypt)*
Hilton on Park Lane W1 *(Curzon Suite)*
Natural History Museum SW7 *(Earth Galleries or North Hall)*
Park Lane Hotel W1 *(Tudor Rose Rm)*
170 Gray's Inn WC1 *(Hall*)*
Skinners' Hall EC4 *(Max*)*
168 Woods River Cruises SE3 *(Silver Barracuda)*
160 The Berners Hotel W1 *(Thomas Ashton Suite*)*
The Dorchester W1 *(Orchid)*
Grocers' Hall EC2 *(Livery Hall*)*
The Landmark W1 *(Drawing Rm or Empire Rm)*
Phillips W1 *(Blenheim Room)*
Roehampton Club SW15 *(Roehampton Room)*
150 Accademia Italiana/European Academy SW1 *(Max*)*
Addington Palace CR9 *(Great Hall)*
Arts Club W1 *(Dining Rm*)*
Arts Depot NW1 *(Max*)*
Baltic Exchange EC3 *(Trading Floor*)*
Barbican Centre EC2 *(Conservatory Terrace)*
Bateaux London WC2 *(Symphony*)*
Dulwich Picture Gallery SE21 *(Max*)*
Hilton on Park Lane W1 *(Grand Ballroom - Section 3)*
Hyde Park Hotel SW1 *(Knightsbridge Suite)*
Loseley Park, Surrey *(Tithe Barn*)*
Mirabelle W1 *(Max*)*
National Liberal Club SW1 *(Terrace *)*
One Whitehall Place SW1 *(Reading And Writing Room)*
Penshurst Place and Gardens, Kent *(Baron's Hall*)*

Quo Vadis W1 *(Private Rm*)*
Ranger's House SE10 *(Marquee*)*
Searcy's SW1 *(Max*)*
The South Bank Centre SE1 *(Hong Kong & Chelsfield Rm)*
140 Beaulieu, Hants *(Domus)*
Hilton on Park Lane W1 *(Crystal Palace Rm)*
The Imagination Gallery WC1 *(Atrium and Mezzanine*)*
Motcomb's Club SW1 *(Max*)*
National Liberal Club SW1 *(David Lloyd George)*
The Queen Elizabeth II Conference Centre SW1 *(Caxton Lounge)*
Royal Albert Hall SW7 *(Picture Gallery)*
139 Saddlers' Hall EC3 *(Max*)*
130 Apothecaries' Hall EC4 *(Hall*)*
Lincoln's Inn WC2 *(Old Hall)*
124 National Liberal Club SW1 *(Dining Rm *)*
120 Café de Paris W1 *(Restaurant*)*
The Caledonian Club SW1 *(Members Dining Rm*)*
Gladwins EC3 *(Max*)*
The Grosvenor House Hotel W1 *(Albemarle)*
Highclere Castle, Berks *(Library*)*
The Imagination Gallery WC1 *(Gallery)*
Inter-Continental W1 *(Apsley)*
The Mayfair Inter-Continental W1 *(Danziger Suite)*
Monkey Island Hotel, Berks *(River Rm*)*
Museum of London EC2 *(Lord Mayor's Coach Gallery*)*
Natural History Museum SW7 *(Spencer Gallery)*
Park Lane Hotel W1 *(Garden Rm)*
Phyllis Court, Oxon *(Grandstand)*
The Queen Elizabeth II Conference Centre SW1 *(Pickwick Suite)*
The Royal College of Pathologists SW1 *(Lecture Room*)*
The Savoy WC2 *(River Rm)*
Sheraton Park Tower SW1 *(Trianon Rm*)*
HQS Wellington WC2 *(Court Rm*)*
Windsor Guildhall, Berks *(Guildhall Chamber*)*
115 Mosimann's Belfry SW1 *(Dining Rm*)*
110 Gloucester Hotel SW7 *(Cotswold - Chalford/Dean)*
Harrington Hall SW7 *(Reynolds & Landseer)*
100 Cannizaro House SW19 *(Viscount Melville Suite*)*
The Chelsea Club SW6 *(Sloane Suite*)*
Clandon, Surrey *(Saloon)*
Cumberland Hotel W1 *(Gloucester)*
The Dorchester W1 *(The Terrace)*
Four Seasons Hotel W1 *(Garden Rm)*
The Gibson Hall EC2 *(Garden Room)*
Grocers' Hall EC2 *(Piper Rm)*
Harrington Hall SW7 *(Turner & Constable)*
Hurlingham Club SW6 *(Palm Court Suite)*
Knebworth House, Herts *(Lodge Barn)*
The Lanesborough SW1 *(Belgravia*)*
Leeds Castle, Kent *(Henry VIII Banqueting Hall)*
London Zoo NW1 *(Raffles Bar and Restaurant)*
Museum of Mankind W1 *(Max*)*
Orangery (Kensington Palace) W8 *(Max*)*
Reform Club SW1 *(Coffee Rm or Library)*
Royal Garden Hotel W8 *(Kensington Suite)*
The Sanctuary WC2 *(Max*)*
Scotts W1 *(Restaurant*)*
Tower Bridge SE1 *(Walkways*)*
Waddesdon Manor, The Dairy, Bucks *(West Hall*)*
Westway Studios W11 *(Studio 3)*
98 City Rhodes EC4 *(Max*)*
95 Baltic Exchange EC3 *(Dining Room)*

91	Innholders' Hall EC4 *(Hall*)*
90	Brighton Royal Pavilion, Sussex *(Banqueting Rm (and Great Kitchen)*)*
	Royal Garden Hotel W8 *('The Tenth' Restaurant)*
	Science Museum SW7 *(Director's Suite)*
85	Royal Lancaster W2 *(Gloucester Suite)*
84	Claridge's W1 *(Drawing Room, French Salon or Mirror Room)*
	Penshurst Place and Gardens, Kent *(Sunderland Room)*
80	Addington Palace CR9 *(Norman Shaw Room or Robing Room)*
	Armourers' & Braisers' Hall EC2 *(Livery Hall*)*
	The Berners Hotel W1 *(Ashton Room or Fitzrovia Suite)*
	Brighton Royal Pavilion, Sussex *(Queen Adelaide Suite)*
	Cutty Sark SE10 *(Lower Hold or Tween Decks*)*
	Four Seasons Hotel W1 *(Oak Rm)*
	Hampshire Hotel WC2 *(Penthouse*)*
	Inner Temple Hall EC4 *(Parliament Chamber)*
	Institute of Directors SW1 *(Burton)*
	Kew (Royal Botanic) Gardens, Surrey *(Gallery (entire ground floor))*
	Leeds Castle, Kent *(Terrace Room)*
	Leighton House W14 *(Studio*)*
	The London Planetarium NW1 *(Max*)*
	Merchant Taylors' Hall EC2 *(Parlour)*
	Le Meridien W1 *(Adams)*
	Park Lane Hotel W1 *(Oak Rm)*
	Portman Hotel W1 *(Gloucester Suite)*
	Ranger's House SE10 *(Gallery)*
	Royal Albert Hall SW7 *(Victoria Rm)*
	Stationers' Hall EC4 *(Court Rm)*
75	Bank of England Museum EC2 *(Max*)*
	The Halkin SW1 *(Max*)*
	The Hempel W2 *(I- Thai Restaurant (and Shadow Bar))*
72	One Whitehall Place SW1 *(Meston Suite)*
70	Addington Palace CR9 *(Winter Garden)*
	The Dorchester W1 *(Park Suite)*
	Hever Castle, Kent *(Tudor Suite*)*
	Howard Hotel WC2 *(Fitzalan*)*
	Hyde Park Hotel SW1 *(King Gustav Adolf Suite)*
	Institute of Directors SW1 *(Waterloo)*
	Museum of the Moving Image SE1 *(Hollywood Studio*)*
	Polesden Lacey, Surrey *(Restaurant*)*
	Raffles SW3 *(Max*)*
	Royal Garden Hotel W8 *(Lancaster Suite)*
	Selsdon Park Hotel, Surrey *(Kent Room)*
	Theatre Museum WC2 *(Foyer or Paintings Gallery*)*
	Tower Bridge SE1 *(Engine Rm)*
68	One Whitehall Place SW1 *(River Room)*
	Woods River Cruises SE3 *(Silver Dolphin)*
65	Barbican Centre EC2 *(Conservatory)*
60	Atlantic Bar & Grill W1 *(Private Room)*
	Drapers' Hall EC2 *(Court Rm/Court Dining)*
	Dukes Hotel SW1 *(Marlborough Suite*)*
	Halcyon Hotel W11 *(Restaurant*)*
	Ham House, Surrey *(Great Hall, Orangery (Restaurant*) or Tea Garden)*
	Hartwell House, Bucks *(James Wyatt Rooms*)*
	Highclere Castle, Berks *(Dining Room)*
	Inter-Continental W1 *(Windsor Suite I)*
	Kaspia W1 *(Max*)*
	Knebworth House, Herts *(Banqueting Hall (House) or House)*
	The Lanesborough SW1 *(Wellington Rm)*
	Leeds Castle, Kent *(State Dining Rm)*
	London Capital Club EC4 *(Max*)*
	Middle Temple Hall EC4 *(Parliament Chamber)*
	Museum of London EC2 *(Eighteenth Century Gallery)*

	One Whitehall Place SW1 *(Thames Suite)*
	Phyllis Court, Oxon *(Thames Room)*
	Roehampton Club SW15 *(Garden Room)*
	The Savoy WC2 *(Beaufort)*
	Stone Buildings WC2 *(Max*)*
	Waddesdon Manor, The Dairy, Bucks *(Winter Gardens)*
	HQS Wellington WC2 *(Quarterdeck)*
57	Dyers' Hall EC4 *(Max*)*
54	The Berkeley SW1 *(Belgravia)*
52	The Caledonian Club SW1 *(Stuart)*
50	Addington Palace CR9 *(Music Room)*
	Bath – Assembly Rooms, *(Card Room)*
	The Berners Hotel W1 *(Slater Room)*
	Cabinet War Rooms SW1 *(Max*)*
	Claridge's W1 *(Kensington)*
	The Dorchester W1 *(Holford)*
	English Garden SW3 *(Max*)*
	Howard Hotel WC2 *(Arundel Suite)*
	Imperial War Museum SE1 *(Boardroom 1)*
	Leeds Castle, Kent *(Gate Tower)*
	Mosimann's Belfry SW1 *(Theo Fabergé)*
	National Liberal Club SW1 *(Lady Violet)*
	Portman Hotel W1 *(Berkeley Suite)*
	The Queen Elizabeth II Conference Centre SW1 *(Guild Room)*
	The Ritz W1 *(Marie Antoinette Suite*)*
	Royal Garden Hotel W8 *(Bertie's Bar)*
48	La Tante Claire SW3 *(Max*)*
46	Stationers' Hall EC4 *(Stock Rm)*
45	Harrington Hall SW7 *(Stubbs or Sutherland)*
	Maison Novelli EC1 *(Top Floor*)*
44	Cannizaro House SW19 *(Earl Of Mexborough or Viscount Melville)*
42	The Royal College of Pathologists SW1 *(Council Room)*
	The Stafford SW1 *(The Cellar*)*
40	Addington Palace CR9 *(Library)*
	Brighton Royal Pavilion, Sussex *(Great Kitchen)*
	The Dorchester W1 *(Pavilion)*
	Four Seasons Hotel W1 *(Pine Rm)*
	Gray's Inn WC1 *(Large Pension Rm)*
	The Grosvenor House Hotel W1 *(Spencer Room)*
	Ham House, Surrey *(Orangery (Tea Room))*
	The Hempel W2 *(Room No 17)*
	The Lanesborough SW1 *(Westminster Rm)*
	London Capital Club EC4 *(Boardroom)*
	Le Meridien W1 *(Regency 2)*
	Park Lane Hotel W1 *(Mirror Rm or Orchard Suite)*
	Quaglino's SW1 *(Private Rm)*
	Royal College of Music SW7 *(Donaldson Rm)*
	The Savoy WC2 *(Pinafore)*
	Scotts W1 *(Oyster Terrace)*
	Sheraton Park Tower SW1 *(Balmoral)*
	The Stafford SW1 *(Panel Rm & Sutherland Rm)*
	Temple Island, Oxon *(Indoors*)*
	Windsor Guildhall, Berks *(Maidenhead Room)*
38	Raffles SW3 *(Dining Rm)*
	Sotheby's W1 *(Café)*
37	Thomas Goode Restaurant W1 *(Max*)*
36	Hever Castle, Kent *(Great Hall)*
	Hyde Park Hotel SW1 *(Loggia)*
	Inter-Continental W1 *(Windsor Suite II)*
	Leith's W11 *(Private Rm*)*
	The Mayfair Inter-Continental W1 *(Berkeley Suite)*
35	Institute of Directors SW1 *(Trafalgar II/St James)*
	Maison Novelli EC1 *(Ground Floor or Middle Floor)*
34	The Berkeley SW1 *(Tattersalls)*
	Green's SW1 *(Private Rm 1*)*

PRIVATE VENUES | SEATED CAPACITY

33	The Royal College of Radiologists W1 *(Council Chamber')*
30	The Berkeley SW1 *(Waterloo)*
	Geffrye Museum E2 *(Lecture Theatre')*
	The Halkin SW1 *(Private Rm)*
	Hartwell House, Bucks *(Doric Room)*
	L'Incontro SW1 *(Private Rm')*
	Inner Temple Hall EC4 *(Luncheon Rm)*
	Kew (Royal Botanic) Gardens, Surrey *(Cambridge Cottage Lounge)*
	Knebworth House, Herts *(Dining Parlour)*
	The Landmark W1 *(Champagne Rm)*
	Leighton House W14 *(Dining Rm)*
	Millennium Conference Centre SW7 *(Room 4)*
	Mimmo d'Ischia SW1 *(Private Rm')*
	Mirabelle W1 *(Pine Rm)*
	Mosimann's Belfry SW1 *(Wedgwood)*
	Motcomb's SW1 *(McClue Suite')*
	Penshurst Place, Kent *(Buttery)*
	The Ritz W1 *(Berkeley Suite Reception Rm & Dining Rm)*
	Sheekey's WC2 *(Section')*
	Stone Buildings WC2 *(Dining Room)*
28	The Metropolitan W1 *(Dining-Meeting Room')*
	The Savoy WC2 *(Gondoliers)*
26	Arts Club W1 *(Drawing Rm)*
	English House SW3 *(Max')*
	Windsor Guildhall, Berks *(Ascot Room)*
25	Innholders' Hall EC4 *(Court Rm)*
	L'Oranger SW1 *(Private Room')*
	HQS Wellington WC2 *(Model Rm and Library)*
24	Baltic Exchange EC3 *(Boardroom)*
	Cannizaro House SW19 *(Oak Room)*
	The Chelsea SW1 *(Beauchamp Rm)*
	Inter-Continental W1 *(Hogarth)*
	Mitsukoshi SW1 *(Western Rm')*
	Portman Hotel W1 *(Library)*
	Royal College of Music SW7 *(Council Rm)*
	The Savoy WC2 *(Patience)*
	The Stafford SW1 *(Sutherland Rm)*
22	Apothecaries' Hall EC4 *(Court Rm or Parlour)*
	The Caledonian Club SW1 *(Selkirk)*
	The Capital SW3 *(Cadogan')*
	The Connaught W1 *(Regency Carlos Suite')*
	Middle Temple Hall EC4 *(Queen's Rm)*
	Scotts W1 *(Basement Function Room)*
	Sheraton Park Tower SW1 *(Buckingham Rm)*
	Zen Central W1 *(Private Rm')*
20	Armourers' & Braisers' Hall EC2 *(Court Rm)*
	Bluebird SW3 *(Private Room')*
	Claridge's W1 *(St James's)*
	English Garden SW3 *(Rm 1)*
	Le Gavroche W1 *(Private Rm')*
	Imperial War Museum SE1 *(Boardroom 2)*
	Institute of Directors W1 *(Trafalgar/Spears)*
	The Landmark W1 *(Boardroom)*
	London Capital Club EC4 *(Gresham Room)*
	Merchant Taylors' Hall EC2 *(Library)*
	Millennium Conference Centre SW7 *(Room 7)*
	Neal St WC2 *(Private Rm')*
	Odéon SW1 *(Private Rm')*
	Park Lane Hotel W1 *(Drawing Rm)*
	Le Pont de la Tour SE1 *(Private Rm')*
	The Ritz W1 *(Trafalgar Suite)*
	Royal Albert Hall SW7 *(Henry Cole Rm)*
	Selsdon Park Hotel, Surrey *(Solarium)*
	The South Bank Centre SE1 *(Sunley Pavilion)*
	Stationers' Hall EC4 *(Ante Rm)*
18	The Dorchester W1 *(Penthouse)*
	Dukes Hotel SW1 *(Duke Of Montrose Suite)*

Hartwell House, Bucks *(Octogon Room)*
The Hempel W2 *(Jade Room)*
Howard Hotel WC2 *(Westminster)*
Royal Garden Hotel W8 *(Westminster Room)*
The Savoy WC2 *(Mikado)*
Sheraton Park Tower SW1 *(Explorers)*
The Square W1 *(Private Rm')*
16 Four Seasons Hotel W1 *(Sitting and Dining Rms)*
Fulham Road SW3 *(Private Rm')*
Hilton on Park Lane W1 *(Serpentine Rm)*
Monkey Island Hotel, Berks *(Boardroom)*
Rib Room Hyatt Carlton Tower Hotel SW1 *(Boardroom')*
Scotts W1 *(Ground Floor Private Room)*
Wiltons SW1 *(Private Rm')*
15 The Lanesborough SW1 *(Wilkins Rm)*
14 Claridge's W1 *(Orangery)*
The Lanesborough SW1 *(Wine Cellar)*
Mosimann's Belfry SW1 *(Gucci)*
One Whitehall Place SW1 *(Cellar)*
Reform Club SW1 *(Committe Rm)*
The Stafford SW1 *(Argyll Rm or Pink Rm & Argyll Rm)*
12 The Berkeley SW1 *(Billet)*
The Caledonian Club SW1 *(Oval)*
The Capital SW3 *(Eaton)*
City Rhodes EC4 *(Private Room)*
The Connaught W1 *(Georgian Rm)*
Cutty Sark SE10 *(Captain's Rm)*
Dukes Hotel SW1 *(Sheridan Room)*
English House SW3 *(Front Rm)*
Halcyon Hotel W11 *(Conference Room)*
Hartwell House, Bucks *(Henry Keene Room)*
Howard Hotel WC2 *(Surrey)*
Hyde Park Hotel SW1 *(19 Private Salons)*
Kaspia W1 *(Private Room)*
Mimmo d'Ischia SW1 *(Private Rm)*
Mitsukoshi SW1 *(Tatami Rm)*
La Porte des Indes W1 *(Private Rooms (x2))*
The Savoy WC2 *(Iolanthe)*
Sheekey's WC2 *(Private Rm)*
Suntory SW1 *(Tatami')*
10 The Berkeley SW1 *(Knightsbridge)*
Cannizaro House SW19 *(Boardroom)*
The Capital SW3 *(Sitting Room)*
The Chelsea SW1 *(Chelsea Rm)*
City Miyama EC4 *(Private Rm')*
English Garden SW3 *(Rm 2)*
Green's SW1 *(Private Rm 2)*
Hampshire Hotel WC2 *(Milton)*
London Capital Club EC4 *(Marco Polo)*
Mirabelle W1 *(Oak, Garden and Teppan-Yaki Rms)*
Mosimann's Belfry SW1 *(Veuve Clicquot)*
Royal Garden Hotel W8 *(Windsor Room)*
Les Saveurs W1 *(Private Rm')*
Thomas Goode Restaurant W1 *(Elephant Room)*
8 London Capital Club EC4 *(Wren Room)*
The Stafford SW1 *(Panel Rm or Pink Rm)*
7 Suntory SW1 *(Teppan-Yaki)*
6 English House SW3 *(Blue Rm)*
Mosimann's Belfry SW1 *(Baulthaup)*
The Savoy WC2 *(Sorcerer)*

£M

5500	Alexandra Palace & Park N22 *(Great Hall')*
2500	Café Royal W1 *(Max')*
2200	Alexandra Palace & Park N22 *(West Hall)*
1700	Adrenaline Village SW8 *(Venue')*
1500	Battersea Park SW8 *(British Genius Site')*

226

1200	Ascot Racecourse, Pavilions & Queen Anne Rooms, Berks *(Pavilion (subdivisible)*)*
	Commonwealth Institute W8 *(Comm Galleries*)*
	Sandown Park Racecourse, Surrey *(Surrey Hall*)*
840	London Metropole W2 *(Palace Suite*)*
660	The Brewery EC1 *(Porter Tun*)*
650	Café Royal W1 *(4-Empire Napoleon)*
550	The International Hotel E14 *(Grand Suite*)*
500	Battersea Park SW8 *(Riverside Terraces)*
	London Marriott W1 *(Westminster Suite*)*
	Sandown Park Racecourse, Surrey *(Claremont)*
450	Hothouse Bar & Grill E1 *(Max*)*
	Jongleurs at Camden Lock NW1 *(Max*)*
	Simpsons- in-the-Strand WC2 *(Max*)*
420	Waldorf Hotel WC2 *(Adelphi Suite & Palm Court*)*
400	Babe Ruth's E1 *(Max*)*
	The Brewery EC1 *(King George III)*
	Café Royal W1 *(6-Dubarry)*
	Epsom Downs, Surrey *(Blue Riband Room*)*
	Harrods SW1 *(Georgian Restaurant*)*
	Twickenham Banqueting Centre, • *(Rose Rm*)*
	Whipsnade Wild Animal Park, Beds *(Max*)*
350	Bath – Pump Room, *(Max*)*
	Cabot Hall E14 *(Hall*)*
	Commonwealth Institute W8 *(Art Gallery)*
	Hotel Russell WC1 *(Warncliffe Suite*)*
	Lloyd's of London EC3 *(Captains' Rm*)*
	Lord's NW8 *(Max*)*
	Sandown Park Racecourse, Surrey *(Marquee (permanent In summer))*
330	Twickenham Banqueting Centre, • *(Spirit of Rugby)*
300	Adrenaline Village SW8 *(Club)*
	Ascot Racecourse, Pavilions & Queen Anne Rooms, Berks *(Buckhounds)*
	Ascot Racecourse, Royal Enclosure, Berks *(Paddock Suite*)*
	Barbican Art Gallery EC2 *(Max*)*
	Holiday Inn – Nelson Dock SE16 *(Sweden*)*
	Jongleurs at The Cornet SW11 *(Max*)*
	Langham Hilton W1 *(Ballroom*)*
	London Transport Museum WC2 *(Max*)*
	Planet Hollywood W1 *(Restaurant*)*
	The Selfridge Hotel W1 *(Selfridge Suite*)*
280	Chartered Accountants' Hall EC2 *(Great Hall*)*
	Glaziers' Hall SE1 *(Hall*)*
	Waldorf Hotel WC2 *(Charter 2)*
270	Café Royal W1 *(2-Louis)*
260	Delfina Studio SE1 *(Max*)*
	Institution of Civil Engineers SW1 *(Great Hall*)*
250	Alexandra Palace & Park N22 *(Palace Restaurant)*
	Brick Lane Music Hall EC2 *(Max*)*
	Capital Radio Café WC2 *(Max*)*
	Delfina Studio SE1 *(Rear Gallery)*
	Hop Exchange SE1 *(Wolsey)*
	Sandown Park Racecourse, Surrey *(Wolsey)*
	Syon Park (Conservatory), Middx *(Great Conservatory*)*
240	Churchill W1 *(Chartwell Suite*)*
	Forte Posthouse Regent's Park W1 *(Cambridge & Oxford Suites*)*
	Hendon Hall Hotel NW4 *(Mount Charlotte Suite*)*
	London Metropole W2 *(Windsor Suite)*
	The Oval SE11 *(Max*)*
230	Epsom Downs, Surrey *(Derby Suite)*
220	Bank of England Club SW15 *(Max*)*
	Carpenters' Hall EC2 *(Livery Hall*)*

	Chelsea Harbour Rooms SW10 *(Turner & Carlyle Rms*)*
	RS Hispaniola SW1 *(Max*)*
	Holiday Inn – Nelson Dock SE16 *(Wasa Suite*)*
	The Law Society WC2 *(Common Rm*)*
	Royal Majestic Suite NW6 *(Ground Floor*)*
210	London Metropole W2 *(Berkshire Suite)*
200	BAFTA Centre W1 *(Function Rm*)*
	Bengal Clipper SE1 *(Max*)*
	The Carnarvon Hotel W5 *(Edward Suite*)*
	Church House SW1 *(Harvey Goodwin Suite*)*
	Conrad Hotel SW10 *(Henley Suite*)*
	Cottons Atrium SE1 *(Max*)*
	Denbies Wine Estate, Surrey *(Garden Atrium Conservatory*)*
	Design Museum SE1 *(Collection Gallery*)*
	Hampton Court, Tiltyard, Surrey *(Max*)*
	Limelight W1 *(Max*)*
	Red Fort W1 *(Private Rm*)*
	Regent's College NW1 *(Refectory*)*
	Royal National Theatre SE1 *(Olivier Stalls Foyer*)*
	Stakis St Ermins SW1 *(Ballroom*)*
	Tower Thistle E1 *(Tower Suite*)*
	The Viceroy NW1 *(Max*)*
	Whipsnade Wild Animal Park, Beds *(Griffin Suite or Phoenix Suite)*
190	The Chesterfield Hotel W1 *(Max*)*
	St Bartholomew's Hospital EC1 *(Great Hall*)*
180	Bath – Pump Room, *(Pump Rm)*
	The Brewery EC1 *(Queen Charlotte)*
	Drones SW1 *(Max*)*
	Epsom Downs, Surrey *(Jockey Club Room)*
	The Insurance Hall EC2 *(Great Hall*)*
	Painters' Hall EC4 *(Livery Hall*)*
	Pinewood Studios, Bucks *(Ballroom*)*
	The Rembrandt Hotel SW7 *(Max*)*
	Sandown Park Racecourse, Surrey *(Saddle Rm)*
	Winchester House SW15 *(River Lawn (marquee)*)*
170	Butchers' Hall EC1 *(Great Hall*)*
	The International Hotel E14 *(Royal Lounge)*
	Royal Society of Arts WC2 *(All Vaults*)*
	The Rubens SW1 *(Max*)*
168	Ironmongers' Hall EC2 *(Banqueting Hall*)*
160	Amadeus Centre W9 *(Upper Hall*)*
	Simpsons- in-the-Strand WC2 *(South Rm)*
150	41 Queen's Gate Terrace SW7 *(Pillar Suite*)*
	Aquarium E1 *(Max*)*
	Belvedere W8 *(Max*)*
	Bombay Brasserie SW7 *(Conservatory*)*
	Church House SW1 *(Hoare Memorial Hall)*
	Dartmouth House W1 *(Max*)*
	Delfina Studio SE1 *(Front Gallery)*
	Denbies Wine Estate, Surrey *(Denbies Suite)*
	The Dog And Fox Ballroom SW19 *(Ballroom*)*
	East India Club SW1 *(Max*)*
	Ham Polo Club, Surrey *(Club House*)*
	RS Hispaniola WC2 *(Main Deck*)*
	Institution of Mechanical Engineers SW1 *(Marble Hall*)*
	Limelight W1 *(Gallery & Dome)*
	Ormond's Restaurant & Club SW1 *(Restaurant*)*
	Queen's Eyot, Berks *(Permanent Marquee*)*
	Royal National Theatre SE1 *(Terrace Café)*
	Theatre Royal WC2 *(Grand Salon*)*
144	HMS Belfast SE1 *(Ship Co's Dining Hall*)*
	Churchill W1 *(Chartwell II)*
140	Basil Street Hotel SW3 *(Parrot Club*)*

Hamilton Suite W1 *(Conservatory & Red Room*)*	St Stephen' Constitutional Club SW1 *(Dining Rm)*

Hamilton Suite W1
(Conservatory & Red Room)*
Leander Club, Berks *(Max*)*
The Royal Air Force Club W1
(Ballroom)*
The Rubens SW1 *(Old Masters Restaurant)*
135 Browns W1 *(Max*)*
The Kenilworth WC1
(Bloomsbury Suite)*
130 Alexandra Palace & Park N22
(Loneborough Rm)
Café Royal W1 *(5-Marquise)*
Cavalry & Guards Club W1
(Coffee Rm)*
Feng Shang NW1 *(Max*)*
Royal Aeronautical Society W1
(Argyll Rm & Hawker Rm)*
Winchester House SW15
(Front Lawn (marquee))
120 Ascot Racecourse, Royal
Enclosure, Berks *(Jockey Club)*
Barber-Surgeons' Hall EC2 *(Max*)*
Café Royal W1 *(6-Dauphin)*
Champenois EC2 *(Max*)*
Church House SW1
(Bishop Partridge Hall)
City of London Club EC2
(Main Dining Rm)*
Conrad Hotel SW10 *(Henley I)*
Farmers' & Fletchers' Hall EC1
(Max)*
Frederick's N1 *(Max*)*
Glaziers' Hall SE1 *(River Rm)*
The Grosvenor SW1 *(Gallery Rm*)*
Groucho Club W1 *(First Floor (entire)*)*
Horwood House, Bucks *(Restaurant*)*
London Metropole W2
(Westminster Suite)
Royal National Theatre SE1 *(Ovations)*
Sandown Park Racecourse, Surrey
(Cavalry Bar)
St John's Gate EC1 *(Chapter Hall*)*
Staple Inn WC1 *(Hall*)*
Trinity House EC3 *(Library*)*
The Washington W1
(Restaurant (Madisons))*
White House Hotel NW1 *(Albany*)*
110 Bath – Pump Room, *(Concert Rm)*
The Chesterfield Hotel W1
(Charles/Queens Suites)
Cobden's Club W10 *(Max*)*
Euten's WC2 *(Max*)*
Kensington Palace Thistle W8
(Duchess)*
London Metropole W2 *(Park Suite or
Thames Suite)*
St Stephen' Constitutional
Club SW1 *(Max*)*
Winchester House SW15 *(River Rm)*
100 Aquarium E1 *(Private Room)*
The Brewery EC1 *(Smeaton's Vaults or
Sugar Rms)*
Browns WC2 *(Courtroom 1*)*
Café Royal W1 *(1-Derby & Queensbury)*
Cobden's Club W10 *(The Grand Hall)*
Conrad Hotel SW10
(Compass Rose or Thames)
Dartmouth House W1
(Long Drawing Rm)
Glaziers' Hall SE1 *(Library & Court Rm)*
ICA SW1 *(Brandon or Nash*)*
Institution of Civil Engineers SW1
(Smeaton Rm)
Irish Club SW1 *(Ball Room*)*
Kew Bridge Steam Museum, Middx
(Steam Hall)*
Langham Hilton W1 *(Portland Suite)*
Mortons Club W1 *(Restaurant & Bar*)*
Palace Theatre W1 *(Stalls Bar*)*
Pinewood Studios, Bucks
(Great Gatsby Rm)
Quayside E1 *(Max*)*
Royal Horseguards Thistle
Hotel SW1 *(Max*)*
Saint WC2 *(Max*)*
Saint John EC1 *(Max*)*
Shakespeare Globe Centre SE1
(Restaurant)*

St Stephen' Constitutional
Club SW1 *(Dining Rm)*
St Thomas' Hospital SE1
(Governors' Hall)*
Stakis St Ermins SW1 *(Balcony)*
Vanderbilt Hotel SW7 *(Max*)*
Waldorf Hotel WC2 *(Minstrel Suite)*
The Westbury W1 *(Mount Vernon Rm*)*
Westminster Conference
Centre SW1 *(Lecture Hall*)*
97 Tallow Chandlers' Hall EC4
(Livery Hall)*
95 Royal Society of Arts WC2
(Benjamin Franklin Rm)
90 Cavalry & Guards Club W1
(Peninsula Rm)
Chelsea Harbour Rooms SW10
(Turner Rm)
Epsom Downs, Surrey *(Boardroom)*
Groucho Club W1 *(Soho Room)*
Kensington Palace Thistle W8
(Marchioness)
National Army Museum SW3
(Art & Uniform Galleries)*
Planet Hollywood W1 *(VIP Suite)*
Regent's College NW1
(Herringham Hall)
Spanish Club W1 *(Alfonso XIII Rm*)*
Waxy O'Conners W1 *(College Bar*)*
85 Britannia Intercontinental
Hotel W1 *(Manhattan*)*
Horniman Museum and
Gardens SE23 *(Conservatory*)*
80 Bank of England Club SW15
(Redgates Lodge)
Brewers' Hall EC2 *(Livery Hall*)*
Butchers' Hall EC1
*(Large Court Rm & Small Court Rm or
Taurus Suite)*
Café Royal W1 *(1-Domino)*
The Carnarvon Hotel W5
(Creffield Suite)
The Cavendish SW1 *(Park*)*
Chartered Accountants' Hall EC2
(Main Reception Rm)
Chelsea Physic Garden SW3
(Reception Room)*
Dartmouth House W1 *(Ballroom)*
Doggetts Coat & Badge SE1
(Restaurant)*
Fulham Palace SW6 *(Drawing Rm or
Great Hall*)*
The Grafton W1 *(Southampton Suite*)*
Guards Museum SW1 *(Royal Gallery*)*
RS Hispaniola WC2 *(Top Deck)*
House of Detention EC1 *(Max*)*
Institution of Civil Engineers SW1
(Brunel Rm or Council Rm)
Kensington Palace Thistle W8 *(Park)*
London Metropole W2
(Aspects (Rooftop Restaurant))
Montana SW6 *(Max*)*
The Mountbatten WC2 *(Earl*)*
My Fair Lady NW1 *(Max*)*
Pinewood Studios, Bucks *(Green Rm)*
RUSI Building SW1 *(Lecture Theatre*)*
Singapura WC2 *(Max*)*
Spring Grove House, Middx
(Winter Garden Room)*
St Andrew's Court House EC4
(Court Room)*
Sutton House E9 *(Max*)*
The Westbury W1 *(Pine Rm)*
75 The Founders' Hall EC1 *(Livery Hall*)*
The Insurance Hall EC2 *(Ostler Suite)*
Planet Hollywood W1 *(Screening Rm)*
72 The Ark SE1 *(Long Gallery*)*
Limelight W1 *(Club VIP (Basement))*
Watermen & Lightermen's
Hall EC3 *(Freemen's Rm*)*
70 Belvedere W8 *(Lower level)*
Bombay Bicycle Club SW12 *(Max*)*
Brown's Hotel W1 *(Clarendon* or
Niagra & Roosevelt combined)*
Café du Jardin WC2 *(Downstairs*)*
Chelsea Harbour Rooms SW10
(Carlyle Rm)
Downstairs At 190 SW7 *(Max*)*

Elena's L'Etoile W1 (Max*)
Granita N1 (Max*)
The Grosvenor SW1 (Bessborough Rm)
Horwood House, Bucks (Eyre)
Hothouse Bar & Grill E1 (Lower Floor)
Kenwood House, Old Kitchen NW3 (Max*)
Orangery (Holland Park) W8 (Max*)
Pewterers' Hall EC2 (Livery Rm*)
Royal Majestic Suite NW6 (First Floor)
Sandown Park Racecourse, Surrey (Persimmon)
The Washington W1 (Richmond Suite)
Wôdka W8 (Max*)

66 The Brewery EC1 (The James Watt)
60 Al Basha W8 (Private Rm*)
Amadeus Centre W9 (Lower Hall)
Avenue House N3 (Drawing Room*)
Basil Street Hotel SW3 (Brompton Rm)
HMS Belfast SE1 (Gun Rm)
Belvedere W8 (Top level)
Beotys WC2 (Private Rm*)
Browns WC2 (Courtroom 2)
Cabot Hall E14 (Sebastian Rm)
Café du Marché EC1 (Max*)
Churchill W1 (Library)
Commonwealth Institute W8 (Bradley)
Cuba Libre N1 (Max*)
The Grafton W1 (Arlington Suite)
Hollington House Hotel, Berks (Cedar Suite*)
Irish Club SW1 (Ulster Rm)
Ivy WC2 (Private Rm*)
Jason's W9 (Restaurant with Terrace*)
The Law Society WC2 (Old Council Chamber)
Lloyd's of London EC3 (Conference Rm)
The London Toy And Model Museum W2 (Max*)
The Mountbatten WC2 (Broadlands)
Neal's Lodge SW18 (Conservatory*)
Oxford & Cambridge Club SW1 (Marlborough*)
Painters' Hall EC4 (Court Rm)
Polygon Bar & Grill SW4 (Max*)
The Rembrandt Hotel SW7 (Elizabeth & Victoria (Queen Suite))
Royal Society of Arts WC2 (Vault 1)
Shakespeare Globe Centre SE1 (Banqueting Room or Exhibition Hall)
Soho Soho W1 (Salon Privée*)
Trinity House EC3 (Court Rm)
Westminster Conference Centre SW1 (Cambridge Rm)
56 The Bankers Club EC2 (Dining Rm*)
55 Cibo W14 (Max*)
52 Athenaeum Hotel W1 (Westminster Suite*)
50 Alexandra Palace & Park N22 (Palm Court 5)
HMS Belfast SE1 (Wardroom)
Bleeding Heart EC1 (Bistro (ground floor)*)
Café Lazeez SW7 (Max*)
Café Royal W1 (Cellars)
Cavalry & Guards Club W1 (Balaclava Rm)
Churchill W1 (Marlborough Suite)
City of London Club EC2 (Garden Rm)
Cobden's Club W10 (Restaurant)
Conrad Hotel SW10 (Harbour)
Dartmouth House W1 (Small Drawing Room)
Euphorium N1 (Max*)
Forte Posthouse Regent's Park W1 (Trinity Suite)
Freud Museum NW3 (Max*)
Goring Hotel SW1 (Archive Room*)
Groucho Club W1 (Gennaro Room)
Hamilton House EC4 (Max*)
Holiday Inn – Mayair W1 (Stratton Suite*)
Holiday Inn – Nelson Dock SE16 (Denmark Suite)
Hotel Russell WC1 (Library)
Ironmongers' Hall EC2 (Luncheon Rm)

The Law Society WC2 (Members Dining Rm)
National Army Museum SW3 (Templer Galleries)
Peacock House W14 (Max*)
Quayside E1 (Private Rm)
Royal Horseguards Thistle Hotel SW1 (Thames)
The Rubens SW1 (Rembrandt Rm)
Sheraton Belgravia SW1 (Dining Rm*)
Soho House W1 (Sitting Room, Study & Bar*)
Spring Grove House, Middx (Music Room)
Sutton House E9 (Marriage Suite (Great and Little Chambers) or Wenlock Barn (including Café-Bar/Linenfold Parlour))
University Women's Club W1 (Drawing Rm or Library*)
Villandry Dining Rooms W1 (Max*)
Waldorf Hotel WC2 (Somerset)
Waxy O'Conners W1 (Restaurant)
West Wycombe Caves, Bucks (Banqueting Hall*)

48 41 Queen's Gate Terrace SW7 (Art Deco Room)
The Ark SE1 (East Gallery)
Churchill W1 (Blenheim)
Hotel Russell WC1 (Ormond Suite)
Royal Society of Arts WC2 (Tavern Rm)
Rules WC2 (Greene Rm)
45 The Brewery EC1 (City Cellars)
Brown's Hotel W1 (Roosevelt)
Butchers' Hall EC1 (Large Court Rm)
Capital Radio Café WC2 (VIP Lounge)
The Golden Hinde SE1 (Max*)
Institution of Mechanical Engineers SW1 (Council)
Julie's Restaurant & Wine Bar W11 (Gothic Rm*)
London Marriott W1 (Hamilton Rm)
Peg's Club WC2 (Dining Rm*)
Simpsons- in-the-Strand WC2 (Smoking Rm)
40 Ascot Racecourse, Pavilions & Queen Anne Rooms, Berks (King Edward VII)
Bleeding Heart EC1 (Private Room)
Boyd's W8 (Max*)
Brown's Hotel W1 (Kipling or Niagara)
Browns WC2 (Courtroom 3)
Cabot Hall E14 (St Lawrence Rm)
Chartered Institute of Public Finance & Accountancy WC2 (Committee Rm 4*)
The Chesterfield Hotel W1 (Conservatory)
Drones SW1 (Private Rm)
L'Escargot W1 (Barrell Vaulted Rm*)
La Famiglia SW10 (Private Rm*)
Formula Veneta SW10 (Private Rm*)
Hamilton Suite W1 (Hamilton Rm)
Hendon Hall Hotel NW4 (Garrick)
Holiday Inn – Nelson Dock SE16 (Rising Star)
Irish Club SW1 (Leinster Room)
Jason's W9 (Restaurant)
Kensington Palace Thistle W8 (Countess Princess)
The Rembrandt Hotel SW7 (Elizabeth)
Royal Aeronautical Society W1 (Council Rm & Bar)
Royal Institute of British Architects W1 (South Rm*)
RSJ SE1 (Private Room (Basement)*)
Rules WC2 (Charles Dickens Rm)
RUSI Building SW1 (Library)
Singapura WC2 (Private Room)
Spanish Club W1 (Presidentian Rm)
Staple Inn WC1 (Council Chamber)
Tower Thistle E1 (Beaufort, Mortimer Suite or Raleigh or Spencer)
Waxy O'Conners W1 (Mezzanine)
The Westbury W1 (Brighton Rm)
White House Hotel NW1 (Chester)

	Whittington's EC4 *(Restaurant*)*
37	Watermen & Lightermen's Hall EC3 *(Court Rm)*
36	The Ark SE1 *(West Gallery)*
	The Cadogan SW1 *(Max*)*
	Empress Garden W1 *(Private Rm 1*)*
	Hotel Russell WC1 *(Bedford Suite)*
	The Kenilworth WC1 *(Louis XV)*
	Langham Hilton W1 *(Regent/ Welbeck Rooms)*
	Seahorse, Middx W1 *(Max*)*
35	Basil Street Hotel SW3 *(Basil Rm)*
	Bath – Pump Room, *(Smoking or Drawing Room)*
	Belgo Centraal WC2 *(Private Room*)*
	Charcos SW3 *(Downstairs*)*
	City of London Club EC2 *(Visitors Rm)*
	First Floor W11 *(Private Rm*)*
	Groucho Club W1 *(New Room)*
	La Pomme d'Amour W11 *(Private Rm*)*
	RUSI Building SW1 *(Reading Rm)*
	Village Bistro N6 *(Max*)*
	White Tower W1 *(Private Room 2*)*
	Winston Churchill's Britain At War Experience SE1 *(Max*)*
34	Chartered Institute of Public Finance & Accountancy WC2 *(Council Chamber)*
32	The Carnarvon Hotel W5 *(Gunnersbury Suite)*
	Carpenters' Hall EC2 *(Luncheon Room)*
	Julie's Restaurant & Wine Bar W11 *(Garden Rm)*
	Mortons Club W1 *(Private Room)*
	Orsino W11 *(Private Room*)*
30	The Bankers Club EC2 *(Private Dining Rms)*
	Bloomsbury Square Training Centre WC1 *(Cellars Restaurant*)*
	Brewers' Hall EC2 *(Court Rm)*
	Brinkley's SW10 *(Grosvenor I)*
	Britannia Intercontinental Hotel W1 *(Grosvenor I)*
	Chartered Accountants' Hall EC2 *(Members' Rm)*
	Church House SW1 *(Westminster)*
	Churchill W1 *(Randolph or Spencer)*
	Commonwealth Institute W8 *(Tweedsmuir)*
	Coopers' Hall EC2 *(Max*)*
	Dan's SW3 *(Conservatory*)*
	Doggetts Coat & Badge SE1 *(Boardroom/Terrace Bar)*
	Downstairs At 190 SW7 *(Private Rm)*
	French House W1 *(Max*)*
	Freud Museum NW3 *(House)*
	Gilbert's SW7 *(Max*)*
	Hendon Hall Hotel NW4 *(Johnson or Sheridan)*
	The Insurance Hall EC2 *(Pipkin Rm)*
	Launceston Place W8 *(Private Area*)*
	Limelight W1 *(Library or Study Bar)*
	Marquis W1 *(Downstairs Room*)*
	Mon Plaisir WC2 *(Private Rm*)*
	Odette's NW1 *(Conservatory*)*
	Royal Aeronautical Society W1 *(Sopwith Rm)*
	The Rubens SW1 *(Rubens)*
	Shepherd's SW1 *(Private Rm*)*
	Stakis St Ermins SW1 *(York or Clarence)*
	Le Suquet SW3 *(Private Rm 1*)*
	Sweetings EC4 *(Max*)*
	Tallow Chandlers' Hall EC4 *(Parlour)*
	The Washington W1 *(Richmond I (Winchester)*
	Wódka W8 *(Private Room)*
28	Athenaeum Hotel W1 *(Devonshire Suite)*
	Brown's Hotel W1 *(Hellenic)*
	La Dordogne W4 *(Private Section*)*
	Fung Shing W1 *(Private Rm*)*
	Scone E14 *(Max*)*
	St Stephen' Constitutional Club SW1 *(Garden Rm)*
	The Westbury W1 *(Regency Rm)*
26	The Ark SE1 *(Refectory)*

	The Berkshire W1 *(Sonning Suite*)*
	Frederick's N1 *(Clarence Room)*
	Hollington House Hotel, Berks *(Oak Room)*
	Mao Tai SW6 *(Private Rm*)*
25	Belgo Centraal WC2 *(Private Room)*
	Busabong Too SW10 *(Mezzanine*)*
	La Capannina W1 *(Private Rm*)*
	Chez Bruce SW17 *(Private Room*)*
	The Grosvenor SW1 *(Warwick Rm)*
	London Marriott W1 *(John Adams Suite)*
	The London Toy And Model Museum W2 *(Conservatory)*
	Poissonnerie de l'Avenue SW3 *(Private Rm*)*
	Rules WC2 *(King Edward VII Rm)*
	The Selfridge Hotel W1 *(Drawing Rm)*
	St John's Gate EC1 *(Council Chamber)*
	The Washington W1 *(Richmond 2 (Fairfax))*
	ZeNW3 NW3 *(Private Rm*)*
24	Butchers' Hall EC1 *(Small Court Rm)*
	Café Royal W1 *(B-Penthouse)*
	Cavalry & Guards Club W1 *(Waterloo Rm)*
	Elena's L'Etoile W1 *(Private Rm)*
	Gay Hussar W1 *(First Floor*)*
	Holiday Inn – Nelson Dock SE16 *(Copenhagen)*
	Julie's Restaurant & Wine Bar W11 *(Banqueting Rm)*
	Marquis W1 *(Ground Floor Room)*
	Le Mesurier EC1 *(Max*)*
	Westminster Conference Centre SW1 *(Gloucester)*
23	The Insurance Hall EC1 *(Council Chamber)*
22	Bombay Bicycle Club SW12 *(Private Room)*
	L'Escargot W1 *(Private Rm)*
	RSJ SE1 *(Private Rm Ground Floor)*
	Sheraton Belgravia SW1 *(Study and Library)*
20	Ajimura WC2 *(Max*)*
	Avenue House N3 *(Salon)*
	HMS Belfast SE1 *(Admiral's Quarters)*
	Belvedere W8 *(Middle level)*
	The Berkshire W1 *(Sandhurst Suite)*
	Boisdale SW1 *(Private Room*)*
	Brasserie St Quentin SW3 *(Private Rm*)*
	Browns W1 *(Room 54)*
	The Cadogan SW1 *(Langtry Dining)*
	The Cavendish SW1 *(Mayfair)*
	Church House SW1 *(Jubilee)*
	The Founders' Hall EC1 *(Parlour)*
	Groucho Club W1 *(Bloomsbury Room)*
	The Guinea W1 *(Boardroom*)*
	Holiday Inn – Mayair W1 *(Presidential Suite)*
	Ken Lo's Memories SW1 *(Private Rm*)*
	Leven is Strijd E14 *(Max*)*
	Lexington W1 *(Private Room*)*
	Limelight W1 *(Annexe)*
	Lindsay House W1 *(Private Rm*)*
	National Army Museum SW3 *(Council Chamber)*
	Oxford & Cambridge Club SW1 *(Edward VII)*
	The Rembrandt Hotel SW7 *(Princes)*
	The Royal Air Force Club W1 *(Drawing Room or Mezzanine Suite)*
	Royal Society of Arts WC2 *(Folkestone Rm)*
	Saint John EC1 *(Private Room)*
	San Martino SW3 *(Private Rm*)*
	Sandown Park Racecourse, Surrey *(Smaller Rms)*
	St Andrew's Court House EC4 *(Archive Room)*
	Stakis St Ermins SW1 *(Cameo)*
	Theatre Royal WC2 *(Board Rm or Royal Retiring Rm)*
	Trinity House EC3 *(Luncheon Room)*
	Vanderbilt Hotel SW7 *(Vanderbilt)*
	The Viceroy NW1 *(Private Rm)*
	Village Bistro N6 *(Ground Floor)*

Waldorf Hotel WC2 *(Kingsway)*
White Tower W1 *(Private Rm 1)*
Zen SW3 *(Private Rm*)*
18 Chartered Accountants' Hall EC2 *(Small Reception Rm)*
The Chesterfield Hotel W1 *(Library)*
Frederick's N1 *(Sussex Rm)*
The Mountbatten WC2 *(Viceroy)*
St Bartholomew's Hospital EC1 *(Treasurer's Rm)*
St Thomas' Hospital SE1 *(Grand Committee Rm)*
17 Hollington House Hotel, Berks *(Millard Dining Room)*
Julie's Restaurant & Wine Bar W11 *(Conservatory)*
16 Basil Street Hotel SW3 *(Mezzanine Rm)*
Cavalry & Guards Club W1 *(Double Bridal Rm)*
Cobden's Club W10 *(Private Room)*
Euphorium N1 *(Private Area)*
The Grosvenor SW1 *(Belgrave)*
The Insurance Hall EC2 *(Morgan Owen Rm)*
RUSI Building SW1 *(Council Room)*
The Selfridge Hotel W1 *(Conservatory)*
Soho House W1 *(Library)*
Le Suquet SW3 *(Private Rm 2)*
Westminster Conference Centre SW1 *(Kent)*
Winchester House SW15 *(Turner Rm)*
15 Kensington Palace Thistle W8 *(Baroness)*
London Marriott W1 *(Dukes Suite)*
14 L'Amico SW1 *(Private Rm*)*
Ascot Racecourse, Pavilions & Queen Anne Rooms, Berks *(Crocker Bulteel)*
La Dordogne W4 *(Private Rm)*
Julie's Restaurant & Wine Bar W11 *(The Tomb (wb))*
Launceston Place W8 *(Private Rm)*
Painters' Hall EC4 *(Painted Chamber)*
Royal National Theatre SE1 *(Richardson Rm)*
St Bartholomew's Hospital EC1 *(Peggy Turner Rm)*
St John's Gate EC1 *(Lord Prior's Dining Room)*
Sutton House E9 *(Linenfold Parlour)*
12 Bentleys W1 *(Private Rm*)*
Brown's Hotel W1 *(Lord Byron)*
Cabot Hall E14 *(Cape Breton Rm or Newfoundland Rm)*
Conrad Hotel SW10 *(Nelson)*
Empress Garden W1 *(Private Rm 2)*
Forte Posthouse Regent's Park W1 *(Pembroke Suite)*
Gay Hussar W1 *(Second Floor)*
Goring Hotel SW1 *(Drawing Rm)*
The Grosvenor SW1 *(Wilton Rm)*
Hodgson's WC2 *(Private Rm*)*
Hotel Russell WC1 *(Boardrooms 1,2,6,7)*
Imperial City EC3 *(Private Vault*)*
Lindsay House W1 *(Private Rm)*
London Metropole W2 *(Boardroom)*
Pomegranates SW1 *(Private Rm*)*
Royal Aeronautical Society W1 *(Hawker Rm)*
Royal Horseguards Thistle Hotel SW1 *(Boardroom)*
Soho House W1 *(Study)*
St Andrew's Court House EC4 *(Panelled Room)*
St Bartholomew's Hospital EC1 *(Henry VIII Committee Rm)*
Waldorf Hotel WC2 *(Westminster or Waterloo or Tavistock)*
11 Browns W1 *(Room 53)*
10 22 Jermyn St SW1 *(Max*)*
Alexandra Palace & Park N22 *(Palm Court 1)*
Brewers' Hall EC2 *(Committee Rm)*
Britannia Intercontinental Hotel W1 *(Grosvenor II)*
Bubb's EC1 *(Private Rm*)*
Cabot Hall E14 *(Nova Scotia Rm)*

The Cavendish SW1 *(Duke)*
Empress Garden W1 *(Private Rm 3)*
Holiday Inn – Mayair W1 *(Burlington)*
Julie's Restaurant & Wine Bar W11 *(The Gallery (wb))*
Langham Hilton W1 *(Cumberland Rm)*
Monkeys SW3 *(Private Rm*)*
The Rembrandt Hotel SW7 *(Victoria)*
Tatsuso EC2 *(Private Rm*)*
Trinity House EC3 *(Reading Room)*
9 Odette's NW1 *(Private Rm)*
8 L'Amico SW1 *(Private Rm)*
Athenaeum Hotel W1 *(Apartments or Richmond Suite)*
Brown's Hotel W1 *(Graham Bell)*
The Chesterfield Hotel W1 *(Stanhope Suite)*
Conrad Hotel SW10 *(Wellington)*
Goring Hotel SW1 *(Breakfast Rm)*
The Grosvenor SW1 *(Hanover)*
Hotel Russell WC1 *(Boardrooms 3,4,5)*
The Insurance Hall EC2 *(President's Rm)*
The Royal Air Force Club W1 *(Boardroom)*
Tower Thistle E1 *(Lewin)*
White Tower W1 *(Private Rooms 3 ,4 ,5 (each))*
6 Browns W1 *(Room 52)*
The International Hotel E14 *(Panorama Conference Suite)*
4 Theatre Royal WC2 *(Duke of Bedford)*

£B-E

1000 Crystal Palace Park SE20 *(Max*)*
200 The Worx I N1 *(Max*)*
The Worx II N1 *(Max*)*
35 Fan Museum SE10 *(Orangery*)*

£B-M

2000 Lee Valley Cycle Circuit E15 *(Max*)*
1000 Honourable Artillery Co EC1 *(Marquee*)*
800 London Astoria WC2 *(Max*)*
Royal Horticultural Halls SW1 *(New Hall*)*
700 Blackheath Concert Halls SE3 *(Great Hall*)*
650 New Connaught Rms WC2 *(Balmoral*)*
600 Equinox at the Empire WC2 *(Max*)*
500 Bow Film Studios E15 *(Max*)*
Cecil Sharp House NW1 *(Kennedy Hall*)*
Grosvenor Rooms NW2 *(Grosvenor Suite*)*
Royal College of Art SW7 *(Henry Moore Gallery*)*
Royal Horticultural Halls SW1 *(Old Hall)*
Stoke Newington Town Hall N16 *(Assembly Room*)*
450 Porchester Centre W2 *(Ballroom*)*
Syon Park (Banqueting), Middx *(Max*)*
440 The London Hippodrome WC2 *(Max*)*
400 Bagleys N1 *(3 Studios (each)*)*
Dulwich College SE21 *(Christenson Hall and Upper Dining Rms*)*
Hammersmith Town Hall W6 *(Assembly Hall*)*
350 Honourable Artillery Co EC1 *(Albert Rm)*
International House E1 *(Max*)*
The London Hippodrome WC2 *(Auditorium)*
London Transport Conference Facilities E14 *(Restaurant*)*
320 Imperial College SW7 *(Main Dining Hall*)*
300 Chelsea Old Town Hall SW3 *(Main Hall*)*

Duke of York's HQ SW3 (Cadogan Hall*)
Equinox at the Empire WC2 (Club)
Fulham Town Hall SW6 (Grand Hall*)
Merchant Centre EC4 (Caxton Suite*)
New Connaught Rms WC2 (Edinburgh)
Regency Banqueting Suite N17 (Max*)

250 Academy of Live & Recorded Arts SW18 (Max*)
Congress Centre WC1 (Congress Hall*)
Dulwich College SE21 (Great Hall*)
Goldsmiths College SE14 (Great Hall*)
Le Gothique SW18 (with Academy of Live & Recorded Arts*)
Hollyhedge House SE3 (Max*)
Mall Galleries SW1 (Main Gallery*)
The Old Town Hall, Stratford E15 (Main Hall*)
Thames Leisure EC4 (Regalia*)
Trafalgar Tavern SE10 (Nelson Suite*)

240 Catamaran Cruisers WC2 (Naticia*)
Texas Embassy Cantina WC2 (Max*)

230 Blackheath Concert Halls SE3 (Recital Rm)
The Clink SE1 (Max*)
Westminster Boating Base SW1 (Max*)

225 Break For The Border W1 (Max*)
220 Chelsea Football Club SW6 (Executive Club Rm*)
King's College WC2 (Great Hall*)
Tidal Cruises SE1 (Royal Princess*)

200 Admiral Enterprises SE1 (Max*)
Badbobs WC2 (Bar/restaurant*)
Bagleys N1 (Bunker Bar)
Brompton Oratory – St Wilfrid's Hall SW7 (Max*)
Dolphin Square SW1 (Restaurant*)
Hellenic Centre W1 (Great Hall*)
Lemonia NW1 (Max*)
Naval & Military Club W1 (Coffee Rm*)
New Connaught Rms WC2 (York)
New World W1 (Max*)
Pentland House SE13 (Marquee / Lawn*)
HMS President EC4 (Drill Hall*)
Royal College of Art SW7 (Gulbenkian Upper Gallery)
Royal Over-Seas League SW1 (Hall of India & Pakistan*)
Royal Holloway College, Surrey (Founder's Dining Hall*)
Tinseltown EC1 (Max*)
Whitelands College SW15 (Ruskin Dining Hall*)

190 Will's Art Warehouse SW6 (Max*)
180 Bishopsgate Institute EC2 (Max*)
The Clink SE1 (Winchester Hall)
Grosvenor Rooms NW2 (Executive Suite)
King's College School SW19 (Great Hall*)
London Scottish SW1 (Hall*)
Royal Green Jackets W1 (Hall*)

175 The London Hippodrome WC2 (Balcony – Restaurant)
172 Honourable Artillery Co EC1 (Long Rm)
160 Abbaye EC1 (Max*)
Conway Hall WC1 (Large Hall*)
Eatons EC3 (Banqueting Suite*)
Fulham House SW6 (Main Hall*)
Kingswood House SE21 (Golden Room, Jacobean Room*)

150 606 Club SW10 (Max*)
Beckton Alpine Centre E6 (Max*)
Embargo SW10 (Max*)
Fulham Town Hall SW6 (Concert Hall)
George Inn SE1 (Max*)
King's College, Hampstead Site NW3 (Bay Hall*)
London School of Economics WC2 (Senior Dining Rm*)
Mermaid Theatre EC4 (Blackfriars Room*)

Music Room At Grays W1 (Exhibition Hall*)
Rose Garden Buffet NW1 (Rose Garden Restaurant*)
Royal Holloway College, Surrey (Picture Gallery)
School of Pharmacy WC1 (Assembly Hall*)
St Botolph's Hall EC2 (Upper Hall*)
St John's Hill SW11 (Drill Hall*)
St Martin In The Fields WC2 (Max*)
Tidal Cruises SE1 (Viscountess)
Victoria & Albert Museum Café SW7 (Max*)
Whitewebbs Museum of Transport, Middx (Meeting Room*)

148 Mainstream Leisure SW15 (Elizabethan*)
146 Syon Park (Banqueting), Middx (Garden Rm)
140 Cecil Sharp House NW1 (Trefusis Hall)
Froebel Institute College SW15 (Portrait Room*)
School of Pharmacy WC1 (Refectory)
Strand Palace Hotel WC2 (Exeter Suite*)
Syon Park (Banqueting), Middx (Peacock Room)

132 Tidal Cruises SE1 (Hurlingham)
130 Polish Hearth Club SW7 (Ballroom*)
Royal Veterinary College NW1 (Max*)

124 Docklands Sailing & Watersports Centre E14 (Function Room*)
120 Brasserie Rocque EC2 (Max*)
City Cruises SE16 (Millennium*)
Footstool SW1 (Max*)
Guy's Hospital SE1 (Robens Suite*)
Lansdowne Club W1 (Ballroom*)
Old Refectory W8 (Max*)
The Players' Theatre WC2 (Lower Supper Room/Bar*)
Polish Hearth Club SW7 (Restaurant)
Royal Institution of Great Britain W1 (Max*)
Syon Park (Banqueting), Middx (Lakeside Rm)
Texas Embassy Cantina WC2 (Upstairs)
Thames Leisure (The Miyuki Maru)

110 Dickens Inn E1 (Nickleby Suite*)
Royal Geographical Society SW7 (Max*)

108 Catamaran Cruisers WC2 (Pridia)
106 Tidal Cruises SE1 (Old London)
100 Abbaye EC1 (Basement Restaurant)
The Battersea Barge Bistro SW8 (Max*)
Beckton Alpine Centre E6 (Function Room)
Brompton Oratory – St Wilfrid's Hall SW7 (St Joseph's Hall or St Wilfrid's Hall (incl Billiards Room))
The Candid Arts Trust EC1 (Ground Floor Gallery*)
The Chelsea Gardener SW3 (Max*)
Chelsea Old Town Hall SW3 (Small Hall)
Crown River Cruises EC4 (Salient*)
Grosvenor Rooms NW2 (Pearl Suite)
Jazz Café NW1 (Max*)
Lauderdale House N6 (Max*)
Legends W1 (Upstairs*)
The Little Ship Club EC4 (Max*)
Mandrake Club (PizzaExpress) W1 (Max*)
Pentland House SE13 (Hall)
Pizza On The Park SW1 (Basement*)
Porchester Centre W2 (Baths)
Royal Geographical Society SW7 (Main Hall)
Southwark Cathedral SE1 (Function Room*)
Throgmorton's EC2 (Oak Rm*)
Turk Launches, Surrey (New Southern Belle*)

90 Chelsea Old Town Hall SW3 (Cadogan Suite)

City Cruises SE16 *(Eltham or Mayflower Garden)*	Burgh House NW3 *(Max*)*
Gecko NW1 *(Max*)*	Chez Gérard (Opera Terrace) WC2 *(Terrace*)*
The Little Ship Club EC4 *(Dining Rm)*	Chislehurst Caves, Kent *(Max*)*
80 Archduke Wine Bar SE1 *(Max*)*	The Conservatory SW11 *(Max*)*
Bonjour Vietnam SW6 *(Basement*)*	The Courtyard, St Peter's Hall W11 *(Cafe)*
Bramah Tea & Coffee Museum SE1 *(Max*)*	The Cross Keys SW3 *(Conservatory*)*
Canning House SW1 *(Max*)*	Dulwich College SE21 *(Old Library)*
The Coliseum WC2 *(Terrace Bar*)*	Durrants Hotel W1 *(Edward VII Rm)*
The Courtyard, St Peter's Hall W11 *(Upper Hall*)*	Floating Boater W2 *(Prince Regent*)*
Hammersmith Town Hall W6 *(Small Hall)*	Gunnersbury Park W3 *(Temple)*
The Irish Centre W6 *(Hall*)*	Honourable Artillery Co EC1 *(Queen's Rm)*
Jazz Café NW1 *(Restaurant)*	The Hudson Club SW7 *(Restaurant*)*
Kingswood House SE21 *(Charles Suite)*	The London Hippodrome WC2 *(Private Function Rm)*
Mars WC2 *(Max*)*	Maidenhead Steam Navigation, Berks *(Edwardian)*
The Old Town Hall, Stratford E15 *(Council Chamber)*	Mall Galleries SW1 *(North Gallery)*
Photographers' Gallery WC2 *(Max*)*	Music Room At Grays W1 *(Gallery)*
Royal College of Art SW7 *(Gulbenkian Lower Gallery)*	Naval & Military Club W1 *(Palmerston Rm or Egremont)*
Royal Over-Seas League SW1 *(St Andrew's Hall)*	New Connaught Rms WC2 *(Durham)*
St Andrew Golf Club EC4 *(Max*)*	Pall Mall Deposit W10 *(Max*)*
Syon Park (Banqueting), Middx *(Terrace Rm)*	Poetry Society WC2 *(Restaurant*)*
76 Maidenhead Steam Navigation, Berks *(Georgian)*	HMS President EC4 *(Gun Rm)*
75 Bakers' Hall EC3 *(Livery Hall*)*	Rose Garden Buffet NW1 *(Prince Regent Rm)*
Dulwich College SE21 *(Cricket Pavilion)*	Secret Garden SE5 *(Garden*)*
Mall Galleries SW1 *(East Gallery)*	Thames Luxury Cruises EC3 *(Golden Salamander)*
New Connaught Rms WC2 *(Ulster)*	Tuttons WC2 *(Max*)*
Thames Luxury Cruises EC3 *(Captain James Cook*)*	**48** Antelope SW1 *(Upstairs*)*
Upper Refectory Suite SW3 *(Max*)*	Beckton Alpine Centre E6 *(Restaurant)*
72 Duke of York's HQ SW3 *(London Irish Mess)*	Lansdowne Club W1 *(Thirties Rm)*
70 El Barco Latino WC2 *(Max*)*	The Players' Theatre WC2 *(Mezzanine Supper Room)*
Borscht & Tears SW3 *(Private Rm*)*	Strand Palace Hotel WC2 *(Drake Suite or Grenville Suite)*
Café L'Institute SW7 *(Cafe*)*	Syon Park (Banqueting), Middx *(Conservatory Lounge)*
Canal Brasserie W10 *(Max*)*	**45** Poetry Society WC2 *(Max)*
City Cruises SE16 *(Westminster)*	St Botolph's Hall EC2 *(Lower Hall)*
Dora House SW7 *(The Studio*)*	St John's Hill SW11 *(Sergeant's Mess)*
Froebel Institute College SW15 *(Terrace Rm*)*	**40** George Inn SE1 *(Talbot)*
Gordon's Wine Bar WC2 *(Max*)*	Guy's Hospital SE1 *(Court Room)*
Gunnersbury Park W3 *(Orangery or Small Mansion*)*	Imperial College SW7 *(Dining Rm (170 Queensgate))*
Mermaid Theatre EC4 *(River Rm)*	Jazz Café NW1 *(Cocktail Bar)*
Naval & Military Club W1 *(Regimental Rm)*	King's College School SW19 *(Dalziel Room)*
Royal College of Art SW7 *(Senior Common Rm Dining Rm)*	Lemonia NW1 *(Private Room)*
Royal Veterinary College NW1 *(Clarence Rm or Northumberland Rm)*	Mr Kong WC2 *(Private Basement*)*
Le Studio Café N1 *(Restaurant*)*	Paulo's W6 *(Max*)*
YHA City of London EC4 *(Roof Top Marquee*)*	HMS President EC4 *(Captain's Quarters)*
65 The Leathermarket SE1 *(Tannery Restaurant*)*	Royal Geographical Society SW7 *(Tea Rm)*
60 Abbaye EC1 *(Wine Bar)*	Ship SW18 *(Max*)*
Bankside Gallery SE1 *(Max*)*	Thames Leisure EC4 *(The Tideway)*
Bow Wine Vaults EC4 *(Larger Section*)*	Turk Launches, Surrey *(MV Yarmouth Belle)*
Chelsea Football Club SW6 *(Sponsors Lounge)*	Tuttons WC2 *(Conservatory)*
The Clink SE1 *(Museum)*	Victoria & Albert Museum Café SW7 *(Painted Rm)*
Crown River Cruises EC4 *(Suerta)*	West Zenders WC2 *(Private Rm*)*
Durrants Hotel W1 *(Spy Room*)*	Wine Gallery SW10 *(Private Rm*)*
Equinox at the Empire WC2 *(The Square)*	**38** Secret Garden SE5 *(Restaurant)*
Le Gothique SW18 *(Patio)*	**36** Crown River Cruises EC4 *(Spirit of London)*
Imperial College SW7 *(Council Chamber)*	Honourable Artillery Co EC1 *(Medal Rm)*
HMS President EC4 *(Wardroom)*	Mainstream Leisure SW15 *(Lady Rose of Regent's)*
Le Studio Café N1 *(Tea Room)*	**35** Boudin Blanc W1 *(Private Rm*)*
Whitechapel Art Gallery E1 *(Max*)*	The Lady Daphne SE1 *(afloat or stationary*)*
56 Strand Palace Hotel WC2 *(Essex Suite)*	Tuttons WC2 *(Larger Vault)*
55 Dolphin Square SW1 *(Chichester Suite)*	**34** Foxtrot Oscar SW3 *(Max*)*
George Inn SE1 *(George)*	**32** Engineer NW1 *(Large Room*)*
The House of St Barnabas-in-Soho W1 *(Council Room* or Soho Room)*	New Connaught Rms WC2 *(Penthouse)*
54 Catamaran Cruisers WC2 *(Abercorn)*	Royal Over-Seas League SW1 *(Mountbatten Rutland or Wrench)*
52 Fulham House SW6 *(Dining Room)*	**30** Anchor SE1 *(Lower Chart Rm*)*
50 Anchor SE1 *(Upper Chart Rm*)*	Bow Wine Vaults EC4 *(Smaller Section)*
Blackheath Concert Halls SE3 *(Café Bar)*	

233

Brasserie du Marché aux Puces W10 *(Private Rm*)*
Coopers Arms SW3 *(Private Rm*)*
The Courtyard, St Peter's Hall W11 *(North Hall)*
French Institute SW7 *(Salon de Réception*)*
Frocks E9 *(Basement*)*
The Sun WC2 *(Max*)*
Westminster College (Battersea) SW11 *(Restaurant*)*
28 Jason's Trip W9 *(Lace Plate II*)*
Maidenhead Steam Navigation, Berks *(Belle)*
27 The Candid Arts Trust EC1 *(Banquet Room)*
25 Chez Gerard, Dover St W1 *(Mezzanine or Private Rm*)*
The Dickens' House Museum WC1 *(Max*)*
Fox & Anchor EC1 *(Private Rm*)*
Front Page SW3 *(Private Rm*)*
Pitcher & Piano W1 *(Panelled Room*)*
24 Docklands Sailing & Watersports Centre E14 *(Teaching Room)*
Durrants Hotel W1 *(Oak Rm)*
Lansdowne Club W1 *(Shelburne Rm)*
Pall Mall Deposit W10 *(Bar)*
Royal Geographical Society SW7 *(Council Rm)*
22 Anchor SE1 *(Shakespeare Rm)*
Bakers' Hall EC3 *(Court Rm)*
Floating Boater W2 *(Lapwing)*
20 Congress Centre WC1 *(Board Rm)*
Crown & Goose NW1 *(Private Rm*)*
Dora House SW7 *(Salon)*
Duke of York's HQ SW3 *(Mercury House)*
Fulham House SW6 *(Reception Room)*
George Inn SE1 *(Lobby)*
Gopal's of Soho W1 *(Private Rm*)*
The Jenny Wren NW1 *(Max*)*
Paulo's W6 *(Downstairs Room)*
Pitcher & Piano W1 *(Casy Area)*
Royal Veterinary College NW1 *(Cambridge Rm or Connaught Rm)*
Surrey Docks Watersports Centre SE16 *(Quay Room/Quay Lounge*)*
Tuttons WC2 *(Smaller Vault)*
18 Caravan Serai W1 *(Max*)*
Hellenic Centre W1 *(Conference Room)*
Wine Gallery SW10 *(Private Rm)*
16 The Battersea Barge Bistro SW8 *(Captain's Cabin)*
Engineer NW1 *(Mirror Room)*
Royal Over-Seas League SW1 *(Bennet-Clark)*
15 Naval & Military Club W1 *(Octagon)*
YHA City of London EC4 *(Chapel)*
14 Royal Geographical Society SW7 *(Everest Rm)*
12 Chas Newens Marine Co SW15 *(Panache, Majestic or Pomery*)*
Chelsea Football Club SW6 *(Box)*
The Coliseum WC2 *(Stoll Rm)*
Durrants Hotel W1 *(Armfield Rm)*
Ikkyu W1 *(Tatami Rm*)*
Royal Veterinary College NW1 *(College Principal's Suite)*
Ship SW18 *(Private Room)*
11 Royal Over-Seas League SW1 *(Park)*
10 The Little Ship Club EC4 *(Chart Rm)*
Royal Geographical Society SW7 *(Reading Rm)*
8 The Coliseum WC2 *(Arlen Rm)*

£B

900 The Ministry of Sound SE1 *(Max*)*
800 Wandsworth Civic Suite SW18 *(Max*)*
650 Hammersmith Palais W6 *(Max*)*
500 Chuen Cheng Ku W1 *(Max*)*

400 Battersea Town Hall SW11 *(Grand Hall*)*
300 The Ministry of Sound SE1 *(The Box and Main Bar)*
250 Brockwell Lido SE24 *(Function Room*)*
The London Welsh Centre WC1 *(Main Hall*)*
Davy's – Skinkers SE1 *(Max*)*
200 Davy's – Bangers EC2 *(Max*)*
Holy Trinity Brompton Church Hall SW7 *(Max*)*
International Students W1 *(Theatre*)*
Nôtre Dame Hall WC2 *(Max*)*
Polish Social & Cultural Association W6 *(Malinova Rm*)*
Westminster Cathedral Hall SW1 *(Max*)*
180 Central Club (YWCA) WC1 *(Queen Mary Hall*)*
150 Abbey Community Centre SW1 *(Main Hall*)*
Africa Centre WC2 *(Main Hall*)*
Battersea Town Hall SW11 *(Lower Hall)*
Polish Social & Cultural Association W6 *(Lowiczanka Restaurant)*
The Tattershall Castle SW1 *(Steamers Discotheque*)*
Turnmills EC1 *(Max*)*
University of London Union WC1 *(Room 101*)*
Wessex House SW11 *(Max*)*
130 Westminster College (Victoria) SW1 *(Vincent Room (Restaurant)*)*
120 Davy's – City Flogger EC3 *(Max*)*
Davy's – Colonel Jaspers EC1 *(Max*)*
Davy's – Crown Passage Vaults SW1 *(Max*)*
HQ NW1 *(Max*)*
International Students W1 *(Portland Rm)*
WKD NW1 *(Max*)*
110 Holderness House EC2 *(Hall*)*
100 Balls Brothers SE1 *(Max*)*
Captain Kidd E1 *(Max*)*
Davy's – Chopper Lump W1 *(Max*)*
Coates Karaoke Bar & Restaurant EC2 *(Max*)*
Davy's – Colonel Jaspers SE10 *(Max*)*
Davy's – Davy's of Creed Lane EC4 *(Max*)*
Davy's – Davys' at Russia Court EC2 *(Max*)*
Davy's – The Habit EC3 *(Max*)*
Leadenhall Wine Bar EC3 *(Max*)*
Davy's – Lees Bag W1 *(Max*)*
London Rowing Club SW15 *(Max*)*
Slug & Lettuce SW15 *(Max*)*
Davy's – Tumblers W8 *(Max*)*
Davy's – The Vineyard E1 *(Max*)*
Walkers of St James's SW1 *(Max*)*
94 Balls Brothers SW1 *(Max*)*
90 Cittie of Yorke WC1 *(Main Bar*)*
Hop Cellars SE1 *(Malt Rm*)*
St Bride Foundation Institute EC4 *(Bridewell Hall*)*
85 Davy's – Burgundys Ben's EC1 *(Max*)*
Davy's – City Boot EC2 *(Max*)*
80 Africa Centre WC2 *(Rear Hall)*
Davy's – Bishop of Norwich EC2 *(Max*)*
Davy's – The Chiv W1 *(Max*)*
Crown & Greyhound SE21 *(Max*)*
Earlsfield Library SW18 *(Max*)*
Kettners W1 *(Oak Rm*)*
Lundonia House WC1 *(Ground Floor*)*
Davy's – Truckles Of Pied Bull Yard WC1 *(Max*)*
Turnmills EC1 *(Café Gaudi)*
75 Davy's – City FOB EC3 *(Max*)*
Davy's – Tapster SW1 *(Max*)*
Vats WC1 *(Restaurant*)*
74 Simpsons Tavern EC3 *(Restaurant*)*

70	Corney & Barrow EC4 *(Max*)*
	Davy's – Guinea Butt SE1 *(Max*)*
	The Horniman At Hay's SE1 *(Frederick John Horniman Rm*)*
	Larry's Wine Bar WC2 *(Max*)*
	Seashell NW1 *(Upstairs Rm*)*
	Slug & Lettuce N1 *(Max*)*
65	Cittie of Yorke WC1 *(Cellar Bar)*
	Davy's – Dock Blida W1 *(Max*)*
	Davy's – The Mug House SE1 *(Max*)*
	The White Horse SW6 *(Private Rm*)*
60	Alma SW18 *(Private Rm*)*
	Balls Brothers EC2 *(Weekday function*)*
	Balls Brothers EC3 *(Weekday function*)*
	Brockwell Lido SE24 *(Cafe-restaurant)*
	Circa W1 *(Downstairs* or Upstairs)*
	Davy's – The Cooperage SE1 *(Max*)*
	Corney & Barrow EC2 *(Max*)*
	Davy's – Davys at Canary Wharf E14 *(Private Room*)*
	Hammersmith Palais W6 *(VIP Bar)*
	Hollands W11 *(Conservatory and Balcony*)*
	The Horniman At Hay's SE1 *(Gallery)*
	Leadenhall Wine Bar EC3 *(Top-floor Room)*
	Mudchute Park and Farm E14 *(Cafe*)*
	La Paquerette EC2 *(Max*)*
	Rock Garden WC2 *(Max*)*
	Slug & Lettuce SW18 *(Palms Wine Bar)*
	University of London Union WC1 *(Room 1*)*
	Victoria Pump House SW11 *(Max*)*
	WKD NW1 *(Mezzanine)*
	Ye Olde Cheshire Cheese EC4 *(Cellar Bar*)*
56	Glassblower W1 *(Max*)*
55	Hop Cellars SE1 *(Restaurant)*
	Ye Olde Cheshire Cheese EC4 *(Johnson's or Williams Rm)*
54	Davy's – Docks Bar & Diner E1 *(Max*)*
50	Abbey Community Centre SW1 *(Bar)*
	The Barley Mow W1 *(Max*)*
	Captain Kidd E1 *(The Gallows)*
	Davy's – City Vaults EC1 *(Max*)*
	The Clachan W1 *(Highland Bar*)*
	Corney & Barrow EC3 *(Max*)*
	Duke of Clarence W11 *(Conservatory*)*
	The Freemason's Arms WC2 *(Max*)*
	Hop Cellars SE1 *(Porter Rm)*
	The Lamb Tavern EC3 *(Dining Rm*)*
	Le Mercury N1 *(Private Rm*)*
	Newham City Farm E16 *(Room*)*
	Queens Ice Bowl W2 *(Private Room*)*
	Simpsons Tavern EC3 *(Grill)*
	Spaghetti House W1 *(Private Rooms x 2*)*
45	Davy's – The Davys of Long Lane EC1 *(Max*)*
	Shampers W1 *(Brasserie or Wine Bar*)*
	Davy's – Shotberries EC2 *(Max*)*
42	Crown & Greyhound SE21 *(Restaurant)*
40	The Argyll Arms W1 *(Palladium Bar*)*
	Balls Brothers EC4 *(Weekday function*)*
	Bill Bentley's EC2 *(Max*)*
	Captain Kidd E1 *(The Observation Deck)*
	Davy's – The Chiv W1 *(Dining Rm)*
	Cittie of Yorke WC1 *(Front Bar)*
	The Crown and Two Chairmen W1 *(Upstairs Bar*)*
	Hollands W11 *(Conservatory)*
	Kettners W1 *(Edward Room)*
	Phene Arms SW3 *(Upstairs Rm*)*
	Pizzeria Condotti W1 *(Private Rm*)*
	Rodos WC2 *(Private Rm*)*
	Shelleys W1 *(Max*)*
	St Bride Foundation Institute EC4 *(Farringdon Rm)*
38	Pimlico Wine Vaults SW1 *(Private Rm*)*
36	Calthorpe Arms WC1 *(Private Rm*)*
	Westminster College (Victoria) SW1 *(Escoffier)*
35	Britannia W8 *(Max*)*

	Slug & Lettuce SW18 *(Room 2)*
33	Davy's – Crusting Pipe WC2 *(Max*)*
30	Davy's – Bishops Parlour EC2 *(Max*)*
	Corney & Barrow EC4 *(Max)*
	The Crown Tavern EC1 *(Upstairs Bar*)*
	Davy's – Davys at Canary Wharf E14 *(Private Room)*
	Deacons EC4 *(Max*)*
	Drakes EC4 *(Max*)*
	Davy's – Gyngleboy W2 *(Max*)*
	Kettners W1 *(Blue Rm)*
	The Plough WC2 *(Max*)*
28	Corney & Barrow EC2 *(Max)*
25	The Catherine Wheel W8 *(Private Room*)*
	Corney & Barrow EC3 *(Max)*
	Slug & Lettuce SW1 *(Max*)*
23	Davy's – Crusting Pipe WC2 *(Private Room)*
22	Two Chairmen SW1 *(Max*)*
20	Duke of Albemarle W1 *(Max*)*
	The Golden Lion SW1 *(Theatre Bar)*
	Holderness House EC2 *(Rifleman's Bar)*
	Davy's – Skinkers SE1 *(Boardroom)*
18	Davy's – City Pipe EC1 *(Boardroom*)*
16	Kettners W1 *(Soho Rm)*
	Phene Arms SW3 *(Terrace)*
12	Balls Brothers SE1 *(Private Rm 2)*
	Davy's – Bottlescrue EC1 *(Private Rm*)*
	Costa's Grill W8 *(Private Rm*)*
	Davy's – Skinkers SE1 *(Second private room)*
10	Davy's – Boot & Flogger SE1 *(Private Rm*)*
	Davy's – Crusting Pipe WC2 *(Private Room)*
	Deacons EC4 *(Private Rm)*
	Lundonia House WC1 *(Club)*
	Ye Olde Cheshire Cheese EC4 *(Director's Rm)*
8	Balls Brothers SW1 *(Private Rm)*
	Balls Brothers SE1 *(Private Rm)*
	Davy's – Davys Wine Vaults SE10 *(Private Room*)*
	Davy's – The Mug House SE1 *(Private Rm)*
6	Balls Brothers EC2 *(Weekday function)*

Function rooms listed by capacity for dinner-dances

* largest entry for venue

£E

340	Mezzo W1 *(Mezzo*)*
300	Blenheim Palace, Oxon *(Max*)*
	Madame Tussaud's NW1 *(Grand Hall*)*
250	Victoria & Albert Museum SW7 *(Dome, Medieval Treasury (& Pirelli Garden)*)*
150	Brocket Hall, Herts *(Max*)*
	Queen's House SE10 *(Max*)*
125	Annabel's W1 *(Max*)*
120	Spencer House SW1 *(Max*)*
80	Moyns Park, Essex *(Great Hall)*

£M-E

1500	The Grosvenor House Hotel W1 *(Great Rm*)*
1300	Royal Lancaster W2 *(Nine Kings Suite*)*
1000	Hilton on Park Lane W1 *(Grand Ballroom*)*
	Royal Albert Hall SW7 *(Cabaret or Ball*)*
	Spitalfields Market E1 *(Marquee (winter)*)*
700	Inter-Continental W1 *(Grand Ballroom*)*
650	Hurlingham Club SW6 *(Max*)*
600	The Queen Elizabeth II Conference Centre SW1 *(Fleming Room*)*
	Royal Lancaster W2 *(Westbourne Suite)*
550	Park Lane Hotel W1 *(Ballroom*)*
540	Cumberland Hotel W1 *(Production Box*)*
500	The Grosvenor House Hotel W1 *(Ballroom)*
	Natural History Museum SW7 *(Central Hall*)*
	Westway Studios W11 *(Max*)*
450	The Dorchester W1 *(Ballroom*)*
400	Portman Hotel W1 *(Ballroom*)*
	Reform Club SW1 *(Max*)*
	Royal Garden Hotel W8 *(Palace Suite*)*
	The Savoy WC2 *(Lancaster Rm*)*
	Woods River Cruises SE3 *(Silver Sturgeon*)*
380	Millennium Conference Centre SW7 *(Lower Level*)*
375	Banqueting House SW1 *(Max*)*
360	Cumberland Hotel W1 *(Carlisle)*
350	Arts Depot NW1 *(Max*)*
	Royal Albert Hall SW7 *(Arena)*
325	Four Seasons Hotel W1 *(Ballroom*)*
310	The Landmark W1 *(Ballroom*)*
300	Hyatt Carlton Tower SW1 *(Ballroom*)*
	Imperial War Museum SE1 *(Exhibition Hall*)*
	Inter-Continental W1 *(Westminster)*
	Phyllis Court, Oxon *(Ballroom*)*
	La Porte des Indes W1 *(Max*)*
	Royal Air Force Museum NW9 *(Battle of Britain Hall*)*
	Science Museum SW7 *(Flight Gallery*)*
280	Lincoln's Inn WC2 *(Great Hall*)*
	Millennium Conference Centre SW7 *(Ground Level (open))*
260	The Mayfair Inter-Continental W1 *(Crystal Rm*)*
	National Liberal Club SW1 *(Max*)*
250	Gloucester Hotel SW7 *(Cotswold Suite & Courtfield Suite*)*
	Inner Temple Hall EC4 *(Parliament Chamber*)*
240	Barbican Centre EC2 *(Garden Rm*)*
	The Gibson Hall EC2 *(Hall*)*
	London Zoo NW1 *(Regency Suite*)*
230	Bath – Assembly Rooms, *(Ballroom*)*

	Knebworth House, Herts *(Manor Barn (incl Bulwer Room)*)*
225	Middle Temple Hall EC4 *(Hall*)*
220	Leeds Castle, Kent *(Fairfax Hall With Terrace Room*)*
210	Le Meridien W1 *(Georgian*)*
200	Bath – Assembly Rooms, *(Tea Room)*
	Harrington Hall SW7 *(Harrington*)*
	Hyde Park Hotel SW1 *(Ballroom*)*
	Institute of Directors SW1 *(Nash*)*
	Kew (Royal Botanic) Gardens, Surrey *(Max*)*
	The Queen Elizabeth II Conference Centre SW1 *(Caxton Lounge)*
	Royal College of Music SW7 *(Concert Hall*)*
	Science Museum SW7 *(East Hall)*
192	Claridge's W1 *(Ballroom*)*
180	The Berkeley SW1 *(Ballroom*)*
	The Imagination Gallery WC1 *(Max*)*
	Roehampton Club SW15 *(Max*)*
	The Roof Gardens W8 *(Max*)*
	The Savoy WC2 *(Abraham Lincoln & Manhattan Rms)*
175	Stationers' Hall EC4 *(Livery Hall*)*
170	Gray's Inn WC1 *(Hall*)*
	Serpentine Gallery W2 *(Max*)*
	Skinners' Hall EC4 *(Max*)*
168	Woods River Cruises SE3 *(Silver Barracuda)*
160	Beaulieu, Hants *(Brabazon*)*
	Clandon, Surrey *(Restaurant*)*
150	Accademia Italiana/European Academy SW1 *(Max*)*
	Baltic Exchange EC3 *(Trading Floor*)*
	Bateaux London WC2 *(Symphony*)*
	Inter-Continental W1 *(Piccadilly)*
	The London Dungeon SE1 *(Max*)*
	Le Meridien W1 *(Edwardian)*
	Natural History Museum SW7 *(North Hall)*
	Park Lane Hotel W1 *(Tudor Rose Rm*)*
	Searcy's SW1 *(Max*)*
	Selsdon Park Hotel, Surrey *(Tudor Room*)*
140	Motcomb's Club SW1 *(Max*)*
130	Hilton on Park Lane W1 *(Curzon Suite)*
120	Arts Club W1 *(Dining Rm*)*
	The Berners Hotel W1 *(Thomas Ashton Suite*)*
	The Caledonian Club SW1 *(Max*)*
	The Dorchester W1 *(Orchid)*
	Museum of London EC2 *(Max*)*
	Phyllis Court, Oxon *(Grandstand)*
	Roehampton Club SW15 *(Roehampton Room)*
	The Savoy WC2 *(River Rm)*
	Sheraton Park Tower SW1 *(Trianon*)*
	Windsor Guildhall, Berks *(Guildhall Chamber*)*
110	The Landmark W1 *(Drawing Rm or Empire Rm)*
	National Liberal Club SW1 *(David Lloyd George)*
100	The Chelsea SW1 *(Sloane Suite*)*
	Knebworth House, Herts *(Lodge Barn)*
	Mirabelle W1 *(Max*)*
	Monkey Island Hotel, Berks *(River Rm*)*
	The Sanctuary WC2 *(Max*)*
90	Hilton on Park Lane W1 *(Crystal Palace Rm)*
	Lincoln's Inn WC2 *(Old Hall)*
85	Harrington Hall SW7 *(Turner & Constable)*
80	Beaulieu, Hants *(Domus)*
	Four Seasons Hotel W1 *(Garden Rm)*
	The Grosvenor House Hotel W1 *(Albemarle)*
	The London Planetarium NW1 *(Max*)*
70	Harrington Hall SW7 *(Reynolds & Landseer)*
	The Mayfair Inter-Continental W1 *(Danziger Suite)*

Museum of the Moving Image SE1 (Max*)
Raffles SW3 (Max*)
Royal Garden Hotel W8 (Kensington Suite)
Royal Lancaster W2 (Gloucester Suite)
68 Woods River Cruises SE3 (Silver Dolphin)
60 The Caledonian Club SW1 (Members Dining Rm)
Cannizaro House SW19 (Viscount Melville Suite*)
The Dorchester W1 (Park Suite)
Four Seasons Hotel W1 (Oak Rm)
Halcyon Hotel W11 (Restaurant*)
Hampshire Hotel W2 (Penthouse*)
The Lanesborough SW1 (Belgravia*)
Leeds Castle, Kent (Terrace Room)
Park Lane Hotel W1 (Garden Rm)
Phyllis Court, Oxon (Thames Room)
Roehampton Club SW15 (Garden Room)
50 Cabinet War Rooms SW1 (Max*)
Dukes Hotel SW1 (Marlborough Suite*)
Park Lane Hotel W1 (Oak Rm)
The Queen Elizabeth II Conference Centre SW1 (Guild Room)
Royal Garden Hotel W8 (Lancaster Suite)
40 Inter-Continental W1 (Windsor Suite I)
30 Inter-Continental W1 (Windsor Suite II)
16 Hyatt Carlton Tower SW1 (Boardroom)
15 Inter-Continental W1 (Hogarth)

£M

5000 Alexandra Palace & Park N22 (Great Hall*)
2000 Alexandra Palace & Park N22 (West Hall)
1500 Battersea Park SW8 (British Genius Site*)
1200 Commonwealth Institute W8 (Comm Galleries*)
1000 Ascot Racecourse, Pavilions & Queen Anne Rooms, Berks (Pavilion (subdivisible)*)
Sandown Park Racecourse, Surrey (Surrey Hall*)
720 London Metropole W2 (Palace Suite*)
660 The Brewery EC1 (Max*)
550 The Brewery EC1 (Porter Tun)
Café Royal W1 (4-Empire Napoleon*)
500 London Marriott W1 (Westminster Suite*)
450 Hothouse Bar & Grill E1 (Max*)
The International Hotel E14 (Grand Suite*)
Jongleurs at Camden Lock NW1 (Max*)
420 Waldorf Hotel WC2 (Adelphi Suite & Palm Court*)
360 Epsom Downs, Surrey (Blue Riband Room*)
350 Cabot Hall E14 (Hall*)
Lord's NW8 (Max*)
Sandown Park Racecourse, Surrey (Claremont)
310 Bath – Pump Room, (Max*)
300 The Brewery EC1 (King George III)
Café Royal W1 (6-Dubarry)
Hotel Russell WC1 (Wharncliffe Suite*)
Jongleurs at The Cornet SW11 (Max*)
Sandown Park Racecourse, Surrey (Marquee (permanent in summer))
Twickenham Banqueting Centre, • (Rose Rm*)
280 Twickenham Banqueting Centre, • (Spirit of Rugby)
250 Ascot Racecourse, Royal Enclosure, Berks (Paddock Suite*)
Brick Lane Music Hall EC2 (Max*)
Commonwealth Institute W8 (Art Gallery)

Holiday Inn – Nelson Dock SE16 (Sweden*)
230 Lloyd's of London EC3 (Captains' Rm*)
224 The Selfridge Hotel W1 (Selfridge Suite*)
220 Waldorf Hotel WC2 (Charter 2)
Hop Exchange SE1 (Max*)
Institution of Civil Engineers SW1 (Great Hall*)
Langham Hilton W1 (Ballroom*)
200 Alexandra Palace & Park N22 (Palace Restaurant)
Ascot Racecourse, Pavilions & Queen Anne Rooms, Berks (Buckhounds)
BAFTA Centre W1 (Max*)
Café Royal W1 (2-Louis)
Chartered Accountants' Hall EC2 (Great Hall*)
Chelsea Harbour Rooms SW10 (Turner & Carlyle Rms*)
Design Museum SE1 (Max*)
Epsom Downs, Surrey (Derby Suite)
Forte Posthouse Regent's Park W1 (Cambride & Oxford Suites*)
Glaziers' Hall SE1 (Hall*)
Hendon Hall Hotel NW4 (Mount Charlotte Suite*)
Limelight W1 (Max*)
Regent's College NW1 (Refectory*)
Royal Majestic Suite NW6 (Ground Floor*)
Sandown Park Racecourse, Surrey (Wolsey)
Stakis St Ermins SW1 (Ballroom*)
192 Churchill W1 (Chartwell Suite*)
180 Bank of England Club SW15 (Max*)
The Carnarvon Hotel W5 (Edward Suite*)
Holiday Inn – Nelson Dock SE16 (Wosa Suite)
London Metropole W2 (Windsor Suite)
The Oval SE11 (Max*)
The Rembrandt Hotel SW7 (Max*)
Winchester House SW15 (River Lawn (marquee)*)
170 Bath – Pump Room, (Pump Rm)
London Metropole W2 (Berkshire Suite)
160 Amadeus Centre W9 (Max*)
Church House SW1 (Harvey Goodwin Suite*)
Conrad Hotel SW10 (Henley Suite*)
Hampton Court, Tiltyard, Surrey (Max*)
Tower Thistle E1 (Tower Suite*)
150 41 Queen's Gate Terrace SW7 (Pillar Suite*)
Barbarella SW6 (Max*)
Dartmouth House W1 (Max*)
The Law Society WC2 (Common Rm*)
Limelight W1 (Gallery & Dome)
Pinewood Studios, Bucks (Ballroom*)
Royal Society of Arts WC2 (All Vaults*)
Syon Park (Conservatory), Middx (Great Conservatory*)
The Viceroy NW1 (Max*)
140 Epsom Downs, Surrey (Jockey Club Room)
Kensington Palace Thistle W8 (Duchess*)
The Rubens SW1 (Old Masters Restaurant*)
130 Royal Aeronautical Society W1 (Max*)
120 Basil Street Hotel SW3 (Parrot Club*)
The Brewery EC1 (Queen Charlotte)
Butchers' Hall EC1 (Max*)
Frederick's N1 (Max*)
The Grosvenor SW1 (Gallery Rm*)
The International Hotel E14 (Royal Lounge)
Sandown Park Racecourse, Surrey (Saddle Rm)
Trinity House EC3 (Max*)
110 Champenois EC2 (Max*)
100 Alexandra Palace & Park N22 (Loneborough Rm)
Ascot Racecourse, Royal Enclosure, Berks (Jockey Club)

The Brewery EC1 *(Smeaton's Vaults or Sugar Rms)*
Café Royal W1 *(S-Marquise)*
ICA SW1 *(Max*)*
Irish Club SW1 *(Ball Room*)*
The Kenilworth WC1 *(Bloomsbury Suite*)*
Mortons Club W1 *(Restaurant & Bar*)*
The Royal Air Force Club W1 *(Running Horse/Buttery*)*
Simpsons-in-the-Strand WC2 *(South Rm*)*
St Stephen' Constitutional Club SW1 *(Dining Rm*)*
Vanderbilt Hotel SW7 *(Max*)*
The Washington W1 *(Restaurant (Madisons)*)*
White House Hotel NW1 *(Albany*)*

96 HMS Belfast SE1 *(Ship Co.'s Dining Hall*)*
City of London Club EC2 *(Main Dining Rm*)*

90 Cobden's Club W10 *(Max*)*

85 Britannia Intercontinental Hotel W1 *(Manhattan*)*

80 The Carnarvon Hotel W5 *(Creffield Suite)*
Churchill W1 *(Chartwell I)*
Conrad Hotel SW10 *(Compass Rose or Thames)*
Fulham Palace SW6 *(Max*)*
Guards Museum SW1 *(Max*)*
The International Hotel E14 *(Buckingham)*
Leander Club, Berks *(Max*)*
London Metropole W2 *(Westminster Suite)*
My Fair Lady NW1 *(Max*)*
Sutton House E9 *(Wenlock Barn (including Café-Bar/Linenfold Parlour)*)*
Waldorf Hotel WC2 *(Minstrel Suite)*
The Westbury W1 *(Mount Vernon Rm*)*

75 Kensington Palace Thistle W8 *(Marchioness)*

72 Limelight W1 *(Club VIP (Basement))*

70 Bath – Pump Room, *(Concert Rm)*
Café Royal W1 *(I-Derby & Queensbury)*
Epsom Downs, Surrey *(Max*)*
The Grafton W1 *(Southampton Suite*)*
Royal Majestic Suite NW6 *(First Floor)*
Sandown Park Racecourse, Surrey *(Cavalry Bar)*

66 The Brewery EC1 *(The James Watt)*

60 HMS Belfast SE1 *(Gun Rm)*
Café Royal W1 *(I-Domino)*
The Cavendish SW1 *(Park*)*
Chelsea Harbour Rooms SW10 *(Carlyle Rm)*
Cuba Libre N1 *(Max*)*
The Grafton W1 *(Arlington Suite)*
Kew Bridge Steam Museum, Middx *(Steam Hall*)*
London Metropole W2 *(Thames Suite)*
Oxford & Cambridge Club SW1 *(Max*)*
Royal Society of Arts WC2 *(Benjamin Franklin Rm)*
The Washington W1 *(Richmond Suite)*
The Westbury W1 *(Pine Rm)*

50 HMS Belfast SE1 *(Wardroom)*
Brown's Hotel W1 *(Clarendon*)*
The Founders' Hall EC1 *(Livery Hall*)*
The Grosvenor SW1 *(Bessborough Rm)*
The Mountbatten WC2 *(Earl*)*
Spanish Club W1 *(Alfonso XIII Rm*)*
West Wycombe Caves, Bucks *(Max*)*

40 Athenaeum Hotel W1 *(Max*)*
City of London Club EC2 *(Garden Rm)*
Sandown Park Racecourse, Surrey *(Persimmon)*
White House Hotel NW1 *(Chester)*
White Swan Water W9 *(Max*)*

30 Hendon Hall Hotel NW4 *(Garrick)*

20 The Grafton W1 *(Duchess or Warren)*
Hendon Hall Hotel NW4 *(Johnson or Sheridan)*

The International Hotel E14 *(Beaufort)*

£B-E

1000 Crystal Palace Park SE20 *(Max*)*
200 The Worx I N1 *(Max*)*
The Worx II N1 *(Max*)*

£B-M

2000 Lee Valley Cycle Circuit E15 *(Max*)*
1000 Honourable Artillery Co EC1 *(Marquee*)*
800 Lee Valley Leisure Centre N9 *(Great Hall*)*
London Astoria WC2 *(Max*)*
700 Blackheath Concert Halls SE3 *(Max*)*
650 Royal Horticultural Halls SW1 *(New Hall*)*
600 Equinox at the Empire WC2 *(Max*)*
580 Badbobs WC2 *(Max*)*
560 New Connaught Rms WC2 *(Balmoral*)*
500 Stoke Newington Town Hall N16 *(Assembly Room*)*
450 Grosvenor Rooms NW2 *(Grosvenor Suite*)*
Porchester Centre W2 *(Ballroom*)*
440 The London Hippodrome WC2 *(Max*)*
400 Royal College of Art SW7 *(Henry Moore Gallery*)*
Royal Horticultural Halls SW1 *(Old Hall)*
350 Hammersmith Town Hall W6 *(Assembly Hall*)*
The London Hippodrome WC2 *(Auditorium)*
Syon Park (Banqueting), Middx
340 Strand Palace Hotel WC2 *(Max*)*
300 Blackheath Concert Halls SE3 *(Great Hall)*
Cecil Sharp House NW1 *(Kennedy Hall*)*
Dulwich College SE21 *(Christenson Hall and Upper Dining Rms*)*
Honourable Artillery Co EC1 *(Albert Rm)*
Regency Banqueting Suite N17 *(Max*)*
280 International House E1 *(Max*)*
250 Chelsea Old Town Hall SW3 *(Main Hall*)*
Duke of York's HQ SW3 *(Cadogan Hall*)*
Hollyhedge House SE3 *(Max*)*
Merchant Centre EC4 *(Caxton Suite*)*
New Connaught Rms WC2 *(Edinburgh)*
Thames Leisure EC4 *(Regalia*)*
240 Catamaran Cruisers WC2 *(Noticia*)*
230 Fulham Town Hall SW6 *(Grand Hall*)*
220 Chelsea Football Club SW6 *(Max*)*
Tidal Cruises SE1 *(Royal Princess*)*
200 Academy of Live & Recorded Arts SW18 *(Max*)*
Badbobs WC2 *(Bar/restaurant)*
Break For The Border W1 *(Max*)*
Congress Centre WC1 *(Congress Hall*)*
Dulwich College SE21 *(Great Hall)*
Goldsmiths College SE14 *(Great Hall*)*
Le Gothique SW18 *(with Academy of Live & Recorded Arts*)*
Hellenic Centre W1 *(Great Hall*)*
Naval & Military Club W1 *(Max*)*
The Old Town Hall, Stratford E15 *(Main Hall*)*
Pentland House SE13 *(Max*)*
Trafalgar Tavern SE10 *(Nelson Suite*)*
180 Grosvenor Rooms NW2 *(Executive Suite)*
King's College School SW19 *(Great Hall*)*

175 The London Hippodrome WC2 *(Balcony – Restaurant)*
170 Royal Holloway College, Surrey *(Founder's Dining Hall°)*
Westminster Boating Base SW1 *(Max°)*
160 Abbaye EC1 *(Max°)*
The Clink SE1 *(Max°)*
King's College WC2 *(Great Hall)*
HMS President EC4 *(Drill Hall°)*
150 Beckton Alpine Centre E6 *(Max°)*
Eatons EC3 *(Banqueting Suite°)*
King's College, Hampstead Site NW3 *(Bay Hall°)*
London Scottish SW1 *(Hall°)*
Mermaid Theatre EC4 *(Max°)*
New Connaught Rms WC2 *(York)*
St John's Hill SW11 *(Drill Hall°)*
Tidal Cruises SE1 *(Viscountess)*
Whitewebbs Museum of Transport, Middx *(Meeting Room°)*
148 Mainstream Leisure SW15 *(Elizabethan°)*
140 Conway Hall WC1 *(Large Hall°)*
Froebel Institute College SW15 *(Main Hall°)*
Fulham House SW6 *(Main Hall°)*
Will's Art Warehouse SW6 *(Max°)*
132 Tidal Cruises SE1 *(Hurlingham)*
130 Bishopsgate Institute EC2 *(Max°)*
Naval & Military Club W1 *(Coffee Rm)*
125 Dolphin Square SW1 *(Restaurant°)*
120 Blackheath Concert Halls SE3 *(Recital Rm)*
Lansdowne Club W1 *(Max°)*
Royal Green Jackets W1 *(Hall°)*
Strand Palace Hotel WC2 *(Exeter Suite)*
Thames Leisure EC4 *(The Miyuki Maru)*
Victoria & Albert Museum Café SW7 *(Max°)*
110 The Clink SE1 *(Winchester Hall)*
Dickens Inn E1 *(Nickleby Suite°)*
Royal Geographical Society SW7 *(Max°)*
St Martin In The Fields WC2 *(Max°)*
106 Tidal Cruises SE1 *(Old London)*
100 The Battersea Barge Bistro SW8 *(Max°)*
Cecil Sharp House NW1 *(Trefusis Hall)*
Crown River Cruises EC4 *(Salient)*
Fulham Town Hall SW6 *(Concert Hall)*
Grosvenor Rooms NW2 *(Pearl Suite)*
Lauderdale House N6 *(Max°)*
The Little Ship Club EC4 *(Max°)*
Royal Over-Seas League SW1 *(Hall of India & Pakistan°)*
Throgmorton's EC2 *(Oak Rm°)*
90 Brasserie Rocque EC2 *(Max°)*
City Cruises SE16 *(Eltham or Mayflower Garden°)*
Footstool SW1 *(Max°)*
80 Guy's Hospital SE1 *(Robens Suite°)*
Old Refectory W8 *(Max°)*
Royal Over-Seas League SW1 *(St Andrew's Hall)*
St Andrew Golf Club EC4 *(Max°)*
76 Maidenhead Steam Navigation, Berks *(Georgian°)*
70 City Cruises SE16 *(Westminster)*
60 Crown River Cruises EC4 *(Suerita)*
Equinox at the Empire WC2 *(The Square)*
The Old Town Hall, Stratford E15 *(Council Chamber)*
Turk Launches, Surrey *(New Southern Belle°)*
Whitechapel Art Gallery E1 *(Max°)*
50 Maidenhead Steam Navigation, Berks *(Edwardian)*
Thames Luxury Cruises EC3 *(Golden Salamander°)*
40 Floating Boater W2 *(Prince Regent°)*
Kingswood House SE21 *(Charles Suite°)*
Thames Leisure EC4 *(The Tideway)*
36 Crown River Cruises EC4 *(Spirit of London)*

Mainstream Leisure SW15 *(Lady Rose of Regent's)*
24 Jason's Trip W9 *(Lace Plate II°)*

£B

650 Hammersmith Palais W6 *(Max°)*
550 Wandsworth Civic Suite SW18 *(Max°)*
350 Battersea Town Hall SW11 *(Grand Hall°)*
200 Polish Social & Cultural Association W6 *(Malinova Rm°)*
Davy's – Skinkers SE1 *(Max°)*
160 Nôtre Dame Hall WC2 *(Max°)*
Polish Social & Cultural Association W6 *(Ball Room)*
150 Central Club (YWCA) WC1 *(Queen Mary Hall°)*
Lea Rowing Club E5 *(Max°)*
The London Welsh Centre WC1 *(Main Hall°)*
University of London Union WC1 *(Max°)*
130 St Etheldreda's Crypt EC1 *(Max°)*
110 Battersea Town Hall SW11 *(Lower Hall)*
Holdernesse House EC2 *(Hall°)*
Polish Social & Cultural Association W6 *(Lowiczanka Restaurant)*
100 Balls Brothers SE1 *(Max°)*
Coates Karaoke Bar & Restaurant EC2 *(Max°)*
Slug & Lettuce SW15 *(Max°)*
The Tattershall Castle SW1 *(Steamers Discotheque°)*
90 Cittie of Yorke WC1 *(Main Bar°)*
Hop Cellars SE1 *(Max°)*
75 St Bride Foundation Institute EC4 *(Bridewell Hall°)*
70 Corney & Barrow EC4 *(Max°)*
Hop Cellars SE1 *(Malt Rm)*
Larry's Wine Bar WC2 *(Max°)*
65 Davy's – The Mug House SE1 *(Max°)*
60 Circa W1 *(Downstairs°)*
Davy's – The Cooperage SE1 *(Max°)*
Lundonia House WC1 *(Ground Floor°)*
WKD NW1 *(Mezzanine°)*
50 Captain Kidd E1 *(Max°)*
Crown & Greyhound SE21 *(Max°)*
40 Cittie of Yorke WC1 *(Cellar Bar)*
Vats WC1 *(Restaurant°)*

ALPHABETICAL INDEX

ALPHABETICAL INDEX

ALPHABETICAL INDEX

ALPHABETICAL INDEX

ALPHABETICAL INDEX